SCIENCE FICTION

This is a volume in the
Arno Press collection

SCIENCE FICTION

ADVISORY EDITORS

R. Reginald

Douglas Menville

See last pages of this volume
for a complete list of titles

CONTEMPORARY SCIENCE FICTION AUTHORS

First Edition

Compiled and Edited by

R. Reginald

ARNO PRESS
A New York Times Company
New York — 1975

Reprint Edition 1974 by Arno Press Inc.

Copyright © 1970 by Unicorn & Son, Publishers.
New material Copyright © 1974 by R. Reginald.
All rights reserved; no part of this book may
be reproduced in any form without the expressed
written consent of the author.

Reprinted by permission of R. Reginald

Reprinted from a copy in the California State
College, San Bernardino Library

First published 1970 as STELLA NOVA: THE CONTEMPORARY
SCIENCE FICTION AUTHORS; reprinted 1974 by Arno Press
Inc., with additions and changes by the author.

SCIENCE FICTION
ISBN for complete set: 0-405-06270-2
See last pages of this volume for titles.

Manufactured in the United States of America

―――――●―――――

Library of Congress Cataloging in Publication Data

Reginald, R
    Contemporary science fiction authors.

    (Science fiction)
    Reprint, with new introd. and index, of the 1970 ed.
published by Unicorn, Los Angeles, under title: Stella
Nova.
    Includes index.
    1. Science fiction, American--Bio-bibliography.
2. Science fiction, English--Bio-bibliography.
I. Title. II. Series.
[Z1231.F4R43 1974]   823'.0876   74-16517
ISBN 0-405-06332-6

CONTEMPORARY

SCIENCE FICTION

AUTHORS

First Edition

Compiled and Edited by

R. Reginald

*Rededicated to
Fran Polek,
who taught me how to fly*

INTRODUCTION

<u>Contemporary</u> <u>Science</u> <u>Fiction</u> <u>Authors</u> is a continuing biobibliographical dictionary of the science fiction and fantasy fields. This first edition, originally published in 1970, includes bibliographies of 483 authors active during the years 1960-1968, and biographies of the 308 writers who responded to questionnaires mailed out by the author. Certain corrections, amendments, and changes have been made for this reprint edition, but the text remains essentially the same. The authors are arranged in alphabetical order according to the names under which they are commonly known, with several exceptions. Authors who have employed a variety of pennames can be located under their real names, if they have been used, or under their most common pseudonyms. Pennames are followed by single asterisks, house pseudonyms by three asterisks.

Each entry includes a bibliography of the author's science fiction and fantasy books, listed in chronological order down the page according to their respective dates of publication. A typical book entry contains the following information: identification number, year of publication, publisher, series number (where applicable), book title, and miscellaneous bibliographical information in parentheses, including type and format of each book, and some information regarding reprints. The key to the abbreviations can be found in a table following this introduction. I have also attempted to provide the author's first known publication or sale, series tie-ins, and works in progress at the time of compilation (1969).

Biographies, when provided by the author, are arranged into four paragraphs. The first section includes the author's full name, date and place of birth, education, awards or honors, and city of residence at the time of compilation. The second section provides the names of the author's parents, spouses (with dates of marriages, divorces (following slashes), and deaths (following dashes)), and children (including ages or dates of birth). The third paragraph details the author's career, and lists any organizations to which the author belonged at the time of compilation. The fourth section includes any sidelights or statements provided by the author in response to specific questions.

The title-index gives title and author only. A pseudonym listing has also been provided for the convenience of the user.

The assistance of the following groups or individuals is gratefully acknowledged: Bill Hughes, the late Ted Carnell, Fran Polek, Jack Salmon, Kornel Skovajsa, Gonzaga University, Anne McCaffrey and SFWA, Linda Balch, Richard Witter and his F&SF Book Co., Audrey Worthy, Charles Nuetzel, and

Brian Aldiss, Piers Anthony, Alan Frank Barter, Gerald Bishop, Ned Brooks, Gary Buck, Steve Burgess, Phil Harbottle, Harry Harrison, Laurence M. Janifer, Sam Moskowitz, John Norman, Alan E. Nourse, Mark Owings, Emil Petaja, Elinor Poland, Robert Sabella, Teddi Sands, Hans Stefan Santesson, James R. Sieger, Bob Stahl, Mary Standish, and Bob Tralins.

Many thanks also to the authors who took time to respond so generously, and to Mrs. Linda Evans, who helped me in amending the original text.

The following publications were consulted while compiling this book: Whitaker's Cumulative Book Index, Cumulative Book Index, Books in Print, Paperbound Books in Print, Contemporary Authors, Who's Who, Who's Who in America, Seekers of Tomorrow (Moskowitz), Index to the Science Fiction Magazines 1926-1950 (D. Day), Index to the Science-Fantasy Publishers (Owings & Chalker), Harry Harrison's Bibliographia (Biamonti), Science Fiction Published in 1967, 1968 (Burger), Science Fiction Title Changes (Viggiano & Franson), Australian Science Fiction Index (Stone), Index to the Weird Fiction Magazines (Cockcroft), An Annotated Checklist of Science Fiction Bibliographical Works (Lerner), A Checklist of Fantastic Literature in Paperbound Books (B. Day), The Supplemental Checklist of Fantastic Literature (B. Day), A Handbook of Science Fiction and Fantasy, 2nd edition (Tuck), Baycon Program Book, Locus (ed., C. & M. Brown), Science Fiction Times (ed., Dietz), Luna (ed., Dietz), Pegasus (ed., Burger), Speculation (ed., Weston), SFWA Bulletin (ed., successively by Knight, Carr, Panshin), F&SF Book Co. List (ed., Witter), Stephen's Book Service List (ed., Takacs), The Fantasy Collector (ed., Cazedessus).

CONTENTS

Author Section 1
Title Index. 311
Pseudonym Index 366
Afterword. 368

ABBREVIATIONS

a	An abridged edition.
ASFA	Australian Science Fiction Association (publisher)
Beacons	Beaconsfield (publisher)
e	An expanded edition.
FKP	First known publication.
FPCI	Fantasy Publishing Company Inc. (publisher)
FPP	First professional publication.
FPS	First professional sale.
FSF	First professional science fiction sale.
FSP	First professional science fiction publication.
H-P	Simultaneous hard and soft cover publication.
H-W	Harris-Wolfe (publisher)
i	Author's name is incomplete as listed.
NAL	New American Library (publisher)
nf	Nonfiction.
P	Paperbound edition.
Pap Lib	Paperback Library (publisher)
P.E.N.	Internation Association of Poets, Playwrights, Editors, Essayists, and Novelists
Phil Lib	Philosophical Library (publisher)
Pop Lib	Popular Library (publisher)
P-P	Simultaneous paperbound editions of two title variations.
RH	Reprinted in hardcover.
RHa	Reprinted in hardcover in abridged form.
RHav	Reprinted under another title in an abridged hardcover edition.
RHe	Reprinted in hardcover in expanded form.
RHev	Reprinted under another title in an expanded hardcover edition.
RHv	Reprinted in hardcover under a variant title.
RP	Reprinted in paperback.
RPa, RPav	as above
RPe, RPev	as above
RPv	Reprinted in paperback under a variant title.
s	A single-author short story collection.
S&S	Simon & Schuster (Publisher)
SER	Series.
SF&F	Science-Fiction & Fantasy Publishers (publisher)
u	Author's full name is unknown (i.e., he won't tell).
VN	D. Van Nostrand (publisher)
West	Westminster Press (publisher)
WIP	Work in progress (as of 1969)
@	An anthology of short stories by more than one author.
*	Signifies a penname when appended to an author's name.
***	A house pseudonym (a penname used by more than one author).

R. COX ABEL

1) 1966 Library 33 with Charles Barren (q.v.)
   Panther Trivana 1. (H-P)

JOHN ADAMS

1) 1960 Badger SF When the Gods Came. (P/RH)

NOTE: John Adams is a possible pseudonym.

EDMOND G. ADDEO

with Richard M. Garvin (q.v.)
1) 1968 Sherbourne The Fortec Conspiracy. (RP)
2) 1968 Sherbourne The Talbot Agreement.

NOTE: Edmond G. Addeo is a member of Science Fiction Writers of America.

RAY AINSBURY

1) 1962 Consul When the Moon Ran Wild. (P)

BRIAN W. ALDISS

1) 1955 Faber The Brightfount Diaries.
2) 1957 Faber Space, Time and Nathaniel. (s/RP)
3) 1958 Faber Non-Stop. (RP)
3A) 1959 Criterion Starship. (a/RP)
4) 1959 Ace Vanguard from Alpha. (P)
5) 1959 Signet No Time Like Tomorrow. (s/P)
6) 1959 Faber The Canopy of Time. (s/RP)
7) 1960 Ace Bow Down to Nul. (P)
8) 1960 Signet Galaxies Like Grains of Sand. (s/P)
9) 1961 Beacon The Male Response. (P/RH)
7A) 1961 Digit The Interpreter. (P)
10) 1961 Ballantine The Primal Urge. (P)
11) 1961 Penguin Penguin Science Fiction. (@/P)
4A) 1961 Digit Equator. (P)
12) 1962 Signet The Long Afternoon of Earth. (P/RHev)
13) 1962 Faber Hothouse. (12/e/RP)
14) 1962 Faber Best Fantasy Stories. (@)

BRIAN W. ALDISS (continued)

15)	1963 Penguin	More Penguin Science Fiction. (@/P)	
16)	1963 Faber	The Airs of Earth. (s/RP)	
17)	1964 Signet	Starswarm. (s/P)	
18)	1964 Faber	The Dark Light-Years. (RP)	
19)	1964 Penguin	Yet More Penguin Science Fiction. (@/P)	
20)	1964 Faber	Greybeard. (RHa/RP)	
21)	1964 Faber	Introducing SF. (@/RP)	
22)	1965 Faber	Earthworks. (RP)	
23)	1965 Faber	Best Science Fiction Stories of Brian W. Aldiss. (s)	
23A)	1966 Harcourt	Who Can Replace a Man? (s/RP)	
24)	1966 Faber	The Saliva Tree and Other Strange Growths. (s/RP)	
25)	1967 Faber	An Age.	
25A)	1968 Doubleday	Cryptozoic! (RP)	
28)	1968 Faber	Report on Probability A.	
29)	1968 Macdonald	Farewell Fantastic Venus! (@/RPav)	
29A)	1968 Dell	All About Venus. (@/a/P)	

with Harry Harrison (q.v.)

26)	1967 Doubleday	Nebula Award Stories Two. (@/RP)
27)	1968 Berkley	Best SF: 1967. (@/P-P)
27A)	1968 Sphere	Year's Best Science Fiction No. 1. (@/P-P)

NOTE: Mr. Aldiss' bibliography is complicated by the fact that many of his English books have been altered in their American editions. A list of these may prove enlightening: No Time Like Tomorrow is roughly based on Space, Time and Nathaniel; Galaxies Like Grains of Sand on Canopy of Time; The Long Afternoon of Earth on Hothouse; Starswarm on The Airs of Earth; Neanderthal Planet on Intangibles, Inc.

FPS: "A Book in Time,"   The Bookseller, February, 1954.
FSF: "Criminal Record,"   Science Fantasy, July, 1954.

WIP:		1969 Sphere	Year's Best Science Fiction No. 2. (@/P/RHv/with Harry Harrison)
		1969 Sidgwick	A Brian Aldiss Omnibus. (7A/10/24)
		1969 Faber	Intangibles, Inc. (s)
30A)		1969 Putnam	Best SF: 1968. (@/with Harry Harrison)
		1969 Avon	Neanderthal Planet. (s/P)
		1969 Faber	Barefoot in the Head.
		1970 Sphere	Year's Best Science Fiction No. 3. (@/P/with Harry Harrison)
		1970 Putnam	Best SF: 1969. (@/with Harry Harrison)
		Doubleday	The Astounding-Analog Reader. (@/ with H. Harrison)
			The Shape of Further Things. (nf)

***   ***   ***   ***   ***

Brian Wilson Aldiss--born August 18, 1925 at Dereham, Norfolk, England--Hugo Award, Best Short Fiction, 1962, "Hothouse;" Nebula Award, Best Novella, 1965, "The Saliva Tree;" Guest of Honor, 23rd World Science Fiction Convention (Loncon II), 1965; Voted Britain's Most Popular Science Fiction Writer by the British Science

BRIAN W. ALDISS (continued)

Fiction Association, 1968--North Abingdon, Berkshire, England.

Son of Stanley & May (Wilson) Aldiss--(2) Margaret Manson: December 11, 1965--1) Clive Aldiss (1955); Wendy Caroline Aldiss (1959); 2) Timothy Aldiss (1967).

Literary Editor, <u>Oxford Mail</u>, 1958-DATE; Editor, Penguin Science Fiction Novels, 1961-1964; Co-Editor, <u>Science Fiction Horizons</u>, 1964-1965; Free-Lance Writer and Editor--Member: Science Fiction Writers of America; British Science Fiction Association (President, 1960-1964); Society of Authors.

The following statement was written in response to several key questions provided by the editors: these queries are typical of those throughout CSFA.

What in your opinion is the current state of science fiction?

"Since sf is the sum of the writings of a great many individuals (I can name thirty without trouble in Great Britain alone), it makes more sense to talk about individual writers. Science fiction may be awful at any given period, but one writer may be brilliant enough to compensate for all the rest--like the English theatre in the time of George Bernard Shaw.

"So let me speak up for my own country, and not produce a distorted echo of yours. The feeling over here is extremely creative; I believe the activity is minor on the whole, but that does not necessarily make it less stimulating. Among a number of speculative and science-fictional writers whom I admire are Pamela Zoline, David Masson, Charles Platt, Langdon Jones, and John Sladek. Two of these, you will note, are American. I would certainly add another American, Tom Disch, were he still over here. Cross-fertilization has been going on--and the flower that has attracted the young Americans is <u>New Worlds</u>, edited by the legendary (but by no means mythical) Mike Moorcock.

"The writers I name are more noted for quality than quantity. Of the better-established authors, I need say nothing (Arthur Clarke can speak for himself!). But it is also worth noting that cross-fertilization has been proceeding in other directions--with several artists such as Richard Hamilton and Paolozzi, who enjoy reading sf, and who plough their imagery back into the field; and with several poets, such as D.M. Thomas, Bill Butler, Peter Redgrove, and Robert Conquest.

"The benefits of this cross-fertilization are, I believe, apparent. SF has long been guilty of ancestor-worship; now everyone is looking outwards and forwards instead. A different sort of writing is emerging, which lives in the present-future interface--an evaluative species of fiction more related to movements in the other arts than to the pulp traditions on which the old sf is based. I know that some people find this makes this sort of writing harder to understand: but this is generally because they are more familiar with the pulps; for anyone unfamiliar with the pulps, the conventions there are hard to understand.

"The only writers whose work means a great deal to me nowadays (once it was otherwise) are Philip K. Dick for his subtilty, my buddy Harry Harrison for his vigor, Kurt Vonnegut for his irony, and J.G. Ballard in some of his short stories--oh, and people who are capable of being absolutely outrageous with a straight face, like Alfred Bester, Fred Pohl, William Tenn, and Charles Harness on occasions. I also have an abiding admiration for H.G. Wells, especially his excellently dark <u>The Island of Dr. Moreau</u>."

BRIAN W. ALDISS (continued)

What role have you played, to your mind, in determining the field's course?
"Not an easy question for a fairly modest man to answer! But I'll say again--I believe only in the work of individual writers, not in sf as a whole: in the chaps in the corporation, not the corporation. And I have always stood for individual work--which is, perhaps, why I once had a reputation for being obscure; there's little help for anyone, in life or letters, unless he finds and is himself. Fashion is a distraction: yet permanence must move with the times. I have always attempted to write my own thing, and have been helped in this by being as conscious of the general cultural heritage as of the specifically science-fictional one.

"When I began writing sf stories, I was told they were just not sf, presumably because I did not load in technology like an exoskeleton round my characters. Now nobody worries (much, anyway), and perhaps I have softened things up in this way. Perhaps I'm still doing it. I really do not know if my anti-novel, Report on Probability A, is sf, or if my undoubtedly best novel, Barefoot in the Head is sf; nor do I care--that sort of minute pigeon-holing is for publishers' minds. I'd like to think that my general policy of non-violence was also catching on a bit. As an editor, I have been instrumental in securing better payments for authors, and have helped familiarise the general reading public with good sf writers. My Penguin series, for instance, brought several unfamiliar American names forward. I have twice been instrumental in helping Moorcock's New Worlds through a crisis, as well as maintaining a fair level of criticism over a number of years.

"This begins to sound like a politician's speech! Well, I believe more and more in the arts of diplomacy. I live, think and breathe writing, and hate the petty bickering and self-advertisement that writers get up to. Fortunately, in writing one escapes all that: the act of writing is a form of possession, a visionary state that at the moment of involvement has little reference to others."

Where is sf going, and what will it become?
"Again, one can only speak of individuals, and I can't see how one writer should presume to speak for others. Some chaps will turn into old hacks, some chaps are hacks, some chaps will stop writing, some will go round the twist, and so on. But sf isn't an army of starship troopers marching on to glory or ignominy; it's just individuals. I don't suffer from the 'Anxious Ownership Syndrome towards sf that afflicts many of the field's eager beavers.

"Nor do I foresee exactly where I am going personally, though I have all the usual private and stereotyped dreams of success to warm me when my typewriter feels cold. I count success not only in cash terms. At present, my writing is greatly intensifying and gathering strength, and--barring accidents!--nothing can stop me developing. In general terms, I shall continue to explore the human design in times of change. We shall never run out of change!"

KINGSLEY AMIS

1) 1960 Harcourt New Maps of Hell. (nf/RP)

        with Robert Conquest (q.v.)
2) 1961 Gollancz Spectrum. (@/RP/RPa)
3) 1962 Gollancz Spectrum 2. (@/RP)

KINGSLEY AMIS (continued)

4)	1963 Gollancz	Spectrum 3.	(@/RP)
5)	1965 Gollancz	Spectrum 4.	(@/RP)
6)	1966 Gollancz	Spectrum 5.	(@/RP)
FPS:	1954 Gollancz	Lucky Jim.	
FSF:	1960 Harcourt	New Maps of Hell.	(nf)
WIP:		Spectrum 6.	(@/with Robert Conquest)

***   ***   ***   ***   ***

Kingsley William Amis--born April 16, 1922, at London, England--B.A. (1st Class Honors), St. John's College, Oxford University, 1947; M.A., Oxford University, 1948; M.A., Cambridge University, 1961--Somerset Maugham Award, 1955, Lucky Jim--Barnet, Hertfordshire, England.

Son of William Robert & Rosa Annie (Lucas) Amis--(1) Hilary Ann Bardwell: 1948/1965; (2) Elizabeth Jane Howard: 1965--1) Philip Nicol William Amis; Martin Louis Amis; Sally Myfanwy Amis.

Lecturer in English, University of Swansea, 1949-1961; Visiting Fellow in Creative Writing, Princeton University, 1958-1959; Fellow, Peterhouse, Cambridge University, 1961-1963; Visiting Professor, Vanderbilt University, 1967-1968; Free-Lance Writer, 1963-DATE.

CHESTER ANDERSON

2)	1967 Pyramid	The Butterfly Kid. (P)
1)	1964 Pyramid	with Michael Kurland (q.v.) Ten Years to Doomsday. (P)

NOTE: Chester V.J. Anderson is a member of Science Fiction Writers of America. A partial biography may be found on the reverse cover of his second novel.

POUL ANDERSON

1)	1952 Winston	Vault of the Ages. (RP)
2)	1954 Ballantine	Brain Wave. (H-P)
3)	1955 Ace	No World of Their Own. (P)
4)	1956 Ace	Planet of No Return. (P/RH)
5)	1957 Avalon	Star Ways. (RP)
7)	1958 Ace	The Snows of Ganymede. (P)
8)	1958 Ace	War of the Wing-Men. (P)
9)	1959 Avalon	Virgin Planet. (RP)
10)	1959 Ace	War of Two Worlds. (P)
11)	1959 Ace	We Claim These Stars! (P)
12)	1959 Lippincott	The Enemy Stars. (RP)
13)	1960 Doubleday	The High Crusade. (RP)
14)	1960 Ballantine	Guardians of Time. (s/P/RH)
15)	1960 Torquil	Twilight World. (RP)
16)	1960 Ace	Earthman, Go Home! (P)
17)	1961 Ace	Mayday Orbit. (P)

POUL ANDERSON (continued)

18)	1961 Doubleday		Three Hearts and Three Lions. (RP)	
19)	1961 Ballantine		Strangers from Earth. (s/P)	
20)	1961 Pyramid		Orbit Unlimited. (P)	
21)	1962 Ballantine		After Doomsday. (P/RH)	
22)	1962 Ace		The Makeshift Rocket. (P)	
23)	1962 Ace		Un-Man and Other Novellas. (s/P)	
24)	1963 Berkley		Shield. (P/RH)	
25)	1963 Ace		Let the Spacemen Beware! (P)	
26)	1964 Doubleday		Time and Stars. (s/RP)	
27)	1964 Doubleday		Trader to the Stars. (s/RP)	
28)	1964 Pyramid		Three Worlds to Conquer. (P)	
29)	1965 Doubleday		The Star Fox. (RP)	
30)	1965 Chilton	1	Agent of the Terran Empire.	
31)	1965 Chilton	2	Flandry of Terra.	
32)	1965 Doubleday		The Corridors of Time. (RP)	
33)	1966 Doubleday		The Trouble Twisters. (RP)	
34)	1966 Chilton	3	Ensign Flandry. (RP)	
36)	1967 Ace		World Without Stars. (P)	
37)	1968 Signet		The Horn of Time. (s/P)	

with Gordon R. Dickson (q.v.)
6)   1957 Gnome   Earthman's Burden.

with Christian Molbech
35)   1966 Doubleday   The Fox, the Dog, and the Griffin.

SER: Flandry.

FPS: "Tomorrow's Children,"   Astounding, March, 1947 (with F.N. Waldrop).

WIP: 1969 Macmillan   Seven Conquests. (s)
       1969 Signet   Beyond the Beyond. (s/P)
       1969 Macmillan   Tales of the Flying Mountains. (s)
       1969 Doubleday   Satan's World.
       1969 Doubleday   Nebula Award Stories Four. (@)

***   ***   ***   ***   ***

Poul William Anderson--born November 25, 1926, at Bristol, Pennsylvania--B.S., University of Minnesota, 1948--Hugo Award, Best Short Fiction, 1961, "The Longest Voyage;" 1964, "No Truce with Kings;" Guest of Honor, 17th World Science Fiction Convention (Detention), 1959; First Annual Macmillan Cock Robin Award, 1959-- Orinda, California.

Son of Anton William & Astrid (Hertz) Anderson--Karen June Millichamp Kruse: December 12, 1953--Astrid May Anderson (14).

Free-Lance Writer, 1948-DATE--Member: Science Fiction Writers of America; Mystery Writers of America; The Scowrers (Secretary, 1957-1962); Institute for 21st Century Studies; American Institute for the Advancement of Science; The Elves', Gnomes', and Little Men's Science Fiction, Chowder, and Marching Society.

POUL ANDERSON (continued)

Mr. Anderson comments on science fiction:

"In my opinion, the current state of the field is very healthy. Magazines seem to be doing about as well as they ever did; that isn't saying much, but then, it never was much, as witness the short lives of most. SF has, however, become a recognized part of trade book and paperback book publishing. Though modest, the profits are real. I don't foresee any boom, unless one of the artificial kind that is quickly followed up by a bust, but I do hope for steady, continued growth.

"More important is the growth in skill, technique, range, and straight literary quality. For this we have not only a number of bright new writers to thank, but a number of old ones, from Heinlein and Leiber on down, who have apparently been stimulated to contribute their own innovations.

"I think the genre is headed toward at least partial reunion with the so-called 'mainstream'--now that each is learning the language of the other--and that this is desireable. At the same time, I hope the straight <u>science</u> fiction story can continue to flourish.

"I wouldn't attempt to judge my own influence on the field. What I've tried to do is keep introducing fresh ideas, especially about the potentialities of science, technology, and the universe; to put forward a realistic rather than romantic view of life; and to maintain a literary standard. It is for others to say how far this attempt may have succeeded or failed.

"As for the 'new wave,' this strikes me as being mainly an artifact of a few enthusiasts like Judith Merril. Most of the writers who are popularly associated with it deny any such categorization: Ballard, Delany, Zelazny, etc. Most of what is advanced under the label is not to my taste; it strikes me as utterly self-indulgent. But some of the--to be more precise--neo-Joycean or neo-Kafkaesque writing is good, and does a service by introducing these techniques to science fiction."

WILLIAM C. ANDERSON

1)	1963 Crown	<u>Penelope.</u>
2)	1964 Crown	<u>Adam M-1.</u>
3)	1966 Crown	<u>Pandemonium on the Potomac.</u>
4)	1968 Crown	<u>The Gooney Bird.</u> (RP)
FPS:	1963 Crown	<u>Penelope.</u>
WIP:	19<u>69</u>	<u>The Apoplectic Palm Tree.</u>

***   ***   ***   ***   ***

William Charles Anderson--born May 7, 1920 at La Junta, Colorado--attended Boise Junior College, 1939; Fort Hays College, 1943; University of Maryland, 1949; Degree in Military Science and Tactics, Air Force Command and Staff College, 1960 --Distinguished Flying Cross; Legion of Merit--Blue Jay, California.

Son of Robert Smith & Fanny (Holly) Anderson--(1) Wilma Y. Duncan: August 17, 1941/1948; (2) Dortha Marie Power: 1948--1) Anne Anderson (27); 2) Scott Anderson (18);

WILLIAM C. ANDERSON (continued)

Holly Anderson (16).

Officer, United States Air Force, 1942-1964 (retired with rank of Lieutenant Colonel); Free-Lance Writer of motion picture and television scripts, and novels, 1964-DATE --Member: Air Force Association.

NOTE: Col. Anderson served in the Space Branch of the Pentagon, 1960-1964.

He writes:
"Although I love science fiction, particularly humorous, I have found it the least successful commercially of any of my books. Fantasy, particularly, is a rough commodity to sell in this day and age. Currently pornography seems to reign. It will be a great day when fantasy comes back into the picture."

---

*PIERS ANTHONY

1)	1967 Ballantine		Chthon. (P)	
2)	1968 Pyramid	1	Sos the Rope. (P)	
4)	1968 Ballantine	-1	Omnivore. (P/RH)	
			with Robert E. Margroff (q.v.)	
3)	1968 Ace		The Ring. (P)	
FPS:	"Possible to Rue,"		Fantastic, April, 1963.	
WIP:	1969 Avon		The Macroscope. (P)	
		-2	Paleo.	
			The Rumpleskin Brat. (with Robert E. Margroff)	
		2	Var the Stick.	

*** *** *** *** ***

Piers Anthony Dillingham Jacob--born August 6, 1934 at Oxford, England--B.A., Goddard College (Major in Creative Writing), 1956--Winner, $5000 Pyramid Publications/Magazine of Fantasy and Science Fiction/Kent Productions Science Fiction Novel Award, 1968, Sos the Rope--St. Petersburg, Florida/Gulfport, Florida.

Son of Alfred Bennis & Norma (Sherlock) Jacob--Carol Marble: June 23, 1956-- Penelope Carolyn Jacob (October 12, 1967).

Technical Writer, Electronics Communications, Inc., 1959-1962; English Teacher, Admiral Farragut Academy, 1965-1966; Free-Lance Writer, 1966-DATE--Member: Science Fiction Writers of America.

NOTE: Mr. Anthony became a naturalized American citizen in 1958.

*CHRISTOPHER ANVIL

1) 1964 Monarch   The Day the Machines Stopped. (P)

FKP: "The Prisoner,"   Astounding, February, 1956.

NOTE: Christopher Anvil is a penname of Harry C (?hristopher) Crosby. He is a past member of Science Fiction Writers of America.

---

*E. L. ARCH

1) 1963 Avalon   Bridge to Yesterday.
2) 1964 Avalon   The Deathstones.
3) 1964 Avalon   Planet of Death.
4) 1965 Avalon   The First Immortals.
5) 1966 Avalon   The Double-Minded Man.
6) 1967 Avalon   The Man with Three Eyes.

FPS: 1951 Reilly   Hidden Valley of Oz. (as Rachel Cosgrove)

***   ***   ***   ***   ***

Rachel Ruth Cosgrove Payes--born December 11, 1922 at Westernport, Maryland --B.S., West Virginia Wesleyan College, 1943; Registered Medical Technologist, ASCP--Shrub Oak, New York.

Daughter of Jacob & Martha (Brake) Cosgrove--Norman M. Payes: September 12, 1954--Robert Payes (10); Ruth Payes (9).

Medical Technologist, various hospitals in Pennsylvania and West Virginia, 1943-1946; Research Associate in Pharmocology, Research Division, American Cyanamid Company, 1946-1957; Free-Lance Writer, 1957-DATE--Member: Science Fiction Writers of America.

---

*RON ARCHER

                with Dave Van Arnam (q.v.)
1) 1967 Pyramid   Lost in Space. (P)

NOTE: Ron Archer is a penname of Ted White (q.v.)

BRUCE ARISS

1) 1963 Avalon   Full Circle.

FPS: "Dreadful Secret of Jonas Harper," What's Doing Magazine, November, 1948.

WIP: The Fourth Eye.

BRUCE ARISS (continued)

***   ***   ***   ***   ***

Bruce Wallace Ariss, Jr.--born October 10, 1911 at Underwood, Washington--
B.A., University of California at Berkeley, 1934--Monterey, California.

Son of Bruce Wallace & Anna (Kirwin) Ariss--Jean McLellan Fitch: July 27, 1934--
Bruce Wallace Ariss III (1937); Dinah G. Ariss (1941); Brien J. Ariss (1944);
Andrea C. Ariss (1947); Holly J. Ariss (1950).

"Divided time between writing, art work, murals, illustrating, TV and motion picture art directing, script writing, magazine and newspaper journalism, art advertising, and copywriting. At present Designer and Illustrator for Defense Language Institute at the Presidio of Monterey"--Member: Pi Delta Epsilon; Carmel Art Association.

NOTE: Mr. Ariss did the illustrations for Reginald Bretnor's <u>Through Time and Space with Ferdinand Feghoot</u> (q.v.).

He writes:
"I believe the greatest value of science fiction is neither entertainment nor the exercise of the fancy (though both of these are important), but the wonderful opportunity it affords for social satire. Jonathan Swift and H.G. Wells are excellent examples of what I mean. The short-sighted bumbling of mankind can be most easily demonstrated by projecting our current follies into a <u>reductio ad absurdum</u> in the future."

ISAAC ASIMOV

1)	1950 Doubleday		Pebble in the Sky. (RP)	
2)	1950 Gnome		I, Robot. (s/RP)	
3)	1951 Doubleday		The Stars, Like Dust. (RP/RPv)	
4)	1951 Gnome	1	Foundation. (RP/RPav)	
6)	1952 Doubleday		The Currents of Space. (RP)	
7)	1952 Gnome	2	Foundation and Empire. (RP/RPv)	
9)	1953 Gnome	3	Second Foundation. (RP/RPv)	
10)	1954 Doubleday		The Caves of Steel. (RP)	
3A)	1954 Ace		The Rebellious Stars. (P)	
12)	1955 Doubleday		The Martian Way. (s/RP)	
4A)	1955 Ace	1A	The 1000 Year Plan. (a/P)	
7A)	1955 Ace	2	The Man Who Upset the Universe. (P)	
13)	1955 Doubleday		The End of Eternity. (RP)	
15)	1957 Doubleday		The Naked Sun. (RP)	
17)	1957 Doubleday		Earth Is Room Enough. (s/RP)	
9A)	1958 Avon	3	2nd Foundation: Galactic Empire. (P)	
19)	1959 Doubleday		Nine Tomorrows. (s/RP)	
20)	1961 Doubleday		Triangle. (1/3/6)	
21)	1962 Doubleday		The Hugo Winners. (@/RP)	

ISAAC ASIMOV (continued)

23)	?1963 Doubleday	0	The Foundation Trilogy.	(4/7/9)
24)	1964 Doubleday		The Rest of the Robots.	(6/10/s/RPa)
25)	1966 Doubleday		Tomorrow's Children.	(@)
26)	1966 Bantam		Fantastic Voyage.	(P/RH)
23A)	1966 Sidgwick	0	An Isaac Asimov Omnibus.	(4/7/9)
27)	1967 4 Square		Through a Glass Clearly.	(s/P)
28)	1968 Doubleday		Asimov's Mysteries.	(s/RP)

as *Paul French

5)	1952 Doubleday	-1	David Starr, Space Ranger.
8)	1953 Doubleday	-2	Lucky Starr and the Pirates of the Asteroids.
11)	1954 Doubleday	-3	Lucky Starr and the Oceans of Venus.
14)	1956 Doubleday	-4	Lucky Starr and the Big Sun of Mercury.
16)	1957 Doubleday	-5	Lucky Starr and the Moons of Jupiter.
18)	1958 Doubleday	-6	Lucky Starr and the Rings of Saturn.

with Groff Conklin

22) 1963 Collier   50 Short Science Fiction Tales. (@/P)

SER: 1) Foundation Trilogy;   2) Lucky Starr.

FPS: "Marooned Off Vesta,"   Amazing, March, 1939.

WIP: 1969 Doubleday   Nightfall and Other Stories. (s)

***   ***   ***   ***   ***

Isaac Asimov--born January 2, 1920 at Petrovichi, Russia--B.S., Columbia University, 1939; M.A., Columbia University, 1941; Ph.D. (Chemistry), Columbia University, 1948--Hugo Award, Special Award, 1963; Best All-Time Series, 1966, The Foundation Series; Guest of Honor, 13th World Science Fiction Convention (Clevention), 1955--West Newton, Massachusetts.

Son of Judah & Anna Rachel (Berman) Asimov--Gertrude Blugerman: July 26, 1942-- David Asimov (August 20, 1951); Robyn Asimov (February 19, 1955).

Instructor, Boston University School of Medicine, 1949-1951; Assistant Professor, 1951-1955; Associate Professor, 1955-DATE; Contributing Science Editor, Venture, January, 1958-July, 1958; The Magazine of Fantasy and Science Fiction, February, 1959-February, 1963; Science Editor, March, 1963-DATE; Free-Lance Writer and Editor, 1939-DATE--Member: Science Fiction Writers of America; Authors' Club; American Chemical Society; Sigma Xi.

NOTE: Mr. Asimov moved to the United States in 1923, and became a United States citizen in 1928.

- -

JOHN AYLESWORTH

1)   1963 Avon   Fee, Fei, Fo Fum. (P)

FPS: 1963 Avon   Fee, Fei, Fo Fum. (P)

***   ***   ***   ***   ***

John B. Aylesworth (u)--born August 18, 1938, at Toronto, Ontario, Canada--attended Forest Hill Collegiate--Los Angeles, California.

Son of Fredrick & Marie Aylesworth--Nancy: July 1, 1961--John Aylesworth (6); Cynthia Aylesworth (4); William Aylesworth (3); Thomas Aylesworth (1).

Has been a television writer for Canadian Broadcasting Company, Perry Como Show, Judy Garland Show, "Frank Sinatra--the Man and His Work," "Herb Alpert Special;" currently Producer, Jonathan Winters Show.

NIGEL BALCHIN

1)   1943 Collins   The Small Back Room.
2)   1967 Collins   Kings of Infinite Space. (RP)

NOTE: Nigel Marlin Balchin was born in 1908. A complete biography may be found in Who's Who. He could not be located.

B.N. BALL

1)   1964 Hamilton   Tales of Science Fiction. (@/RP)
2)   1965 Dobson   Sundog. (RP)
3)   1968 Dobson   1 Timepiece.

FPS: an article on the Communist invasion of Tibet, Birmingham Town Crier, 1948.
FSF: "The Pioneer,"   New Worlds, February, 1962.

WIP: 1969 Dobson   2 Timepit.
                          3 Timepivot.

***   ***   ***   ***   ***

Brian Neville Ball--born June 19, 1932 in England--B.A., London University, 1960; M.A., Sheffield University, 1968--Doncaster, Yorkshire, England.

Son of Walter & Elsie (Booth) Ball--Margaret Snead: August, 1955--Jane Ball (11); Amanda Ball (5).

Teacher, various secondary schools, 1955-1965; College Lecturer, College of

B.N. BALL (continued)

Education, 1965-DATE; Free-Lance Writer--Member: Doncaster R.U.F.C.

Mr. Ball writes:
"I've given some thought to why I like writing sf: I think it's the wrestle with metaphysics that excites me. Then there's the topsy-turvy nature of science fiction. If you recall the Royal Hatcheries of Barsoom, as I try to do when I get over-serious, you'll see what I mean: I think didacticism is not for this genre. The sf writer, if he can preserve his sense of what is and isn't asinine, can intuitively put his finger into lots of interesting plum-filled metaphysical pies, and draw out awesomely rich speculative plums."

JOHN BALL

1)	1958 Duell	Operation Springboard.
1A)	1960 Hutchinson	Operation Space.
2)	1960 Duell	Spacemaster I.
FPS:	1947 Rutgers	Records for Pleasure. (nf)
FSF:	1958 Duell	Operation Springboard.

*** *** *** *** ***

John Dudley Ball, Jr.--born July 8, 1911 at Schenectady, New York--B.A., Carroll College, 1934--Edgar Award, Best Novel, 1965, In the Heat of the Night; British Critics Award, Best Novel of the Year, 1966, In the Heat of the Night; Academy Award, Best Picture of the Year, Best Story of the Year, "In the Heat of the Night"--Encino, California.

Son of John Dudley & Alena L. (Wiles) Ball--Patricia M. Hamilton: August 22, 1942 --John Dudley Ball III (March 2, 1952).

Has served as a newspaper writer and editor; Director of Public Relations, Institute of the Aerospace Sciences, 1958-1961; Editor-in-Chief; DMS Publications, 1961-1963; Free-Lance Writer, 1964-DATE--Member: Aviation Space Writers Association; Trained Cormorants (Scion Society of the Baker Street Irregulars; President, 1964-DATE); Japanese-American Citizens League (Chapter President, 1969).

J.G. BALLARD

1)	1962 Berkley	The Wind from Nowhere. (P/RH)
2)	1962 Berkley	The Voices of Time. (s/P)
3)	1962 Berkley	The Drowned World. (P/RH)
4)	1962 Berkley	Billenium. (s/P)
5)	1963 Gollancz	The Four-Dimensional Nightmare. (RP)
6)	1963 Berkley	Passport to Eternity. (s/P)

J.G. BALLARD (continued)

7)	1964 Berkley	Terminal Beach. (s/RH)
8)	1964 Berkley	The Burning World. (P/RHv)
8A)	1965 Cape	The Drought. (RP)
9)	1965 Doubleday	The Drowned World and The Wind from Nowhere.
10)	1966 Berkley	The Impossible Man. (s/P)
11)	1966 Cape	The Crystal World. (RP)
12)	1967 Panther	The Day of Forever. (s/P)
13)	1967 Cape	The Disaster Area.
14)	1967 Panther	The Overloaded Man. (s/P)
FPS:	"Prima Belladonna,"	Science Fantasy, December, 1956.
FPP:	"Escapement,"	New Worlds, December, 1956 (simultaneous).
WIP:	1969 Cape	The Atrocity Exhibition.
	1969 Putnam	The Best Science Fiction Stories of J.G. Ballard. (s)

***   ***   ***   ***   ***

James Graham Ballard--born November 15, 1930 at Shanghai, China--attended King's College, Cambridge University--Weybridge, Surrey, England.

Son of James & Edna (Johnstone) Ballard--Helen Mary Matthews: 1954-1964--James Ballard (13); Fay Ballard (11); Beatrice Ballard (9).

Free-Lance Writer.

Mr. Ballard responded to questions in the following manner:
   "The current state of sf--extremely interesting, at least in Britain--in the USA less so--American sf writers seem pallid and unadventurous; possibly the commercial publishing scene dominates them--most sf anyway is being produced by other means--science itself, the visual arts, and so on--the sort of imaginative sf that is required now is beyond the range or abilities of most of its present writers, if not all. Where is the new wave headed--towards becoming the most important literature of the last decades of the twentieth century, in fact, the new mainstream--and about time, too. Science Fiction has been in continuous evolution since Wells--there is nothing particularly unique about modern sf of the 40's and 50's--that has now lost its relevance and vitality, and a new, far more relevant science fiction has appeared."

OWEN BARFIELD

2)	1963 Faber	Worlds Apart.
3)	1965 Faber	Unancestral Voice.
4)	1968 Eerdmans	The Silver Trumpet.
		as *G.A.L. Burgeon
1)	1950 Gollancz	This Ever Diverse Pair.

OWEN BARFIELD (continued)

FPS: 1925
FSF: 1950 Gollancz   This Ever Diverse Pair. (as *G.A.L. Burgeon)

***   ***   ***   ***   ***

Arthur Owen Barfield--born November 9, 1898 at London, England--B.A., Wadham College, Oxford University, 1921; B. Litt., Oxford University, 1922; M.A., Oxford University, 1934; B.C.L., Oxford University, 1934--Dartford, Kent, England.

Son of Arthur Edward & Elizabeth (Shoults) Barfield--Matilda Christian Douie: April 11, 1923--Alexander Barfield; Lucy Barfield.

Lawyer, 1934-1960; Chairman, International Help for Children, 1954-DATE--Member: International P.E.N.; Royal Society of Literature (Fellow); Anthroposophical Society in Great Britain (Honorary Treasurer, 1960-1964); Athenaeum Club.

CHARLES BARREN

1) 1966 Library 33 Panther   with R. Cox Abel (q.v.)
Trivana 1. (H-P)

NOTE: Charles Barren was born in 1913. A complete biography may be found in Contemporary Authors.

WILLIAM E. BARRETT

1) 1939 Lippincott   Flight from Youth.
2) 1960 Doubleday   The Edge of Things. (1/s)
3) 1963 Doubleday   The Fools of Time. (RP)

FPS: "The Music of Madness," Weird Tales, March, 1926.

***   ***   ***   ***   ***

William Edmund Barrett--born November 16, 1900 at New York, New York--attended Manhattan College--Citation, Regis College, 1956; Litt.D., Creighton University, 1961--Denver, Colorado.

Son of John Joseph & Eleanor Margaret (Flannery) Barrett--Christine M. Rollman: February 15, 1925--William Edmund Barrett, Jr.; Marjorie Christine Barrett.

Advertising Manager, Westinghouse Co., 1923-1929; Free-Lance Writer, 1929-DATE; Member: P.E.N.; Colorado Authors League (President, 1943-1944); National Press Club.

ALAN FRANK BARTER

1) 1966 Macmillan   with Raymond Wilson (q.v.)
                    Untravelled Worlds. (@/P)

FPS: 1966 Macmillan Untravelled Worlds. (@/P/with Raymond Wilson)

***   ***   ***   ***   ***

Alan Frank Barter--born August 20, 1933 at Cardiff, South Wales--B.A., Cambridge University, 1957; M.A., Cambridge University, 1960--Sedbergh, Yorkshire, England.

Son of Edwin & Catherine Irene (Thomas) Barter--Susan Fembridge: August 1, 1959--Andrew Barter (7); Mark Barter (5).

Schoolmaster, Dulwich College, 1958-1962; Sedbergh School, 1962-DATE (currently Head of English Department)--Member: various golf clubs.

NOTE: Mr. Barter played rugby for Cambridge University, and later attained the final trial in rugby for Wales.

Some remarks by Mr. Barter on his collaborator may be found in the entry of Raymond Wilson (q.v.).

- -

ERLE BARTON

1) 1963 Badger SN   The Unseen. (P)
2) 1964 Badger SF   The Planet Seekers. (P)

NOTE: Erle Barton is a probable pseudonym, R. Lionel Fanthorpe (q.v.) being the likely author of all or most of the works under this name.

- -

BEN BARZMAN

1) 1960 Collins   Out of This World. (RP)
2) 1960 Putnam   Twinkle, Twinkle Little Star. (RPv)
2A) 1962 Pap Lib   Echo X. (P)

- -

ROBERT BATEMAN

1) 1963 Dobson   When the Whites Went. (RP)

FPS: 1957 Museum   Instructions to Young Athletes. (nf)
FSF: 1963 Dobson   When the Whites Went.

ROBERT BATEMAN (continued)

WIP: "a vague project for an sf book later this year."

***   ***   ***   ***   ***

Robert Moyes Carruthers Bateman--born June 21, 1922 at Manchester, England--Ifield, Sussex, England.

Son of Gerald Ashworth & Agnes Helen (Moyes) Bateman--(1) Anne Marion Bohan: June 1, 1944/1957; (2) Margot Winifred Wardle: September 20, 1957--1) Geoffrey Bateman (22); Jacquelin Bateman (21); Felicity Bateman (13); 2) Lucy Emma Bateman (7).

Has been in television broadcasting and reporting most of his life; Chief Sub-Editor, Independent Television News, Ltd., 1955-1956; Sports Editor, 1956-DATE --Member: various philatelic organizations.

JOHN BAXTER

1) 1966 Ace   The Off-Worlders. (P)
2) 1968 Angus   The Pacific Book of Australian Science Fiction. (@/RP)

FKP: "Vendetta's End,"   Science Fiction Adventures, November, 1962.

NOTE: John Martin Baxter is an Australian writer.

PETER S. BEAGLE

1) 1960 Viking   A Fine and Private Place. (RP)
2) 1968 Viking   The Last Unicorn. (RP)

FPS: "Telephone Call,"   Seventeen, 1956.
FSF: 1960 Viking   A Fine and Private Place.

WIP: see below

***   ***   ***   ***   ***

Peter Soyer Beagle--born April 20, 1939, at New York, New York--B.A., University of Pittsburgh, 1959; graduate study at Stanford University, 1960-1961--Wallace Stegner Fellowship, 1960-1961--Santa Cruz, California.

Son of Simon & Rebecca (Soyer) Beagle--Enid Nordeen: May 8, 1964--Vickie (15); Kalisa (10); Daniel (7).

Free-Lance Writer--Member: Science Fiction Writers of America; Authors Guild;

PETER S. BEAGLE (continued)

Dramatists Guild; P.E.N.

"Work in Progress:
"I am about to start work on the screenplay of The Last Unicorn, which will hopefully be done as a live movie. After that, I'll start on a new novel--it could be considered a fantasy, but the setting will be realistic 20th century Berkeley, and it won't always be easy to tell when something unquestionably supernatural is happening. My main interest as a writer is in this common ground that the Perfectly Serious shares with the Absurd, the matter-of-fact with the terrifying, the costume with the skin, the mask with the face. I don't know if this is the only way to deal with America (which is certainly as fantastic a country as Middle-Earth or Prydain, and almost as real), but it concerns and challenges me right now. If I can get that continually shifting frontier mapped--at least for a moment--then I'll try something else. I think of fantasy as a way of seeing rather than a definite state or style, and I like it."

JACK BEECHING

1) 1968 Cape   The Dakota Project.

THORNTON BELL

1) 1964 Badger SF   Space Trap. (P)
2) 1964 Badger SN   Chaos. (P)

NOTE: Thornton Bell is a probable pseudonym, R. Lionel Fanthorpe (q.v.) being the likely author of all or most of the works under this name.

MARGOT BENNETT

1) 1968 Eyre   The Curious Masters.

FKP: "An Old-Fashioned Poker for My Uncle's Head," The Magazine of Fantasy and Science Fiction, May, 1954.

DONALD R. BENSEN

1) 1963 Pyramid   The Unknown. (@/P)
2) 1964 Pyramid   The Unknown Five. (@/P)

FPS: reviews for The Saturday Review.
FSF: 1963 Pyramid   The Unknown. (@/P)

DONALD R. BENSEN (continued)

***   ***   ***   ***   ***

Donald Roynold Bensen--born October 3, 1927 at Brooklyn, New York--A.B., Columbia University, 1950--New York, New York.

Son of Roynold & Dorothy (Thatcher) Bensen--Anne McCurdy: October 11, 1957 --Nicholas Thatcher Bensen (February 18, 1965).

Production Manager, Funk & Wagnalls, 1951-1952; Assistant Editor, Peoples Book Club, 1952-1956; Editor, Pyramid Books, 1957-1968; Executive Editor, Berkley Books, 1968-DATE--Member: Trap Door Spiders; Witch Doctors.

RAFE BERNARD

1)	1954 Ward, Lock		The Wheel in the Sky. (RP)
2)	1967 Corgi		The Halo Highway. (P)
2A)	1967 Pyramid	3	Army of the Undead. (P)

SER: The Invaders (British edition unnumbered).

ALFRED BESTER

1)	1953 Shasta	The Demolished Man. (RP)
2)	1953 Dial	Who He?
3)	1956 Sidgwick	Tiger! Tiger! (RP/RPv)
3A)	1957 Signet	The Stars My Destination. (P)
4)	1958 Signet	Starburst. (s/P)
5)	1959 Panther	The Rat Race. (P)
6)	1964 Signet	The Dark Side of Earth. (s/P)
7)	1967 Sidgwick	An Alfred Bester Omnibus. (1/3/6)

FKP: "The Broken Axiom," Thrilling Wonder, April, 1939.

NOTE: Alfred Bester was born in 1913. A former member of Science Fiction Writers of America, he received a Hugo Award, Best Novel, 1953, The Demolished Man, and was Book Editor, The Magazine of Fantasy and Science Fiction, October, 1960-July, 1962. A complete biography may be found in Contemporary Authors.

LLOYD BIGGLE, JR.

1)	1961 Ace	The Angry Espers. (P/RH)
2)	1963 Doubleday	All the Colors of Darkness. (RP)
3)	1965 Doubleday	The Fury Out of Time. (RP)

LLOYD BIGGLE, JR. (continued)

4)	1966 Doubleday	Watchers of the Dark. (RP)
5)	1967 Doubleday	The Rule of the Door and Other Fanciful Regulations. (s/RP)
6)	1968 Doubleday	The Still, Small Voice of Trumpets. (RP)
FKP:	"Gypped,"	Galaxy, July, 1956.

NOTE: Lloyd Biggle, Jr. was born in 1923. He was the first Secretary/Treasurer of Science Fiction Writers of America, serving from 1965-1967. A complete biography may be found in Contemporary Authors.

OTTO O. BINDER

6)	1967 Bantam	The Avengers Battle the Earth-Wrecker. (P)
		as *Eando Binder
1)	1948 Prime	Lords of Creation. (RP)
2)	1965 Belmont	Anton York, Immortal. (P)
3)	1965 Pap Lib	Adam Link--Robot. (P)
4)	1965 Avalon	with Earl Andrew Binder as *Eando Binder Enslaved Brains.
5)	1966 Ballantine	with Craig Tennis Dracula. (P)
FPS:	"The First Martian,"	Amazing, October, 1932 (with Earl Andrew Binder as *Eando Binder).
WIP:	1969 Belmont 1	Secret of the Flying Saucers. (P)

***   ***   ***   ***   ***

Otto Oscar Binder--born August 26, 1911 at Bessemer, Michigan--attended Crane City College, 1929-31; Northwestern University, 1932; University of Chicago, 1932-1933--Chestertown, New York.

Son of Michael & Marie (Payer) Binder--Ione Frances Turek: November 2, 1940 --Mary Lorine Binder (died March 27, 1967, age 14).

Editor-in-Chief, Space World, 1959-1962; Publisher, 1962-1963; Free-Lance Writer (mainly of comics), 1930-DATE.

NOTE: Mr. Binder mentions that he never obtained a college degree, being short of credits and money at the time. "But NASA, on contracting me as a writer in 1965 for one year, to write high school educational material on the Mercury, Gemini, and Apollo Programs, told me this in effect gave me an honorary M.S.

OTTO O. BINDER (continued)

degree (for my long background in writing science articles, and for editorship of <u>Space World</u>). Hence, the Goddard Space Flight Center of NASA offered me a post as public relations technical writer on the basis of these qualifications. So I can teach science today in high school, if I wish."

He also comments:

"According to Sam Moskowitz, my single original contribution to science fiction--that is, introducing a new category of stories--is the <u>first person robot story</u>, as per my Adam Link series. They were not the first robot stories, of course, but the first in the first person, and with a new depth in 'humanizing' robots, as I think Sam puts it.

"My impression of the sf field today is that the magazines have fallen into some kind of semi-limbo, and show little sign of change or improvement or appeal; whereas the paperback book market is thriving and boisterous, with many new and quite good novel-length tales appearing with perennial regularity. And I have (as of this past year) decided to join this book market, already having a contract for a novel for Belmont Books. This 'return to the fold,' as it were, is now in full gear since moving from New Jersey to a small, quiet town in upstate New York.

"As for where the field is headed, I think it will always be a stimulating glimpse into the future, near or far, or into strange lands in unknown universes. By combining both a semi-scientific and therefore 'logical' basis to stories, plus pure entertainment value, I think sci-fi is here to stay--at least in the paperbacks. The magazines?...who knows.

"At any rate, I hope to show up more and more in the pbs from now on, having a file full of what I think are good new ideas. In a sense, this is a return to my 'first love,' as I was out of the field almost entirely between 1942 and 1965, and a sort of anticipatory glow came from my switchover (from the comics field, where I wrote such main characters as Captain Marvel of old and Superman of today)."

JEROME BIXBY

1) 1964 Ballantine. <u>Space by the Tale</u>. (s/P)
2) 1964 Brandon <u>Devil's Scrapbook</u>. (s/P)

FPS: "Tubemonkey," <u>Planet Stories</u>, Winter, 1949.

***   ***   ***   ***   ***

Drexel Jerome Lewis Bixby--born January 11, 1923 at Los Angeles, California-- Crestline, California.

Son of Rex Vancil & Ila (Lewis) Bixby--(2) Linda Burman: December 27, 1967-- Russell Albert Bixby; Jan Emerson Bixby; Leonardo Brook Bixby.

Editor, <u>Planet Stories,</u> Summer, 1950-July, 1951; <u>Two Complete Science-Adventure</u>

JEROME BIXBY (continued)

Books, Winter, 1950-Summer, 1951; Associate Editor, Galaxy, Thrilling Wonder Stories, and Startling Stories during the early 1950's; Owner, Exoterica, Bullhead City, Arizona, 1963-1964; Walden Realty Company, Bullhead City, Arizona, 1964-1965 (both now defunct); Free-Lance Writer--Member: Writers Guild of America, West.

NOTE: Mr. Bixby states that his primary interest is symphonic composition, and that his hobbies are architecture, painting, and psychical research. He mentions: "Have recently concentrated entirely on film work, and have lost touch with current sf. I doubt that I've made any contribution to the field, as such ... wish I had."

THOMAS BLAKE

1) 1968 Vantage   U.N. Confidential--A.D. 2000.

JAMES BLISH

#	Year	Publisher		Title
1)	1951	Greenberg		Jack of Eagles. (RP/RPv)
2)	1953	Galaxy		The Warriors of Day. (P)
3)	1955	Putnam	3	Earthman, Come Home. (RP)
4)	1956	Faber	1	They Shall Have Stars. (RP/RPv)
1A)	1956	Avon		ESPer. (P)
5)	1957	Gnome		The Seedling Stars. (RP)
4A)	1957	Avon	1	Year 2018. (P)
6)	1957	Faber		Fallen Star. (RP/RPv)
7)	1958	Avon	4	The Triumph of Time. (P/RHv)
8)	1958	Ballantine	-4	A Case of Conscience. (P/RH)
6A)	1958	Ballantine		The Frozen Year. (P)
9)	1958	Avon		VOR. (P)
10)	1959	Signet		Galactic Cluster. (s/P/RH)
7A)	1959	Faber	4	A Clash of Cymbals.
12)	1961	Putnam	+1	The Star Dwellers. (RP)
13)	1961	Ballantine		So Close to Home. (s/P)
14)	1961	Berkley		Titan's Daughter. (P)
15)	1962	Ballantine		The Night Shapes. (P)
16)	1962	Putnam	2	A Life for the Stars. (RP)
17)	1964	Faber	-1	Doctor Mirabilis.
19)	1965	Faber		Best Science Fiction Stories of James Blish. (s)
20)	1965	Putnam	+2	Mission to the Heart Stars.
21)	1966	Ballantine		New Dreams This Morning. (@/P)
22)	1967	Bantam		Star Trek. (s/P)
24)	1968	Bantam		Star Trek 2. (s/P)
25)	1968	Doubleday	-2	Black Easter. (RP)
26)	1968	Weybright		The Vanished Jet.

JAMES BLISH (continued)

11)	1959 Avalon		with Robert A.W. Lowndes (q.v.) The Duplicated Man. (RP)
18)	1964 Advent		as *William Atheling, Jr. The Issue at Hand. (nf/s/RP)
23)	1967 Doubleday		with Norman L. Knight (q.v.) A Torrent of Faces. (RP)

SER: 1) Cities in Flight;   2) After Such Knowledge
NOTE: the Star Trek volumes are collaborations based on scripts originally used for the program.

FPS: "Emergency Refueling,"   Super Science Stories, March, 1940.

WIP: 1969 Bantam   Star Trek 3. (s/P)
     1969 Bantam   an untitled Star Trek novel. (P)
          Doubleday   Anywhen. (s)
          Avon   King Log. (P)
          Doubleday   And All the Stars a Stage.
          Doubleday -3 The Day After Judgment.
          Dell   Beep. (P)

***   ***   ***   ***   ***

James Benjamin Blish--born May 23, 1921 at Orange, New Jersey--B.Sc., Rutgers University, 1942; graduate study at Columbia University, 1945-1946--Hugo Award, Best Novel, 1959, A Case of Conscience; Guest of Honor, 18th World Science Fiction Convention (Pittcon), 1960--Brooklyn, New York/Marlow, Berkshire, England.

Son of Asa Rhodes & Dorothea (Schneewind) Blish--(1) Mildred Virginia Kidd: May 23, 1947/1963; (2) Judith Ann Lawrence: November 9, 1963--1) Elisabeth Blish; Charles Benjamin Blish.

Editor, Vanguard Science Fiction, June, 1958 (only issue); Trade Newspaper Editor, 1947-1951; Public Relations Counsel, Hill and Knowlton, Inc, 1951-1969; Free-Lance Writer; Editor, Kalki (a journal of the James Branch Cabell Society), 1967-DATE--Member: Science Fiction Writers of America (Vice-president, 1966-1968); History of Science Society.

He writes:
"1. Current State of Science Fiction. Flourishing.
2. Where It Is Headed. I don't know.
3. Opinion of 'New Wave': valuable experimentation with all the botches you would expect of any experiment.
4. What My Own Work Has Contributed: technical criticism, and a few precedents in the realm of subject matter?"

ROBERT BLOCH

1)	1945 Arkham	The Opener of the Way. (s)
2)	1945 Utopian	The Sea Witch. (P)
3)	1960 Arkham	Pleasant Dreams: Nightmares. (s/RPav)
4)	1961 S & S	Blood Runs Cold. (s/RP)
3A)	1961 Belmont	Nightmares. (s/a/P)
5)	1962 Belmont	More Nightmares. (s/P)
6)	1962 Belmont	Terror. (P)
7)	1962 Belmont	Yours Truly, Jack the Ripper. (s/P)
8)	1962 Gold Medal	Atoms and Evil. (s/P)
9)	1962 Advent	The Eighth Stage of Fandom. (nf/s/RP)
10)	1963 Belmont	Horror-7. (s/P)
11)	1963 Pyramid	Bogey Men. (s/P)
12)	1965 Tandem	The House of the Hatchet. (s/P)
13)	1965 Pyramid	Tales in a Jugular Vein. (s/P)
14)	1965 Pyramid	The Skull of the Marquis de Sade. (s/P)
15)	1966 Award	Chamber of Horrors. (s/P)
16)	1967 4 Square	Torture Garden. (s/P)
17)	1967 Belmont	The Living Demons. (s/P)
18)	1967 Tandem	The Night Walker. (s/P)
19)	1968 Belmont	Ladies' Day and This Crowded Earth. (P)

FPS:	"The Secret in the Tomb,"	Weird Tales, May, 1935.
FPP:	"The Feast in the Abbey,"	Weird Tales, January, 1935.
WIP:	1969 Mirage	Dragons and Nightmares. (s)

***   ***   ***   ***   ***

Robert Albert Bloch--born April 5, 1917 at Chicago, Illinois--Hugo Award, Best Short Story, 1959, "The Hell-Bound Train;" Guest of Honor, 6th World Science Fiction Convention (Torcon), 1948; E.E. Evans Memorial Award; Screen Guild Award; Mystery Writers of America Special Scroll, 1961; Trieste Science Fiction Film Festival Award, 1965; Ann Radcliffe Television Award, 1966; Ann Radcliffe Literature Award, 1969--Los Angeles, California.

Son of Raphael A. & Stella (Loeb) Bloch--(1) Marion Holcombe: October 2, 1940/1963; (2) Eleanor Alexander: October 16, 1964--1) Sally Ann Bloch (25).

Copywriter for an advertising agency, 1942-1953; Radio Program Writer, 1945 (adapted 39 of his stories for the radio series, Stay Tuned for Terror); Television Panelist, 1954-1959; Free-Lance Television and Screen Writer, 1960-DATE--Member: Science Fiction Writers of America; Mystery Writers of America; Writers' Guild; Count Dracula Society; Academy of Motion Picture Arts and Sciences.

Mr. Bloch writes:
"Science is catching up with science fiction, and science fiction is catching up--stylistically--with mainstream writing. Hopefully, this augurs a wider general audience for the genre, though perhaps the media-shift will be to film and television. Through the years, most of my work has been on the peripheral

ROBERT BLOCH (continued)

edges of science fiction proper--fantasy, weird-horror and suspense, together with a smattering of humor. To the extent that psychopathology is classifiable as a branch of medical science, my other novels--The Scarf, Spiderweb, Shooting Star, The Will to Kill, The Kidnaper, Psycho, The Dead Beat, Firebug, The Couch, The Star-Stalker, and The Todd Dossier--all contain these elements as they pertain to an examination of subjective reality. I cannot lay claim to playing any significant part in the development of science fiction except insofar as I have attempted in a small way to focus attention on man rather than machines. And I do feel that the exploration of outer space must eventually give way to an exploration of inner space--i.e., the human psyche--if science fiction is to attain maturity. The monsters and marvels moving unnoticed in our midst deserve, I believe, the fuller consideration of writers and readers alike."

ERNEST J. BLOW

1) 1963 Consul   Appointment in Space. (P)

TOM BOARDMAN, JR.

1) 1965 4 Square   The Unfriendly Future. (@/P)
2) 1965 Penguin   Connoisseur's Science Fiction. (@/P)
3) 1966 4 Square   An ABC of Science Fiction. (@/P)
4) 1968 Dobson   Science Fiction Horizons No. 1. (@)

FPS: Science Fiction criticism to Books and Bookmen, 1959.

***   ***   ***   ***   ***

Thomas Volney Boardman, Jr.--born December 20, 1930 at Bronxville, New York--attended Haileybury and Imperial Service College--London, England.

Son of Thomas Volney & Dorothy C. Boardman--Joyce Parkinson: September 20, 1952 --Thomas Volney Boardman IV (September 16, 1953); Mary Jean Boardman (May 4, 1955).

Publisher and Editor of books; currently Export Manager for a large British publishing group; also Science Fiction Editor, Macdonald & Co, Ltd.; and a science fiction book reviewer--Member: Science Fiction Writers of America; British Science Fiction Association; Mystery Writers of America; Crime Writers Association.

J.F. BONE

1) 1962 Bantam   The Lani People. (P)

J.F. BONE (continued)

FKP: "Survival Type,"   <u>Galaxy</u>, March, 1957.

NOTE: Jesse Franklin Bone was born in 1916. A physician, Dr. Bone is a member of Science Fiction Writers of America.

BEN BOVA

1) 1959 Winston   <u>The Star Conquerors.</u>
2) 1964 Holt   <u>Star Watchman.</u>
3) 1967 Holt   <u>The Weathermakers.</u>
4) 1968 Holt   <u>Out of the Sun.</u>

FPS: 1959 Winston   <u>The Star Conquerors.</u>

WIP: 1969 Holt   <u>The Dueling Machine.</u>
       Holt   <u>Escape!</u>

***   ***   ***   ***   ***

Benjamin William Bova--born November 8, 1932 at Philadelphia, Pennsylvania --B.S., Temple University, 1954--Arlington, Massachusetts.

Son of Benjamin & Giove (Caporiccio) Bova--Rosa Cucinotta: November 28, 1953 --Michael Francis Bova (11); Regina Marie Bova (9).

Editor, <u>Upper Darby News</u>, 1953-1956; Technical Editor, Martin Aircraft Company (on Vanguard Project), 1956-1958; Screen Writer, Physical Science Study Committee, Massachusetts Institute of Technology, 1958-1959; Science Writer, Avco Everett Research Lab, 1960-1964; Manager of Marketing, 1964-DATE; Free-Lance Writer--Member: Science Fiction Writers of America; National Association of Science Writers; American Association for the Advancement of Science.

In answer to the editors' questions, Mr. Bova writes:
   "1) The current state of sf seems healthy and vigorous--more so than I've ever seen it before. 2) I can't make a general statement about a 'wave.' There are many 'New Wave' writers that I enjoy reading, others who leave me cold. Same for 'old wave' writers. I do get bothered by stories that are scientifically <u>wrong</u>--after all, the name of the game is science fiction. 3) My contributions to the field have been totally negligible."

ETTA BOWDEN
with Phil Bowden (q.v.)

1) 1965 Vantage   <u>Mercy Island.</u>

PHIL BOWDEN

1) 1965 Vantage   with Etta Bowden (q.v.)
                      Mercy Island.

---

*JOHN BOYD

1) 1968 Weybright   The Last Starship from Earth. (RP)

FPS: 1968 Weybright   The Last Starship from Earth.
FPP: 1968 Weybright   The Slave Stealer (as Boyd Upchurch) (simultaneous).

WIP: 1969 Weybright   The Pollinators of Eden.
                      The Rakehells of Heaven.

***   ***   ***   ***   ***

Boyd Bradfield Upchurch--born October 3, 1919 at Atlanta, George--A.B., University of Southern California, 1947--Los Angeles, California.

Son of Ivie Doss & Margaret (Blake) Upchurch--Fern Gillaspy: January 26, 1944 --no children.

Professional Salesman of Photoengravings--Member: Science Fiction Writers of America.

LEIGH BRACKETT

1)	1951 Pemberton	Shadow Over Mars. (P)
2)	1952 Gnome	The Starmen. (RPv)
3)	1953 Ace	The Sword of Rhiannon. (P/RH)
4)	1955 Doubleday	The Long Tomorrow. (RP)
2A)	1955 Ace	The Galactic Breed. (P)
5)	1955 Ace	The Big Jump. (P)
1A)	1961 Ace	The Nemesis from Terra. (P)
6)	1963 Ace	Alpha Centauri--Or Die! (P)
7)	1964 Ace	People of the Talisman. (P)
8)	1964 Ace	The Secret of Sinharat. (P)
9)	1967 Ace	The Coming of the Terrans. (s/P)

FPS: "Martian Quest,"   Astounding, February, 1940.

***   ***   ***   ***   ***

Leigh Douglass Brackett--born December 7, 1915 at Los Angeles, California --Jules Verne Award for Fantasy; Spur Award, Best Novel, 1963, Follow the Free Wind; Guest of Honor, 22nd World Science Fiction Convention (Pacificon II), 1964 --Lancaster, California/Kinsman, Ohio.

LEIGH BRACKETT (continued)

Daughter of William Franklin & Margaret (Douglass) Brackett--Edmond Moore Hamilton: December 31, 1946--no children.

Free-Lance Writer--Member: Science Fiction Writers of America; Western Writers of America; Authors League; Writers Guild of America.

Miss Brackett makes the following comments:
"On the current state of science fiction: Magazine-wise, from a writer's standpoint, not good; though there are excellent magazines, there are not enough of them to provide an adequate short story market for the beginner, wherein to learn his trade. In the artistic sense, from the reader's standpoint, very good indeed; there is great variety, a type of sf to suit every taste. Some of the more pretentious works seem to have more pretense than substance, but then I could never read Faulkner, either. On the 'new wave:' Like the 'nouvelle vague' in the films, some good, some bad, some just ho-hum. Experimentation is healthy, and the experiments that don't succeed seem just to die of attrition. I have nothing against anyone writing any sort of sf that comes into his head; the only thing I object to strenuously is an effort on the part of any group to impress its image on the field as a kind of dogma...science fiction must be this and no other. Of course it never works anyway. Years and decades ago both space opera and sword-and-sorcery were read out of the party, but I notice that they're both still around and flourishing. The public, as someone once said, still drives its dark trade in heroes. As for an opinion on how my own stories have contributed to the development of the genre...frankly, I have no idea, and it would require someone with a more objective viewpoint than I could possibly ever have to comment on this."

RAY BRADBURY

1)	1947	Arkham	Dark Carnival. (s)
2)	1950	Doubleday	The Martian Chronicles. (s/RP)
2A)	1951	Hart-Davis	The Silver Locusts. (s/RP)
3)	1951	Doubleday	The Illustrated Man. (s/RP)
4)	1952	Bantam	Timeless Stories for Today and Tomorrow. (@/P)
5)	1953	Doubleday	The Golden Apples of the Sun. (s/RP)
6)	1953	Ballantine	Fahrenheit 451. (s/H-P/RPa)
7)	1955	Ballantine	The October Country. (s/H-P/RPa/RPav)
8)	1955	Hart-Davis	Switch on the Night.
9)	1956	Bantam	The Circus of Dr. Lao and Other Improbable Stories. (@/P)
10)	1959	Doubleday	A Medicine for Melancholy. (s/RP)
10A)	1959	Hart-Davis	The Day It Rained Forever. (s/RP)
11)	1962	S & S	Something Wicked This Way Comes. (RP)
12)	1962	Doubleday	R Is for Rocket. (s/RP)
7A)	1962	4 Square	The Small Assassin. (s/a/P)
13)	1964	S & S	The Machineries of Joy. (s/RP)
14)	1965	Vintage	The Vintage Bradbury. (s/P)

RAY BRADBURY (continued)

15)	1966 Doubleday	S Is for Space. (s)
16)	1966 Doubleday	Twice 22. (s/10)
FPS:	"Pendulum,"	Super Science Stories, November, 1941 (with Henry L. Hasse).
WIP:	1969 Knopf	I Sing the Body Electric. (s)

***   ***   ***   ***   ***

Ray Douglas Bradbury--born August 22, 1920 at Waukegan, Illinois--Benjamin Franklin Award, Best Short Story in an American Magazine, 1953-1954, "Sun and Shadow;" Commonwealth Club of California Gold Medal, 1954, Fahrenheit 451; $1000 Award, National Institute of Arts and Letters, for Contribution to American Literature, 1954; Boys' Clubs of America Junior Book Award, 1956, Switch on the Night--Los Angeles, California.

Son of Leonard Spaulding & Esther (Moberg) Bradbury--Marguerite Susan McClure: September 27, 1947--Susan Bradbury; Ramona Bradbury; Bettina Bradbury; Alexandra Bradbury.

Free-Lance Writer--Member: Science Fiction Writers of America; Writers Guild of America.

RUSSELL BRADDON

1)	1964 Heinemann	The Year of the Angry Rabbit. (RP)
2)	1968 Joseph	The Inseperables.

NOTE: Russell Reading Braddon was born in 1921. A complete biography may be found in Contemporary Authors.

MARION ZIMMER BRADLEY

1)	1961 Ace	1	The Door Through Space. (P)
2)	1962 Ace		Seven from the Stars. (P)
3)	1962 Ace	2	The Planet Savers. (P)
4)	1962 Ace	3	The Sword of Aldones. (P)
5)	1963 Monarch		The Colors of Space. (P)
6)	1964 Ace		The Dark Intruder and Other Stories. (s/P)
7)	1964 Ace	4	Falcons of Narabedla. (P)
8)	1964 Ace	5	The Bloody Sun. (P)
9)	1965 Ace	6	Star of Danger. (P)

SER: Darkovan

MARION ZIMMER BRADLEY (continued)

FPS:	"Centaurus Changeling,"	The Magazine of Fantasy and Science Fiction, April, 1954.
FPP:	"Keyhole,"	Vortex #2 (1953)
	"Women Only,"	Vortex #2 (1953) (simultaneous).
WIP:	1969 Ace	The Brass Dragon. (P)

***   ***   ***   ***   ***

Marion Eleanor Zimmer Bradley Breen--born June 3, 1930 at Albany, New York--B.A., Hardin-Simmons University, 1964--Staten Island, New York.

Daughter of Leslie R. & Evelyn (Conklin) Zimmer--(1) R.A. Bradley: 1949/1964; (2) Walter Breen: 1964--1) David Stephen Bradley (November, 1950); 2) Patrick Russell Breen (October, 1964); Moira Evelyn Breen (January, 1966).

Free-Lance Writer--Member: Mystery Writers of America; Fantasy Amateur Press Association.

R. BRETNOR

1)	1953 Coward	Modern Science Fiction: Its Meaning and Its Future. (nf/@)
		as *Grendel Briarton
2)	1962 Paradox	Through Time and Space with Ferdinand Feghoot. (s/P)
FPS:	"Maybe Just a Little One,"	Harper's Magazine, August, 1947.

***   ***   ***   ***   ***

Reginald Bretnor--born July 30, 1911 at Vladivostok, Russia--Berkeley, California.

Widower--no children.

"Wrote propaganda for OWI and Dept. of State's OIICA, 1943-1947. Have been freelancing since."--Member: Science Fiction Writers of America; Mystery Writers of America; American Ordnance Association; National Rifle Association; Japanese Sword Society of the United States.

LEO BRETT

1)	1960 Badger SF	Exit Humanity. (P/RH)

LEO BRETT (continued)

2)	1960 Badger SF	The Microscopic Ones. (P)
3)	1960 Badger SF	The Faceless Planet. (P)
4)	1961 Badger SF	March of the Robots. (P)
5)	1961 Badger SF	Mind Force. (P)
6)	1961 Badger SN	Black Infinity. (P)
7)	1962 Badger SN	Nightmare. (P)
8)	1962 Badger SN	Face in the Night. (P)
9)	1962 Badger SN	The Immortals. (P)
10)	1963 Badger SN	They Never Come Back. (P)
11)	1963 Badger SN	The Forbidden. (P)
12)	1963 Badger SN	From Realms Beyond. (P)
13)	1963 Badger SF	The Alien Ones. (P/RH)
14)	1963 Badger SF	Power Sphere. (P/RH)

NOTE: Leo Brett is a probable pseudonym, R. Lionel Fanthorpe (q.v.) being the likely author of all or most of the works appearing under this name.

DEWEY C. BROOKINS

1)	1965 Vantage	Flying High.
FPP:	1965 Vantage	Flying High.

***   ***   ***   ***   ***

Dewey C. Brookins--born June 4, 1904 at Dothan, Alabama--attended United States Naval College and General Motors Trade Schools--Montgomery, Alabama.

Son of Frank & Eolin Brookins--(2) Rebecca: 1951--Wanda Brookins (1952).

Has been a United States Naval Inspector; automobile salesman; newspaper columnist; lecturer on the Bible.

FREDRIC BROWN

1)	1949 Dutton	What Mad Universe. . (RP)
2)	1951 Shasta	Space on My Hands. (s/RP)
3)	1953 Dutton	The Lights in the Sky Are Stars. (RP)
5)	1954 Dutton	Angels and Spaceships. (s/RP/RPv)
3A)	1954 Boardman	Project Jupiter. (RP)
6)	1955 Dutton	Martians, Go Home. (RP)
5A)	1956 Bantam	Star Shine. (s/P)
7)	1957 Dutton	Rogue in Space. (RP)
8)	1958 Bantam	Honeymoon in Hell. (s/P)
9)	1961 Bantam	The Mind Thing. (P)

FREDRIC BROWN (continued)

10)	1961 Bantam	<u>Nightmares and Geezenstacks</u>. (s/P)
11)	1968 Lancer	<u>Daymares</u>. (s/P)

		with Mack Reynolds (q.v.)
4)	1953 Shasta	<u>Science Fiction Carnival</u>. (@/RPa)

FPS:	"The Moon for a Nickel,"	<u>Detective Story</u>, 1936.
FSF:	"Not Yet the End,"	<u>Captain Future</u>, Winter, 1941.

***   ***   ***   ***   ***

Fredric William Brown--born October 29, 1906 at Cincinnati, Ohio--attended Hanover College, one year; University of Cincinnati, one year--Edgar Award, Best First Mystery Novel, 1948, <u>The Fabulous Clipjoint</u>,--Tucson, Arizona.

Son of Karl Lewis & Emma Amelia (Graham) Brown--(1) Helen Ruth: 1929/1947; (2) Elizabeth Charlier: 1948--1) James Ross Brown (1930); Linn Lewis Brown (1932)

"I was an office worker until 1936 (age 30), when I became a proofreader, and started selling stories. Worked at both proofreading and writing, off and on, until 1947; since then have been a full-time writer. Have written slightly more in the mystery field than in science fiction, but prefer the latter."

HARRISON BROWN

		with Chloe Zerwick (q.v.)
1)	1968 Doubleday	<u>The Cassiopeia Affair</u>. (RP)

FPS:	1946 S&S	<u>Must Destruction Be Our Destiny</u>? (nf)
FSF:	1968 Doubleday	<u>The Cassiopeia Affair</u>. (with Chloe Zerwick)

***   ***   ***   ***   ***

Harrison Scott Brown--born September 26, 1917 at Sheridan, Wyoming--B.S., University of California, 1938; Ph.D., Johns Hopkins University, 1941--American Association for the Advancement of Science Award, 1948; American Chemical Society Award, 1951; Lasker Award, 1958; LL.D., University of Alberta, 1960; D.Sc., Rutgers University, 1964; D.Sc., Amherst University, 1966--La Canada, California.

Son of Harrison H. & Agatha (Scott) Brown--(2) Rudd Owen: November 11, 1949--Eric Scott Brown (25).

Assistant Director of Chemistry, Clinton Laboratories, 1943-1946; Assistant Professor, Institute for Nuclear Studies, University of Chicago, 1946-1948; Associate Professor, 1948-1951; Professor of Geochemistry, California Institute of Technology, 1951-DATE; Professor of Science of Government, California Institute of Technology, 1967-DATE--Member: National Academy of Sciences

HARRISON BROWN (continued)

(Foreign Secretary); Philosophical Society; Phi Beta Kappa; American Association for the Advancement of Science; American Chemical Society.

JAMES GOLDIE BROWN

1)	1966 Macmillan	From Frankenstein to Andromeda.	(@/P/RH)
FPS:	1957 Longmans	School Certificate Revision in English.	(nf/P)
FSF:	1966 Macmillan	From Frankenstein to Andromeda; an Anthology of Science Fiction.	(@/P)

***   ***   ***   ***   ***

James Goldie Brown--born May 21, 1901 at Christchurch, New Zealand--M.A. (Second Class Honors in English and French), University of Canterbury, Christchurch, 1921; M.A. (First Class Honors in History), University of Canterbury, Christchurch, 1936--Auckland, New Zealand.

Son of James Taylor & Lily (Fraser) Brown--Eileen Katharine Percy: January 21, 1925--James Gerald Brown (43); Elaine Katharine Brown (39); Juliet Anne Brown (35); Andrew Fraser Brown (30).

Teacher, various schools in New Zealand and Fiji, 1919-1928; Mt. Albert Grammar School, 1928-1967; since 1967 has taught a course in letter and report writing for the employees of the Auckland city council; retirement pending.

JOHN BRUNNER

2)	1959 Ace	Threshold of Eternity.	(P)
3)	1959 Ace	The 100th Millenium.	(P/RPe)
4)	1959 Gollancz	The Brink.	
5)	1959 Ace	Echo in the Skull.	(P)
6)	1959 Ace	The World Swappers.	(P)
7)	1960 Ace	Slavers of Space.	(P/RPe)
8)	1960 Ace	The Skynappers.	(P)
9)	1960 Ace	The Atlantic Abomination.	(P)
10)	1960 Ace	Sanctuary in the Sky.	(P)
12)	1961 Ace	Meeting at Infinity.	(P)
13)	1962 Ace	Secret Agent of Terra.	(P)
15)	1962 Ace	The Super Barbarians.	(P)
16)	1962 Ace	Times Without Number.	(P)
17)	1962 Gollancz	No Future in It.	(s/RP)
18)	1963 Pyramid	The Dreaming Earth.	(P)
20)	1963 Ace	Listen! The Stars!	(P)
21)	1963 Ace	The Astronauts Must Not Land.	(P)

JOHN BRUNNER (continued)

22)	1963 Ace	The Space-Time Juggler. (P)
23)	1963 Ace	Castaways' World. (P)
24)	1963 Ace	The Rites of Ohe. (P)
25)	1964 Ace	To Conquer Chaos. (P)
26)	1964 Ace	Endless Shadow. (P)
27)	1964 Ballantine	The Whole Man. (P/RH/RHv)
27A)	1965 Faber	Telepathist. (RP)
29)	1965 Ace	Enigma from Tantalus. (P)
30)	1965 Ace	The Repairmen of Cyclops. (P)
31)	1965 Ace	The Altar on Asconel. (P)
32)	1965 Mayflower	Now Then! (s/P)
33)	1965 Ace	The Day of the Star Cities. (P)
34)	1965 Faber	The Long Result. (RP)
35)	1965 Ballantine	The Squares of the City. (P)
36)	1966 Compact	No Other Gods But Me. (s/P)
37)	1966 Ace	A Planet of Your Own. (P)
38)	1967 Ballantine	Out of My Mind. (s/P)
39)	1967 Signet	The Productions of Time. (P)
40)	1967 Ace	Born Under Mars. (P)
41)	1967 Doubleday	Quicksand. (RP)
42)	1968 4 Square	Out of My Mind. (s/P)
43)	1968 4 Square	Not Before Time. (s/P)
44)	1968 Ace	Bedlam Planet. (P)
45)	1968 Lancer	Into the Slave Nebula. (7/e/P)
46)	1968 Belmont	Father of Lies. (P)
47)	1968 Ace	Catch A Falling Star. (3/e/P)
48)	1968 Doubleday	Stand on Zanzibar. (RP)
1)	?1951 an English house	under a house pseudonym title not revealed. (P)

as *Keith Woodcott

11)	1961 Ace	I Speak for Earth. (P)
14)	1962 Ace	The Ladder in the Sky. (P)
19)	1963 Ace	The Psionic Menace. (P)
28)	1965 Ace	The Martian Sphinx. (P)

NOTE: Numbers 42 and 43 are roughly based about Number 38.
FPS: ?1951   Paperback novel published under a house pseudonym.

WIP:	1969 Ballantine	Double, Double. (P)
	1969 Ace	The Jagged Orbit. (P)
	1969 Pyramid	Black Is the Color. (P)
	1969 Belmont	The Evil That Men Do. (P)
	1969 Dell	Timescoop. (P)
	1969 Dell	The Usurpers of Carrig. (13/e/P)
	Dell	A Funny Thing Happened on My Way to the Future. (s/P)

JOHN BRUNNER (continued)

Ace	Times Without Number. (16/e/P)
Norton	The Devil's Work.
	More Things in Heaven. (21/e)

***   ***   ***   ***   ***

John Kilian Houston Brunner--born September 24, 1934 at Oxfordshire, England--British Fantasy Award, 1966--London, England.

Son of Anthony & Felicity (Whittaker) Brunner--Marjorie Rosamond Sauer: July 12, 1958--no children.

Editor, Spring Books, 1956-1958; Free-Lance Writer, 1958-DATE--Member: Science Fiction Writers of America; Crime Writers Association; P.E.N.; Society of Authors; National Union of Journalists; World Future Society; Authors Guild.

NOTE: Mr. Brunner wrote the script for The Terrornaughts, a movie version of Murray Leinster's The Wailing Asteriods.

---

*ALGIS BUDRYS

1)	1954 Lion	False Night. (P/RPe)
2)	1958 Ballantine	Man of Earth. (P)
3)	1958 Pyramid	Who? (P/RH)
4)	1959 Pyramid	The Falling Torch. (P)
5)	1960 Ballantine	The Unexpected Dimension. (s/P/RH)
6)	1960 Gold Medal	Rogue Moon. (P)
7)	1961 Regency	Some Will Not Die. (1/e/P)
8)	1963 Berkley	Budrys' Inferno. (s/P)
9)	1964 Gollancz	The Furious Future. (RP)
10)	1967 Gold Medal	The Amsirs and the Iron Thorn. (P/RHv)
10A)	1968 Gollancz	The Iron Thorn.

FPS: either "The High Purpose," Astounding, November, 1952; or "Walk to the World," Space, November, 1952.

***   ***   ***   ***   ***

Algirdas Jonas Budrys--born January 9, 1931, at Konigsberg, East Prussia--attended University of Miami, 1947-1949; Columbia University, 1951-1952--Edgar Award, Best Short Story, 1966--Evanston, Illinois.

Son of Jonas & Regina (Kashuba) Budrys--Edna F. Duna: July 24, 1954--Jeffrey John Budrys; Steven Paul Budrys; Timothy Charles Budrys; David James Budrys.

Investigations Clerk, American Express Company, 1950-1951; Assistant Editor, Gnome Press, 1952; Galaxy, 1953; Editorial Work, Royal Publications, 1958-1961;

*ALGIS BUDRYS (continued)

Editor-in-Chief, Regency Books, 1961-1963; Editorial Director, Playboy Press, 1963-1965; President and Creative Director, Commander Publications, 1965-1966; Public Relations Account Executive, Theodore R. Sills, Inc., and Young & Rubicam, Inc., 1966-DATE; Free-Lance Writer and Book Critic (Galaxy Bookshelf, February, 1965-DATE)--Member: Science Fiction Writers of America; Old Town Bicycle Club.

(H.) K(ENNETH) BULMER

3)	1952	Panther	Encounter in Space. (P)	
4)	1953	Panther	The Stars Are Ours. (H-P)	
5)	1953	Panther	Space Salvage. (P)	
6)	1953	Panther	Galactic Intrigue. (H-P)	
7)	1953	Panther	Empire of Chaos. (H-P)	
13)	1954	Warren	Challenge. (P)	
14)	1954	Hamilton	World Aflame. (H-P)	
16)	1957	Ace	City Under the Sea. (P/RH)	
17)	1959	Ace	The Secret of ZI. (P/RHv)	
18)	1959	Ace	The Changeling Worlds. (P)	
19)	1960	Ace	The Earth Gods Are Coming. (P)	
20)	1961	Ace	Beyond the Silver Sky. (P)	
21)	1961	Ace	No Man's World. (P)	
19A)	1961	Digit	Of Earth Foretold. (P)	
21A)	1962	Digit	Earth's Long Shadow. (P)	
22)	1962	Digit	The Wind of Liberty. (P)	
23)	1962	Digit	The Fatal Fire. (P)	
24)	1963	Digit	Defiance. (P)	
25)	1963	Ace	The Wizard of Starship Poseidon. (P)	
26)	1964	Ace	The Million Year Hunt. (P)	
27)	1964	Ace	Demons' World. (P)	
28)	1965	Ace	Land Beyond the Map. (P)	
27A)	1965	Compact	The Demons. (P)	
29)	1965	Ace	Behold the Stars. (P)	
30)	1966	Ace	Worlds for the Taking. (P)	
31)	1967	Ace	To Outrun Doomsday. (P)	
32)	1967	Ace	The Key to Irunium. (P)	1
33)	1967	Ace	Cycle of Nemesis. (P)	
34)	1968	Ace	The Key to Venudine. (P)	2
35)	1968	Doubleday	The Doomsday Men. (RP)	

with A.V. Clarke

1)	1952	Hamilton	Space Treason. (P)
2)	1952	Hamilton	Cybernetic Controller. (P)

as *Philip Kent

8)	1953	Pearson	Mission to the Stars. (P)
9)	1953	Pearson	Vassals of Venus. (P)

(H.) K(ENNETH) BULMER (continued)

11)	1954 Pearson		Slaves of the Spectrum. (P)
12)	1954 Pearson		Home Is the Martian. (P)
			as *Karl Maras
10)	1953 Comyns		Zhorani. (P)
15)	1955 Gaywood		Peril from Space. (P)
FPS:	1952 Hamilton		Space Treason. (P/with A.V. Clarke)
WIP:	1969 Ace		The Star Venturers. (P)
	1969 Macdonald		The Ulcer Culture.
	1969 Pap Lib		Kandar. (P)
	1969 Ace	3	The Wizards of Senchuria. (P)
17A)	19<u>69</u> Hale		The Patient Dark.

***   ***   ***   ***   ***

Henry Kenneth Bulmer--born January 14, 1921 at London, England--Horsmonden, Kent, England.

Son of Walter Ernest & Hilda Louise (Corley) Bulmer--Pamela Kathleen Buckmaster: March 7, 1953--Deborah Louise Bulmer; Lucy Ellen Bulmer; Kenneth Laurence Bulmer.

Representative of various paper merchandising and office equipment firms, 1947-1954; Free-Lance Writer, 1954-DATE--Member: Science Fiction Writers of America; Horsmonden Players (Secretary, 1964-1965).

Mr. Bulmer provided the following incidental note: "A.V. (Aubrey Vincent) Clarke was a BNF of the middle fifties, and we shared a flat together which became known as 'The Epicentre,' and for a time was the centre point around which fandom revolved. He has dropped out now, though, of fandom and sf, unfortunately."

The following is an excerpt from Mr. Bulmer's letter:
"...As for the new wave, the current new wave, that is, for we have new waves rolling in every so often, thank goodness, the freedom of modern idiom and construction can be of great benefit, though they also do give rise to a whole lot of rubbish. Many new young writers have not bothered to learn how to write; but I suppose this was always so. There are a lot of new writers in the new wave who are very good indeed. One of the more interesting aspects of the current nouvelle vague is the tone of writers; that is, their attitude to their material. It is a truism to say that the new wave has taken two different forms either side of the Atlantic ditch, and there are relationships between the four angles (there could be others, of course); but as I believe that sf is a truly international literary (I use the word from necessity here) field, eventually this present ferment will resolve into a new and better form. Then a new new wave will come along to stir things up again. If it doesn't, then sf will be dead.

(H.) K(ENNETH) BULMER (continued)

"The task of picking names today that will be considered important in, say, twenty years' time is near-insuperable. I shall not attempt it. But I will say with easy assurance that many of the 'top' names in the field today will be forgotten, whilst other practitioners who today are not held in high esteem will be seen in their true perspective. This is one reason why contemporary praise, although heady, is not important. Or, rather, is important only if it impairs the creativity of the artist in question.

"As you probably know, City Under the Sea has recently been issued over here in hardcover, and I was amused to find a review in the Sunday Times, a favourable review, which failed to mark what I would suggest is nowadays the most important aspect of this old book: that it discusses in some detail the needs of the present and future that can be fulfilled under the sea with all the current experiments going on. This was a prophetic book in that sense, although the essential task of sf is not prophecy in a narrow sense, and was a pretty early one too, contemporary with Arthur Clarke's undersea book // The Deep Range--ed. //; as far as I could tell, it was factually correct, and not a fairy-tale fantasy full of scientific errors, as almost all underwater books had been up to that time. Underwater, that is, in the naked man-in-sea sense, not submarine activity.

"I leave to others any assessment of my own 'contribution to the development of sf.' All I can say is that the underlying philosophy of my work has so far not been analysed or even understood by sf critics and reviewers, although, like most other writers, I have been subjected to uninformed attacks. In one sense (and this could be construed as a failure) it is impossible to deal with my books as single units; they form parts of a greater whole, the later ones especially, but also some of the earlier pbs. Anyway, enough of that..."

----

*ANTHONY BURGESS

1)	1962 Heinemann	A Clockwork Orange.	(RP)
2)	1962 Heinemann	The Wanting Seed.	(RP)
FPS:	1956 Heinemann	Time for a Tiger.	
FSF:	1962 Heinemann	A Clockwork Orange.	(RP)

***　　　***　　　***　　　***　　　***

John Anthony Burgess Wilson--born February 25, 1917 at Manchester, England--B.A. (Honors), Manchester University, 1940--Lija, Malta.

Son of Joseph & Elizabeth (Burgess) Wilson--(1) Llewela Isherwood Jones: January 22, 1942-March 20, 1968; (2) Liliana Macellari: September 9, 1968--1) Paolo Andrea Wilson (4).

Lecturer, Central Advisory Council for Adult Education in the Forces, 1946-1948; Lecturer in Phonetics, Ministry of Education, 1948-1950; Educational Officer, Colonial Service, 1954-1959; Free-Lance Writer--Member: P.E.N.

*ANTHONY BURGESS (continued)

"Some views of sf:
    "The form fascinates me as much as it did when I first read H.G. Wells, and, having written two books which I am assured are in the genre, I have often considered writing more. (I have, in fact, written a long short sf story published in the Hudson Review last year, but have shied from anything longer.) The trouble with sf at the moment is that it has been shunted from the main literary stream to a quirky back-channel. It receives the same critical respect as detective fiction receives, and this is overqualified, merely indulgent. The best sf is literature like Bellow, Malamud, Henry James or Joyce for that matter. Lord of the Flies is sf, so really is Finnegans Wake. But sf writers are themselves responsible for the subliterary regard in which the form is increasingly held. They are interested in language and write extremely well, but they are not much concerned with character and lack the big architectonic gift. I've just been reading Pavane by Keith Roberts, a study of present-day and future England as they might have been if the Counter-Reformation had prevailed in 1588. A wonderful idea, and wonderful writing, but the creator's mind isn't big enough to encompass it. He has to write scrappily, episodically, picking at the theme in short studies. Are not perhaps all our sf writers becoming content to be small, coterie, quirky people and refusing to compete with the so-called bigger world of 'general fiction?' This worries me."

WILLIAM R. BURKETT, JR.

1)   1965 Doubleday   Sleeping Planet. (RP)

FPS: "Sleeping Planet,"   Analog, July-September, 1964.

WIP: an sf adventure tale with Richard Laurence Baron.

***   ***   ***   ***   ***

William R. Burkett, Jr. (u)--born August 31, 1943 at Augusta, Georgia--Jacksonville, Florida/Neptune Beach, Florida.

Son of William R. & Frances (DeLong) /Lines /Burkett--Wanda Yvonne Kleppe: April 1, 1968--no children.

Has been a student, copyboy, novelist, reporter, feature writer, soldier, Sunday editor, free-lance writer; now with the Civil Service (Navy Public Relations)--Member: Authors Guild of America; National Rifle Association.

JOHN COLEMAN BURROUGHS

1)   1967 Ballantine   Treasure of the Black Falcon. (P)

JOHN COLEMAN BURROUGHS (continued)

FPS: "Man Without a World," *Thrilling Wonder Stories*, June, 1939 (with Hulbert Burroughs).

WIP: <u>Danton Doring</u> (both writing and illustrating).

***   ***   ***   ***   ***

John Coleman Burroughs--born February 28, 1913 at Chicago, Illinois--B.A., Pomona College, 1934--Malibu, California.

Son of Edgar Rice & Emma (Hulbert) Burroughs--(1) Jane Ralston: December 12, 1936/September 28, 1961; (2) Mary Nalon: December 16, 1961--1) John Ralston Burroughs (26); Danton Burroughs (24); Dian Burroughs (20); Kimberly Burroughs (13); Stacy Burroughs (11).

Free-Lance Writer and Illustrator--Honorary Member: Burroughs Bibliophiles; Member: Phi Beta Kappa.

WILLIAM BURROUGHS

1) 1959 Olympia   <u>The Naked Lunch.</u> (RP)
2) 1961 Olympia   <u>The Soft Machine.</u> (RP)
3) 1962 Olympia   <u>The Ticket That Exploded.</u> (RP)
4) 1964 Grove   <u>Nova Express.</u> (RP)

<u>NOTE</u>: William Seward Burroughs was born in 1914. A complete biography may be found in <u>Contemporary Authors</u>.

SAMUEL HOLROYD BURTON

1) 1966 Longmans   <u>Science Fiction.</u> (@)

MARTIN CAIDIN

1) 1964 Dutton   <u>Marooned.</u> (RP)
2) 1967 Dutton   <u>No Man's World.</u>
3) 1967 Meredith   <u>The Last Fathom.</u>
4) 1968 Dutton   <u>The God Machine.</u> (RP)
5) 1968 McKay   <u>Four Came Back.</u>

FPS: 1950 McBride   <u>Jets, Rockets and Guided Missiles.</u> (nf)
FSF: 1964 Dutton   <u>Marooned.</u> (RP)

MARTIN CAIDIN (continued)

WIP· 1969 Meredith   The Mendelov Conspiracy.

***   ***   ***   ***   ***

Martin Caidin--born September 14, 1927 at New York, New York--eight writing awards--Cocoa Beach, Florida.

Grace: November 1, 1952/pending--Jamie Caidin (13); Pamela Caidin (10).

Free-Lance Writer--Member: Aviation Writers Association; American Rocket Society; British Interplanetary Society; United States Naval Institute; American Aviation Historical Society; Aircraft Owners and Pilots Association.

Mr. Caidin is also a pilot and broadcaster. His novel Marooned was sold to Columbia Pictures and is slated for release in late 1969. Of it he writes: "It's going to be a dillie. At least $15 million worth. I just spent some time on the sets. Full-size Apollo, Voskhod and X-24 Lifting Body spacecraft, as well as a slew of models of various sizes, all of them absolutely authentic to every last nut and bolt. The astronauts have been using the sound stage as a sort of grandiose playroom..."

----

*IAN CAMERON

1) 1961 Hutchinson   The Lost Ones.

NOTE: Ian Cameron, penname of Donald Gordon Payne, was born in 1924. A complete biography may be found in Contemporary Authors.

JOHN W. CAMPBELL

1) 1947 Hadley   The Mightiest Machine. (RP)
2) 1948 Shasta   Who Goes There? (s/RP/RPv)
3) 1949 Fantasy   The Incredible Planet. (s)
4) 1951 Fantasy   The Moon Is Hell! (RP)
5) 1951 Dutchess   Brigands of the Moon. (P)
6) 1952 Atlas   From Unknown Worlds. (@/H-P)
7) 1952 S & S   The Astounding Science Fiction Anthology.
                           (@/RPa/RPav)
8) 1952 Shasta   The Cloak of Aesir. (s)
2A) 1952 Kemsley   The Thing and Other Stories. (s/P)
9) 1953 Fantasy   The Black Star Passes. (RP)
7A) 1954 Grayson   The First Astounding Science Fiction Anthology.
                           (@/a/RP)
7B) 1954 Grayson   The Second Astouding Science Fiction Anthology.
                           (@/a/RP)

JOHN W. CAMPBELL (continued)

7C)	1956 Berkley	Astounding Tales of Space and Time. (@/a/P)	
10)	1957 Fantasy	Islands of Space (RP)	
11)	1960 Gnome	Invaders from the Infinite. (RP)	
12)	1962 Doubleday	Prologue to Analog. (@/RP)	
13)	1963 Doubleday	Analog 1. (@/RP)	
14)	1964 Doubleday	Analog 2. (@/RP)	
15)	1965 Doubleday	Analog 3. (@/RP)	
16)	1965 Dobson	The Analog Anthology. (12/13/14)	
17)	1966 Doubleday	Analog 4. (@)	
18)	1966 Ace	The Planeteers. (s/P)	
19)	1966 Ace	The Ultimate Weapon. (P)	
20)	1966 Doubleday	Collected Editorials from Analog. (nf/s)	
21)	1967 Doubleday	Analog 5. (@)	
22)	1968 Doubleday	Analog 6. (@/RP)	

FPS: "When the Atoms Failed," Amazing, January, 1930.

WIP: 1969 Doubleday   Analog 7. (@)

***   ***   ***   ***   ***

John Wood Campbell--born June 8, 1910 at Newark, New Jersey--B.S., Duke University, 1932--Hugo Award, Best Professional Magazine, 1953, 1955, 1957, Astounding; 1961, 1962, 1964, 1965, Analog; Guest of Honor, 5th World Science Fiction Convention (Philcon), 1947; 12th World Science Fiction Convention (SFcon), 1954; 15th World Science Fiction Convention (Loncon I), 1957--New York, New York.

Son of John Wood & Dorothy (Strahern) Campbell--(1) Dona Stuart: 1931/1950; (2) Margaret Winter: 1951--Philinda Campbell Hammond (28); Leslyn S. Campbell (23).

Editor, Astounding/Analog, October, 1937-DATE.

JOHN CARNELL

1)	1946 Pendulum	Jinn and Jitters. (@/P)
2)	1954 Museum	Gateway to Tomorrow. (@/RP)
3)	1954 Boardman	No Place Like Earth. (@/RP)
4)	1955 Boardman	The Best from New Worlds. (@/P)
5)	1955 Museum	Gateway to the Stars. (@)
6)	1964 Penguin	Lambda I and Other Stories. (@/P)
7)	1964 Dobson	New Writings in SF 1. (@/RP)
8)	1964 Dobson	New Writings in SF 2. (@/RP)
9)	1965 Dobson	New Writings in SF 3. (@/RP)
10)	1965 Dobson	New Writings in SF 4. (@/RP)

JOHN CARNELL (continued)

11)	1965 Corgi	Weird Shadows from Beyond.	(@/P)
12)	1965 Dobson	New Writings in SF 5.	(@/RP)
13)	1965 Dobson	New Writings in SF 6.	(@/RP)
14)	1966 Dobson	New Writings in SF 7.	(@/RP)
15)	1966 Dobson	New Writings in SF 8.	(@/RP)
16)	1966 Dobson	New Writings in SF 9.	(@/RP)
17)	1967 Corgi	New Writings in SF 10.	(@/RH)
18)	1967 Corgi	New Writings in SF 11.	(@/RH)
19)	1968 Dobson	New Writings in SF 12.	(@/RP)
20)	1968 Dobson	New Writings in SF 13.	(@/RP)
FPS:	Articles to	Disc, a Jazz magazine.	
FSF:	"Probability Zero,"	Astounding, August, 1942.	
WIP:	1969 Dobson	New Writings in SF 14.	(@/RP)
		other editions of New Writings in SF.	

***   ***   ***   ***   ***

Edward John Carnell--born April 8, 1912 at Plumstead, London, England--Hugo Award, Best Professional British Magazine, New Worlds, 1957--Plumstead, London, England.

Son of William John and Louise Carnell--Irene Cloke: June 17, 1939--Michael John Carnell (24); Leslyn Hilary Carnell (21).

Editor, New Worlds, October, 1946 (#1)-April, 1964 (#141); Science Fantasy, Winter, 1951/1952-April, 1964·(#64); Science Fiction Adventures (British), March, 1958 (#1)-May, 1963 (#32) (all issues); has been an apprentice printer, printing house manager, deputy buyer for commercial printing and stationary, buyer for a bookstore chain; Literary Agent specializing in science fiction, 1964-DATE--Honorary Member: British Science Fiction Association.

Mr. Carnell was the Publicity Director of the British Interplanetary Society, 1936-1938, and edited the BIS Journal during the same period. Also was the Secretary of the original British Science Fiction Association, 1937-1939, and editor of the BSFA Journals until September, 1939. Gained first part-assisted passage to a Worldcon (forerunner of the present day TAFF) in 1949 to Cincinatti. Chairman, 15th World Science Fiction Convention (Loncon I), London, 1957.

ELMER J. CARPENTER

1)	1967 Flagship	Moonspin.	(P)

TERRY CARR

1) 1963 Ace   Warlord of Kor. (P)
5) 1966 Doubleday   Science Fiction for People Who Hate Science
                         Fiction. (@/RP)
7) 1967 Ace   New Worlds of Fantasy. (@/P)

                      with Ted White (q.v.) as *Norman Edwards
2) 1964 Monarch   Invasion from 2500. (P)

                      with Donald A. Wollheim (q.v.)
3) 1965 Ace   World's Best Science Fiction: 1965. (@/P)
4) 1966 Ace   World's Best Science Fiction: 1966. (@/P)
6) 1967 Ace   World's Best Science Fiction: 1967. (@/P)
8) 1968 Ace   World's Best Science Fiction: 1968. (@/P)

FPS: "Blind Clarinet," sold in 1961 to Ted White for his anthology, The Soul of Jazz; paid for but never published, as the book was rejected by Regency Books.
FPP: "Who Sups with the Devil," The Magazine of Fantasy and Science Fiction, May, 1962.

WIP: 1969 Gold Medal   The Others. (@/P)
      1969 Ace   World's Best Science Fiction: 1969.
                             (@/P/RH/with Donald A. Wollheim).
      1969 Ace   New Worlds of Fantasy #2. (@/P)

***   ***   ***   ***   ***

Terry Gene Carr--born February 19, 1937 at Grant's Pass, Oregon--attended City College of San Francisco, 1954-1957; University of California at Berkeley, 1957-1958--Hugo Award, Best Amateur Publication, 1959, Fanac; TAFF Representative, 1965, 23rd World Science Fiction Convention (Loncon II)--Brooklyn, New York.

Son of Leslie Clarence & Marcella Woods (Drummond) Carr--(1) Norah Veronica Clarice Van Dycke (Miriam Dyches Carr Knight): January 31, 1959/1961; (2) Carol Ann Newmark: September 7, 1961--no children.

Free-Lance Writer, 1961-1962; Associate Editor, Scott Meredith Literary Agency, 1962-1964; Ace Books, 1964-1967; Editor, Ace Books, 1967-DATE; Founding Editor, Ace Science Fiction Special Line, 1968-DATE--Member: Science Fiction Writers of America (Chairman, Election Committee, 1966); Fantasy Amateur Press Association.

Editor, SFWA Bulletin, August 1967-June, 1968; Founder, Science Fiction Writers of America Forum, 1967-1968.

LIN CARTER

1) 1965 Ace   1   The Wizard of Lemuria. (P)

LIN CARTER (continued)

2)	1966 Ace	2	Thongor of Lemuria. (P)
3)	1966 Ace		The Star Magicians. (P)
4)	1966 Ace		The Man Without a Planet. (P)
6)	1967 Belmont		The Flame of Iridar. (P)
8)	1967 Pap Lib	3	Thongor Against the Gods. (P)
10)	1968 Belmont		The Thief of Thoth. (P)
11)	1968 Belmont		Tower at the Edge of Time. (P)
12)	1968 Pap Lib	4	Thongor in the City of Magicians. (P)
14)	1968 Pap Lib	5	Thongor at the End of Time. (P)

with *David Grinnell (Donald A. Wollheim, q.v.)
5) 1967 Avalon   Destination: Saturn. (RP)

with Robert E. Howard
7) 1967 Lancer   King Kull. (s/P)

with Robert E. Howard and L. Sprague de Camp (q.v.)
9) 1967 Lancer   -5   Conan. (s/P)
15) 1968 Lancer -9   Conan the Wanderer. (s/P)

with L. Sprague de Camp (q.v.)
13) 1968 Lancer -8   Conan of the Isles. (P)

SER: 1) Thongor; 2) Conan.

FPS: "Masters of the Metropolis," The Magazine of Fantasy and Science Fiction, April, 1957 (with Randall Garrett).

WIP:	1969 Belmont		Giant of World's End. (P)
	1969 Ballantine		Tolkien: A Look Behind the Lord of the Rings. (nf/P)
	1969 Lancer	-10	Conan of Cimmeria. (s/P/with Robert E. Howard and L. Sprague de Camp)
	1969 Belmont		The Purloined Planet. (P)
	1969 Belmont		Beyond the Gates of Dream. (s/P)
	1969 Ace		Star Thief. (P)
	1969 Signet		Lost World of Time. (P)
	1969 Ballantine		The Young Magicians. (@/P)
	1969 Ballantine		Dragons, Elves and Heroes. (@/P)

***   ***   ***   ***   ***

Linwood Vrooman Carter--born June 9, 1930 at St. Petersburg, Florida--graduate of an art school; attended Columbia University, two years--Jamaica, New York.

Son of Mr. & Mrs. Raymond L. Carter--(2) Noel Vreeland: August 17, 1963--no children.

Free-Lance Writer; Editorial Consultant, Ballantine Adult Fantasy Series, 1969-DATE --Member: Science Fiction Writers of America.

CURTIS W. CASEWIT

1) 1960 Avalon   The Peacemakers. (RP)

FPS: "The Mask,"   Weird Tales, March, 1952.

***   ***   ***   ***   ***

Curtis W. Casewit (u)--born May 21, 1922 at Mannheim, Germany--attended Florence Language School, 1933-1938; University of Denver; University of Colorado --Edgar Award, Best Book Reviewer, 1956; Writer's Digest Short Story Contest Award, 1955; Dutton Article Award, 1964; 1966--Denver, Colorado.

Charlotte Fischer-Lamberg: July, 1954--Carla Casewit; Stephen Casewit; Niccolo Casewit.

Department Store Book Buyer, Denver, Colorado, 1959-1964; Free-Lance Writer, 1964-DATE --Member: Society of Magazine Writers; Society of American Travel Writers.

Mr. Casewit notes:
"Current state of sf? Vastly improved, sophisticated, brilliant, fresh --but of no value to the free-lance writer who makes a living from his craft. Markets have shrunk to very, very few--motion pictures only by big names; novels not much in demand. Pure science will eventually replace sf; we've reached the point where we'll finally take off to the planets."

CHRISTOPHER CERF

1) 1966 Vintage   The Vintage Anthology of Science Fantasy. (@/P)
2) 1968 Doubleday   The World's Largest Cheese. (s)

FPS: parody pieces to Mademoiselle, July, 1961.
FSF: 1966 Vintage   The Vintage Anthology of Science Fantasy. (@/P)

***   ***   ***   ***   ***

Christopher Bennett Cerf--born August 19, 1941 at New York, New York--B.A., Harvard University, 1963--New York, New York.

Son of Bennett Alfred & Phyllis (Fraser) Cerf--unmarried.

Editor, Random House, 1963-DATE--Member: The Nectarine Organization.

Editor, Harvard Lampoon, 1962-1963.

JACK L. CHALKER

1)	1961 Anthem	The New H.P. Lovecraft Bibliography. (nf/P)
2)	1963 Anthem	In Memoriam: Clark Ashton Smith. (nf/H-P)
3)	1965 Anthem	Mirage on Lovecraft. (nf/P)
		with Mark Owings (q.v.)
4)	1966 Anthem	The Index to the Science-Fantasy Publishers. (nf/P)
		with Mark Owings (q.v.) as *Mark Owings
5)	1967 Mirage	The Necronomicon: A Study. (nf/P)
FPP:	1961 Anthem	The New H.P. Lovecraft Bibliography. (nf/P)

***   ***   ***   ***   ***

Jack Laurence Chalker--born December 17, 1944 at Norfolk, Virginia--B.S., Towson State College; M.L.A., Johns Hopkins University--Baltimore, Maryland.

Son of Lloyd A. & Nancy H. Chalker--unmarried.

Publisher/Editor, Anthem Series and Mirage Press, 1961-DATE--Member: Baltimore Science Fiction Society; Maryland Association for Science-Fantasy; Washington Science Fiction Association; Council for Geographic Education: National Rifle Association; Associate Member: Science Fiction Writers of America.

NOTE: Mr. Chalker compiled and edited the official bibliography of H.P. Lovecraft.

JONATHAN CHANCE

1)	1968 Hale	The Light Benders.

A. BERTRAM CHANDLER

1)	1961 Avalon	The Rim of Space. (RP)
2)	1961 Ace	Bring Back Yesterday. (P)
3)	1961 Ace	Rendezvous on a Lost World. (P)
4)	1963 Ace	Beyond the Galactic Rim. (s/P)
5)	1963 Ace	The Ship from Outside. (P)
6)	1963 Monarch	The Hamelin Plague. (P)
7)	1964 Jenkins	The Deep Reaches of Space. (RP)
8)	1964 Avalon	Glory Planet.
9)	1964 Ace	Into the Alternate Universe. (P)
10)	1964 Ace	The Coils of Time. (P)
11)	1965 Ace	The Alternate Martians. (P)

A. BERTRAM CHANDLER (continued)

12) 1965 Ace   Empress of Outer Space. (P)
13) 1965 Ace   Space Mercenaries. (P)
14) 1967 Ace   Contraband from Outerspace. (P)
15) 1967 Ace   Nebula Alert. (P)
16) 1967 Ace   The Road to the Rim. (P)
17) 1968 Horwitz False Fatherland. (P)

FPS: "'This Means War!'"   Astounding, May, 1944.

WIP: 1969 Ace   The Rim Gods. (P)
17A)   1969 Dell   Spartan Planet. (P)
        1969 Lancer   Catch the Star Winds. (s/P)

***   ***   ***   ***   ***

Arthur Bertram Chandler--born March 28, 1912 at Aldershot, England--Certificate of Competency as Master of a Foreign Going Steamship--Woollahra, New South Wales, Australia.

Son of Arthur Robert & Ida Florence (Calver) Chandler--(1) Joan Margaret Barnard: /1962; (2) Susan Schlenker: 1962--1) Penelope Anne Chandler; Christopher John Chandler; Jennifer Lynn Chandler.

Ship Captain; has served on tramp steamers, cargo and passenger liners, troop transports, Pacific Islands traders, coasters (Australia and New Zealand), and trans-Tasman freighters--Member: Science Fiction Writers of America; Australian Society of Authors; British Interplanetary Society (Fellow); Merchant Service Guild of Australia.

Hobbies: navigation, pilotage, cookery, nudism--Allergies: work.

LOUIS CHARBONNEAU

1)   1958 Doubleday   No Place on Earth. (RP)
2)   1960 Zenith   Corpus Earthling. (P)
3)   1963 Bantam   The Sentinel Stars. (P)
4)   1965 Bantam   Psychedelic-40. (P/RHv)
4A) 1965 Jenkins   The Specials.
5)   1967 Bantam   Down to Earth. (P)
6)   1968 Bantam   The Sensitives. (P)

NOTE: #6 was based on an original movie script by Deane Romano.

FPS: a radio dramatic script, c. 1950.
FSF: 1958 Doubleday   No Place on Earth.

WIP: A Falling World.

LOUIS CHARBONNEAU (continued)

***   ***   ***   ***   ***

Louis Henry Charbonneau--born January 20, 1924 at Detroit, Michigan--A.B., University of Detroit, 1948; M.A., University of Detroit, 1950--Pacific Palisades, California.

Son of Louis Henry & Mary Ellen (Young) Charbonneau--Hilda: December 15, 1945--no children.

Instructor, University of Detroit, 1948-1952; Copywriter, Mercury Advertising, Los Angeles, 1952-1956; Los Angeles Times, 1956-DATE; Free-Lance Writer--Member: Science Fiction Writers of America.

NOTE: Mr. Charbonneau's father is the Dean of the University of Detroit School of Law.

PAUL CHARKIN

1)	1959 Badger SF	Light of Mars. (P)
2)	1960 Badger SF	The Other Side of Night. (P)
3)	1963 Digit	The Living Gem. (P)
FPS:	"The Wrong Glass,"	The Socialist Leader, 1952.
WIP:		Dolls of Ecstasy.

***   ***   ***   ***   ***

Paul Samuel Charkin--born July 20, 1907 at Muswell Hall, North London, England--East Twickenham, Middlesex, England.

Son of Samuel & Louise Frances Estelle (Walden) Charkin--unmarried.

"Started my career as a clerk in my father's business, and when that was closed during the industrial depression of the 1930's, became a tramp, door-knocking canvasser and high-pressure salesman. Entered business as a House Agent and a Radio Salesman, and failed at both. The War saw me conscripted into A.R.P. duties (which I hated), and then to Red Cross work, which was more interesting"--Founding Member: Richmond Arts Club; Richmond Writers Circle.

CHARLES CHILTON

1)	1954 Jenkins	Journey Into Space. (RP)
2)	1956 Jenkins	The Red Planet. (RP)

CHARLES CHILTON (continued)

3) 1960 Jenkins   The World in Peril. (RP)

NOTE: Charles Frederick William Chilton is a British writer.

----

*JOHN CHRISTOPHER

1)	1954 Grayson		The Twenty-Second Century. (s/RP)	
2)	1955 Joseph		The Year of the Comet. (RPv)	
3)	1956 Joseph		The Death of Grass. (RP)	
3A)	1957 S & S		No Blade of Grass. (RP)	
2A)	1958 Avon		Planet in Peril. (P)	
4)	1962 Eyre		The World in Winter. (RP)	
4A)	1962 S & S		The Long Winter. (RP)	
5)	1964 Hodder		Cloud on Silver. (RP)	
5A)	1964 S & S		Sweeney's Island. (RP)	
6)	1965 Hodder		The Possessors. (RP)	
7)	1965 Hodder		A Wrinkle in the Skin. (RP)	
7A)	1966 S & S		The Ragged Edge. (RP)	
8)	1967 Hodder		The Little People. (RP)	
9)	1967 Hamilton	1	The White Mountains.	
10)	1967 Hamilton	2	The City of Gold and Lead.	
11)	1968 S & S		Pendulum. (RP)	
12)	1968 Hamilton	3	The Pool of Fire.	

FPS: "Christmas Tree,"   Astounding, February, 1949 (as Christopher Youd).

WIP: 1969 Hamilton   The Lotus Caves.
      1969 Hamilton   The Guardians.

***   ***   ***   ***   ***

Christopher Samuel Youd--born April 16, 1922 at Huyton, Lancaster, England--attended Peter Symonds' School, Winchester, England--Le Foulon, Guernsey, Channel Islands, Great Britain.

Married in 1946--has son born in 1951, and four daughters born respectively in 1953, 1955, 1957, 1959.

"Started writing seriously in 1947 with the help (still gratefully acknowledged) of the Rockefeller Foundation;" Free-Lance Writer, 1958-DATE--Member: Science Fiction Writers of America.

CURT CLARK

1) 1967 Ace   Anarchaos. (P)

CURT CLARK (continued)

FKP: "Nackles," The Magazine of Fantasy and Science Fiction, January, 1964.

RONALD CLARK

1) 1962 Cape   Queen Victoria's Bomb; the Disclosures of Professor Franklin Huxtable, M.A., Cantab., A Novel.

FPS: "London's Climbing Nursery," The Vauxhall Motorist, c. 1937.
FSF: "The Man Who Went Back," Evening Standard, c. 1949.

***   ***   ***   ***   ***

William Ronald Clark--born November 2, 1916 at Merton Park, London, England --attended Kings College, Wimbledon--London, England.

Son of Ernest & Ethel Clark--(1) Irene Tapp: 1938/1953; (2) Pearla Doris Odden: 1953--no children.

Free-Lance Writer.

ARTHUR C. CLARKE

1)	1951 Sidgwick	Sands of Mars.	(RP)
2)	1952 Winston	Islands in the Sky.	(RP)
3)	1953 Ballantine	Childhood's End.	(H-P)
4)	1953 Gnome	Against the Fall of Night.	(RHe/RP)
5)	1953 Ballantine	Expedition to Earth.	(s/H-P)
6)	1953 Sidgwick	Prelude to Space.	(RP/RPv)
7)	1955 Ballantine	Earthlight.	(H-P)
8)	1956 Ballantine	Reach for Tomorrow.	(s/H-P)
9)	1956 Harcourt	The City and the Stars.	(4/ê/RP)
10)	1957 Harcourt	The Deep Range.	(RP)
11)	1957 Ballantine	Tales from the White Hart.	(s/P/RH)
12)	1958 Harcourt	The Other Side of the Sky.	(s/RP)
13)	1959 Harcourt	Across the Sea of Stars.	(3/7/s)
6A)	1961 Lancer	Master of Space.	(P)
14)	1961 Harcourt	A Fall of Moondust.	(RP)
15)	1962 Harcourt	From the Oceans, From the Stars.	(9/10/s)
16)	1962 Harcourt	Tales of Ten Worlds.	(s/RP)
A)	1962 Digit	The Mind Masters.	(P)
17)	1963 Holt	Dolphin Island.	(RP)
18)	1963 Harcourt	Glide Path.	(RP)
19)	1964 Harper	Boy Beneath the Sea.	

ARTHUR C. CLARKE (continued)

20)	1965 Sidgwick	An Arthur C. Clarke Omnibus. (3/5/6)
21)	1965 Harcourt	Prelude to Mars. (1/6/s)
22)	1966 Delacorte	Time Probe. (@/RP)
23)	1967 Harcourt	The Nine Billion Names of God. (s)
24)	1968 NAL	2001: A Space Odyssey. (RP)
25)	1968 Sidgwick	A Second Arthur C. Clarke Omnibus. (1/7/14)
26)	1968 Harcourt	The Lion of Commare and Against the Fall of Night.

FPS: "Man's Empire of Tomorrow, Tales of Wonder, Winter, 1938.
FSF: "Loophole," Astounding, April, 1946.

WIP:
6B)   1969 Lancer   The Space Dreamers. (P)

***   ***   ***   ***   ***

Arthur Charles Clarke--born December 16, 1917 at Minehead, Somersetshire, England--B.Sc. (First Class Honors), King's College, University of London, 1948--International Fantasy Award, 1952, The Exploration of Space; Hugo Award, Best Short Story, 1956, "The Star;" Guest of Honor, 14th World Science Fiction Convention (Nycon II), 1956; Kalinga Prize, 1961; Ballantine Medal, Franklin Institute, 1963--Colombo, Ceylon.

Son of Charles Wright & Norah (Willis) Clarke--Marilyn Mayfield: 1953/1964-- no children.

Auditor, British Civil Service, 1936-1940; Assistant Editor, Science Abstracts, 1949-1950; Free-Lance Writer--Member: Science Fiction Writers of America; Society of Authors; British Interplanetary Society (Chairman, 1946-1947, 1950-1953); International Academy of Astronautics; American Rocket Society (Senior Member); American Astronautical Society (Fellow); Association of British Science Writers; Royal Astronomical Society; Ceylon Astronomical Society (President); British Astronomical Association; Association of Visiting Scientists (London).

I.F. CLARKE

1)	1961 Library	The Tale of the Future: A Checklist. (nf)
2)	1966 Oxford	Voices Prophesying War, 1763-1984. (nf)

NOTE: Ignatius Frederick Clarke.

---

*HAL CLEMENT

1)	1950 Doubleday	Needle. (RF/RPv)
2)	1952 Gnome	Iceworld.

*HAL CLEMENT (continued)

3)	1954 Doubleday	1	Mission of Gravity. (RP)
4)	1956 Page		The Ranger Boys in Space.
5)	1957 Ballantine		Cycle of Fire. (P/RH)
1A)	1957 Avon		From Outer Space. (P)
6)	1964 Ballantine		Close to Critical. (P/RH)
7)	1965 Ballantine		Natives of Space. (s/P)

FPS: "Proof,"   Astounding, June, 1942.

WIP: 1969 Doubleday   Small Changes. (s)
                               2   Starlight.

***   ***   ***   ***   ***

Harry Clement Stubbs--born May 30, 1922, at Somerville, Massachusetts--B.S., Harvard University, 1943; M.Ed., Boston University, 1947; M.S., Simmons College, 1963--Milton, Massachusetts.

Son of Harry Clarence & Marjorie (White) Stubbs--Mary Elizabeth Myers: July 19, 1952--George Clement Stubbs (June 6, 1953); Richard Myers Stubbs (September 11, 1954); Christine Stubbs (August 29, 1959).

Teacher of Science, Milton Academy, Milton, Massachusetts, 1949-DATE; Free-Lance Writer--Member: Science Fiction Writers of America; New England Science Fiction Association; Authors Guild; American Association for the Advancement of Science; Association of Lunar and Planetary Observors; Meteoritical Society; Bond Astronomical Society; New England Association of Chemistry Teachers (Division Chairman, 1961-1962).

In response to questions, Mr. Stubbs wrote:
    "I feel very happy about the current state of sf. It seems to be increasing in popularity; the groups and individuals who have strong opinions on what it ought to be and do are different enough to minimize the risk of its getting into a rut. Most of its readers and writers seem ready to grant that it must face the criteria of literature in general, and story telling in particular, and not just live by its own standards. The only contribution of which I have been conscious in my own work is the maintaining of a high science standard. (Unless you want to include an error I seem to have started: an organism living in symbiosis with another is a symbiont, not a symbiote)."

MILDRED CLINGERMAN

1)   1961 Ballantine   A Cupful of Space. (s/P)

FPS: "Minister Without Portfolio," The Magazine of Fantasy and Science Fiction, February, 1952.

MILDRED CLINGERMAN (continued)

***   ***   ***   ***   ***

Mildred Clingerman--born March 14, 1918 at Allen, Oklahoma--attended University of Arizona, 1941.--Tucson, Arizona.

Daughter of Arthur & Meda (Bush) McElroy--Stuart Kendall Clingerman: May 29, 1937--Kendall Clingerman Bradley (28); Kurt Clingerman (26).

Has been a teacher at the University of Arizona--Member: Tucson Press Club.

STANTON A. COBLENTZ

1) 1945 Wings — When the Birds Fly South.
2) ?1945 Utopian — Youth Madness. (P)
3) 1949 FPCI — The Sunken World. (RP)
4) 1950 Avon — Into Plutonian Depths. (P)
5) 1950 FPCI — After 12000 Years.
6) 1952 FPCI — The Planet of Youth. (RP)
7) 1955 Fantasy — Under the Triple Suns.
8) 1957 Avalon — Hidden World. (RP)
9) 1958 Avalon — The Blue Barbarians.
10) 1960 Avalon — Next Door to the Sun.
11) 1961 Avalon — The Runaway World.
12) 1964 Avalon — The Moon People.
13) 1964 Arcadia — The Last of the Great Race.
14) 1964 Arcadia — The Lost Comet.
15) 1964 Avalon — The Lizard Lords.
16) 1966 Avalon — Lord of Tranerica.
17) 1967 Avalon — The Crimson Capsule.
18) 1968 Avalon — The Day the World Stopped.

NOTE: The texts of the two Arcadia Books were extensively mutilated.

FPS: "The Sunken World," Amazing Stories Quarterly, Summer, 1928.

***   ***   ***   ***   ***

Stanton Arthur Coblentz--born August 24, 1896 at San Francisco, California--A.B., University of California at Berkeley, 1917; M.A., University of California at Berkeley, 1919--Commonwealth Club of California Silver Medal for Poetry, 1953; Lyric Foundation Traditional Poetry Award of $1000, 1953--Mill Valley, California.

Son of Mayer & Mattie (Arndt) Coblentz--Flora Bachrach: June 23, 1922--no children.

Feature Writer, San Francisco Examiner, 1919-1920; Book Reviewer, New York Times and New York Sun, 1920-1938; Founder/Editor, Wings, 1933-1960;

STANTON A. COBLENTZ (continued)

Free-Lance Writer and Poet--Member: Authors League of America.

In a personal letter, Mr. Coblentz states:
"...As for my opinion of the present state of science fiction: naturally my own preferences run toward the older type, such as was published in the heyday of Amazing. But I realize that this is an opinion only, and an opinion that may be dictated by prejudices... As for my contributions to the genre-- I think that this is a question which should be answered by others. I don't believe, however, that anyone would deny that my best work has been in my novels such as The Sunken World, and I personally believe that my satire has been one of the most original features of my work..."

THEODORE R. COGSWELL

1) 1962 Pyramid   The Wall Around the World. (s/P)
2) 1968 Belmont   The Third Eye. (s/P)

FPS: "The Specter General,"   Astounding, June, 1952.

***   ***   ***   ***   ***

Theodore Rose Cogswell--born March 10, 1918 at Coatesville, Pennsylvania --B.A., University of Colorado, 1948; M.A., University of Denver, 1949; graduate study at University of Minnesota, 1949-1953; University of Denver, 1956-1957; --listed in Directory of American Scholars--Chinchilla, Pennsylvania.

Son of DeWitt Russell & Marguerite (Rose) Cogswell--(1) Marjorie Mills: 1948/1963; (2) Coralie Norris: 1964--1) Megan Mills Cogswell; Cathleen Bradford Cogswell.

Instructor, University of Minnesota, 1949-1953; University of Kentucky, 1953-1956; 1957-1958; Assistant Professor, Ball State College, 1958-1965; Keystone Junior College, 1965-DATE--Member: Science Fiction Writers of America; Modern Language Association; Veterans of Foreign Wars; Mensa; Conference on College Composition and Communication; National Council of Teachers of English.

NOTE: Mr. Cogswell was Director, Proceedings of the Institute for Twenty-First Century Studies, 1959-1963. In an incidental note, he was also an ambulance driver for the Spanish Republican Army, 1937-1938.

EVERETT B. COLE

1) 1961 Gnome   The Philosophical Corps.

FKP: "Philosophical Corps,"   Astounding, March, 1951.

NOTE: Everett B. Cole could not be located.

WALTER R. COLE

1) 1964 Cole   A Checklist of Science Fiction Anthologies. (nf)

FPP: 1964 Cole   A Checklist of Science Fiction Anthologies. (nf)

WIP: A supplement to the above, covering sf anthologies published from 1964-1968 --tentatively scheduled for publication in Spring, 1970.

***   ***   ***   ***   ***

Walter Randall Cole--born April 19, 1933 at Brooklyn, New York--attended college for two years--N3F Amateur Award, 1965--Brooklyn, New York.

Son of Ernest Tomasuolo (stepfather) & Rose (Balgley)--unmarried.

Associate Editor, Science Fiction Times,-April, 1969; now connected with Luna Publications, Oradell, New Jersey--Member: National Fantasy Fan Federation; New York Science Fiction Society.

Mr. Cole writes:
"Science fiction, at the present time, is rapidly growing, and it is beginning to receive the literary recognition it long deserved. The 'new wave' is basically a hodge podge of words that contain very little sensible meaning. Granted that new trends must be considered to avoid stagnation in the field, but the type of material presently published in New Worlds (the forerunner of 'new wave' writing) scarcely makes it worthwhile to read. Certainly very little reader interest (at least from this reader) is retained in this material.
  "Insofar as my own contribution to the field may be considered, it is limited professionally to the publication of my checklist. One did hope that editors would amend the continuously repetitive method of selecting stories for anthologies, and that the Checklist would be an aid in resolving that situation. The work is, I feel, a valuable reference work, and should be treated as such."

JAMES NELSON COLEMAN

1) 1967 Berkley   Seeker from the Stars. (P)

WIP: 1969 Berkley   The Null-Frequency Impulser. (P)

D.G. COMPTON

1) 1965 Hodder   The Quality of Mercy. (RP)
2) 1966 Hodder   Farewell, Earth's Bliss.
3) 1967 Hodder   The Silent Multitude. (RP)
4) 1968 Hodder   Synthajoy. (RP)

D.G. COMPTON (continued)

FPS:	"Fully Furnished,"	A radio play, 1955.
FSF:	1965 Hodder	The Quality of Mercy. (RP)

WIP: "I've been researching into the real world of computers, their genuine possibilities and particularly the holy enthusiasm with which they seem to fire their more sophisticated operators. For it is with these people that I think lies whatever danger there may be. There's a book on these lines coming along."

***   ***   ***   ***   ***

David Guy Compton--born August 19, 1930 at London, England--Liverpool, England.

Son of George & Nuna (Davey) Compton--Elizabeth Tillotson: 1951/pending--Margaret Compton (17); Robin Compton (daughter 15); James Compton (10).

"Typical writer's first ten years bumming around with long-suffering wife and children; then a serious settling down to the job of writing, utter poverty, final survival."

Mr. Compton writes:
"For me I think the writing of sf is a sign of weakness. I write about the future because this enables me to write about the present once removed, and therefore more easily. I am wary of the sf label, partly because in this country among the majority of readers it is still something of a dirty word, and partly because I am wary of labels. Certainly my next novel, The Palace, isn't remotely sf. And anyway, I have till recently thought of myself as a playwright, doing rather 'experimental' things for radio in this country and Germany. That I should have written books still surprises me."

ROBERT CONQUEST

1)	1955 Ward/Lock	A World of Difference. (RP)
		with Kingsley Amis (q.v.)
2)	1961 Gollancz	Spectrum. (@/RP/RPa)
3)	1962 Gollancz	Spectrum 2. (@/RP)
4)	1963 Gollancz	Spectrum 3. (@/RP)
5)	1965 Gollancz	Spectrum 4. (@/RP)
6)	1966 Gollancz	Spectrum 5. (@/RP)
FPS:	1938	
FSF:	1955 Ward/Lock	A World of Difference.
WIP:		Spectrum 6. (@/with Kingsley Amis)

ROBERT CONQUEST (continued)

***　　　***　　　***　　　***　　　***

George Robert Acworth Conquest--born July 15, 1917 at Malvern, England--B.A., Magdalen College, Oxford University, 1939; also attended Winchester College, 1931-1935; University of Grenoble, 1935-1936--P.E.N. Prize for Long Poem, 1945; Festival of British Verse Prize, 1951; Order of the British Empire--London, England.

Son of R. Folger W. & Rosamund A. (Acworth) Conquest--(1) Joan Watkins: 1942/1948; (2) Tatiana Mihailova: 1948/1962; (3) Caroleen Macfarlane: April 4, 1964--1) John Conquest (1943); Richard Conquest (1945).

With British Foreign Service, 1946-1956; Fellow, London School of Economics, 1956-1958; Lecturer in English, Buffalo University, 1959-1960; Literary Editor, Spectator, 1962-1963; Senior Fellow, Columbia University Russian Institute, 1964-1965; Free-Lance Writer--Member: Science Fiction Writers of America; Author's Society; British Interplanetary Society; Travellers Club.

Mr. Conquest provided the following statement:
"As to the Nouvelle Vague, I have little patience with it. We all grew up with the experimentalist arts, but everything worth doing had already been done forty years ago, and tedious repetitions of repetitions, largely of what turned out to be non-viable among the early stuff, simply means unreadability; or rather, it can only be read by an adolescent on the first step of what he conceives to be thrilling sophistication. As Pasternak, one of the subtlest of experimentalists, remarked after long experience: 'The support has been taken out from under that modern trend...this striving, though true and original in its source, was not self-dependent enough to stand up.'
"As practised nowadays, I regard the whole business as largely a piece of self-indulgence by authors, and the taste for it on the part of readers little more than an exercise in self-congratulation on their supposed cleverness and sensitivity.
"This is not to say that occasional bursts of talent may not appear in it, for it has always been the case that some creative authors and other artists have lacked judgment and discipline, and have diverted their talents according to the current fashions through weakness or silliness.
" But in fact, by the time the New Wave reached science fiction it was a pretty tired ripple. It is worth adding that science fiction is a particularly unsuitable area for this sort of thing. It has always been an axiom that logical fantasy must be as clearly expressed as possible, for reasons so obvious they surely don't need developing here.
"Again while fiction of extreme introspection is perfectly legitimate if one likes, that sort of thing, to use for it expressions like 'Inner Space' and claim it is anything to do with science fiction is a mere semantic trick: nor will the use of a few sf properties and an otherwise symbolist or far-in scene transform it into sf.
"Are we really offered Ballard in exchange for Heinlein? They are both capable writers in principle, and both capable of occasional lapses, even when

ROBERT CONQUEST (continued)

doing their best. And Heinlein was always at least as subtle, as cunning, and as imaginative a writer as Ballard. But Ballard is now as often as not just plain silly--and in such a tediously, dreary old way: it might have shocked Queen Victoria, it might have surprised Sinclair Lewis, it might have been thought the last word in novelty by Harriet Monroe. But since shock, surprise, and novelty are the only virtues of this method (apart from an implicit claim to be deeply symbolic of everything, which can hardly be taken seriously); once those effects are exhausted, all that is left is an empty imitativeness. The semi-educated have always gone for inessential, extrinsic, eye-catching gimmickry in the arts. The fact that many of them still do so should not be taken to be of any significance, except to the sociologist.

"SF proper is already wide-ranging enough. It is perfectly capable of developing wonder and terror, as well as cool satire (in the genuine and original sense), and fantastic naturalism.

"All this may sound a little puritanical, and by all means let people write and read what they like; but it needs saying that the vast fashion-bound novelty trade, in the other arts, only dominates a market not worth having, and has not there achieved the monopoly or even the prestige which it so loudly claims for itself.

"I regard myself as an amateur. But I think I now see what the faults are in the modest efforts at science fiction I have published; when I write some more, I would hope, particularly, to make it livelier, more colourful, and in a sense, more fantastic. However, as in every other field, one shouldn't write in ways that do not really appeal to one--and particularly not by following the mode."

Mr. Conquest adds this note in a later letter:
"Basic objection to new waveries--parochialism. They're stuck in the tiny horizon of ideas and techniques which chance to be momentarily trendy. Rather like insisting on Jules Verne writing in the tone of The Yellow Book."

COLIN COOPER

1)	1968 Faber	The Thunder and Lightning Man.
FPS:	"Design for Danger,"	a radio play, 1956.
FSF:	"Host Planet Earth,"	a serial in six parts, British Broadcasting Corporation, 1967.
WIP:	1969 Faber	Outcrop.
		an untitled third novel.

***   ***   ***   ***   ***

Colin Symons Cooper--born July 5, 1926 at Birkenhead, England--special prize in national competition organized by The Observer (in conjunction with London Weekend Television) for the TV play, "The Funeral of H.M. Queen Victoria"-- London, England.

COLIN COOPER (continued)

Son of Frederick Arthur & Clara Violette (Symons) Cooper--Maureen Elizabeth Goodwin: September 2, 1966--Daniel Goodwin Cooper (July 14, 1967); Ben Symons Cooper (August 24, 1968).

Has had miscellaneous employment in the aircraft industry, a garage equipment company, agricultural goods manufacturing, a hospital, and a human development research project for the University of London; has also been a travelling salesman; Free-Lance Writer--Member: Society of Authors; Writer's Guild of Great Britain.

Mr. Cooper writes:
"I believe that sf must continue to extend its boundaries. SF must not feel itself to be confined in any way to antique concepts of style or subject matter. The best of the sf writers have shown that there is no imaginable subject that cannot be treated within an sf context. Far too many people--readers as well as non-readers--have the impression that sf is a narrow literary field concerned solely with spaceships. In 'Macbeth' and Crime and Punishment respectively, Shakespeare and Dostoievsky showed to what heights a crime story could be pushed. SF has yet to produce writers of similar calibre, but the time will come. It must come. Despite the superb work done by its pioneers, sf is still a very young literary form--a precocious child, perhaps, but nevertheless one that still has a long way to go before achieving what I, personally, am convinced it is capable of."

EDMUND COOPER

1)	1958 Ballantine	Deadly Image.	(P/RHv)
1A)	1958 Hutchinson	The Uncertain Midnight.	
2)	1958 Ballantine	Tomorrow's Gift.	(s/P)
3)	1959 Ballantine	Seed of Light.	(P/RH)
4)	1960 Digit	Voices in the Dark.	(s/P)
5)	1963 Panther	Tomorrow Came.	(s/P)
6)	1964 Faber	Transit.	(RP)
7)	1966 Hodder	All Fools' Day.	(RP)
8)	1967 Hodder	A Far Sunset.	(RP)
9)	1968 Mayflower	News from Elsewhere.	(s/P)
10)	1968 Hodder	Five to Twelve.	(RP)

FPS:	"The Unicorn,"	Everybody's Magazine, 1951.	
FSF:	"The Jar of Latakia,"	Authentic, September, 1954.	
WIP:	1969 Hodder	Sea-Horse in the Sky.	
	1969 Berkley	Square Root of Tomorrow.	(s/P)

EDMUND COOPER (continued)

***   ***   ***   ***   ***

Edmund Cooper (u)--born April 30, 1926 at Marple, Cheshire, England--Arundel, Sussex, England.

Son of Joseph & Harriet (Fletcher) Cooper--(1) Joyce Plant: 1946/1963; (2) Valerie Makin: 1963--1) Glynis Cooper (1947); Daryl Cooper (1955); Troy Cooper (1958); Guy Cooper (1960); 2) Shaun (1960); Justine (1962); Regan (1963); Jason Cooper (1964).

Mr. Cooper has been a labourer, civil servant, merchant seaman, teacher and journalist; currently Free-Lance Writer--Member: Science Fiction Writers of America; P.E.N.

Mr. Cooper provided the following statement:
   "I think the main value of sf is as a form of social criticism. If it makes people wonder where society is heading, it is doing a good job. I have no patience with galatic cowboys and Indians. I have no patience with comic strip gimmickry. I don't like moronic supermen using faster-than-light drive to go for a Saturday night burnup round the galaxy.
   "Most sf is trash, and most sf writers should be doing something useful--like building roads. The good ones--people like Clarke and Vonnegut--are not only entertaining; they are making contributions to progress.
   "In my own novels, I try to deal with serious themes (the problems of automation and leisure, colour, xenophobia, social prejudice, and so on) in sf terms. I try not to be too solemn about it. I am an entertainer, and I have to keep the reader reading.
   "It seems important to me, also that the characters used in sf should be credible. Many writers do not bother to develop characters. They are cardboard cut-outs.
   "I try to ensure that the people I write about are people in whom I, at least, can believe."

ALFRED COPPEL

1)	1960 Gold Medal		Dark December. (P/RH)
2)	1968 Harcourt	1	as *Robert Cham Gilman The Rebel of Rhada. (RP)
FPS:	"Age of Unreason,"		Astounding, December, 1947.
WIP:	1969 Harcourt	2	The Navigator of Rhada. (as *Robert Cham Gilman)
	1970 Harcourt	3	The Starkahn of Rhada. (as *Robert Cham Gilman)

ALFRED COPPEL (continued)

***　　　***　　　***　　　***　　　***

Alfredo José de Marini y Coppel Jr.--born November 9, 1921 at Oakland, California --attended Stanford University, 1940-1942--Palo Alto, California.

Son of Alfredo José & Ana Roumalda (de Arana) de Marini y Coppel--Elisabeth Schorr: March 10, 1943--Elisabeth Ann Coppel (25); Alfred Coppel III (23).

Free-Lance Writer--Member: Authors Guild.

PAUL COREY

1) 1968 Hale　　　　　The Planet of the Blind. (RP)

FPS: "Their Forefathers Were Presidents," Story, July, 1934.
FSF: "Operation Survival," New Worlds, December, 1962.

WIP:　　　　　　　　A Simple Ear.
　　　　　　　　　　Second of Nine.

***　　　***　　　***　　　***　　　***

Paul Frederick Corey--born July 8, 1903 in Shelby County, Iowa--B.A., University of Iowa, 1925--Sonoma, California.

Son of Edwin Olney & Margaret Morgan (Brown) Corey--Ruth Lechlither: February 1, 1928--Anne Margaret Corey (May 26, 1941).

With Encyclopaedia Britannica, 1927-1928; National Encyclopaedia, 1930-1931; Free-Lance Writer, April, 1931-DATE--Member: Authors League of America.

Mr. Corey provided the following comments on his career:
　　"Science fiction writing is sort of my fourth incarnation. In the '30's I wrote proletarian' short stories, and appeared in most of the little magazines of that decade (including Blast and The Anvil), and in mags that paid like Story and several others. The only sales of any consequence moneywise were to Scribner's and Farm Journal. One story of this period had a definite fantasy flavor, and was called 'The Farmer and the Gold Stone.
　　"My first Middle Western Farm Novel was published in September, 1939, and started my second incarnation: books, mainly novels. A trilogy: Three Miles Square, 1939; The Road Returns, 1940; County Seat, 1941; all farm fiction, followed by a fourth, Acres of Antaeus, 1946, and all adult stuff. In 1944 my first 'teenage' novel was published, The Red Tractor, and this was followed by four more: Five Acre Hill, Shad Haul, Corngold Farm, and Milk Flood. The latter, although written in the '40's was not published until 1956. Two non-fiction books, Buy an Acre and Build a Home, were also written and published during this period; they had a do-it-yourself or how-to slant. The only thing I did at that time with a

PAUL COREY (continued)

fantasy or sf flavor was an article for Look, 'Hitler Can Invade America by Air. As a result, I became a guerilla warfare specialist connected with the First Service Command Tactical School (1942).

"The Joe McCarthy era brought my novel writing to an end, and I swung to the how-to and do-it yourself field. I wrote about the houses I had built myself (Homemade Homes) in 1950. Then I started designing furniture, photographing the construction steps, and telling people how to build the stuff. Articles of this kind appeared in all the mechanics mags, plus Woman's Home Companion, Country Gentleman, True, etc. And there was also the usual how-to stuff: how to weather strip, etc. Fawcett brought out a book of my furniture articles: Furniture You Can Build. And so during the '50's I wrote sf only in my spare time.

"Fiction is my first love, though, and science fiction, which I have always fancied, seemed to me the only way I could say some of the things I had wanted to say after the J. McC. era. And by the '60's furniture was so easy to buy that no one was interested in building it themselves. Other types of mechanics magazine material bored me, and so I decided to go all out for sf. However, the only American editor who gave me any encouragement (and he didn't publish) was Anthony Boucher. Most of the others didn't bother to read me, except one or two editors of the new magazines, and they wrote me long fatuous criticisms, or even marked up my manuscripts, and said nothing that can't also be said about Clarke or Bradbury or Heinlein, or any other of the sf pros. And they're still doing it, and I submit things to them only for kicks now. But it was the reaction of the sf stuffed-shirts here who prompted me to try Britain, and E. J. Carnell took the first one I submitted to him while he still edited New Worlds. After he became an all-out literary agent, he sold my novel The Planet of the Blind, and used a short story ('If You're So Smart') for New Writings in SF14. I'm not sure that he really digs me, but everything he's had to say about my work makes a considerable spot of sense to me. So my fourth incarnation, so to speak, is now given over pretty much to sf.

"Just a note on my farm fiction period: 'The Middle-Western Farm Novel in the Twentieth Century' is a doctoral dissertation by a Roy Meyer, published by the University of Nebraska Press, 1966. He rates me along with Rolvaag, Hamlin Garland, and Willa Cather, and says that my books have made 'the most important contribution during the past generation to farm fiction.' And Frank Paluka (that's his real name), Head of Special Collections, University of Iowa Library wrote me: 'You may be interested to know that one scholar who was here last Fall (1965), and was much interested in our Corey papers was a Mlle. Danine Mouraille from Nice, France, who is doing her doctoral thesis for the Sorbonne on "The Rural World of the Middle West in America 1871 to 1950."'

"So much for posterity: I can now enjoy myself with sf writing and reading."

GEORGE CORSTON

1)	1968 Hale	Aftermath.
FPS:	1968 Hale	Aftermath.

GEORGE CORSTON (continued)

***   ***   ***   ***   ***

Michael George Corston--born July 14, 1932 at Kenton, Middlesex, England--Harrow & Wembley, Middlesex, England.

Josephine: July 14, 1963--no children.

With British Civil Service.

JUANITA COULSON

1)	1967 Ace	Crisis on Cheiron. (P)
2)	1968 Ace	The Singing Stones. (P)
FPS:	"Another Rib,"	The Magazine of Fantasy and Science Fiction, June, 1963 (as *John Jay Wells with Marion Zimmer Bradley).
WIP:	1970 Dell	War of the Wizards. (P)
		What Do You Mean, We?
		World He Never Made.
		Praedar's Planet.

***   ***   ***   ***   ***

Juanita Ruth Coulson--born February 12, 1933 at Anderson, Indiana--B.A., Ball State University, 1954; M.A., Ball State University, 1961--Hugo Award, Best Amateur Publication, 1965, Yandro; Ralph Holland Memorial Award from Fan Art Show, 1962--Hartford City, Indiana.

Daughter of Grant E. & Ruth Margaret (Oemler) Wellons--Robert Stratton Coulson: August 22, 1954--Bruce Edward Coulson (11).

Housewife--Member: Science Fiction Writers of America.

Mrs. Coulson writes:
   "My education is in teaching, and I did teach for one year. I have also worked in a book bindery, and operated a home mimeography business for the past ten years. I have always wanted to be a writer, but only within the past five years have I accepted the discipline necessary to the profession."

---

*RICHARD COWPER

1)   1967 Dobson   Breakthrough. (RP)

*RICHARD COWPER (continued)

2)	1968 Dobson	Phoenix.
FPS:	1958 Hutchinson	The Golden Valley (as *Colin Murry)
FSF:	1967 Dobson	Breakthrough.

***   ***   ***   ***   ***

John Middleton Murry--Born May 9, 1926 at Bridport, Dorset, England--B.A., (2nd Class Honors), Oxford University, 1950; Diploma of Education, University of Leicester, 1951--Llantwit Major, Glamorgan, South Wales.

Son of J. Middleton & Violet (le Maistre) Murry--Ruth Jezierski: July 27, 1950--Jacqueline (14); Helen (13).

Teacher of English, Whittinghame College, 1952-1967; Head of English Department, Atlantic College, 1967-DATE; Free-Lance Writer--Member: Authors' Society.

LUTHER COX

1)	1968 Exposition	The Earth Is Mine.

----

*EDMUND CRISPIN

1)	1955 Faber	Best SF: Science Fiction Stories. (@/RP)
2)	1956 Faber	Best SF Two. (@/RP)
3)	1958 Faber	Best SF Three. (@/RP)
4)	1961 Faber	Best SF Four. (@/RP)
5)	1962 Faber	Best Tales of Terror. (@/RP)
6)	1963 Faber	Best SF Five. (@)
7)	1965 Faber	Best Tales of Terror Two. (@)
8)	1966 Faber	Best SF Six. (@)
9)	1968 Faber	The Stars and Under. (@)
FPS:	1944 Gollancz	The Case of the Gilded Fly.
FSF:	1955 Faber	Best SF: Science Fiction Stories. (@)
WIP:	Faber	Best SF Seven. (@)

***   ***   ***   ***   ***

Robert Bruce Montgomery--born October 2, 1921 at Chesham Bois, England--B.A., St. John's College, Oxford University, 1943; attended Merchant Taylors' School--Totnes, Devon, England.

Son of Robert Ernest & Marion (Blackwood) Montgomery--unmarried.

*EDMUND CRISPIN (continued)

Schoolmaster, Shrewsbury School, 1943-1946; under his own name, is a composer and conductor, chiefly of film music; Mystery Critic, London Sunday Times (April, 1967-DATE); Free-Lance Writer and Editor, particularly of mystery novels and stories, 1946-DATE--Member: British Science Fiction Association (Chairman).

M.A. CUMMINGS

1) 1968 Flagship   Exile and Other Tales of Fantasy. (s/P)

FKP: "The Brides of Ool," Planet Stories, Summer, 1955.

NOTE: Monette A. Cummings.

RICHARD A. CURTIS

1) 1968 Dell   Future Tense. (@/P)

FPS: a mystery story to Ellery Queen's Mystery Magazine, in the early 1960's
FSF: "Introduction to 'The Saint,'" Cavalier, April, 1968.

***   ***   ***   ***   ***

Richard Alan Curtis--born June 23, 1937 at Bronx, New York--B.A., Syracuse University; M.A., University of Wyoming--New York, New York.

Son of Charles & Betty Curtis--Joanne Stone: August 17, 1966--no children.

Free-Lance Writer and Editor.

PETER DAGMAR

1) 1962 Digit   Alien Skies. (P)
2) 1962 Digit   Spykos 4. (P)
3) 1963 Digit   Sands of Time. (P/RH)
4) 1963 Digit   Once in Time. (P)

MILDRED E. DANFORTH

1) 1963 Digit   From Outer Space. (P)

LEONARD DAVENTRY

1) 1965 Gollancz   A Man of Double Deed. (RP)

WIP: 1969 Doubleday   Reflections in a Mirage and The Ticking Is in
                           Your Head.

NOTE: Leonard John Daventry was born in 1915. A winner of the Atlantic
Literary Award in 1946, he is currently a member of Science Fiction Writers of
America. A complete biography may be found in Contemporary Authors.

AVRAM DAVIDSON

2) 1962 Berkley   Or All the Seas with Oysters. (s/P)
3) 1963 Doubleday   The Best from Fantasy and Science Fiction
                           Twelfth Series. (@/RP)
4) 1964 Doubleday   The Best from Fantasy and Science Fiction
                           Thirteenth Series. (@, RP)
5) 1964 Pyramid   Mutiny in Space. (P)
6) 1965 Doubleday   The Best from Fantasy and Science Fiction
                           Fourteenth Series. (@/RP)
7) 1965 Ace   What Strange Stars and Skies. (s/P)
8) 1965 Pyramid   Masters of the Maze. (P)
9) 1965 Ace   Rogue Dragon. (P)
10) 1965 Berkley   Rork! (P/RH)
11) 1966 Ace   The Kar-Chee Reign. (P)
12) 1966 Ace   Clash of Star-Kings. (P)
13) 1966 Berkley   The Enemy of My Enemy. (P)

                           with Ward Moore (q.v.)
1) 1962 Pyramid   Joyleg. (P)

FPS: To Orthodox Jewish Life Magazine, 1946.
FSF: "My Boy Friend's Name Is Jello," The Magazine of Fantasy and Science
Fiction, July, 1954.

WIP: 1969 Doubleday   1   The Phoenix and the Mirror.
      1969 Ace   -1   The Island Under the Earth. (P)
           Ace   -2   The Sixlimbed Folk. (P)
           Ace   -3   The Cap of Grace. (P)
      1970 Doubleday   Bumberboom.
      1970 Doubleday   an untitled collection.

SER: 1) Vergil Magus; 2) The Cap of Grace.

***   ***   ***   ***   ***

Avram Davidson--born April 23, 1923 at Yonkers, New York--attended New York

AVRAM DAVIDSON (continued)

University, 1940-1942, 1947-1948; Yeshiva University, 1947-1948; Pierce College 1950-1951--Hugo Award, Best Short Story, 1958, "Or All the Seas with Oysters; Best Professional Magazine, 1963, Magazine of Fantasy and Science Fiction; Edgar Award, Best Short Story, 1962, "The Affair at the Lahore Cantonment;" Ellery Queen Award, 195? The Necessity of His Condition"--San Rafael, California Belize British Honduras

Son of Harry Jonas & Lillian (Adler) Davidson--Grania Kaiman: divorced--Ethan Michael Anders.

Executive Editor, The Magazine of Fantasy and Science Fiction, April, 1962-November, 1964; Free-Lance Writer, 1964-DATE--Member: Science Fiction Writers of America, Worshipful Company of the Ailing Cockroach; Serendipitous Order of Beavers.

"I don't know where science fiction, mankind, or, for that matter, me is going. I can no longer read sf, and consider my present and recent work to be fantasy alone

----

L.P. DAVIES

1) 1964 Jenkins   The Paper Dolls. (RP)
2) 1965 Jenkins   The Artificial Man. (RP)
3) 1966 Jenkins   Psychogeist. (RP)
4) 1966 Jenkins   The Lampton Dreamers.
5) 1967 Jenkins   Twilight Journey. (RP)
6) 1968 Jenkins   The Alien.

FPS: "Because Josie Didn't Go Straight Home," Family Star, 1959.
FSF: "The Wall of Time,"   London Mystery Magazine, 1960.

WIP: 1969 Doubleday   Dimension A.
        1969 Jenkins   Genesis Two.

***   ***   ***   ***   ***

Leslie Purnell Davies--born October 20, 1914 at Crewe, Cheshire, England--Fellow of the British Optical Association; Degree in Optometry, Manchester University, 1939--Deganwy, Caernarvon, North Wales.

Son of Arthur & Annie (Sutton) Davies--Wynne Tench: 1942--no children.

Has been a pharamacist, optometrist, painter in Rome, postmaster in Birmingham; now a Free-Lance Writer with 250 short story credits--Member: Science Fiction Writers of America.

L.P. DAVIES (continued)

The following remarks by Mr. Davies are taken from two private letters:
   "As you say, my books are hard to classify. The Artificial Man, for instance, was issued as sf in England, but as a Crime Club in the States. Privately, I called this hybrid type of writing 'Psychofiction.' And I prefer this format because I like my theme to have a firm foothold in normality. Outer Space has been exploited ad nauseum. The human mind has, to my way of thinking, far greater potential--from a writer's point of view--than B.E.M.'s on some obscure fictional world."
   2)"...You may be right in that many British writers are turning to the inner mind for their themes, but your American writers seem to be going--judging by the SFWA Award nominations--in the reverse direction. Please don't get me wrong--their writing is excellent, and makes me very envious--that of Robert Silverberg in particular. But I beg to say that science fiction should be what its name implies--fiction about science. And science doesn't seem to play any part at all in this so-called 'New Wave.' I abhor categories, but, for the sake of potential readers, they are a necessary evil. And because readers in general are God Almighty I think we should at least play the game with them and break sf down into other categories: Fantasy, Space Fiction, Science Fiction and Psychofiction.
   "And not only would this help the reader, it would also make life easier for the writer. My first novel, The Paper Dolls, was rejected by eight publishers before it finally found a home. And two of those publishers were honest enough to admit in their letters that they had rejected it mainly because the story didn't fit into any of their categories. And the publisher who did accept said: 'We don't know what to call it. So we will issue it as "suspense," leave it to the reader to decide for himself, and hope for the best.'"

BRADFORD M. DAY

1)	1952 SF & F	A Checklist of Fantastic Magazines. (nf/P)
2)	1953 SF & F	An Index to the Weird and Fantastica in Magazines. (nf/P)
3)	1954 SF & F	Past and Future and The Last Generation. (@/P)
4)	1955 SF & F	Talbot Mundy Biblio. (nf/P)
5)	1956 SF & F	Edgar Rice Burroughs Biblio. (nf/P)
6)	1961 SF & F	The Complete Checklist of Science-Fiction Magazines. (nf/P)
7)	1963 SF & F	Sax Rohmer: A Bibliography. (nf/P)
8)	1963 SF & F	The Supplemental Checklist of Fantastic Literature. (nf/P)
9)	1964 SF & F	Bibliography of Adventure: Mundy, Burroughs, Rohmer, Haggard. (nf/P)
10)	1965 SF & F	The Checklist of Fantastic Literature in Paperbound Books. (nf/P)
FPP:	1952 SF & F	A Checklist of Fantastic Magazines. (nf/P)

BRADFORD M. DAY (continued)

*** *** *** *** ***

Bradford M. Day (u)--born September 20, 1916 at Marblehead, Massachusetts--Denver, New York.

Son of Bradford M. & B. Edna Day--married in 1945--six children.

Publisher/Editor, Science-Fiction and Fantasy Publications, 1952-DATE; Owner of Woodhaven Bookland (a bookstore).

L. SPRAGUE de CAMP

1)	1941 Holt		Lest Darkness Fall. (RP)
4)	1948 Fantasy		Divide and Rule. (RP)
6)	1949 Shasta		The Wheels of If. (s)
9)	1951 Doubleday		Rogue Queen. (RP)
10)	1951 FPCI		The Undesired Princess.
11)	1953 Twayne		The Continent Makers. (s)
12)	1953 Hermitage		Science Fiction Handbook. (nf)
14)	1953 Twayne		The Tritonian Ring. (RP)
15)	1953 Hamilton		Sprague de Camp's New Anthology of Science Fiction. (@/H-P)
16)	1954 Ace	1	Cosmic Manhunt. (P)
19)	1957 Avalon		Solomon's Stone.
20)	1958 Avalon	2	The Tower of Zanid. (RP)
21)	1960 Avalon		The Glory That Was.
23)	1962 Avalon	3	The Search for Zei. (RP)
24)	1963 Doubleday		A Gun for Dinosaur. (s/RP)
25)	1963 Avalon	4	The Hand of Zei. (RPa)
26)	1963 Pyramid		Swords and Sorcery. (@/P)
27)	1965 Pyramid		The Spell of Seven. (@/P)
16A)	1966 Compact	1	A Planet Called Krishna. (P)
30)	1967 Pyramid		The Fantastic Swordsmen. (@/P)
32)	1968 Mirage		The Conan Reader. (nf/s)
37)	1968 Pyramid		The Goblin Tower. (P)

with Fletcher Pratt

2)	1941 Holt	-1	The Incomplete Enchanter. (RP)
3)	1942 Holt		The Land of Unreason. (RP)
5)	1948 Gnome		The Carnelian Cube. (RP)
7)	1950 Gnome	-2	The Castle of Iron. (RP)
13)	1953 Twayne		Tales from Gavagan's Bar. (s)
22)	1960 Avalon	-3	Wall of Serpents.

with P. Schuyler Miller

8)	1950 Fantasy		Genus Homo. (RF)

L. SPRAGUE de CAMP (continued)

			with Robert E. Howard
17)	1955 Gnome	+6	Tales of Conan. (s)
28)	1966 Lancer	01	Conan the Adventurer. (s/P)
29)	1967 Lancer	04	Conan the Usurper. (s/P)
35)	1968 Lancer	08	Conan the Freebooter. (s/P)

			with Björn Nyberg
18)	1957 Gnome	+7	The Return of Conan. (RPev)

			with Robert E. Howard and Lin Carter (q.v.)
31)	1967 Lancer	05	Conan. (s/P)
36)	1968 Lancer	09	Conan the Wanderer. (s/P)

			with Robert E. Howard and Björn Nyberg
33)	1968 Lancer	06	Conan the Avenger. (18/e/P)

			with Lin Carter (q.v.)
34)	1968 Lancer	07	Conan of the Isles. (P)

SER: 3), 4) Conan.

FPS: "The Isolinguals,"   Astounding, September, 1937.

WIP: 1969 Lancer   10   Conan of Cimmeria. (s/P/with Robert E. Howard and Lin Carter).
     Lancer   Conan the Buccaneer. (P/with Lin Carter)
     Lancer   Conan of Aquilonia. (P/with Lin Carter)

***   ***   ***   ***   ***

Lyon Sprague de Camp--born November 27, 1907, at New York, New York--B.S., California Institute of Technology, 1930; graduate study at Massachusetts Institute of Technology, 1932; M.S., Stevens Institute of Technology, 1933--International Fantasy Award, 1952, Lands Beyond; Cleveland Science Fiction Association Award, 1953, Tales from Gavagan's Bar; Atheneum Press Fiction Award, 1958, An Elephant for Aristotle; Guest of Honor, 24th World Science Fiction Convention (Tricon), 1966--Villanova, Pennsylvania.

Son of Lyon & E. Beatrice (Sprague) de Camp--Catherine A. Crook: August 18, 1939--Lyman Sprague de Camp; Gerard Beekman de Camp.

Editor, Inventors Foundation, 1933-1936; Fowler-Becker Publishing Company, 1937-1938; Writer, 1938-DATE--Member: Science Fiction Writers of America; Hydra Club; Trap Door Spiders Club; Philadelphia Science Fiction Society; Hyborian Legion; Association Phonétique Internationale; History of Science Society; Society for the History of Technology.

MIRIAM ALLEN deFORD

1) 1964 Pap Lib   Space, Time and Crime. (@/P)

FPS: 1907, magazine and title of story now unknown.
FSF: "The Last Generation,"   Harper's Magazine, 1946.

WIP: 1969 Ballantine   Xenogenesis. (s/P)

***   ***   ***   ***   ***

Miriam Allen deFord--born August 21, 1888 at Philadelphia, Pennsylvania--attended Wellesley College, 1907-1908; A.B., Temple University, 1911; graduate study at University of Pennsylvania, 1911-1912--Edgar Award, Best Non-Fiction, 1961, The Overbury Affair; MWA Scroll for Non-Fiction, 1965, Murderers Sane and Mad; Committee for Economic Development $500 Award for Essay Competition, 1958; Watts Essay Competition, R.P.A., 1964; Many poetry awards--San Francisco, California.

Daughter of Moïse & Frances (Allen) deFord--(1) Armistead Collier: February 14, 1915/1921; (2) Maynard Shipley: April 16, 1921-June 8, 1934--no children.

Open Forum Reporter, Boston, 1913-1915; Public Stenographer, San Diego, 1915; Insurance Claims Adjuster, 1918-1923; subsequent career chiefly in newspaper writing and reporting, including: Staff Correspondent, Federated Press, 1921-1956; Labor's Daily, 1956-1958--Member: Science Fiction Writers of America (Chairman, Election Committee, 1965); Mystery Writers of America (Director); Authors Guild; Poetry Society of America; American Civil Liberties Union; American Humanist Association; A.D.A.; Rationalist Press Association (London); United World Federalists.

----

*ALLEN DeGRAEFF

3) 1963 Collier   Human and Other Beings. (@/P)

                          with Basil Davenport as *Basil Davenport
1) 1958 Dodd   Deals with the Devil. (@/RP)
2) 1960 Ballantine   Invisible Men. (@/P)
4) 1967 VN   Famous Monster Tales. (@)

FSF: 1958 Dodd   Deals with the Devil. (@/with Basil Davenport as
                            *Basil Davenport)

***   ***   ***   ***   ***

Albert Paul Blaustein--born October 12, 1921 at New York, New York--A.B., University of Michigan, 1951; J.D., Columbia University, 1948--Cherry Hill, New Jersey.

*ALLEN DeGRAEFF (continued)

Son of Karl Allen & Rose (Brickman) Blaustein--Phyllis Midgen: December 21, 1948--Mark Allen Blaustein (January 12, 1950); Eric Barry Blaustein (July 11, 1951); Dana Beth Blaustein (January 31, 1957).

Reporter, City News Bureau, Chicago, Illinois, 1941-1942; Lawyer, 1948-1950, 1952-1955; Assistant Professor of Law and Law Librarian, New York Law School, 1953-1955; Associate Professor of Law, Rutgers University, 1955-1959; Professor of Law and Law Librarian, 1959-1969; Professor of Law, 1969-DATE; Associate Editor, The Young Lawyer, 1950;Founding Editor, Public Relations Bulletin, 1953-1954; Special Studies Consultant, Survey of the Legal Profession, 1948-1955; Professional Relations Adviser, National Association of Claimants' Compensation Attorneys, 1955-1957; Consultant, United States Commission on Civil Rights, 1962-1963; Consultant on Desegregation Problems, School District of Pennsylvania, 1963-1964; Law Library Consultant, Haile Selassie I University, Addis Ababa, Ethiopia, 1963-1968; SAILER Program, Institution of International Education and International Legal Center, for legal institutions in Liberia, Ghana, Nigeria, Congo (Kinshasa), Zambia, Lesotho, Malawi, Tanzania, Kenya, and Sudan; Consultant on legal materials for the drafting of the 1967 South Vietnamese Constitution, United States Information Service, 1966-1967; Consultant on legal research and law book resources, Ministry of Justice and National Assembly, South Vietnam, for United States Agency for International Development, 1967-- Member: American Association of Law Libraries (Chairman, Publications Committee, 1965-DATE); Association of American Law Schools (Chairman, Legislation Round Table Council, 1965-1967); Association of the Bar of the City of New York; American Law Institute; Camden County Bar Association.

NOTE: Professor Blaustein designed the United States postage stamp commemorating the American Bar Association, 1953. He also has served as an expert witness on the legal aspects of population control for the United States Senate Committee, 1966.

SAMUEL R. DELANY

1)	1962 Ace		The Jewels of Aptor. (P/RPe)
2)	1963 Ace	1	Captives of the Flame. (P/RPev)
3)	1964 Ace	2	The Towers of Toron. (P)
4)	1965 Ace	3	City of a Thousand Suns. (P)
5)	1965 Ace		The Ballad of Beta-2. (P)
6)	1966 Ace		Empire Star. (P)
7)	1966 Ace		Babel-17. (P/RH)
8)	1967 Ace		The Einstein Intersection. (P/RH)
9)	1968 Ace		The Jewels of Aptor. (1/e/P/RH)
10)	1968 Doubleday		Nova.
11)	1968 Sphere	1A	Out of the Dead City. (2/e/P)

SER: The Fall of the Towers.

SAMUEL R. DELANY (continued)

FPS:	an article on folk music,	Seventeen Magazine, 1960.
FSF:	1962 Ace	The Jewels of Aptor. (P)

***   ***   ***   ***   ***

Samuel Ray Delany, Jr.--born April 1, 1942 at New York, New York--attended City College of New York, two years--Nebula Award, Best Novel, 1966, Babel 17; 1967, The Einstein Intersection; Best Short Story, 1967, "Aye, and Gomorrah --San Francisco, California.

Son of Samuel Ray & Margaret Carey (Boyd) Delany--Marilyn Terry Hacker: August 24, 1961--no children.

Free-Lance Writer, 1967-DATE--Member: Science Fiction Writers of America.

"Youth spent between city house in New York's Harlem and country home in Hopewell Junction, New York. Year in Europe; currently live in San Francisco. Primary interest is the speculative novel. .I have only been able to support myself solely through writing in the past two years. Speculative fiction, nevertheless, provides a fascinating internal adventure for the writer."

----

*LESTER del REY

1)	1948 Prime	...And Some Were Human. (s/RP)
2)	1952 Winston	Marooned on Mars. (RP)
4)	1953 Winston	Attack from Atlantis. (RP)
7)	1954 Winston	Step to the Stars. (RP)
9)	1956 Winston	Mission to the Moon.
10)	1956 Ballantine	Nerves. (H-P)
12)	1958 Ballantine	Robots and Changelings. (s/P)
13)	1959 Avalon	Day of the Giants. (RP)
14)	1961 Holt	Moon of Mutiny. (RP)
15)	1962 Regency	The Eleventh Commandment (P)
16)	1963 Holt	Outpost of Jupiter.
17)	1963 Galaxy.	The Sky Is Falling and Badge of Infamy. (P)
18)	1965 West.	The Runaway Robot. (RP)
19)	1965 Ballantine	Mortals and Monsters. (s/P)
20)	1966 West	Tunnel Through Time. (RP)
21)	1966 Holt	Rocket from Infinity.
22)	1966 Lancer	Siege Perilous. (P)
23)	1966 Belmont	The Scheme of Things. (P)
24)	1966 Holt	The Infinite Worlds of Maybe.
25)	1968 West	Prisoners of Space.
		as *Philip St. John
3)	1952 Winston	Rocket Jockey.
6)	1954 Winston	Rockets to Nowhere.

*LESTER del REY (continued)

3A)	1955 Hutchinson	Rocket Pilot.
		as *Erik Van Lhin
5)	1953 Winston	Battle on Mercury.
11)	1956 Avalon	Police Your Planet.
		with Frederik Pohl (q.v.) as *Edson McCann
8)	1955 S & S	Preferred Risk. (RP)

NOTE: #s 18/20/22/25/22A were written by Paul W. Fairman, but are also listed here because they appeared under Mr. del Rey's name.

FPS: "The Faithful,"   Astounding, April, 1938.

WIP:
22A) 1969 Lancer   The Man Without a Planet. (P)

NOTE: Ramon Felipe San Juan Mario Silvio Enrico Smith Heathcourt-Brace Sierra y Alvarez del Rey y de los Uerdes was born in 1915. He has held the following positions: Editor, Space Science Fiction, May, 1952-September, 1953; Publisher, Science Fiction Adventures, November, 1952 (as *R. Alvarez); Editor, November, 1952-September, 1953 (as *Philip St. John); Fantasy Fiction, February/March, 1953-August, 1953; Associate Editor, February/March, 1953-November, 1953 (as *John Vincent); Editor, November, 1953 (with Harry Harrison as *Cameron Hall); Managing Editor, Galaxy, June, 1968-May, 1969; Feature Editor, July, 1969-DATE; Managing Editor, If, June, 1968-May, 1969; Feature Editor, July, 1969-DATE; Managing Editor, International Science Fiction, June, 1968; Editor, Worlds of Fantasy, #1 (1968). Mr. del Rey was Guest of Honor, 25th World Science Fiction Convention (NyCon 3), 1967.

GRAEME de TIMMS

1)	1963 Digit	Three Quarters. (P)
2)	1963 Digit	Split. (P)

DIANE DETZER

8)	1968 Avalon	Planet of Fear.
		as *Adam Lukens
1)	1959 Avalon	The Sea People.
2)	1960 Avalon	Conquest of Life.
3)	1961 Avalon	Sons of the Wolf. (RF)
4)	1962 Avalon	The Glass Cage.
5)	1962 Avalon	The World Within.

DIANE DETZER (continued)

6)	1963 Avalon	Alien World.
7)	1963 Avalon	Eevalu.

as *Jorge de Reyna
9)   1968 Avalon   Return of the Starships.

FPS: "Follow the Fleet,"   Ridgefield Press, Fall, 1939.
FSF: "The Tomb,"   Science Fiction, November, 1958.

***   ***   ***   ***   ***

Diane Detzer de Reyna (u)--born May 13, 1930 at Ridgefield, Connecticut--attended Barnard College; Pennsylvania State University; Heffleyn Browne Secretarial School--Newtown, Connecticut.

Daughter of Captain (USN) August J. & Dorothy Detzer--married--Peter de Reyna (17); Margaret de Reyna (9).

"Wrote personal articles at 9, newspaper reviews for a New England newspaper at 16; outside jobs have always generally been secretarial; presently working for Silvermine Publishers, Norwalk, Connecticut"--Member: Newtown Chess Club.

CHARLES V. DE VET

with Katherine MacLean (q.v.)
1)   1962 Ace   Cosmic Checkmate. (P)

FPS: "The Unexpected Weapon,"   Amazing, September, 1950.

***   ***   ***   ***   ***

Charles Vincent De Vet--born October 28, 1911 at Fayette, Michigan--B.S., Ferris State Teachers College, 1938; graduate study at the University of Michigan, 1939-1940--St. Paul, Minnesota.

Son of John & Lucille (Feastre) De Vet--Elenore Derwin: November 10, 1936 --Charles F. De Vet (28); Annette De Vet Benidt (31).

Teacher, various Michigan high schools, 1934-1940; served with the Postal Transport Service, 1940-1968; now retired.--Member: Science Fiction Writers of America.

PHILIP K. DICK

1)	1955 Ace	Solar Lottery. (P/RHv)
2)	1955 Rich	A Handful of Darkness. (s/RP)

PHILIP K. DICK (continued)

3)	1956 Ace	The World Jones Made. (P/RH)
1A)	1956 Rich	The World of Chance. (RP)
4)	1956 Ace	The Man Who Japed. (P)
5)	1957 Ace	Eye in the Sky. (P)
6)	1957 Ace	The Cosmic Puppets. (P)
7)	1957 Ace	The Variable Man and Other Stories. (s/P)
8)	1959 Lippincott	Time Out of Joint. (RP)
9)	1960 Ace	Dr. Futurity. (P)
10)	1960 Ace	Vulcan's Hammer. (P)
11)	1962 Putnam	The Man in the High Castle. (RP)
12)	1963 Ace	The Game-Players of Titan. (P)
13)	1964 Ballantine	Martian Time-Slip. (P)
14)	1964 Ace	The Simulcra. (P)
15)	1964 Belmont	The Penultimate Truth. (P/RH)
16)	1964 Ace	Clans of the Alphane Moon. (P)
17)	1965 Doubleday	The Three Stigmata of Palmer Eldritch. (RP)
18)	1965 Ace	Dr. Bloodmoney, or How We Got Along After the Bomb. (P)
19)	1966 Doubleday	Now Wait for Last Year. (RP)
20)	1966 Ace	The Crack in Space. (P)
21)	1966 Ace	The Unteleported Man. (P)
22)	1967 Pyramid	The Zap Gun. (P)
23)	1967 Berkley	Counter-Clock World. (P)
25)	1968 Doubleday	Do Androids Dream of Electric Sheep? (RP)
		with Ray Nelson (q.v.)
24)	1967 Ace	The Ganymede Takeover. (P)
FPS:	"Beyond Lies the Wub,"	Planet Stories, July, 1952.
WIP:	1969 Ace	The Preserving Machine. (s/P)
	1969 Doubleday	Ubik.
	1969 Berkley	Galactic Pot-Healer. (P)

***   ***   ***   ***   ***   ***

Philip Kindred Dick--born December 16, 1928 at Chicago, Illinois--attended University of California at Berkeley, 1950--Hugo Award, Best Novel, 1963, The Man in the High Castle--San Rafael, California.

Son of Joseph Edgar & Dorothy (Kindred) Dick--(1) Jeanette: 1949/August 10, 1950; (2) Kleo: 1951/May 2, 1957; (3) Ann: 1958/April 17, 1966; (4) Nancy: April 18, 1967--3) Laura Dick (6); 4) Isolde Dick (2).

In the retail record business through 1951; Free-Lance Writer, 1951-DATE --Member: Science Fiction Writers of America.

GORDON R. DICKSON

1)	1956	Ace		Alien from Arcturus. (P)
2)	1956	Ace		Mankind on the Run. (P)
4)	1960	Ace	1	The Genetic General. (P)
5)	1960	Ace		Time to Teleport. (P)
6)	1960	Holt	-1	Secret Under the Sea. (RP)
7)	1961	Pyramid		Naked to the Stars. (P)
8)	1961	Ace		Delusion World. (P)
9)	1961	Ace		Spacial Delivery. (P)
10)	1962	Doubleday	2	Necromancer. (RP/RPv)
11)	1963	Holt	-2	Secret Under Antarctica.
10A)	1963	Macfadden	2	No Room for Man. (P)
12)	1964	Holt	-3	Secret Under the Carribbean.
13)	1965	Holt		Space Winners.
14)	1965	Bantam		The Alien Way. (P)
15)	1965	Berkley		Mission to Universe. (P)
16)	1967	Berkley		The Space Swimmers. (P/RH)
18)	1967	Dell	3	Soldier, Ask Not. (P)

with Poul Anderson (q.v.)
3) 1957 Gnome   Earthman's Burden.

with Keith Laumer (q.v.)
17) 1967 Doubleday   Planet Run. (RP)

SER: 1) Childe ("Dorsai") Cycle.

FPS: "Trespass!"   Fantastic Story Quarterly, Spring, 1950
                            (with Poul Anderson).

WIP: 1969 Putnam   Spacepaw. (RP)
     1969 Doubleday   None But Man.
     1969 Dell   Wolfling. (P)
     1969 Dell   Hour of the Horde. (P)
          Doubleday   Danger--Human. (s)
          Crowell   Mutants. (s)
          Dell   Alien Art. (P)
          Lippincott   Sleepwalkers World.
          Lippincott   Outposter.
          Putnam   Pilgrim and Professional.
          Doubleday 4 Tactics of Mistake.

***   ***   ***   ***   ***

Gordon Rupert Dickson--born November 1, 1923 at Edmonton, Alberta, Canada--B.A., University of Minnesota, 1948; graduate study, University of Minnesota, 1948-1950 --Hugo Award, Best Short Fiction, 1965, "Soldier, Ask Not;" Nebula Award, Best Novelette, 1966, "Call Him Lord"--Minneapolis, Minnesota.

GORDON R. DICKSON (continued)

Son of Gordon Fraser & Maude Leola (Ford) Dickson--unmarried.

Free-Lance Writer, 1950-DATE--Member: Science Fiction Writers of America (President, 1969-1970).

Mr. Dickson comments on his work:
"The 'Dorsai' Cycle was originally intended to consist of nine volumes, three historical novels, three contemporary novels, and three science fiction novels of the future, so that the whole Cycle spans a stretch of time from the early fourteenth century to the late twenty-fourth century--or roughly a thousand years.
"The science fiction end of it, as you may know has grown. Already published are <u>Dorsai</u> //<u>The Genetic General</u>--ed.//, <u>Necromancer</u>, <u>Soldier Ask Not;</u> and the upcoming <u>Tactics of Mistake</u> will be published by Doubleday.
"In addition to these titles, the final act of the Cycle--which, by the way, is correctly named the Childe Cycle--are to be <u>Armageddon</u> and <u>Childe</u>.
"Of the three contemporary, and the three historical novels, none are finished at the present time, and only two have prospective titles. The first historical--the one that starts the Cycle--is to be titled <u>Hawkwood</u>, being a fictionalized biography of Sir John Hawkwood, a painting of whom can still be seen in the Duomo in Florence (unless the recent flood managed to damage it along with the many other art treasures in that city).
"The first book, or perhaps the second (but most likely the first), of the three contemporary novels is currently titled <u>Stoneman's Walk</u>. While the Hawkwood title is firm, the other may be changed around.
" I expect it may take me fifteen years before the Cycle is finally finished. But it is a project very dear to my heart, and if I keep writing long enough, it most assuredly will be done."

T. E. DIKTY

13)	1955 Fell	The Best Science Fiction Stories and Novels: 1955. (@/RPav)
14)	1956 Fell	The Best Science Fiction Stories and Novels: 1956. (@/RPav)
13A)	1957 Crest	Five Tales from Tomorrow. (@/a/P)
14A)	1958 Crest	Six from Worlds Beyond. (@/a/P)
15)	1958 Advent	The Best Science Fiction Stories and Novels: Ninth Series. (@)
16)	1960 Fell	Every Boy's Book of Outer Space Stories. (@)
17)	1966 Fell	Great Science Fiction Stories About Mars. (@)
18)	1967 Fell	Great Science Fiction Stories About the Moon. (@)

with Everett F. Bleiler

1)	1949 Fell	The Best Science Fiction Stories: 1949. (@)
2)	1950 Fell	The Best Science Fiction Stories: 1950. (@)
3)	1951 Fell	The Best Science Fiction Stories: 1951. (@)
4)	1952 Garden City	The Science-Fiction Omnibus. (1/2)

T.E. DIKTY (continued)

5)	1952 Fell	Year's Best Science Fiction Novels: 1952. (@)
6)	1952 Farrar	Imagination Unlimited. (@/RPa)
7)	1952 Fell	The Best Science Fiction Stories: 1952. (@)
8)	1953 Fell	Year's Best Science Fiction Novels: 1953. (@)
9)	1953 Fell	The Best Science Fiction Stories: 1953. (@)
10)	1954 Fell	Year's Best Science Fiction Novels: 1954. (@)
11)	1954 Fell	The Best Science Fiction Stories: 1954. (@)
12)	1955 Bantam	Frontiers in Space. (@/P)

FPS: 1949 Fell   The Best Science Fiction Stories: 1949
                        (@/with Everett F. Bleiler)

***   ***   ***   ***   ***

Thaddeus Eugene Dikty--born June 16, 1920 at Port Clinton, Ohio--Naperville, Illinois.

Son of Ignatius & Eleanor Dikty--Julian May: January 10, 1953--Sam Dikty (14); David Dikty (12); Barbara Dikty (11).

Free-Lance Editor.

THOMAS M. DISCH

1)	1965 Berkley		The Genocides. (P/RH)
2)	1966 Ace		Mankind Under the Leash. (P)
3)	1966 Compact		One Hundred and Two H Bombs. (s/P)
4)	1967 Berkley		Echo Round His Bones. (P)
5)	1968 Hart-Davis		Camp Concentration.
7)	1968 Hart-Davis		Under Compulsion. (s)
			with John T. Sladek (q.v.) as *Thom Demijohn.
6)	1968 Doubleday		Black Alice.

SER: The Prisoner.

FPS: "The Double Timer,"   Fantastic, October, 1962.

WIP:	1969 Ace	1	The Prisoner. (P)
7A)	1969 Doubleday		Fun with Your New Head. (s)
			Glandier.

***   ***   ***   ***   ***

Thomas Michael Disch--born February 2, 1940 at Des Moines, Iowa--attended New York University, 1959-1962--Milford, Pennsylvania.

THOMAS M. DISCH (continued)

Son of Felix Henry & Helen Margaret (Gilbertson) Disch--unmarried.

Employed in advertising, Doyle Dane Bernbach, 1963-1964; Free-Lance Writer, 1964-DATE--Member: Science Fiction Writers of America.

GEOFFREY DOHERTY

1)	1959 Murray	Aspects of Science Fiction. (@)
2)	1965 Murray	Second Orbit. (@)
3)	1966 Nelson	Stories from Science Fiction. (@)

FPS:	1956	
FSF:	1959 Murray	Aspects of Science Fiction. (@)

***   ***   ***   ***   ***

Geoffrey Donald Doherty--born February 17, 1927 at Sheffield, England--attended University of Sheffield, 1944-1948--Stoke-on-Trent, Stafford, England.

Son of Michael & Ethel Doherty--married February 18, 1950--Elizabeth Jane Doherty (14); Michael John Doherty (12).

English Teacher, various Grammar Schools, 1950-1962; with various Colleges of Education, 1962-1968; currently Head of the Department of Drama, Alsager College.

CYRIL DONSON

1)	1968 Hale	Born in Space.

JUNE DRUMMOND

1)	1968 Gollancz	The Gantry Episode.

NOTE: June Drummond was born in 1923. A complete biography may be found in Contemporary Authors.

MADELAINE DUKE

1)	1964 Heinemann	Claret, Sandwiches and Sin. (RP)
2)	1967 Heinemann	This Business of Bomfog.

MADELAINE DUKE (continued)

FPS: a short story published in 1945.
FSF: 1964 Heinemann   Claret, Sandwiches and Sin.

WIP: a juvenile sf novel.

***   ***   ***   ***   ***

Madelaine Elizabeth Duke--born August 21, 1925 at Geneva, Switzerland--attended University of St. Andrews; University of Edinburgh: qualified in medicine and science--Ditchling, Sussex, England.

Daughter of Richard & Federica Duke--Dr. Alexander Macfarlane: August, 1946 --no children.

Free-Lance Writer--Member: Society of Authors; P.E.N.; English Speaking Union; New Arts; Hartford Foundation (Fellow).

NOTE: Miss Duke's parents were killed in a German concentration camp at Hinsk in 1942.

BRUCE DUNCAN

1)   1968 Belmont   Mirror Image. (P)

GEORGE W. EARLEY

1)   1968 Sherbourne   Encounters with Aliens: UFOs and Alien
                       Beings in Science Fiction. (@)

FPS: "Moon Gun,"   Journal of the Interplanetary Exploration Society,
                       December, 1960.
FSF: 1968 Sherbourne Encounters with Aliens. (@)

WIP: a second anthology and a swords-and-sorcery novel.

***   ***   ***   ***   ***

George Whiteford Earley--born February 15, 1927 at Warrenton, Virginia--B.S., Miami University (Ohio), 1951--Bloomfield, Connecticut.

Son of Guy B. & Carol B. (Whiteford) Earley--Margaret D. Griffith: 1951--David Earley (16); Kathryn Earley (8); Stephen Earley (12); Christine Elizabeth Earley (0).

With United States Air Force, 1951-1953; "Since 1953 I have been an aerospace administrative engineer, closely associated with a variety of aerospace programs,

GEORGE W. EARLEY (continued)

including space life support systems;" Principal Reviewer of science fiction and related materials, <u>Hartford Sunday Courant</u>, 1956-DATE--Member: Burroughs Bibliophiles; Hyborian Legion; Fellowship of the Ring.

<u>NOTE</u>: Mr. Earley mentions that he worked on development for the Apollo program of both the space suit backpack and the LEM life support program.

A. EARNSHAW
with Eric Thacker (q.v.)

1)	1968 Cape	<u>Musrum.</u>
FPS:	1968 Cape	<u>Musrum.</u> (with Eric Thacker)
WIP:	1969 Cape	<u>Wintersol.</u> (with Eric Thacker)

***   ***   ***   ***   ***

Anthony Earnshaw--born October 9, 1924 at Ilkley, Yorkshire, England--Leeds, England.

Son of Ernest & Dorothy (Myers) Earnshaw--Monica Simpson: 1957/1969--Ruth Earnshaw (December 15, 1957); Frances Earnshaw (January 9, 1959.)

Factory Worker in and around Leeds, 1940-1966; Lecturer, Bradford College of Art, 1966-DATE.

Concerning his life and work, Mr. Earnshaw writes:
    "In the 1940's an interest in surrealism led me to take up painting, and in recent years I have exhibited work in various shows in Britain. My friendship with my co-author and -illustrator Eric Thacker dates from 1942. In 1967 we wrote, drew, and produced <u>Musrum</u> ...to keep ourselves amused...'
<u>Musrum</u> is not sf: the book can best be described as an 'astounding novel. Reality contains every possible and impossible thing. It is the role of sf, as with all imaginative art and literature, to explore and illuminate the frontiers of experience, and thereby pave the way for the fulfillment of desires. 'Mind can only triumph in its most perilous activities; no daring is fatal.'--Paul Eluard."

ROBERT EASSON

1)	1968 Vantage	<u>The Bird, the Ghoul, and in the Name of My Friend.</u>
FPP:	1968 Vantage	<u>The Bird, the Ghoul, and in the Name of My Friend.</u>

ROBERT EASSON (continued)

***　　　　***　　　　***　　　　***　　　　***

Robert Watson Easson--born April 10, 1941 at Aberdeen, Scotland--currently (1968) a senior at Washburn University--Topeka, Kansas.

Son of Alexander & Anne (Watson) Easson--unmarried.

Student.

JACK DENNIS ECKSTROM

1)   1968 Avalon   Time of the Hedrons.

----

*PETER EDGAR

1)   1963 Digit   Cities of the Dead. (P)

NOTE: Peter Edgar is a penname of Peter King-Scott.

G.C. EDMONDSON

1)   1965 Ace   The Ship That Sailed the Time Stream. (P)
2)   1965 Ace   Stranger Than You Think. (s/P)

FPS: to McCall's Magazine.
FSF: "Blessed Are the Meek," Astounding, September, 1955.

WIP: Chapayeca.

***　　　***　　　***　　　***　　　***

José Mario Garry Ordonez Edmondson y Cotton--born October 11, 1922 at Rascuachitlán, Tabasco, Mexico--believed to have an M.D. from a Vienna, Austria, school--San Diego, California.

Thrice married--two sons, two daughters.

"Shod Pancho Villa's horse;" one of the few remaining blacksmiths in the United States; Free-Lance Writer--Member: Science Fiction Writers of America.

In response to our further questioning, Mr. Edmondson wrote the following:
   "My parents' names were Pop & Mom. My eldest daughter, named after a first century BC Roman reformer, has just produced a child named in highly original fashion from Old Testament sources. In English her name is 'bee.' #1 boy is named after a famous loser in the Trojan campaign. He's now

G.C. EDMONSON (continued)

losing another war in Vietnam. #2 boy bears the name of one of history's famous bastards. #2 girl was immortalized by the late Chas. Lutwidge Dodgson. My spouse was done the same honor by Georges Bizet. There is a tiny verse about my natal village, Villa Hermosa de Rascuachitlán, which might be helpful in visualizing the terrain:

> Un pinche petate fué mi cuna
> en tristes pañales me envolvieron.
> Tan rechingada fué mi fortuna
> que pura verga a mamar me dieron.

Though he's eager to disclaim it, I believe the author was Antonio Plazas. If you ever get to San Diego and run into a handsome, extremely virile type with large amounts of charisma, rest assured, it isn't me."

<u>NOTE</u>: ·Mr. Edmondson is just resuming writing after a five year illness.

DAVID EDWARDS

1) 1960 Greenwich   <u>Next Stop, Mars!</u>

CHARLES EINSTEIN

1) 1964 Gold Medal   <u>The Day New York Went Dry.</u> (P)

FSF: "Tunnel 1971,"   <u>Saturn,</u> May, 1957.

***   ***   ***   ***   ***

Charles Einstein (u)--born August 2, 1926 at Boston, Massachusetts--Ph.B., University of Chicago--San Rafael, California.

Son of Harry & Lillian Einstein--married, May 18, 1947--three sons, one daughter.

Free-Lance Writer--Member: Authors League; Writers Guild of America.

JOSEPH ELDER

1) 1968 Trident   <u>The Farthest Reaches.</u> (@)

JOHN ELLIOT

with Fred Hoyle (q.v.)

1)	1962 Souvenir	1	A for Andromeda. (RP)
2)	1964 Souvenir	2	Andromeda Breakthrough. (RP)

NOTE: John Herbert Elliot was born in 1918.

BRUCE ELLIOTT

1) 1968 Belmont   Asylum Earth. (P)

FKP: "Fearsome Fable,"   The Magazine of Fantasy and Science Fiction, February, 1951.

D.E. ELLIS

1) 1961 Digit   A Thousand Ages. (P)

FKP: "Stress,"   New Worlds, September, 1961.

HARLAN ELLISON

1)	1960 Ace	The Man with Nine Lives. (P)
2)	1960 Ace	A Touch of Infinity. (s/P)
3)	1961 Regency	Gentlemen Junkie and Other Stories of the Hung-Up Generation. (s/P)
4)	1962 Pap Lib	Ellison Wonderland. (s/P)
4A)	1964 Pap Lib	Earthman, Go Home! (s/P)
5)	1965 Pyramid	Paingod and Other Delusions. (s/P)
6)	1967 Pyramid	I Have No Mouth and I Must Scream. (s/P)
7)	1967 Belmont	Doomsman. (P)
8)	1967 Doubleday	Dangerous Visions. (@/RPav)
9)	1967 Belmont	From the Land of Fear. (s/P)
10)	1968 Trident	Love Ain't Nothing But Sex Misspelled. (s)

FPS: "The Sword of Parmegon,"   Cleveland News, 1947

WIP:
8A)	1969 Berkley	Dangerous Visions #1. (@/a/P)
8B)	1969 Berkley	Dangerous Visions #2. (@/a/P)
8C)	1969 Berkley	Dangerous Visions #3. (@/a/P)
	1969 Avon	The Beast That Shouted Love at the Heart of the World. (s/P)

HARLAN ELLISON (continued)

1969 Belmont	The Sound of a Scythe. (1/e/P)
1969 Belmont	Partners in Wonder. (s/P)
1969 Doubleday	Demon with a Glass Hand.

"Man Without Time," a television series, sold to Paramount, and under consideration by NBC for the 1970-1971 season.
"Astra/Ella!" a second TV series, sold to Paramount and under consideration by CBS.
Again, Dangerous Visions. (@)

***   ***   ***   ***   ***

Harlan Jay Ellison--born May 27, 1934 at Cleveland, Ohio--attended Ohio State University, 1951-1953--Hugo Award, Best Short Fiction, 1966, "'Repent, Harlequin!' Said the Ticktockman;" Best Short Story, 1968, "I Have No Mouth, and I Must Scream;" Best Drama, 1968, "City on the Edge of Forever,"(On Star Trek.); Nebula Award, Best Short Story, 1965, "'Repent Harlequin!' Said the Ticktockman;" Nova Award, Most Outstanding Contributor to the Field of Science Fiction, 1968; Writers Guild of America Award for Most Outstanding Script in the Category of TV Anthology, 1964-1965 Season, "Demon with a Glass Hand" (on Outer Limits); Writers Guild of America Award for Most Outstanding Script in the Category of TV Dramatic-Episodic, 1966-1967 Season, "City on the Edge of Forever" (on Star Trek)--Sherman Oaks, California.

Son of Louis Laverne & Serita (Rosenthal) Ellison--married and divorced three times--no children.

Founder/Editor, Regency Books, 1961-1962; Free-Lance Writer, 1956-DATE; Free-Lance TV and Film Script Writer, 1962-DATE--Member: Science Fiction Writers of America (Vice President, 1965-1966); Writers Guild of America; Synanon; Congress for Racial Equality; Students' National Coordinating Committee; American Civil Liberties Union; Center for the Study of Democratic Institutions.

Mr. Ellison provided the following statements on himself and science fiction:
"THE CURRENT STATE OF SF: Without doubt, this is the most exciting period in the history of sf. We have at long last shucked-off the restrictions and tunnel-vision of the pulp era (though we still must contend with the reactionaries who prefer to live in the golden days of yesterday, who resist change in almost a microcosmic parallel to the change-resistance in our culture as a whole). The idea that what we wrote was merely escapist fiction, or mild little myths. The taking-of-its-place with the best of contemporary fiction. It is not at all unthinkable to me that among the young men writing today will emerge talents considered on a par with the best of the classic novelists. It is an exhilarating time to be alive, and to be writing, and to be writing in this field. The controversy is spreading and I think is enormously healthy for the field; the range of writing style and new voices makes every year more unpredictable, more enriching. At last sf writers are getting both the recognition and monetary rewards their work has entitled them to, for fifteen years.

HARLAN ELLISON (continued)

"THE NEW WAVE: does not exist. It is the bugaboo of those who need labels and classifications so they can better cope with the uncopeable. It is the categorization of critics. It does not, in actuality, exist. What we are now seeing is the emergence of many individual waves, each one containing a single writer; but all linked by their concern with form, style, the impact of the visual media on the reader, their concern for contemporary events, and a feeling of serious purpose. They are not merely magazine writers, they are men who conceive of themselves as engaged in a holy chore: that of writing. The feel of a changing world is in their writing. Consider them: Zelazny, Delany, Disch, Ballard, Aldiss, Spinrad, Anthony, myself, Dorman, Emshwiller, Silverberg, Brunner. These are all names that ten years ago were either unimportant or unknown. Look where they stand now and compare them with the positions of 'name writers' who have moved on to other fields or have said what they had to say. The common error that is made by detractors of what the new voices are saying is that they believe (erroneously) that the young turks are trying to bury The Old Wave. That is pure horseshit. We respect and admire the men who broke the ground for us, who set the pace, who taught us what we know. We have reverence for them, and when they choose to write at the peak of their form, we laud them. We conceive of 'burying' another writer as an unthinkable sin. There is more than enough room for everyone. If the arteriosclerotic reactionaries were as Christian in their thinking as they demand of others, they would recognize that the natural order is being supremely served by the young men nudging the older, more established writers. Only in this way do we all benefit, all grow.

"MY OWN CONTRIBUTION: I have tried to avoid do-as-I-say-not-as-I-do. In urging other writers--through speeches and articles and the implied directives of Dangerous Visions--to break free, experiment, stretch their muscles, I have tried to offer the honest examples of my own struggles. Brought up on the concepts that sf should never aspire to more than competent pulp writing, and that plot is all, I have fought my own inclinations to write with conformity. 'The Beast That Shouted Love at the Heart of the World' and 'Pretty Maggie Moneyeyes' and several other stories that have been much discussed were my attempts to show other writers what they could do if they refused to accept the artificial parameters imposed on them by decades now dead. Dangerous Visions was the first market in which any writer could have his say, untrammeled by editorial prejudices, even down to such minutiae as guaranteeing each writer his punctuation would be retained, even it if made for a book in which there was no set format. I have frequently--and consciously--offered myself as a target for the detractors of the new work, feeling that my life-style and financial situation made me eminently qualified to take the brunt of insult and calumny. It has worked out precisely that way. Other writers have been able to slip past the assassins, because the canards were being hurled at me and what I've written. I consider it in the nature of dues to be paid. I suppose if a single word for my contribution must be settled on, there are two choices: catalyst or gadfly. I would not be at all upset were time to judge me as one or the other."

- -

ROGER ELWOOD

1)	1964 Pap Lib	Alien Worlds. (@/P)
2)	1965 Pap Lib	Invasion of the Robots. (@/P)
		with Sam Moskowitz (q.v.)
3)	1966 Holt	Strange Signposts. (@)
4)	1967 Tower	The Human Zero and Other Science Fiction Masterpieces. (@/P)
5)	1968 Tower	The Time Curve. (@/P)
WIP:	1969 Macfadden	Alien Earth and Other Stories. (@/P/with Sam Moskowitz)
	1969 Macfadden	Other Worlds, Other Times. (@/P/with Sam Moskowitz)

I. O. EVANS

1)	1944 Warne	Gadget City.
2)	1956 Sidgwick	Jules Verne: Master of Science Fiction. (@)
3)	1965 Arco	Jules Verne and His Work. (nf)
4)	1966 Panther	Science Fiction Through the Ages, Volume 1. (@/P)
5)	1966 Panther	Science Fiction Through the Ages, Volume 2. (@/P)
FPS:	1932 Archer	The Junior Outline of History. (nf)
FSF:	1956 Sidgwick	Jules Verne: Master of Science Fiction. (@)

WIP: "Compilation of a history of Science Fiction."

*** *** *** *** ***

Idrisyn Oliver Evans--born November 11, 1894 at Bloemfontein, South Africa--Tadworth, Surrey, England.

Son of Harry & Sara Winifred (Sutton) Evans--Marie Elizabeth Mumford: March 6, 1937--no children.

British Civil Servant, 1912-1956; Editor (and often translator), "Fitzroy" Edition of Jules Verne, 1958-DATE--Member: Société Jules Verne (Paris); Society of Authors; Society of Civil Service Authors; Royal Geographical Society (Fellow).

NOTE: Mr. Evans served in the 6th Welch Regiment and Special Brigade, Royal Engineers, during the first World War.

Mr. Evans writes:
"Now that science fiction has become a recognised and popular art form, it has had the foreseeable result of attracting a number of authors who are not really interested in or 'committed to' it. Hence a spate of Space Opera and of works including needless vulgar or sexual themes--it has been said that science

I.O. EVANS (continued)

fiction, which at first had an attractive austerity in such matters, has now become 'adult'--which apparently means that it deals with such extraneous matters as adultery!

"On the other hand, it has necessarily become much more factual: now that conditions on, for example, Mars and the Moon are reasonably well known, writers have to adapt their narratives accordingly, instead of giving their imagination free rein.

"Happily there are still authors of outstanding brilliance--notably, Arthur C. Clarke, Robert Heinlein, Isaac Asimov, Eric Frank Russell. Though John Wyndham's recent death is a sad loss, such authors as those named, and a number of others, still maintain the high standards of science fiction."

On Jules Verne, he comments:

"Though not the actual creator of sf, Verne turned it into an established branch of literature, and showed its potentialities. Though himself greatly inspired by Edgar Allan Poe, he was free from that writer's morbidity, and from his addiction to hoaxes. He took science fiction seriously, and gave it that austerity which it has never completely lost. He was more factual than his confrère H.G. Wells, and with a few exceptions he sought to give all his work a sound scientific basis, while making it at the same time attractive as fiction."

Finally, Mr. Evans discussed his own work:

"I have written a few short sf stories that have found publication--and many more that haven't! Some historical stories I wrote years ago for young readers also have more than a touch of sf. My chief contribution to science fiction has, however, been to make better known the works of Jules Verne: not only did I produce an anthology of his sf stories, but I also edited the 'Fitzroy' edition of most of his works. Finding that the original translations of these were largely imperfect, I revised many of them drastically, and I also translated some that were, I believe, hitherto unknown to the English-reading world. My Science Fiction Through the Ages, Part I, is also an innovation, in that I used it to show the historical development of this art form."

WILLIAM H. EVANS

with Ron Ellik

1)   1966 Advent   The Universes of E.E. Smith. (nf/RP)

FPS: 1966 Advent   The Universes of E.E. Smith. (nf/with Ron Ellik)

***   ***   ***   ***   ***

William Harrington Evans--born February 26, 1921 at Salem, Oregon--B.A., Willamette University, 1942; Ph.D., Oregon State University, 1947--Hyattsville, Maryland.

Son of W.D. & Sibyl H. Evans--Buddie: 1965--Stepchildren: Toni (29); Peggy Rae (25).

WILLIAM H. EVANS (continued)

Thermochemist, National Bureau of Standards, 1947-DATE--Member: Fantasy Amateur Press Association (1942-DATE); American Chemical Society; American Physical Society.

NOAH D. FABRICANT

			with Groff Conklin
1)	1963 Collier		Great Science Fiction About Doctors. (@/P)

NOTE: Noah Daniel Fabricant, a Doctor of Medicine, was born in 1904. He could not be located.

PAUL W. FAIRMAN

3)	1964 Monarch		The World Grabbers. (P)
4)	1965 Pyramid	2	City Under the Sea. (P)
8)	1968 Lancer		Rest in Agony. (2/e/P)
10)	1968 Lancer		I, the Machine. (P)
11)	1968 Holt		The Forgetful Robot.

as *Ivar Jorgensen

1)	1963 Monarch	Ten from Infinity. (P)
2)	1963 Monarch	Rest in Agony. (P/RPe)
12)	1968 Belmont	Whom the Gods Would Slay. (P)

as *Lester del Rey

5)	1965 West	The Runaway Robot. (RP)
6)	1966 West	Tunnel Through Time. (RP)
7)	1966 Lancer	Siege Perilous. (P)
9)	1968 West	Prisoners of Space.

UNNUMBERED SER: #4--Voyage to the Bottom of the Sea.

FKP: "No Teeth for the Tiger," Amazing, February, 1950.

WIP:
7A)	1969 Lancer	The Man Without a Planet. (P/as *Lester del Rey)

NOTE: Paul W. Fairman was born in 1916. Among the positions he has held are: Editor, If, March, 1952-September, 1952; Associate Editor, Amazing, August, 1952-March, 1953; Managing Editor, April/May, 1953-November, 1954; April, 1956; June, 1956-August, 1956; Editor, September, 1956-November, 1958; Associate Editor, Fantastic Adventures, August, 1952-March, 1953; Fantastic, Fall, 1952-March/April, 1953; Managing Editor, May/June 1953-October, 1954; August, 1956; Editor, October, 1956-November, 1958; Dream World, February, 1957-August, 1957 (all issues). He is a member of Science Fiction Writers of America.

BRON FANE

1)	1960 Badger SF	Juggernaut.	(P/RHv)
2)	1960 Badger SF	Last Man on Earth.	(P)
3)	1961 Badger SF	Rodent Mutation.	(P)
4)	1963 Badger SF	The Intruders.	(P)
5)	1963 Badger SF	Somewhere Out There.	(P/RH)
6)	1963 Badger SN	Softly by Moonlight.	(P)
7)	1964 Badger SN	Unknown Destiny.	(P)
8)	1964 Badger SF	Nemesis.	(P)
9)	1964 Badger SF	Suspension.	(P)
10)	1964 Badger SN	The Macabre Ones.	(P)
1A)	1965 Arcadia	Blue Juggernaut.	
11)	?1966 Badger SF	U.F.O. 517.	(P)

NOTE: Bron Fane is a probable pseudonym, R. Lionel Fanthorpe (q.v.) being the likely author of all or most of the works appearing under this name.

R. LIONEL FANTHORPE

1)	?1958 Badger SF	The Waiting World.	(P)
2)	1959 Badger SF	Alien from the Stars.	(P/RH)
3)	1959 Badger SF	Hyperspace.	(P)
4)	1959 Badger SF	Space-Borne.	(P)
5)	1959 Badger SF	Fiends.	(P)
6)	1960 Badger SF	Doomed World.	(P)
7)	1960 Badger SF	Satellite.	(P)
8)	1960 Badger SF	Asteroid Man.	(P)
9)	1960 Badger SN	Out of the Darkness.	(P)
10)	1960 Badger SF	Hand of Doom.	(P/RH)
11)	1961 Badger SF	Flame Mass.	(P)
12)	1961 Badger SN	The Golden Chalice.	(P)
13)	1962 Badger SF	Space Fury.	(P/RH)
14)	1963 Badger SF	Negative Minus.	(P)
15)	1965 Badger SF	Neuron World.	(P)
16)	1965 Badger SN	The Triple Man.	(P)
17)	1966 Badger SN	The Unconfined.	(P)
18)	1966 Badger SF	The Watching World.	(P)

NOTE: R(?obert) Lionel Fanthorpe is an enigma. Repeated efforts to contact him have proved futile, though the following information has been determined: 1) he is a real person, one of the few on the Badger list; 2) he was born in Dereham, Norfolk, England on the same street as that of Brian Aldiss (this from Mr. Aldiss); 3) he was once a member of the British Interplanetary Society (from 1952), though he is not as of this date; 4) according to the information contained on his early books, his profession was that of a teacher; 5) it is possible that he may be recently deceased. Contacts with prominent men in British science fiction circles have agreed on the following point: he was probably responsible for the majority of the Badger Science Fiction and Supernatural pocketbook lines, writing

R. LIONEL FANTHORPE (continued)

many of his works under pennames. Recent studies by the editors indicate that the following names were at least partially used by Fanthorpe: Lionel Roberts (Robert Lionel in several reprints); Leo Brett; Bron Fane; Pel Torro; John E. Muller (Marston Johns and Mel Jay in several reprints); Karl Zeigfreid (now confirmed to be a pseudonym). Four further Badger names, Trebor Thorpe, Erle Barton, Neil Thanet, and Lee Barton (the latter two used only in the Supernatural Line), are suspected Fanthorpe pseudonyms; regretably, representative works by these authors were not available for examination. Fanthorpe titles may be identified by the profusion of literary and historical allusions (often accompanied by direct quotes from the original) which fill his books; by the inclusion of poems or poetry fragments, often from his own hand; by long didactic passages (particularly on science or mathematics), explaining some abstruse concept; and/or by descriptive paragraphs containing a patterned repetition of certain words (often colors) or sentence fragments. At times he may also mention himself within the body of his work (see Projection Infinity (Zeigfreid), page 38).

PHILIP JOSÉ FARMER

1)	1957 Ballantine		The Green Odyssey.	(H-P)
2)	1960 Ballantine		Strange Relations.	(s/P/RH)
3)	1960 Beacon		Flesh.	(P/RH)
4)	1960 Beacon		A Woman a Day.	(P)
5)	1961 Ballantine		The Lovers.	(P)
6)	1962 Ballantine		The Alley God.	(s/P)
7)	1962 Ace		Cache from Outer Space.	(P)
8)	1962 Ace		The Celestial Blueprint.	(s/P)
9)	1964 Ballantine		Inside Outside.	(P)
10)	1964 Pyramid		Tongues of the Moon.	(P)
11)	1965 Ballantine		Dare.	(P)
12)	1965 Ace	1	The Maker of Universes.	(P)
13)	1966 Berkley		Night of Light.	(P)
14)	1966 Belmont		The Gate of Time.	(P)
15)	1966 Ace	2	The Gates of Creation.	(P)
4A)	1968 Lancer		The Day of Timestop.	(P)
16)	1968 Ace	3	A Private Cosmos.	(P)
17)	1968 Essex	-1	The Image of the Beast.	(P)

FPS:	"O'Brien and Obrenov,"	Adventure, March, 1946.	
FSF:	"The Lovers,"	Startling Stories, August, 1952.	
WIP:	1969 Essex	-2	A Feast Unknown. (P)
	1969 Ace		Red Orc. (P)
	1969 Doubleday		Lord Tyger.
	1970 Doubleday		Ramstan.

***   ***   ***   ***   ***

Philip José Farmer--born January 26, 1918 at North Terre Haute, Indiana--attended University of Missouri, 1936-1937, 1941; B.A., Bradley University, 1950; graduate study at Arizona State University, 1961-1962--Hugo Award, Best New Science Fiction Author, 1953; Best Novella, 1968, "Riders of the Purple Wage".

PHILIP JOSÉ FARMER (continued)

Son of George & Lucile (Jackson) Farmer--Elizabeth Virginia André: May 10, 1941--Philip Laird Farmer; Kristen Farmer.

Free-Lance Writer--Member: Science Fiction Writers of America; Burroughs Bibliophiles; First Fandom; International Wizard of Oz Club; Society of Technical Writers and Educators; Institution for Reinstitution of Fertility Rites; Citizens League Against the Sonic Boom; REAP (Founder).

Mr. Farmer writes:
"Science Fiction at present is in a state of high flux, in division, in internal conflict, in steady fermentation. In other words, in the best condition it's ever been. Only when a number of writers (no matter how small the minority) experiment with ideas, styles, attitudes, structures, etc., is a field capable of great interest and progress. Today, despite the opposition of a great number of die-hards, of semifossils, the field is jumping with idea-kangaroos. It's very exciting and it may lead to something new. If it doesn't, the field will at least have been exciting during the renaissance period.
"I am for this ferment, although I tend to like heroes more than antiheroes. But not always. I'm really not qualified to evaluate my own contributions; my opinions would be too subjective. However, with perhaps one or two exceptions, none of the critics in this field seem to be capable of evaluating me. We need new critics as well as new writers. Joanna Russ may be what is needed; we'll see."

HOWARD FAST

1)	1961 Bantam	The Edge of Tomorrow. (s/P)
4)	1967 Dial	Hunter and the Trap.
		as *E.V. Cunningham
2)	1962 Doubleday	Phyllis. (RP)
3)	1966 Doubleday	Helen.
FPS:	"Wrath of the Purple,"	Amazing, October, 1932.
WIP:	1969 Morrow	The Man who Zapped an Angel.

***   ***   ***   ***   ***

Howard Melvin Fast--born November 11, 1914 at New York, New York--attended National Academy of Design--Breadloaf Literature Award, 1937; Schomburg Award for Race Relations, 1944; Newspaper Guild Award, 1947; Jewish Book Council of America Annual Award, 1947; International Peace Prize of USSR, 1954; Screen Writers Annual Award, 1960; Secondary Education Board Annual Book Award, 1962--New York, New York.

HOWARD FAST (continued)

Son of Barney & Ida (Miller) Fast--Betty Cohen: June 6, 1937--Rachel Fast; Jonathan Fast.

Foreign Correspondent, <u>Esquire</u> and <u>Coronet</u>, 1945; Public Lecturer; Free-Lance Writer.

Mr. Fast writes:
"Do I think science fiction is improving? Indeed I do. From a rather shaky infancy, it now begins to emerge as perhaps the most valid original art form of the second half of the twentieth century. From rather disasterous pulp writing --often disgraceful--it begins more and more to cherish style and maturity, and to embrace a humanistic philosophy all too rare in these barbaric years. It dares to think to venture, to guess, to hope and to believe--all of which are absent from most modern fiction. And best of all, it has vision, and dares to speak of the possibility of things beyond the reach of our poor senses, and our blood-soaked and wretched 'civilization.' The name 'science fiction' no longer serves, so well and richly does the art grow, and perhaps one of the things most needed now is a new generic title. Having started to read <u>Amazing Stories</u> when I was twelve, I can still remember the genesis of the title. It served then because science was still an early god. Now, I am afraid, science must bend its head in shame. As to my future--of course I will go on. I am just wetting my toes in the field, and I love it. More power to all who practice it!"

JOHN M. FAUCETTE

1)	1968 Ace	<u>Crown of Infinity</u>. (P)
2)	1968 Ace	<u>The Age of Ruin</u>. (P)
FPS:	1968 Ace	<u>Crown of Infinity</u>. (P)

***   ***   ***   ***   ***

John Matthew Faucette Jr.--born September 15, 1943 at New York, New York-- attended Polytechnic Institute of Brooklyn, one year--Third Place, Nassau Open Chess Championship, 1967--New York, New York.

Son of John Matthew & Dorothy Faucette--unmarried.

Free-Lance Writer--Member: United States Chess Federation.

EDWARD L. FERMAN

1)	1966 Doubleday	<u>The Best from Fantasy and Science Fiction Fifteenth Series</u>. (@)
2)	1967 Doubleday	<u>The Best from Fantasy and Science Fiction Sixteenth Series</u>. (@)

EDWARD L. FERMAN (continued)

3)	1968 Doubleday	The Best from Fantasy and Science Fiction Seventeenth Series. (@)
4)	1968 H-W	Once and Future Tales from the Magazine of Fantasy and Science Fiction. (@)
FPS:	1966 Doubleday	The Best from Fantasy and Science Fiction Fifteenth Series. (@)
WIP:	1969 Doubleday	The Best from Fantasy and Science Fiction Eighteenth Series. (@)

***   ***   ***   ***   ***

Edward Lewis Ferman--born March 6, 1937 at New York, New York--B.A., Middlebury College, 1958--New York, New York.

Son of Joseph Wolfe & Ruth (Eisen) Ferman--Audrey Bonchak: May, 1964--Emily Allison Ferman (3).

Editorial Assistant, The Magazine of Fantasy and Science Fiction, November, 1958-January, 1959; Managing Editor, April, 1962-December, 1965; Editor, January, 1966-DATE; Venture Science Fiction, May, 1969-DATE.

JOSEPH W. FERMAN

1)	1964 Ballantine	No Limits. (@/P)
FPS:	1964 Ballantine	No Limits. (@/P)

***   ***   ***   ***   ***

Joseph Wolfe Ferman--born June 8, 1906 at Lida, Lithuania--B.C.S., New York University, 1927--Hugo Award, Best Professional Magazine, 1956, 1958, 1959, 1960, 1963, Magazine of Fantasy and Science Fiction--Rockville Centre, New York.

Son of Wolfe & Esther (Little) Ferman--Ruth Eisen: January 29, 1931--Edward Lewis Ferman (March 6, 1937).

General Manager, The Magazine of Fantasy and Science Fiction, Fall, 1949-July, 1954; Publisher, August 1954-DATE; Editor, December, 1964-December, 1965; Publisher, Venture Science Fiction, January, 1957-July, 1958; May, 1969-DATE--Member: Hundred Million Club; Unity Club of Nassau County; Committee for World Human Rights, Inc. (Charter Member).

CHARLES G. FINNEY

1) 1935 Viking   The Circus of Doctor Lao. (RP)
2) 1937 Vanguard   The Unholy City. (RPe)
3) 1939 Holt   Past the End of the Pavement.
4) 1961 Doubleday   The Old China Hands. (RP)
5) 1964 Pyramid   The Ghosts of Manacle. (s/P)
6) 1968 Pyramid   The Unholy City. (2/e/P)

NOTE: #6 contains an original novella, "The Magician Out of Manchuria."

FPS: 1935 Viking   The Circus of Doctor Lao. (RP)

***   ***   ***   ***   ***

Charles Grandison Finney--born December 1, 1905 at Sedalia, Missouri--attended University of Missouri, 1925-1926--American Booksellers Award, Most Original Novel of 1935, The Circus of Doctor Lao--Tucson, Arizona.

Son of Norton J. & Florence (Bell) Finney--Marie Lucy Doyle: 1939--Sheila Finney Boulay (25); Felice Marie Finney (21).

Has been on staff of Arizona Daily Star, Tucson, Arizona, since 1930, beginning as a proofreader; currently Financial Page Editor.

NOTE: Mr. Finney spent three years with the 15th U.S. Infantry in Tientsin, China (1927-1929).

---

*JACK FINNEY

1) 1955 Dell   The Body Snatchers. (P/RH)
2) 1957 Rinehart   The Third Level. (s/RP)
2A) 1958 Eyre   The Clock of Time. (s/RP)
3) 1963 S & S   I Love Galesburg in the Springtime.
4) 1968 S & S   The Woodrow Wilson Dime.

FKP: "The Third Level,"   The Magazine of Fantasy and Science Fiction, October, 1952.

NOTE: Jack Finney is a penname of Walter Braden Finney.

NICHOLAS FISK

1) 1967 Hamilton   Space Hostages. (RP)

FPS: to Strand Magazine, 1939.

NICHOLAS FISK (continued)

FSF: 1967 Hamilton   Space Hostages.

***   ***   ***   ***   ***

Nicholas Fisk (u)--born October 10, 1923 at London, England--London, England.

Mr. Fisk is married and has four children.

Illustrator, Publisher, Photographer; Director, Icon Books Ltd; Free-Lance Writer, 1939-DATE--Member: Savik Club.

CHARLES L. FONTENAY

1) 1958 Ace   Twice Upon a Time. (P)
2) 1961 Ace   Rebels of the Red Planet. (P)
3) 1964 Monarch   The Day the Oceans Overflowed. (P)

FPS: "Disqualified,"   If, September, 1954.

***   ***   ***   ***   ***

Charles Louis Fontenay--born March 17, 1917 at São Paulo, Brazil--Southern Regional Education Board Fellowship, Vanderbilt University, 1966-1967--Nashville, Tennessee.

Son of Charles Robert & Miriam (Steel) Fontenay--(2) Martha Mae Howard: September 30, 1962--2) Marguerethe Louise Fontenay (5); Charles Howard Blake Fontenay (2).

Newspaper reporter and editor for various Tennessee newspapers and The Associated Press from 1936; with The Nashville Tennessean, 1946-DATE; City Editor, 1965-1968; presently in charge of rewrite operations.

NOTE: Mr. Fontenay entered the United States as an infant, and was raised at Union City, Tennessee.

Mr. Fontenay writes:
   "My agent would be extremely happy were I able to list some "Work in Progress, as he has been bugging me off and on for three years. Unfortunately, I have been unable to get any one of several ideas to jell, primarily due to my concentration upon a work in the philosophy of history, to be published by the University of Tennessee Press. This would seem rather far removed from the field of science fiction, but the scientific research that was necessary for me to do during the period that I was turning out science fiction stories regularly and frequently (in order to make them accurate and authoritative), was one of the major lines that led me into my non-fiction work (dealing with evolutionary biology, analytic psychology, anthropology and philosophy). I still plan to get back to writing

CHARLES L. FONTENAY (continued)

some science fiction, but I have already found that I can't write 'message' fiction of any kind. I can only write the kind I like best to read, which is the bang-up adventure type solidly grounded in genuine scientific possibility."

GEORGE C. FOSTER

1) 1963 Digit   The Change. (P)

NOTE: George Cecil Foster.

GARDNER F. FOX

1)	1962 Pyramid		Five Weeks in a Balloon. (P)
2)	1964 Pap Lib		Escape Across the Cosmos. (P)
3)	1964 Ace		The Arsenal of Miracles. (P)
4)	1964 Ace	1	Warrior of Llarn. (P)
6)	1965 Ace		The Hunter Out of Time. (P)
7)	1966 Ace	2	Thief of Llarn. (P)

as *Bart Somers

5)	1965 Pap Lib	-1	Beyond the Black Enigma. (P)
8)	1967 Pap Lib	-2	Abandon Galaxy! (P)

as *Simon Majors

9) 1967 Pap Lib   The Druid Stone. (P)

SER: 2) Commander Craig Galactic Adventure

FPS: "The Weirds of the Woodcarver," Weird Tales, September, 1944.

WIP: 1969 Belmont   Kothar-Barbarian Swordsman. (P)

***   ***   ***   ***   ***

Gardner Francis Fox--born May 20, 1911 at Brooklyn, New York--A.B., St. John's University, 1932; LL.B., St. John's University, 1935--Alley Award, 1963 --Yonkers, New York.

Son of Leon Francis & Julia Veronica (Gardner) Fox--Lynda J. Negrini: November 14, 1937--Jeffrey Francis Fox (20); Lynda Anne Fox Taylor (26).

Free-Lance Writer; has been writing comics (Batman, Superman, Flash, Green Lantern, etc.) since 1937--Member: Science Fiction Writers of America; Authors Guild.

H. BRUCE FRANKLIN

1) 1966 Oxford   *Future Perfect.* (nf/RP)

FSF: 1966 Oxford   *Future Perfect.* (nf/RP)

***   ***   ***   ***   ***

Howard Bruce Franklin--born February 28, 1934 at Brooklyn, New York--B.A., Amherst College, 1955; Ph.D., Stanford University, 1961--Palo Alto, California.

Son of Robert & Florence (Cohen) Franklin--Jane Morgan: February 11, 1956 --Karen Franklin; Gretchen Franklin; Robert Franklin.

Assistant Professor of English and American Literature, Stanford University, 1961-1964; Assistant Professor of English and American Literature, Johns Hopkins University, 1964-1965; Associate Professor of English and American Literature, Stanford University, 1965-DATE--Member: Modern Language Association; New University Conference.

MICHAEL FRAYN

1)   1968 Viking   *A Very Private Life.*

FPS: a short story   to *Punch* c. 1955.
FSF: 1968 Viking   *A Very Private Life.*

***   ***   ***   ***   ***

Michael Frayn (u)--born September 8, 1933 at London, England--B.A., Emmanuel College, Cambridge University, 1957--Somerset Maugham Award, 1966, *The Tin Men*; Hawthornden Prize, 1967, *The Russian Interpreter*--London, England.

Gillian Palmer: February 18, 1960--three daughters.

Reporter, *The Manchester Guardian*, 1957-1959; Columnist, 1959-1962; *The London Observer*, 1962-1968; Free-Lance Writer.

GERTRUDE FRIEDBERG

1)   1966 Doubleday   *The Revolving Boy.* (RP)

FPS: "Three Cornered Moon," a play produced in 1933.
FSF: "The Short and Happy Death of George Frumkin," *The Magazine of Fantasy and Science Fiction*, April, 1963.

GERTRUDE FRIEDBERG (continued)

***   ***   ***   ***   ***

Gertrude Tonkonogy Friedberg (u)--B.A., Barnard College, 1929--New York, New York.

Married Charles K. Friedberg, M.D.--Richard Friedberg; Barbara Friedberg.

Free-Lance Writer and Playwright--Member: Science Fiction Writers of America.

H.B. FYFE

1) 1962 Pyramid   D-99. (P)

FPS: "Locked Out,"   Astounding, February, 1940.

***   ***   ***   ***   ***

Horace Bowne Fyfe, Jr.--born September 30, 1918 at Jersey City, New Jersey--B.S. (cum laude), Columbia University--Ridgefield Park, New Jersey.

Son of Horace Bowne & Lillian (Lewis) Fyfe--Adeline Marie Dougherty: September 8, 1946--no children.

Free-Lance Writer--Member: Science Fiction Writers of America.

RAYMOND Z. GALLUN

1) 1956 S & S   People Minus X. (RP)
2) 1961 Pyramid   The Planet Strappers. (P)

FPS: either "The Crystal Ray,"   Air Wonder, November, 1929; or
       "The Space Dwellers,"   Science Wonder, November, 1929.

***   ***   ***   ***   ***

Raymond Zinke Gallun--born March 22, 1910 at Beaver Dam, Wisconsin--attended University of Wisconsin, 1929-1930--Forest Hills, New York.

Son of Adolph & Martha (Zinke) Gallun--Frieda E. Talmey--no children.

"Currently (and for the past five years) employed by Edo Corporation (a manufacturer of sonar equipment). Otherwise a long and various history of occupational--and other--vagabondage--generally quite pleasant, if lowly"--Member: Science Fiction Writers of America.

RAYMOND Z. GALLUN (continued)

Mr. Gallun provided the following pleasant letter:
"About the 'New Wave:' I'm sure I've read stories considered to be in that category, but have not found--or composed for myself--any definition that can be called precise. I guess everybody tries for newness--and I suppose the result does collectively form itself into successive waves. I myself, though, just like good yarns, however they may be classified. So I don't know whether I've taken part in the New Wave or not--Planet Strappers might have been a bit of a beginning there. At least one publisher bounced it for being too 'hard and cycnical,' or words to that effect.

"Paradoxically, the book was written in a very gentle atmosphere: Santa Eulalia del Rio in Ibiza during the fall of 1958--the place seems since to have been smothered in an overload of swank hotels, and has died, as far as I am concerned, along with Acapulco before it. I still remember the old whitewashed farmhouse, with its loft smelling freshly of maize and almonds; and the dog and the local folk who sort of adopted me, and the ruined windmill towers, the goatpaths, and the fishing boat lights at night. Somebody's kind, dusty Shangri-La, with echoes back at least to the Phoenicians (my earliest interest being archeology, and more particularly Egyptology). Planet Strappers was my last go at science fiction, though I really do think I'll be trying it again within a couple of years."

DANIEL F. GALOUYE

1)	1961 Bantam	Dark Universe.	(P/RH)
2)	1963 Bantam	Lords of the Psychon.	(P)
3)	1964 Gollancz	Counterfeit World.	(RPv)
3A)	1964 Bantam	Simulacron-3.	(P)
4)	1964 Corgi	The Last Leap.	(s/P)
5)	1966 Gollancz	The Lost Perception.	(RP/RPv)
5A)	1968 Bantam	A Scourge of Screamers.	(P)
6)	1968 Gollancz	Project Barrier.	(s)

FPS: "Tonight the Sky Will Fall," Imagination, May, 1952.
FPP: "Rebirth," Imagination, March, 1952.

WIP: 1970 Bantam   The Infinite Man. (P)

***   ***   ***   ***   ***

Daniel Francis Galouye--born February 11, 1920 at New Orleans, Louisiana--B.A., Louisiana State University, 1941--New Orleans, Louisiana.

Son of Jean Baptiste & Hilda (Mouney) Galouye--Carmel Barbara Jordan: December 26, 1945--Denise Marie Galouye (22); Jeanne Arlene Galouye (20).

Reporter and writer, New Orleans States-Item, 1946-1955; Chief Editorial Writer, 1955-1960; Associate Editor, 1960-1965; currently retired as a result of latent

DANIEL F. GALOUYE (continued)

wartime injuries; Free-Lance Writer--Member: Science Fiction Writers of America (Chairman, Elections Committee, 1969).

NOTE: Consultant, New Orleans City Mayor's Science Center and Planetarium Committee.

Mr. Galouye provided the following comments on science fiction:

"Science Fiction, I find, is currently in its healthiest state thus far, although the medium appears to be undergoing revolutionary change in at least two directions.

"First, there is the ascendancy of nonperiodical publications, to the apparent detriment of our professional magazines. Hardbound and/or paperback printings are claiming more and more attention--with the end result that periodicals, although probably 'holding their own' circulationwise, are not realizing growth commensurate with the expanding population. Hard- and softcovers have not only walked off with all the benefits accruing from both a growing readership and increased interest in science, but have also rendered magazine submissions more unprofitable to authors in the field. A single book, written over a three- or four-month period, will fetch more income (with subsidiary and foreign-rights earnings taken into consideration) than a whole year's worth of submissions to the periodicals. Unless the magazines can manage a breakthrough in the area of circulation, and become competitive with paperbacks, we may well witness demise of the periodical format. (This would indeed be unfortunate for, oddly enough, successful and repeated publication in SF magazines is a credential that is still generally expected of new novelists by book publishers. In other words: from where are our new writers going to come if opportunity for publication in the magazines becomes increasingly restricted, or perhaps eliminated entirely?)

"Second, revolutionary change involving the so-called 'new wave,' although having profound impact on the field at present, will nevertheless prove to be of ephemeral consequences. Throughout the history of literature, there have been various deviationist schools--flashy stylistic efforts striking off in new directions and demanding attention on the strength of their very bold and unorthodox nature. But, always, these movements have ended up on spur tracks, while literature in general has adhered to the basics of 'story-telling' in the classic sense, as epitomized in the epic narrative. Only when the 'tools of carpentry' become more important than the finished products for which they were designed to construct--only then will 'cute and unorthodox' styles of prose-designing become more important than the fundamental purpose underlying literary effort, i.e., conveying to the reader a precise and clearly-understandable 'idea,' 'intriguing plot' or 'fascinating concept.' When a story is intended only as a showcase for manipulation of words in bizarre arrangements, it may gain the author momentary recognition as a phraseologist, but the story itself is soon forgotten. When the story's ultimate aim is to present a straightforward account of situation-complication-resolution, however, it stands on its own merit and, if sufficiently worthy, will be long and clearly remembered. Phraseologists we'll always have (at present, too many of them--all riding the 'new wave' crest). But there'll always be a much greater demand for down-to-earth story-telling. The nonliterati will stay in the majority.

DANIEL F. GALOUYE (continued)

"It's interesting to note that (in my opinion, at least, and in the opinion of many sf writers whom I know) sf is enjoying an ever greater upsurge elsewhere than in the U.S. This phenomenon no doubt results from admiration of and fascination over America's scientific achievements. And we find that, here again, the works most in demand--or, at least, those considered most presentable by foreign publishers--are the ones which were first published in the U.S. long before the 'new wave' was a gleam in Michael Moorcock's eyes.

"What have my own contributions been to development of the SF genre? Insignificant indeed, relative to the benefits I have derived from association with the field and its personalities."

ALAN GARNER

1)	1960 Collins		The Weirdstone of Brisingamen. (RP)
2)	1963 Collins		The Moon of Gomrath. (RP)
3)	1965 Collins		Elidor. (RP)
4)	1967 Collins		The Old Man of Mow.
5)	1967 Collins		The Owl Service.

RANDALL GARRETT

4)	1962 Doubleday		Unwise Child. (RP)
9)	1966 Doubleday		Too Many Magicians. (RP)

with Robert Silverberg (q.v.) as *Robert Randall

1)	1958 Gnome	1	Shrouded Planet.
2)	1959 Gnome	2	Dawning Light. (RP)

with Larry M. Harris (*Laurence M. Janifer,(q.v.)

3)	1960 Beacon		Pagan Passions. (P)

with *Laurence M. Janifer (q.v.) as *Mark Phillips

5)	1962 Pyramid		Brain Twister. (P)
7)	1963 Pyramid		The Impossibles. (P)
8)	1963 Pyramid		Supermind. (P)

as *Darrel T. Langart

6)	1963 Doubleday		Anything You Can Do... (RP/RPv)

FKP: "The Waiting Game," Astounding, January, 1951.

WIP:
6A) 1969 Lancer   Anything You Can Do... (P)

NOTE: Randall Philip Garrett is a member of Science Fiction Writers of America.

RICHARD M. GARVIN

with Edmond G. Addeo (q.v.)

1) 1968 Sherbourne The Fortec Conspiracy. (RP)
2) 1968 Sherbourne The Talbot Agreement.

WIP: The Twilight Believers.
    The Dallas Pontiff.
    James Cardinal Francis Calannans All Time
        Great Confessions.
    The Nativity According to St. Chrononix, Inc.

***   ***   ***   ***   ***

Richard McClellan Garvin--born August 4, 1934 at Hollywood, California--B.A., San Jose State College, 1957--Mill Valley, California.

Son of John M. & Elizabeth N. Garvin--Carolyn M.: April 29, 1961--Elizabeth Ann Garvin (2).

Owns two bookstores in the Mill Valley area; Free-Lance Writer--Member: Science Fiction Writers of America.

Hobbies: art, music, literature of the outre.

---

*JANE GASKELL

1) 1957 Hutchinson   Strange Evil.
2) 1958 Hutchinson   King's Daughter. (RP)
3) 1963 Hodder   1   The Serpent. (RP)
4) 1965 Hodder   2   Atlan. (RP)
5) 1966 Hodder   3   The City (RP)

FSF: 1957 Hutchinson   Strange Evil.

***   ***   ***   ***   ***

Jane Lynch (u)--born July 7, 1941 at Grange-over-Sands, Lancaster, England --London, England.

Daughter of Andrew Gaskell & Edith (Hackett) Denvil--Gerald Lynch:' May 10, 1963/1968--no children.

"Working since age of 19 in London's Fleet Street as a national daily newspaper feature writer."

Miss Gaskell writes:
    "If I don't provide details, it's literally because I can't. I am grateful and happy that you've asked me--but I know nothing whatsoever about the state of

*JANE GASKELL (continued)

sf at the moment--I avoid sf in my reading, and find good fantasy so rarely that it must work out at one new favorite a decade of my experience."

VANCE A. GEIGLEY

1)   1968 Vantage   Will It End This Way?

FPP: 1968 Vantage   Will It End This Way?

***   ***   ***   ***   ***

Vance Acton Geigley--born October 10, 1907 at Webb City, Missouri--Las Vegas, Nevada.

Son of Joseph D. & Ella Mae Geigley--Mary Catherine Snyder: October 30, 1937--no children.

Mr. Geigley has been involved with mining, and has been a general building contractor and a real estate investor--Member: American Legion; Veterans of Foreign Wars.

RICHARD E. GEIS

1)   1967 Brandon   1   The Sex Machine. (P)
2)   1968 Brandon   2   The Endless Orgy. (P)

FPS: "The Fight Game,"   Adam, January, 1959

WIP: 1969 Essex   The Perverts. (P)

***   ***   ***   ***   ***

Richard Erwin Geis--born July 19, 1927 at Portland, Oregon--attended Vanport College (now Portland State University) for two years--Santa Monica, California.

Son of Erwin Walter & Delores (Dreske) Geis--unmarried.

Free-Lance Writer, 1959-DATE--Member: Science Fiction Writers of America.

NOTE: Mr. Geis is Editor and Publisher of Science Fiction Review (formerly Psychotic).

MARK S. GESTON

1)	1967 Ace	Lords of the Starship.	(P)
FPS:	1967 Ace	Lords of the Starship.	(P)
WIP:	1969 Ace	Out of the Mouth of the Dragon.	(P)

***   ***   ***   ***   ***

Mark Symington Geston--born June 20, 1946 at Atlantic City, New Jersey--A.B. (History), Kenyon College, 1968--Kenyon Review Award for Achievement in Fiction, 1968--New York, New York.

Son of John C. & Mary S. Geston--unmarried.

Student, New York University School of Law, 1968-DATE--Member: Delta Tau Delta; Phi Beta Kappa.

Mr. Geston writes:
"The most fantastic of all novels, those whose substance thrived on magic, were written by Thomas Wolfe, the inspiration (but too much a genius to be a guide) for my own writing."

NOTE: Mr. Geston wrote Lords of the Starship during his sophomore year at Kenyon, and Out of the Mouth of the Dragon in his senior year.

DIANA GILLON

1)	1961 Barrie	with Meir Gillon (q.v.) The Unsleep. (RP)
FSF:	1961 Barrie	The Unsleep. (with Meir Gillon)

***   ***   ***   ***   ***

Diana Pleasance Gillon--born September 1, 1915 at London, England--Diploma in Librarianship, University of London, 1935--Barnet, Hertfordshire, England.

Daughter of Thomas Henry Towler & Evelyn Beatrice (White) Case--Meir Selig Gillon: June, 1937--Evelyn Zvi Raanan Gillon (son; 1941); Richard Benedict Gillon (1944); Dikla Lalage Gillon (daughter; 1945).

Archivist, 1935-1938; Film Critic, Palestine Post, 1941-1948; Book Reviewer (with Meir Gillon) for Reynold's News, Sunday Times, Guardian, etc.; has participated in discussions on films and books for the British Broadcasting Company--Member: P.E.N.; Society of Authors.

NOTE: The Gillons collaborated with Arthur C. Clarke (q.v.) in collecting and collating material for the non-fiction book, The Coming of the Space Age.

DIANA GILLON (continued)

The Gillons write:
"We feel that with truth so rapidly catching up with fiction at the moment, there may well be a slight temporary falling-off in new ideas //in sf--ed.//. But as imaginative writers get used to the new set-up of truth, they will certainly come up with a new crop. SF remains the one really effective way of getting revolutionary ideas across to the reader. Our own Unsleep is, of course, satire of the present (as it was in 1961) told in terms of the future. Successful? Well, the topless dresses didn't really catch on, did they? But apart from that, almost everything we visualised has come true--so perhaps it's been more successful as prophecy than as satire."

MEIR GILLON
with Diana Gillon (q.v.)

1)   1961 Barrie   The Unsleep. (RP)

FSF: 1961 Barrie   The Unsleep. (with Diana Gillon)

***   ***   ***   ***   ***

Meir Selig Gillon--born August 11, 1907 at Sibiu, Transylvania--LL.B., University of London, 1943--Barnet, Hertfordshire, England.

Son of Josef Hirsch & Sara (Weinberger) Goldstein--Diana Pleasance Case: June, 1937--Evelyn Zvi Raanan Gillon (son; 1941); Richard Benedict Gillon (1944); Dikla Lalage Gillon (daughter; 1945).

Civil Servant, Government of Palestine, 1941-1946; with the British Broadcasting Company, 1949-1950; Book Reviewer (with Diana Gillon) for Reynold's News, Sunday Times, Guardian, etc.--Member: P.E.N.; Society of Authors.

NOTE: The Gillons collaborated with Arthur C. Clarke (q.v.) in collecting and collating material for the non-fiction book, The Coming of the Space Age.

The Gillons comment on science fiction and satire:
"In satire, the story must not be so far from present conditions that the parallel is not clear. But given this proviso, the Unnamed Future setting gives the writer freedom to express ideas which if set in present times might bring him into conflict with the Law of Libel, or even, in some places, involve him in political persecution."

MIRRA GINSBURG

1) 1965 Macmillan   The Fatal Eggs and Other Soviet Satire. (@/RP)

MIRRA GINSBURG (continued)

2)	1968 Phillips		Last Door to Aiya. (@)
FPS:	1965 Macmillan		The Fatal Eggs and Other Soviet Satire. (@)
WIP:	1969 Holt		The Useless Planet. (@)

***   ***   ***   ***   ***

Mirra Ginsburg--born in Russia--New York, New York.

Daughter of Joseph & Bronia (Geier) Ginsburg.

Editor and Translator from Russian and Yiddish--Member: P.E.N.

"Soviet Science Fiction is the freest and best <u>published</u> writing in Russia today."

A.A. GLYNN

1) 1963 Badger SF   Plan for Conquest. (P)

NOTE: Alan Anthony Glynn is a British scientist.

TOM GODWIN

1)	1958 Gnome	1	The Survivors. (RPv)
1A)	1960 Pyramid	1	Space Prison. (P)
2)	1964 Pyramid	2	The Space Barbarians. (P)
FKP:	"The Gulf Between,"		Astounding, October, 1953.

H.L. GOLD

1)	1952 Crown	The Galaxy Reader of Science Fiction. (@/RHa)
2)	1954 Crown	The Second Galaxy Reader of Science Fiction. (@)
3)	1955 Crown	The Old Die Rich and Other Science Fiction Stories. (s)
4)	1956 Grayson	The Galaxy Science Fiction Omnibus. (@)
5)	1958 Doubleday	The Third Galaxy Reader. (@/RP)
6)	1958 Doubleday	Five Galaxy Short Novels. (@/RP)
7)	1959 Doubleday	The Fourth Galaxy Reader. (@/RP)
8)	1959 Doubleday	The World That Couldn't Be and Eight Other Novelets from Galaxy. (@/RP)

H.L. GOLD (continued)

9)	1960 Doubleday	Bodyguard and Four Other Short Novels from Galaxy. (@/RP)
10)	1961 Doubleday	The Fifth Galaxy Reader. (@/RP)
1	1961 Doubleday	Mind Partner and Eight Other Novelets. (@/RP)
12,	1962 Doubleday	The Sixth Galaxy Reader. (@)
FPS:	"Inflexure,"	Astounding, October, 1934 (as *Clyde Crane Campbell).

***   ***   ***   ***   ***

Horace Leonard Gold--born April 26, 1914 at Montreal, Canada--Hugo Award, Best Professional Magazine, 1953, Galaxy--La Canada, California.

Son of Henry & Regina Gold--(1) Evelyn: September 3, 1939/February 13, 1957; (2) Muriel; August 21, 1965--1) Eugene Jeffrey Gold (27); Linda Conley (26); Christopher Conley (23); Sherill Conley (11).

Editor, Galaxy, October 1950-October, 1961--Beyond, July, 1953-#10 (1955) (all issues); If, July, 1959-September, 1961; Assistant Editor, Thrilling Wonder, Startling Stories, Captain Future, 1939-1941--Member: Science Fiction Writers of America.

----

*REX GORDON

1)	1955 Heinemann	Utopia 239.
2)	1956 Heinemann	No Man Friday. (RPv)
2A)	1957 Ace	First on Mars. (P)
3)	1959 Ace	First to the Stars. (P)
3A)	1961 Consul	The World of Eclos. (P)
4)	1962 Ace	First Through Time. (P/RHv)
4A)	1964 Gibbs	The Time Factor. (RP)
5)	1966 Ace	Utopia Minus X. (P/RHv)
5A)	1967 Library 33	The Paw of God. (RP)
FPS:	a story	to Cycling Magazine, 1935.
FSF;	1955 Heinemann	Utopia 239.

WIP: The Yellow Fraction: "Unfortunate events following man's one-way journey to a planet of another star. Human society is a product of its environment, so suppose another environment and what do you get? Even on Earth, some of us have some trouble deciding what life is all about, but a planet with odd effects does not make this process any easier, especially if you happen to be selected for...but they don't tell you what it is you are selected for."

*REX GORDON (continued)

***   ***   ***   ***   ***

Stanley Bennett Hough--born February 25, 1917 at Preston, Lancashire, England--attended Radio Technical College, Preston, 1935-1936--Infinity Award, Best Science Fiction Novel of the Year, 1957, No Man Friday (First on Mars)--Truro, Cornwall, England.

Son of Simeon & Eva (Bennett) Hough--Justa Elisabeth Cecilia Wodschow: June 25, 1938--no children.

Radio Operator, 1936-1945; was in the yatching business 1946-1951; Free-Lance Writer--Member: Workers Educational Association (District Vice-Chairman, Southwest District).

Mr. Gordon comments on science fiction:
"In my own work I try to stick to the classical tradition of writing science fiction, not fantasy or horror stories or disguised sex-dreams or sadism. The story has to have a point that is connected with scientific developments that we can envisage. These developments must not contradict the laws of nature as we now know them, unless some likely error in our present knowledge can be demonstrated. Science fiction is for intelligent people, not morons. Supermen are no more acceptable than bug-eyed monsters. Any game is the better for being played according to known rules, and the unexpected should be produced by thinking out new moves in the game, not by making up new rules in order to cheat.

"Science fiction written in this way performs a definite service to the community, demonstrating the real consequences to human life of social tendencies and scientific possibilities that scientists themselves are liable to view only theoretically. It is also a vehicle for philosophic wit, whether about the actual nature of the universe, or Joe Doakes' probable actual reactions to situations that the theorist would tend to regard as ideal, but which might go wrong in practice. In this sense, sf is our modern version of philosophy: a philosophy tied to possible actual events and sense-impressions, which not only gives speculation a new force and realism, but also demands that we look at our ideas realistically and make sure that they actually work--or enables us to demonstrate that other people's ideas don't.

"SF is not only philosophy for the multitude, invented by the genius of the American people (it came up from the grass roots of popular demand, and was not imposed from above), but it is better philosophy because the narrative form demands that all speculations be envisaged and presented in terms of precise events. It is an offshoot of American Pragmatism. It is a vehicle for true scientific speculation, and its social consequences are liable to be enormous."

PHYLLIS GOTLIEB

1)   1964 Gold Medal   Sunburst. (P)

PHYLLIS GOTLIEB (continued)

FPS: a group of poems to a Canadian Broadcasting Company program, "Anthology," 1955.
FSF: "A Grain of Madness," Fantastic, September, 1959.

***   ***   ***   ***   ***

Phyllis Fay Gotlieb--born May 25, 1926 at Toronto, Canada--B.A., University of Toronto, 1948; M.A., University of Toronto, 1950--Toronto, Canada.

Daughter of Leo & Mary (Kates) Bloom--Calvin C. Gotlieb: June 12, 1949--Leo Gotlieb; Margaret Gotlieb; Jane Gotlieb.

Free-Lance Writer--Member: Science Fiction Writers of America; League of Canadian Poets.

Mrs. Gotlieb writes:
"I started writing at the age of eleven, mainly poetry, till the source seemed to dry up at the age of twenty. After I got married my husband suggested I try writing science fiction to break the writer's block. It took me nine years to make the first sale, but by then the poetry had come back, and since that time I have had a dual career (very modest in both divisions) as a Canadian poet and an American science fiction writer; so far the two have not meshed.
"Since I write very slowly and my output is small, I have gotten far more than I have been able to give to sf; it taught me to write in a quick, clean style that has helped my poetry and mainstream writing as well. To science fiction I have tried to bring an unsentimental sense of humanity and depth of character, a feeling that whatever happens out in the depths of space depends ultimately on people of one sort or another, whatever their form or planetary origin. I do my best to understand and present them as completely as I can."

RON GOULART

1) 1968 Doubleday   The Sword Swallower.

FPS: "Letters to the Editor,"   The Magazine of Fantasy and Science Fiction, April, 1952.

WIP: Ace   The Fire Eater. (P)
      Doubleday   Gadget Man.
      Ace   a history of the pulp magazines. (P)

***   ***   ***   ***   ***

Ronald Joseph Goulart--born January 13, 1933 at Berkeley, California--B.A., University of California, 1955--Shoreham, New York.

RON GOULART (continued)

Son of Joseph Silveira & Josephine (Macri) Goulart--Frances Sheridan: June 13, 1964--Sean (7).

With Guild, Bascom & Bonfigli (advertising agency), 1955-1958; Free-Lance Writer, 1960-DATE--Member: Science Fiction Writers of America (Vice-President, 1969-1970); Mystery Writers of America.

The following are excerpts from two letters of Mr. Goulart:
"My wife is also a writer. Over the past three or so years she has done a few pieces for the women's magazine and for some of the children's magazines. She's also done articles and reviews in the jazz field (especially for Jazz and Pop Magazine in its less rock-oriented days). Last week //March 18, 1969--ed.// she signed a contract to do a cook book. For the ladies she usually signs herself Frances Sheridan Goulart.

"I met her while she was working in San Francisco as a copywriter for Guild, Bascom and Bonfigli, an advertising agency that at the time specialized in humorous commercials. This was the same outfit I'd worked for a few years before, in the middle 1950's. When I was at GBB I wrote ads and commercials for Skippy Peanut Butter (which at that dim period in time sponsored a show called 'You Asked For It'), Regal Pale Beer, Foremost Dairies, Mother's Cookies, Chicken of the Sea Tuna, etc. One of the Skippy ads I did showed Casey Stengel eating a cracker. This won several awards at the time and I think eventually was even included in a book with the lovely title of The Hundred Best Ads from the Reader's Digest. The ad also ran in Life and I recall it cost them more to have the dab of peanut butter in color than they paid me in a whole year. GBB also did the Ralston account. I did some TV commercials for the cereals and then did The Chex Press which ran on the backs of all the Chex boxes. There were 55 different ones and the series folded when GBB lost the account.

"My mother was Italian. Her father, Giacomo Macri, came over from the Calabria region of Italy. There have been a couple of famous bandits with this name over there. My father, by the way, is Portuguese and was born in the Azores."

MATTHEW GRANT

1) 1963 Digit   Hyper-Drive. (P)

JOSEPH L. GREEN

1) 1965 Gollancz   The Loafers of Refuge. (RP)

FPS: "Once Around Arcturus,"   If, September, 1962.
FPP: "The Engineer,"   New Worlds, February, 1962.

JOSEPH L. GREEN (continued)

WIP: 1969 Gollancz   An Affair with Genius. (s)
     100000 word novel

***   ***   ***   ***   ***

Joseph Lee Green--born January 14, 1931 at Compass Lake, Florida--Merritt Island, Florida.

Mr. Green is married and has three children.

Free-Lance Writer--Member: Science Fiction Writers of America.

ROBERT GREEN

1) 1968 Hale   The Great Leap Backwards.

?FKP: "No Place Like Where,"   The Magazine of Fantasy and Science Fiction, May, 1964.

NOTE: ?Robert M. Green, Jr. is the probable name of this author.

IRVING A. GREENFIELD

1) 1967 Lancer   Waters of Death. (P/RH)

FPS: 1962 Beacon   The Schemers. (P)
FSF: 1967 Lancer   Waters of Death. (P)

WIP: 1969 Lancer   The Others. (P)
     1969 Belmont   Ecce Veritas. (P)
     1969 Dell   A Time for Every Purpose. (P)

***   ***   ***   ***   ***

Irving A. Greenfield--born February 22, 1928 at Brooklyn, New York--B.A., Brooklyn College, 1950--Brooklyn, New York.

Son of Samuel & Anna (Berkowitz) Greenfield--Anita Grace: September 2, 1950--Richard Greenfield (13); Nathan Greenfield (10).

Was a Free-Lance Technical Writer for several years; Vice-President, Groody Advertising Company, 1957-1965; Free-Lance Writer, 1965-DATE.

THOMAS E. GROULING

1) 1962 Vantage   Project 12.

FPP: 1962 Vantage   Project 12.

***   ***   ***   ***   ***

Thomas Edward Grouling--born June 9, 1940 at Baltimore, Maryland--B.A., University of Baltimore, 1965; M.A., University of Kansas, 1967--listed in Who's Who Among Students in American Universities and Colleges, 1963-1964, and 1964-1965--Atchison, Kansas.

Son of Charles & Anna Grouling--unmarried.

With Credits and Adjustments, Baltimore Office, Best Foods-Corn Products Company, 1957-1961; with Customer Service Department, Sears, Roebuck & Company, Baltimore, Maryland, 1964-1966; Instructor in English and Foreign Student Adviser, St. Benedict's College, 1967-DATE--Member: Modern Language Association.

JAY GROVES

1) 1967 Exposition   Fireball at the Lake.

FPP: 1967 Exposition   Fireball at the Lake.

***   ***   ***   ***   ***

Jay Voelker Groves--born August 4, 1922 at Minneapolis, Minnesota--B.S.Ed., University of Minnesota, 1943; M.A., University of Minnesota, 1946; M.A., West Virginia University, 1967--Buckhannon, West Virginia.

Son of Jay N. & Vivian Groves--Martha Gould: May 25, 1948--Lester Groves (1951); Sarah Groves (1954); Catherine Groves (1956).

Teacher of History and Economics at the college level since 1947; Instructor in Economics, West Virginia Wesleyan College, 1958-DATE--Member: American Economic Association; American Association of University Professors; Civil Air Patrol.

J.W. GROVES

1) 1968 Hale   Shellbreak.

FPS: "The Sphere of Death," Amazing, October, 1931.

J.W. GROVES (continued)

WIP:	19<u>69</u> Hale	Heels of Achilles.

***   ***   ***   ***   ***

John William Groves--born November 6, 1910 at Catford, London, England--London, England.

Son of John William & Edith Rosa (Winterbourne) Groves--Ada May: December 14, 1935--no children.

"I've had no career. Just jobs. And, occasionally, short story sales to the magazines. I switched to novels about the end of 1967."

WYMAN GUIN

1)	1967 Avon	Living Way Out. (s/P)
FPS:	"Trigger Tide,"	Astounding, October, 1950 (as *Norman Menasco).
WIP:	19<u>69</u> Avon	The Standing Joy. (P)

***   ***   ***   ***   ***

Wyman Woods Guin--born March 1, 1915 at Wanette, Oklahoma--Tarrytown, New York.

Son of Joel & Marie (Menasco) Guin--(1) Jean Adolph: 1939-1955; (2) Valerie Carlson: 1956--1) Joel Guin (28); Jennifer Guin (25); 2) Cynthia Guin (9); Kevin Guin (7); Kristen Guin (4).

Employed (successively as Technician in Pharmacology; Advertising Writer; Advertising Manager; Vice President, Marketing) by Lakeside Laboratories, Inc., Milwaukee, 1938-1962; Vice President, Medical Television Communications, Inc, Chicago, 1962-1964; Planning Administrator, L.W. Erolich & Co/Intercon International, 1964-DATE; Free-Lance Writer.

JAMES E. GUNN

2)	1955 Gnome	This Fortress World. (RP)
3)	1958 Bantam	Station in Space. (P)
4)	1961 Bantam	The Joy Makers. (P/RH)
5)	1962 Bantam	The Immortals. (P)
6)	1964 Bantam	Future Imperfect. (s/P)

JAMES E. GUNN (continued)

with Jack Williamson (q.v.)

1) 1955 Gnome   Star Bridge. (RP)

FPS: "Paradox,"   Thrilling Wonder Stories, October, 1949.
FPP: "Communications,"   Startling Stories, September, 1949.

***   ***   ***   ***   ***

James Edwin Gunn--born July 12, 1923 at Kansas City, Missouri--B.S., University of Kansas, 1947; M.A., University of Kansas, 1951--Lawrence, Kansas.

Son of J. Wayne & Elsie (Hutchison) Gunn--Jane Anderson: February 6, 1947 --Christopher Gunn (19); Kevin Gunn (14).

Free-Lance Writer, 1948-1949, 1952-1955; Editor, Western Printing and Lithographing Co, 1951-1952; Managing Editor, Alumni Publications, University of Kansas, 1955-1958; Instructor in English, University of Kansas, 1958-DATE; Administrative Assistant to the Chancellor for University Relations, 1958-DATE --Member: Science Fiction Writers of America; American College Public Relations Association (Chairman, Mid-America District).

Mr. Gunn writes:
"I have the feeling that science fiction is about ready to expand into broader areas of appeal, if the right things happen or are made to happen. It once had a broad, general readership. Then Hugo Gernsback focused it and nourished it with Amazing Stories and its successors and competitors. Now after a period of inbreeding, it seems ready to burst forth again. My hope is that it does not forget its past and its strengths. The period of the magazines was the period when I came to know and love science fiction. That love was the reason I turned to writing science fiction back in 1946 when the idea I had been working on--writing a series of radio plays based on Kansas City history--found no one interested.
"My part in science fiction has been a minor one. I was neither a trail blazer nor a definer. Perhaps I might have done more if I had continued to write full-time, as I did between 1953 and 1955, but offers came along to lead me in other directions. If I have stood for anything, perhaps it was for craftsmanship in writing, for a concern about knowing the techniques of writing and applying them to science fiction. But I have never overdone it: I think technique without content is a meaningless exercise, and I think there is a basic strength that science fiction developed, a way of looking at the universe, that should be retained and developed. Those writers who are bursting out of the field in coruscations of scintillating prose and invention may be leaving their source of strength behind: science fiction's philosophy of rationalism, pragmatism, existentialism...
"But where science fiction is going and how far it goes depends on all of us. I think it has something to give the world, particularly young people, in the way of mind liberation without lawlessness. I hope it has that opportunity."

PETER HAINING

1)	1965	4 Square	The Hell of Mirrors. (@/P)
2)	1966	Mayflower	Where Nightmares Are. (@/P)
3)	1966	Digit	Summoned from the Tomb. (P)
4)	1966	4 Square	Beyond the Curtain of Dark. (@/P)
5)	1966	4 Square	The Craft of Terror. (@/P)
6)	1967	Hale	The Gentlewomen of Evil. (@)
7)	1968	Frewin	The Evil People. (@)
8)	1968	4 Square	Legends for the Dark. (@/P)
9)	1968	Frewin	The Midnight People. (@)
10)	1968	Sidgwick	The Future Makers. (@/RP)
11)	1968	Allen	Dr. Caligari's Black Book. (@)

FPS:	1965	4 Square	The Hell of Mirrors. (@/P)
FSF:	1968	Sidgwick	The Future Makers. (@)

***   ***   ***   ***   ***

Peter Alexander Haining--born April 2, 1940 at Enfield, Middlesex, England--London, England.

Son of William & Joan Haining--Philippa June: October 2, 1965--Richard Alexander Haining (May 11, 1967); Sean Peter Haining (February 12, 1969).

"Five years in journalism as a reporter in the provinces, followed by a period as Feature Editor of a magazine before entering publishing as an editor in 1965;" Editor, New English Library (Publishers of 4 Square Books), 1965-1967; Senior Editor, 1967-1968; Executive Director, 1968-DATE.

Mr. Haining provided the following comment on his work:

"The major part of my work in the Fantasy and Horror genre--I have only stepped very gingerly into Science Fiction, aware as I am of my own deficiencies in this area--has been as an anthologiser. My work has been directed towards discovering either early or neglected work by the major writers in the field, and republishing this in new collections. Apart from this, I've always endeavored to set an overall theme for each book, rather than just collect stories on any subject. This certainly seems to have been welcomed in England, where publishers have noticed the falling off of sales of general collections of Horror and Fantasy stories. While I have tried to encourage new writers, those which have received most of my attention have been writing in the same kind of style as H.P. Lovecraft, and the early works of August Derleth and Ray Bradbury. There are at least two other anthologisers in England concentrating very determinedly on finding new talent, and hence my efforts have been directed more to the past. I am convinced there is still a great weight of material which is worthy of reprinting, and certainly the enthusiasm with which my various projects have been greeted by writers like Bradbury, Bloch, and Derleth gives me encouragement to continue this work. I've also been recently very cheered by the number of my books which have been sold for editions not only in America, but also on the continent of Europe."

JAMES R. HALLUMS

1) 1965 Digit   They Came, They Saw. (P)

- -

1194   EDMOND HAMILTON

1) 1936 Allan   The Horror on the Asteriod. (s)
2) 1945 Utopian   Murder in the Clinic. (P)
3) 1945 Utopian   Tiger Girl. (P)
4) 1949 Fell   The Star Kings. (RP/RPv)
5) 1950 Pemberton   The Monsters of Juntonheim. (P)
6) 1950 Pemberton   Tharkol, Lord of the Unknown. (P)
4A) 1950 Signet   Beyond the Moon. (P)
7) 1951 Fell   City at World's End. (RP)
8) 1959 Ace   The Sun Smasher. (P)
9) 1959 Torquil   The Star of Life. (RP)
10) 1960 Torquil   The Haunted Stars. (RP)
11) 1961 Torquil   Battle for the Stars. (RP)
12) 1964 Ace   Outside the Universe. (P)
13) 1964 Lancer   The Valley of Creation. (P)
14) 1965 Ace   Crashing Suns. (s/P)
15) 1965 Ace   Fugitive of the Stars. (P)
16) 1966 Belmont   Doomstar. (P)
17) 1967 Ace   1 The Weapon from Beyond. (P)
18) 1968 Ace   2 The Closed Worlds. (P)
20) 1968 Ace   3 World of the Starwolves. (P)

                         as ***Brett Sterling
19) 1968 Pop Lib   -1 Danger Planet. (P)

SER: 1) Starwolf;   2) Captain Future.

FPS: "The Monster-God of Mamurth," Weird Tales, August, 1926.

WIP: 1969 Pop Lib   -3 Outlaw World. (P)
       1969 Pop Lib   -4 Quest Beyond the Stars. (P)
       1969 Pop Lib   -5 Outlaws of the Moon. (P)
       1969 Pop Lib   -6 The Comet Kings. (P)
       1969 Pop Lib   -7 Planets in Peril. (P)
       1969 Pop Lib   -8 Calling Captain Future. (P)
       1969 Pop Lib   -9 Captain Future's Challenge. (P)
       1969 Ace   4 The Galactic Hunters. (P)
       1969 Pop Lib   -10 Galaxy Mission. (P)
***   ***   ***   ***   ***

Edmond Moore Hamilton--born October 21, 1904 at Youngstown, Ohio--attended Westminster College, 1919-1921--Guest of Honor, 22nd World Science Fiction Convention (Pacificon II), 1964; Elected to First Fandom Science Fiction Hall of Fame, 1967--Lancaster, California/Kinsman, Ohio.

EDMOND HAMILTON (continued)

Son of Scott B. & Maude (Whinery) Hamilton--Leigh Brackett: December 31, 1946--no children.

"Wrote my first sf story when I was 21 years old, and have been a professional writer exclusively ever since; have about 400 odd published stories"--Member: Science Fiction Writers of America; Authors Guild.

Mr. Hamilton responds to questions:
"What is my opinion of the present state of science fiction? In the first place, I must say that I protest against all attempts to lay down dogmatic rules about sf. It can be many things, and all can be good. But having said that, I record my belief that sf has gotten far away from the literature of anticipation to a mixed bag of psychological fiction and of fantasy. There is, I think, too much coterie writing in sf these days. The thing that troubles me most is that comparatively few science-fictionists seem to have much real interest in the continuing space program now going on. After decades of writing about these things, they are beginning to come true before our eyes, but few seem to care much. If this is true, it would seem to indicate that sf has changed from a broad and often lurid literature dreaming of the future into a small field in which the desire to shine as a 'literary' writer has completely replaced the old burning interest in possible things to come.

"What advice would I give to an aspiring writer? I can do no better than repeat the advice which A. Merritt gave me when I was just starting. He wrote me, 'Do not read too much of other peoples' science fiction. Read books of scientific nature and let your imagination play around the facts therein.'

"What do I think I've contributed to science fiction? That's hard to answer. While I've never confined myself solely to space adventure stories, I've written a great many of them, and perhaps in them indicated my belief that the conquest of space would be the great adventure. And if what Borman and McDivitt and the others are doing is not adventure...what is?"

W.C. HANNA

1) 1964 Arcadia   The Tandar Saga.

VERN HANSEN

1) 1962 Digit   The Whisper of Death. (P)
2) 1963 Digit   Murder with Menaces. (P)
3) 1963 Digit   The Twisters. (P)
4) 1963 Digit   Creatures of the Mist. (P)
5) 1964 Digit   Claws of the Night. (P)
6) 1964 Digit   The Grip of Fear. (P)

WILLIAM HANSMAN

1)   1968 Vantage   The A.G. Man.

FPP: 1968 Vantage   The A.G. Man.

***   ***   ***   ***   ***

William Donald Hansman--born February 13, 1913 at Smiths' Falls, Ontario, Canada--North Hollywood, California.

Marjorie: 1941--Anne Louise Hansman; Donna Marielle Hansman

Engineer.

PHIL HARBOTTLE

1)   1963 Harbottle   John Russell Fearn--An Evaluation. (nf)
2)   1964 Harbottle   E. C. Tubb-An Evaluation. (nf)
3)   1965 Harbottle   The Ultimate Analysis. (nf/RPe)
4)   1968 Harbottle   The Multi-Man. (3/e/P)

FPP: 1963 Harbottle   John Russell Fearn--An Evaluation. (nf)

***   ***   ***   ***   ***

Philip James Harbottle--born October 2, 1941 at Wallsend-on-Tyne, Northumberland, England--Wallsend-on-Tyne, Northumberland, England.

Son of James Pringle & Agnes Talbot (Hardwick) Harbottle--Maureen Doyle: September 27, 1969--no children.

Local Government Officer, 1961-1969, Publications Manager, Ronald E. Graham (Publishers) Pty Ltd., 1969-DATE; Editor, Vision of Tomorrow, August, 1969-DATE--Member: British Science Fiction Association; Brandling Lawn Tennis Club; Associate Member: Science Fiction Writers of America.

Statement of Mr. Harbottle:
  "As Publications Manager and Editor of Ronald E. Graham (Publishers) Pty Ltd., I am at present actively encouraging and soliciting new sf being written by British and Australian writers (Graham is an Australian company publishing and trading in Britain), and illustrations by new and existing artists. This is for a new magazine, Vision of Tomorrow, large slick size, monthly, to appear in August. Three issues bought for and set in print at time of writing//June 3, 1969-ed.//.
  "Also planning a second magazine, working title Mind's Eye, same format. This will carry reprints, revised if need be, of older science fiction deemed of outstanding merit by myself, and approved by the publisher. Principal British authors reprinted: Fearn, Tubb, Bulmer, Temple. American: Hamilton, Williamson.

PHIL HARBOTTLE (continued)

Will use new stories by British, Australian, or American authors as convenient. If the magazine survives, I will work towards a preponderance of new material. Short novels (up to 50,000 words) will be featured. I am NOT in the market for material as yet, except by invitation. Announcements will be made fairly soon, through Science Fiction Writers of America and elsewhere.

"Both magazines will feature orthodox sf. No taboo on themes, especially-- but stories must be understandable, entertaining fiction. I have little interest in the so-called new wave. Nothing against it--quite happy to see it appearing elsewhere--but I don't think it can replace orthodox sf, or rather, orthodox fiction. I believe the field needs a magazine to sustain new writers, and for the magazine to sustain itself it needs a mass audience--which means entertainment, not nausea, however pertinent.

"The magazines will be liberally illustrated, using several new artists, including some of my own work on smaller spots, headings, etc. Articles about sf, in the Lowndes style, will be used, including British sf history by Walter Gillings, John Carnell, and others."

KENNETH HARKER

1) 1966 Compact   The Symmetrians. (P)

CHARLES L. HARNESS

1) 1953 Bouregy   Flight Into Yesterday. (RPv)
1A) 1955 Ace   The Paradox Men. (P/RH)
2) 1966 Compact   The Rose. (s/P/RH)
3) 1968 Berkley   The Ring of Ritornel. (P/RH)

FPS: "Time Trap,"   Astounding, August, 1948.

***   ***   ***   ***   ***

Charles Leonard Harness--born December 29, 1915 at Colorado City, Texas--B.S., George Washington University, 1942; LL.B., George Washington University, 1946-- Clarksville, Maryland.

Son of Conrad T. & Lillian B. Harness--Nell: July 27, 1938--Mollie Shan Harness (21); Charles Bryan Harness (14).

Lawyer--Member: Science Fiction Writers of America; American Patent Law Association.

JOHN BEYNON HARRIS

1A)	1964 Lancer	The Secret People. (P)	

as *John Beynon

1)	1935 Newnes	The Secret People. (RP)
2)	1936 Newnes	The Planet Plane. (RPv)
2A)	1953 Nova	Stowaway to Mars. (P)

as *Johnson Harris

3)	1946 Utopian	Love in Time. (P)

as *John Wyndham

4)	1951 Doubleday	The Day of the Triffids. (RP/RPv)
4A)	1952 Pop Lib	The Revolt of the Triffids. (P)
5)	1953 Joseph	The Kraken Wakes. (RP)
5A)	1953 Ballantine	Out of the Deeps. (H-P)
6)	1954 Dobson	Jizzle. (s/RP)
7)	1955 Joseph	The Chrysalids. (RP)
7A)	1955 Ballantine	Re-Birth. (H-P)
8)	1956 Joseph	The Seeds of Time. (s/RP)
9)	1956 Ballantine	Tales of Gooseflesh and Laughter. (s/P)
10)	1957 Joseph	The Midwich Cuckoos. (RP/RPv)
10A)	1960 Ballantine	The Village of the Damned. (P)
12)	1960 Joseph	Trouble with Lichen. (RP)
13)	1961 Joseph	Consider Her Ways. (s/RP/RPv)
13A)	1961 Ballantine	The Infinite Moment. (s/P)
14)	1964 Joseph	The John Wyndham Omnibus. (4/5/7)
15)	1968 Ballantine	Chocky. (P/RH)

as *John Wyndham and *Lucas Parkes

11)	1958 Joseph	The Outward Urge. (RP)

FPS:	"Worlds to Barter,"	Wonder Stories, May, 1931.

***   ***   ***   ***   ***

John Wyndham Parkes Lucas Beynon Harris--born July 10, 1903 at Knowle, Warwickshire, England--attended Bedales School--Petersfield, Hampshire, England.

Son of George Beynon & Gertrude (Parkes) Harris--Grace Isabel Wilson: July 26, 1963--no children.

Free-Lance Writer--Member: Science Fiction Writers of America; Society of Authors; International P.E.N.

Mr. Harris died on March 11, 1969.

HARRY HARRISON

1)	1960 Bantam		1	Deathworld. (P)
2)	1961 Pyramid		-1	The Stainless Steel Rat. (P)
3)	1962 Bantam			Planet of the Damned. (P/RHv)
4)	1962 Pyramid			War with the Robots. (s/P/RH)
5)	1964 Bantam		2	Deathworld 2. (P/RHv)
5A)	1964 Gollancz		2	The Ethical Engineer.
6)	1965 Doubleday			Bill, the Galactic Hero. (RP)
7)	1965 Gollancz			Two Tales and Eight Tomorrows. (s/RP)
8)	1965 Doubleday			Plague from Space. (RP)
9)	1966 Doubleday			Make Room! Make Room! (RP)
3A)	1967 Dobson			Sense of Obligation.
10)	1967 Doubleday			The Technicolor® Time Machine. (RP)
12)	1968 Dobson			Backdrop of Stars. (@/RPv)
14)	1968 Avon		+1	The Man from P.I.G. (P)
15)	1968 Dell		3	Deathworld 3. (P/RH)
12A)	1968 Berkley			SF: Authors' Choice. (@/P)

with Brian W. Aldiss (q.v.)

11)	1967 Doubleday		Nebula Award Stories Two. (@/P-P)
13)	1968 Berkley		Best SF: 1967. (@/P-P)
13A)	1968 Sphere		Year's Best Science Fiction No. 1. (@/P-P)

with Leon E. Stover (q.v.)

16)	1968 Doubleday		Apeman, Spaceman. (@/RP)

FPS:	"Rock Diver,"		Worlds Beyond, February, 1951.
WIP:	1969 Sphere		Year's Best Science Fiction No. 2. (@/P/RHv/ with Brian Aldiss)
17A)	1969 Putnam		Best SF: 1968. (@/with Brian Aldiss)
	1969 Putnam		Captive Universe. (RP)
	1969 Faber		Blast Off for Boys. (@)
	1969 Macdonald		Four for the Future. (@)
20A)	1969 Doubleday		Worlds of Wonder. (@)
	1970 Doubleday		The Year 2000. (@)
	1970 Doubleday		Spaceship Medic.
	1970 Delacorte		Nova 1. (@)
	1970 Avon	+2	The Man from R.O.B.O.T. (P)
	1970 Putnam		In Our Hands, the Stars.
	1970 Berkley		Harrison's 20. (s/P)
	Delacorte		Nova 2. (@)
	Harper		Science Fiction Classics. (@)
	Doubleday		The Astounding-Analog Reader. (@/with Brian Aldiss.
	Walker	-2	The Stainless Steel Rat's Revenge.
	1970 Sphere		Year's Best Science Fiction No. 3. (@/P/ with Brian Aldiss)
	1970 Putnam		Best SF: 1969. (@/with Brian Aldiss)
	Collier		One Step from Earth. (s)
	Berkley		SF: Authors' Choice 2. (@/P)
			An untitled novel,(with Leon E. Stover)

***   ***   ***   ***   ***

HARRY HARRISON (continued)

Harry Max Harrison--born March 12, 1925 at Stamford, Connecticut--Imperial Beach, California.

Son of Leo & Ria (Kirjassoff) Harrison--Joan Merkler: June 4, 1954--Todd Harrison (1955); Moira Harrison (1959).

Free-Lance Commercial Artist, 1946-1955; Editor, Science Fiction Adventures, December, 1953-May, 1954; Fantasy Fiction, November, 1953 (with Lester del Rey, as *Cameron Hall); SF Impulse, October, 1966-February, 1967; Fantastic, November, 1967-October, 1968; Amazing, December, 1967-September, 1968; Associate Editor, Amazing, November, 1968; Fantastic, December, 1968; Free-Lance Writer and Editor-- Member: Science Fiction Writers of America (Vice-President, 1968-1969); British Science Fiction Association; Knight of St. Fantony.

Mr. Harrison writes:
"There is no New Wave save in the eye of the beholder--there is just good and bad sf. Currently, I feel the state of the short story is bad, the novel improving all the time. There seems to be a growing market for books, and as long as they are being sold, better books will be done. For the first time, financial rewards can justify any amount of effort. My new novel, Captive Universe, was on the 'A' list of the Book of the Month Club, and came within a hair of being a selection. SF has more readers than it ever had before.

"My contributions? I know I wrote Deathworld (among other reasons) because I thought sf at that time was getting too cerebral, and too much of the action and entertainment had gone out of it. The reader reaction to the book seems to have proven I was right. It has been reprinted four times and translated into seven languages. My feelings have changed during the years, and now I see more than enough color and action--at times little else--and so I am plugging for better writing, better thinking, more attention to our specialized craft. With this in mind, I published and edited with Brian W. Aldiss SF Horizons, the first magazine of sf criticism. We only did two issues, but the impact was enough to start other people thinking and working along the same lines. My recent novels have been more like general novels--appealing to mainstream readers--while still being sf pure for the specialized readers. Make Room! Make Room! was like this, and the new novel, In Our Hands, the Stars, takes place in the present time. And Analog is serializing it."

HENRY L. HASSE

1)   1968 Avalon   The Stars Will Wait.

FKP: "The End of Tyme,"   Wonder Stories, November, 1933 (with A. Fedor).

----

*GERALD HATCH

1)	1963 Monarch		The Day the Earth Froze. (P)

Gerald Hatch is a penname of Dave Foley.

JOHN HAY

1)	1968 Hodder		The Invasion.

PETER HEATH

1)	1967 Lancer	1	Assassins from Tomorrow. (P)
2)	1967 Lancer	2	The Mind Brothers. (P)
3)	1968 Lancer	3	Men Who Die Twice. (P)

ROBERT A. HEINLEIN

1)	1947 Scribner	Rocket Ship Galileo.
2)	1948 Scribner	Space Cadet.
3)	1948 Fantasy	Beyond This Horizon. (RP)
4)	1949 Scribner	Red Planet. (RP)
5)	1949 Gnome	Sixth Column. (PRv)
6)	1950 Doubleday	Waldo and Magic, Inc. (RP/RPv)
7)	1950 Shasta	The Man Who Sold the Moon. (s/RP)
8)	1950 Scribner	Farmer in the Sky. (RP)
9)	1951 Scribner	Between Planets. (RP)
10)	1951 Shasta	The Green Hills of Earth. (s/RP)
11)	1951 Dell	Universe. (P/RHe)
12)	1951 Doubleday	The Puppet Masters. (RP)
5A)	1951 Signet	The Day After Tomorrow. (P)
13)	1952 Doubleday	Tomorrow, the Stars. (@/RP)
14)	1952 Scribner	The Rolling Stones.
15)	1953 Scribner	Starman Jones. (RP)
16)	1953 Shasta	Revolt in 2100. (s/RP)
17)	1953 Fantasy	Assignment in Eternity. ,(s/RP)
18)	1954 Doubleday	The Star Beast.
19)	1955 Scribner	Tunnel in the Sky. (RP)
20)	1956 Doubleday	Double Star. (RP)
21)	1956 Scribner	Time for the Stars. (RP)
22)	1957 Doubleday	The Door into Summer. (RP)
23)	1957 Scribner	Citizen of the Galaxy.
24)	1958 Gnome	Methuselah's Children. (RP)
25)	1958 Doubleday	Have Space Suit--Will Travel.

ROBERT A. HEINLEIN (continued)

6A)	1958	Avon	Waldo: Genius in Orbit. (P)
26)	1959	Putnam	Starship Troopers. (RP)
27)	1959	Gnome	The Menace from Earth. (s/RP)
28)	1959	Gnome	The Unpleasant Profession of Jonathan Hoag. (s/RP/RPv)
29)	1960	Digit	Lost Legacy. (P)
30)	1961	Putnam	Stranger in a Strange Land. (RP)
28A)	1962	Pyramid	6 x H. (s/P)
31)	1963	Putnam	Podkayne of Mars. (RP)
32)	1963	Putnam	Glory Road. (RP)
33)	1964	Putnam	Orphans of the Sky. (11/e/RP)
34)	1964	Putnam	Farnham's Freehold. (RP)
35)	1965	Doubleday	Three by Heinlein. (6/12)
36)	1966	Putnam	The Moon Is a Harsh Mistress. (RP)
37)	1966	Sidgwick	A Robert Heinlein Omnibus. (3/7/10)
38)	1966	Ace	The Worlds of Robert A. Heinlein. (s/P)
35A)	1966	Gollancz	A Heinlein Triad. (6/12)
39)	1967	Putnam	The Past Through Tomorrow. (7/10/16/24)

FPS: "Life-Line,"   Astounding, August, 1939.

***   ***   ***   ***   ***

Robert Anson Heinlein--born July 7, 1907 at Butler, Missouri-graduated from United States Naval Academy, 1929; graduate study at University of California at Los Angeles, 1934--Hugo Award, Best Novel, 1956, Double Star; 1960, Starship Troopers; 1962, Stranger in a Strange Land; 1967, The Moon Is a Harsh Mistress; Guest of Honor, 3rd World Science Fiction Convention (Denvention), 1941; 19th World Science Fiction Convention (Seacon), 1961; Boys' Clubs of American Award, 1959; Sequoyah Book Award, 1961--Santa Cruz, California.

Son of Rex Ivar & Bam (Lyle) Heinlein--Virginia Gerstenfeld: 1948--no children.

With United States Navy, 1929-1934; (disabled and retired with rank of Lieutenant,); Free-Lance Writer, 1939-DATE--Member: Science Fiction Writers of America; Authors League; World Future Society; American Association for the Advancement of Science; American Institute of Aeronautics and Astronautics.

Mr. Heinlein mentions:
   "My papers, correspondence, manuscripts, and file copies of editions are being collected by the University of California. Eventually, someone with a taste for this sort of work may make a complete list. But I shan't, as I have trouble enough keeping my contracts straight and finding time to write."

He also adds:
   "I never answer personal questions, nor comment on my own work, nor on that of my colleagues. So I have nothing to say on the 'state of the art.'"

HENRY HARDY HEINS

1) 1964 Grant   A Golden Anniversary Bibliography of
                                           Edgar Rice Burroughs. (nf)

ZENNA HENDERSON

1) 1961 Doubleday   Pilgrimage: The Book of the People. (s/RP)
2) 1965 Doubleday   The Anything Box. (s/RP)
3) 1966 Gollancz   The People: No Different Flesh. (s/RP)

FPS: "Come on, Wagon!" The Magazine of Fantasy and Science Fiction, December, 1951.

***   ***   ***   ***   ***

Zenna Henderson--born November 1, 1917 at Tucson, Arizona--B.A., Arizona State University, 1940; M.A., Arizona State University, 1954--Eloy, Arizona.

Daughter of Louis Rudolph & Emily Vernell (Rowley) Chlarson--Richard Harry Henderson: June 5, 1944/1951--no children.

Teacher, 1940-DATE: has taught mainly in First Grade in Arizona; First Grade Teacher, Eloy West School, 1961-DATE--Member: Science Fiction Writers of America; National Education Association; Arizona Education Association.

Miss Henderson provided the following statement:
     "I am afraid I'm not qualified to comment on the present state of sf--I have read very little of it in the past fifteen years, mainly because--as in American History--my interest dies quickly after the Exploratory period (individuals against environment) turns into Political or Economic history (masses manipulated). From the little I have read, it has lost spontaneity and the light touch. It has fallen in with the contemporary scene: violence, sex, and the erasing of individuality. It tends to be ponderous with theses that aren't that weighty, or that worth wading through. These are the points on which I bias my opinions--I reiterate, I'm not qualified to judge.
     "I began writing about the time I began reading, but began with sf when I decided I should write in the field which I read the most. Lacking a technical background, I turned to people functioning in sf surroundings. But really, my stories are mostly fantasy--adult wishful thinking.
     "As to my contribution--well, from the fan letters I receive (they cover an amazing area as to age, occupations, and geographical locations), the concensus seems to be that I depict the sort of ordinary people who so often get trampled in a technological society; and also the 'goodness' and orderliness of a life that is functioning according to a plan, no matter how much we hack it up. In other words, Man is not the measure of life, God is. I might add that the interpretations of God that I receive are also amazingly divergent. Most of my correspondents seem to draw comfort from my stories, which is pleasant, because comfort is what you cain't hardly get none of no more!"

FRANK HERBERT

1)	1956 Doubleday		The Dragon in the Sea. (RP/RPv)
1A)	1959 Avon		21st Century Sub. (P)
2)	1966 Chilton	1	Dune. (RP)
3)	1966 Ace		The Green Brain. (P)
4)	1966 Berkley		Destination: Void. (P)
5)	1966 Berkley		The Eyes of Heisenberg. (P)
6)	1968 Berkley		The Santaroga Barrier. (P)
7)	1968 Avon		The Heaven Makers. (P)

FKP: "Looking for Something," Startling Stories, April, 1952.

WIP: 1969 Putnam 2 Dune Messiah.

***   ***   ***   ***   ***

Frank Patrick Herbert won a Nebula Award, Best Novel, 1965, and a Hugo Award, Best Novel, 1966, both for Dune.

T. EARL HICKEY

1) 1966 Avalon   The Time Chariot.

PHILIP E. HIGH

1)	1964 Ace	The Prodical Sun. (P)
2)	1964 Ace	No Truce with Terra. (P)
3)	1966 Ace	The Mad Metropolis. (P)
4)	1967 Ace	Reality Forbidden. (P/RH)
5)	1967 Pap Lib	Twin Planets. (P/RH)
6)	1967 Ace	These Savage Futurians. (P/RH)
7)	1968 Ace	The Time Mercenaries. (P)
8)	1968 Hale	Invader on My Back. (RP)

FPS: "The Statics," Authentic, September, 1955.

***   ***   ***   ***   ***

Philip Empson High--born April 28, 1914 at Bedfordshire, England--Invader on My Back included in the archives of the British Museum--Canterbury, Kent, England.

Son of William & Muriel High--Pamela: August 17, 1950--Jacqueline High (11); Beverly High (daughter; 5).

Busdriver; Free-Lance Writer.

DOUGLAS A. HILL

1)	1966 Hart-Davis	Window on the Future. (@)
2)	1966 Panther	Way of the Werewolf. (@/P)
3)	1967 Hart-Davis	The Devil His Due. (@/RP)
FPS:	1965 Hawthorn	The Supernatural. (nf/with Pat Williams)
FSF:	1966 Hart-Davis	Window on the Future. (@)

***　　　***　　　***　　　***　　　***

Douglas Arthur Hill--born April 6, 1935 at Manitoba, Canada--B.A., University of Saskatchewan; graduate study at University of Toronto--Canada Council of Arts Grant for Poetry, 1968--London, England.

Son of William & Cora A. Hill--married 1957--one son, age 5.

Free-Lance Writer, 1959-1962, 1964-DATE; Publisher's Editor, 1962-1964--Member: National Union of Journalists (British); British Folklore Society.

Mr. Hill mentions:
   "Most of my work has been (in the jargon) 'non-creative': as a regular reviewer in the London Tribune; as consultant to publishers; as anthologist; as associate editor of New Worlds (Britain's only sf magazine, and sf's avant-garde leader). My 'creative' work is channeled into poetry (but not sf poetry); and I earn my living writing non-fiction mostly in the fields of folklore, history, and literary subjects."

ERNEST HILL

1)	1968 Ace	Pity About Earth. (P/RH)
FPS:	A poem in a magazine called	New Helios.
FSF:	"The Last Generation,"	New Worlds, January, 1964.
WIP:		John Anderson, My Jo John.

***　　　***　　　***　　　***　　　***

Ernest Hill--born July 14, 1915 at Stourbridge, England--Faversham, Kent, England.

Son of Ernest & Agnes Hill--twice married--Kenneth Hill (31); Raymond Hill (29).

Has been a farmer, policeman, with the R.A.F.; currently Advertising Manager, The Consulting Engineer, a technical journal in the Thomson Group.

Mr. Hill writes:
   "I was brought up in Stratford-upon-Avon, and having moved around the continent during and between wars, I have come to rest in an ancient mill-house where the original water wheel ground the charcoal for some of the first gunpowder used for lethal purposes in Europe. I have only recently found the time to write, but I hope you will see more of me from now on."

CHRISTOPHER HODDER-WILLIAMS

1) 1959 Hodder   Chain Reaction. (RP)
2) 1964 Hodder   The Main Experiment. (RP)
3) 1967 Hodder   The Egg-Shaped Thing.
4) 1968 Hodder   A Fistful of Digits.

John Christopher Glazebrook Hodder-Williams has a partial biography in Contemporary Authors.

LEE HOFFMAN

1)   1967 Belmont   Telepower. (P)

FPS: 1966 Ace   The Legend of Blackjack Sam. (P)
FSF: 1967 Belmont   Telepower. (P)

WIP: 1969 Ballantine   The Caves of Karst. (P)
        1970 Avon   Kyning. (P)

***   ***   ***   ***   ***

Lee Hoffman (u)--born August 14, 1932 at Chicago, Illinois--attended Armstrong Junior College, 1949-1951--Spur Award, Best Novel, 1967, The Valdez Horses--New York, New York.

Larry T. Shaw: /divorced.

Has been a Printer's Devil, Savannah Vocational School; Girl Friday, Hoffman Radio-TV Service; Assistant Editor, Infinity, October, 1956-November, 1958; Science Fiction Adventures, December, 1956-June, 1958 (all issues); with Reprint Department, MD Publications; Claim Handler, Hoffman Motors (no relation); in Printing Production, Arrow Press; Allied Typographers; George Morris Press; Free-Lance Writer, 1965-DATE--Member: Science Fiction Writers of America; Western Writers of America.

---

*J. HUNTER HOLLY

1) 1959 Avalon   Encounter. (RP)
2) 1960 Avalon   The Green Planet. (RP)
3) 1962 Avalon   The Dark Planet.
4) 1962 Monarch   The Flying Eyes. (P)
5) 1963 Avalon   The Running Man. (RP)
6) 1963 Avalon   The Gray Aliens. (RP)

*J. HUNTER HOLLY (continued)

7)	1964 Avon		The Time Twisters. (P)
8)	1965 Avalon		The Dark Enemy.
9)	1966 Avalon		The Mind Traders. (RP)
10)	1967 Ace	10	The Assassination Affair. (P)

SER: The Man From U.N.C.L.E.

FPS: 1952
FSF: 1959 Avalon   Encounter.

WIP: "I have been ill for two years, and so I haven't been writing anything except that Man From U.N.C.L.E. book, I'm trying hard to get started again."

***   ***   ***   ***   ***

Joan Carol Holly--born September 25, 1932 at Lansing, Michigan--B.A., Michigan State University, 1954--Lansing, Michigan.

Daughter of Arthur Hunter & Hazel (Trumbo) Holly--unmarried.

Free-Lance Writer--Member: Science Fiction Writers of America; Authors Guild; Phi Kappa Phi.

Miss Holly mentions:
   "I started to write stories when I was five years old. They were nature stories about animals, etc., and my mother wrote them down for me as I dictated them. You can see that I had an unusually fine mother for her to take the time to do that."

HAYDEN HOWARD

1) 1967 Ballantine   The Eskimo Invasion. (P)

FKP: "It,"   Planet Stories, January, 1952.

John Hayden Howard is a member of Science Fiction Writers of America.

IVAN HOWARD

1) 1963 Belmont   Rare Science Fiction. (@/P)
2) 1963 Belmont   6 and the Silent Scream. (@/P)
3) 1963 Belmont   Novelets of Science Fiction. (@/P)
4) 1963 Belmont   Escape to Earth. (@/P)
5) 1963 Belmont   Way Out. (@/P)
6) 1964 Belmont   Things. (@/P)

FRED HOYLE

1)	1957 Heinemann		The Black Cloud. (RP)
2)	1959 Heinemann		Ossian's Ride. (RP)
6)	1966 Heinemann		October the First Is Too Late. (RP)
7)	1967 NAL		Element 79. (s/RP)
			with John Elliot (q.v.)
3)	1962 Souvenir	1	A for Andromeda. (RP)
5)	1964 Souvenir	2	Andromeda Breakthrough. (RP)
			with Geoffrey Hoyle (q.v.)
4)	1963 Heinemann		Fifth Planet. (RP)
FSF:	1957 Heinemann		The Black Cloud.
WIP:	1969 Heinemann		Rockets in Ursa Major. (with Geoffrey Hoyle)

***　　　***　　　***　　　***　　　***

Fred Hoyle--born June 24, 1915 at Bingley, Yorkshire, England--attended Emmanuel College, Cambridge University--Cambridge, England.

Son of Ben & Mable Hoyle--Barbara Clark: December 28, 1939--Geoffrey Hoyle (January 12, 1941); Elizabeth Hoyle (24).

Lecturer in Mathematics, Cambridge University, 1945-1958; Plumian Professor of Astronomy and Experimental Philosophy, and Director of the Institute of Theoretical Astronomy, Cambridge University, 1958-DATE--Member: Royal Society (Fellow).

GEOFFREY HOYLE

		with Fred Hoyle (q.v.)
1)	1963 Heinemann	Fifth Planet. (RP)
FPS:	1963 Heinemann	Fifth Planet. (with Fred Hoyle)
WIP:	1969 Heinemann	Rockets in Ursa Major. (with Fred Hoyle)

***　　　***　　　***　　　***　　　***

Geoffrey Hoyle--born January 12, 1941 at Scunthorpe, Lincolnshire, England--attended Cambridge University--Cambridge, England.

Son of Fred & Barbara (Clark) Hoyle-- unmarried.

E. MAYNE HULL

with A. E. van Vogt (q.v.)
1) 1948 FPCI   Out of the Unknown. (s)
2) 1954 Fell   Planets for Sale. (RP)
3) 1966 Doubleday   The Winged Man. (RP)

FKP: "The Flight That Failed,"   Astounding, December, 1942.

WIP: 1969 Powell   Out of the Unknown. (1/e/P/with A. E. van Vogt)

Edna Mayne Hull is the wife of A. E. van Vogt. She was Guest of Honor, 4th World Science Fiction Convention (Pacificon I), 1946.

JOHN IGGULDEN

1) 1960 Chapman   Breakthrough. (RP)

John Manners Iggulden was born in 1917. A partial biography may be found in Contemporary Authors.

NEIL D. ISAACS

with Rose A. Zimbardo (q.v.)
1) 1968 Notre Dame   Tolkien and the Critics. (nf/RP)

FSF: 1968 Notre Dame   Tolkien and the Critics. (nf/with Rose A. Zimbardo)

WIP: The Triumph of Artifice, "a study of contemporary modes of fiction, film, and drama, in which I will discuss several matters of interest to you, I think: Tolkien, the fiction of Charles Williams, 2001, Last Year at Marienbad, Blow-Up, Tiny Alice, Juliet of the Spirits, etc."

***   ***   ***   ***   ***   ***

Neil David Isaacs--born August 21, 1931 at New York, New York--A.B., Dartmouth College, 1953; A.M., University of California at Berkeley, 1956; Ph.D., Brown University, 1959--ACLS Aid-in-Grant, 1966; National Endowment for Humanities Fellowship, 1969-1970--Knoxville, Tennessee.

NEIL D. ISAACS (continued)

Son of Maurice B. & Florence (Braun) Isaacs--Esther Reece Karmazine: December 21, 1953--Ian Mark Isaacs (14); Jonathan Dean Isaacs (12); Daniel Reece Isaacs (9); Anne Braun Isaacs (3).

Instructor in English, City College of New York, 1959-1963; Assistant Professor of English, University of Tennessee, 1963-1965; Associate Professor, 1965-DATE-- Member: American Literature Society; Modern Language Association; American Association of University Professors; SAMLA; Medieval Academy of America.

JOHN JAKES

1)	1967 Ace		When the Star Kings Die. (P)
2)	1968 Avon	1	Brak the Barbarian. (P)

SER: Brak the Barbarian

FPS: "Machine,"   The Magazine of Fantasy and Science Fiction, April, 1952.
FPP: "The Dreaming Trees,"   Fantastic Adventures, November, 1950

WIP:	1969 Pap Lib		The Hybrid. (P)
	1969 Ace		The Planet Wizard. (P)
	1969 Pap Lib	2	Brak the Barbarian Versus the Sorceress. (P)
	1969 Ace		Tonight We Steal the Stars. (P)
	1969 Pap Lib	3	Brak the Barbarian Versus the Mark of the Demons. (P)
	1969 Signet		The Last Magicians. (P)
	1969 West		The Secrets of Stardeep.
	1969 Pap Lib		Asylum World. (P)

***   ***   ***   ***   ***

John William Jakes--born March 31, 1932 at Chicago, Illinois--A.B., DePauw University, 1953; M.A., Ohio State University, 1954--Dayton, Ohio.

Son of John A. & Bertha R. Jakes--Rachel Anne Payne: June 15, 1951--Andrea Jakes (15); Ellen Jakes (13); Mike Jakes (11); Victoria Jakes (8).

Free-Lance Writer--Member: Science Fiction Writers of America; Mystery Writers of America; Sigma Delta Chi.

----

*LAURENCE M. JANIFER

3)	1963 Pyramid		Slave Planet. (P)
6)	1964 Pyramid		The Wonder War. (P)
7)	1965 Lancer		You Sane Men. (P)
8)	1966 S&S		Masters' Choice. (@/RPav)
9)	1968 Belmont		Impossible? (s/P)
7A)	1968 Lancer		Bloodworld. (P)
10)	1968 Belmont		A Piece of Martin Cann. (P)

as Larry M. Harris with Randall Garrett (q.v.)

1)	1960 Beacon		Pagan Passions. (P)

with Randall Garrett (q.v.) as *Mark Phillips

2)	1962 Pyramid	1	Brain Twister. (P)
4)	1963 Pyramid	2	The Impossibles. (P)
5)	1963 Pyramid	3	Supermind. (P)

with S. J. Treibich, (q.v.)

11)	1968 Ace	-1	Target: Terra. (P)
FSF:	"Expatriate,"		Cosmos, November, 1953.
WIP:	1969 Ace	-2	The High Hex. (P/with S. J. Treibich)
8A)	1969 Tandem		Masters' Choice 1. (@/a/P)
8B)	1969 Tandem		Masters' Choice 2. (@/a/P)
	1969 Ace	-3	The Wagered World. (P/with S. J. Treibich)

NOTE: Mr. Janifer's reply was among the last received. Until that time, it had been the editors' belief that Laurence M. Janifer was the legalized name of Larry M. Harris. The statement reproduced below refutes that supposition, but unfortunately, the information came too late to alter position of this entry (which should be under "Harris").

*** *** *** *** ***

Larry Mark Harris--born March 17, 1933 at Brooklyn, New York--attended City College of New York--New York, New York.

Son of Bernard N. & Hilda (Warshauer) Harris--unmarried.

Editor, Scott Meredith Literary Agency, 1952-1957; Free-Lance Writer, 1957-DATE-- Member: Mystery Writers of America; Hydra Club.

*LAURENCE M. JANIFER (continued)

Mr. Janifer discusses his change of name:

"'Harris' was a name given to my paternal grandfather when he got off the boat (from Poland), since the poor man spoke no English and had no idea what was going forward. The story of our christening, so to call it, has been a family joke throughout the generations. I determined, though, to be named for my line, rather than by an immigration inspector, and began digging round for the original name. Most of the people who knew it were dead or senile. After six years of searching, in the Summer of 1962, my brother found the name for me, and I immediately resumed it-- or changed it, if you like the phrasing. My mother and brother (the only other people concerned) have not changed, and remain Harrises. 'Janifer' is the simplest spelling of a Polish name meaning, simply, 'inhabitant of, or person from, Janov', a town in what is sometimes Poland and sometimes Russia, depending on how things go. The switch from H. to J. was advised against by several editors, many friends, two agents, and very nearly everyone else. It doesn't seem to have done any public harm or good; it has done me good. It has made for no strain between my Harris family and me. I have never changed my name legally, and have no intent of doing so-- it's an unnecessary complication. I may, of course, use any name I wish as long as there is no intent to defraud involved; very well, I use Janifer. 'Laurence' for the previous 'Larry' was a matter entirely of euphony. It's surprising, when you get to digging, how many Harrises (this by the way) turn out to be remote results of immigration christening. There are lots of other Janifers--at least one other with my spelling in Manhattan alone, and many others all over spelling the name Janover, Jannifer, Janiver, Janoffer, and many other variants; also counted in this confusing tribe are all the people named Janov, Janoff, and their variants. I went to high school with a boy named David Janov, and now buy my paper and typewriter-ribbons from a store owner named Janoff; the world is much too small."

(JULIE ANN JARDINE)

		with *Larry Maddock as *Howard L. Cory
1)	1966 Ace	The Sword of Lankor. (P)
2)	1966 Ace	The Mind Monsters. (P)

FPS: "The Party," Fling, 1958 (as *Corrie Howard with *Larry Maddock).
FSF: "When the Spirit Moves You," Fling, 1959 (as *Corrie Howard with *Larry Maddock).

***   ***   ***   ***   ***

Julie Anne Jardine--born February 6, 1926 at Harbin, Manchuria--Mesa, Arizona.

(JULIE ANN JARDINE)(continued)

Daughter of Mr. & Mrs. Hariton Shohor--(2) Jack Owen Jardine: 1958/February 2, 1967--Sabra Fiona Jardine (10).

Dancer and Stage Performer for thirty years; Free-Lance Writer--Member: Temple Beth Sholem.

Hobbies: Sewing, reading, cooking, her daughter.

F. A. JAVOR

1) 1967 Signet   The Rim-World Legacy. (P)

FKP: "Patriot,"   Astounding, August, 1963.

Frank A. Javor is a member of Science Fiction Writers of America.

WILL F. JENKINS

1)   1931 Brewer   Murder Madness.
2)   1946 Fell   The Murder of the U.S.A. (RP/RPv)
2A) 1950 News Stand   Destroy the U.S.A. (P)

                            as *Murray Leinster
3)   1949 Fell   The Last Spaceship. (RP)
4)   1949 Crestwood   Fight for Life. (P)
5)   1950 Shasta   Sidewise in Time. (s)
6)   1951 Random   Great Stories of Science Fiction. (@)
7)   1953 Shasta   1   Space Platform. (RP)
8)   1953 Shasta   2   Space Tug. (RP)
9)   1954 Ace   Gateway to Elsewhere. (P)
10) 1954 Gnome   The Forgotten Planet. (RP)
11) 1954 Ace   The Brain-Stealers. (P)
12) 1954 Fantasy   Operation: Outer Space. (RP)
13) 1954 Galaxy   The Black Galaxy. (P)
14) 1955 Ace   The Other Side of Here. (P)
15) 1957 Avalon   City on the Moon. (RP)
16) 1957 Gnome   Colonial Survey. (RPv)
16A) 1957 Avon   The Planet Explorer. (P)
17) 1958 Avalon   Out of This World.
18) 1958 Gold Medal   War with the Gizmos. (P)
19) 1959 Gold Medal   The Monster from World's End. (P)
20) 1959 Ace   The Mutant Weapon. (P)

WILL F. JENKINS (continued)

21)	1959 Ace		The Pirates of Zan. (P)
22)	1959 Gold Medal		Four from Planet 5. (P)
23)	1960 Avon		Monsters and Such. (s/P)
24)	1960 Avon		Twists in Time. (s/P)
25)	1960 Avon		The Wailing Asteroid. (P)
26)	1960 Berkley		Men into Space. (P)
27)	1960 Berkley		The Aliens. (s/P)
28)	1961 Berkley		Creatures of the Abyss. (P)
29)	1961 Ace		This World Is Taboo. (P)
30)	1962 Avon		Talents, Inc. (P)
31)	1962 Berkley		Operation Terror. (P)
32)	1964 Pyramid		Doctor to the Stars. (P)
33)	1964 Ace		The Duplicators. (P)
34)	1964 Berkley		The Other Side of Nowhere. (P)
35)	1964 Pyramid		Time Tunnel. (P)
36)	1964 Macfadden		The Greks Bring Gifts. (P)
37)	1964 Berkley		Invaders of Space. (P)
38)	1966 Ace		Space Captain. (P)
39)	1966 Belmont		Get Off My World! (s/P)
40)	1966 Berkley		Checkpoint Lambda. (P)
41)	1967 Pyramid	-1	The Time Tunnel. (P)
42)	1967 Avon		Miners in the Sky. (P)
43)	1967 Avon		Space Gypsies. (P)
44)	1967 Pyramid	-2	Timeslip! (P)
45)	1967 Ace		S.O.S. from Three Worlds. (s/P)
46)	1968 Sidgwick		A Murray Leinster Omnibus. (31/37/40)
47)	1968 Pyramid	+1	Land of the Giants. (P)

SER: 2) Time Tunnel; 3) Land of the Giants. (P)

FPS: Twelve epigrams to   Smart Set Magazine, 1915.
FSF: "Oh, Aladdin!"   Argosy, January 11, 1919.

WIP: 1969 Pyramid   +2   The Hot Spot. (P)
       1969 Pyramid   +3   Unknown Danger. (P)

***   ***   ***   ***   ***

William Fitzgerald Jenkins--born June 16, 1896 at Norfolk, Virginia--<u>Liberty</u> Short-Short Story Award of $1000, 1937, "A Very Nice Family;" Hugo Award, Best Novelette, 1956, "Exploration Team;" Guest of Honor, 21st World Science Fiction Convention (DisCon), 1963--Gloucester, Virginia.

WILL F. JENKINS (continued)

Son of George Briggs & Mary Louise (Murry) Jenkins--Mary Mandola: August 9, 1921--Mary Jenkins Daniels; Elizabeth Jenkins Hardit; Wenllian Jenkins Stallings; Joan P. Jenkins.

Free-Lance Writer, 1915-DATE.

Mr. Jenkins makes this comment on his career:
"The only freakish stuff is that I invented Front Projection, got two patents out on it, and collect occasional sums from the Front Projection Corporation in New York."

He also mentions:
"You ask about my first professional sales. The very first one of all was of six epigrams--no, twelve, to Smart Set Magazine, then edited by H. L. Mencken and George Jean Nathan. This was in 1915, but I can't give you a publication date. As epigrams, they were unsigned and used as fillers, and were undoubtedly scattered through several issues. Groff Conklin once observed that at least eight thousand people went around at cocktail parties, saying negligently that they used to write half the epigrams in Smart Set, and Mencken the other half. I was the one person who did not say that at cocktail parties. I was rarely invited. But I could have said it and proved it."

Mr. Jenkins was recently presented a plague by the Newark Science Fiction Club in celebration of his fifty years writing science fiction.

GEORGE CLAYTON JOHNSON

1) 1967 Delacorte — with William F. Nolan (q.v.) Logan's Run. (RP)

FKP: "The Freeway," Gamma, 1963 (Spring).

RAY W. JOHNSON

1) 1960 Exposition — Astera: The Planet That Committed Suicide.

Ray W. Johnson was born in 1900.

D. F. JONES

1) 1966 Hart-Davis — Colossus. (RP)
2) 1967 Hart-Davis — Implosion.

Dennis Feltham Jones.

GONNER JONES

1) 1968 Faber   The Dome.

NEIL R. JONES

1) 1967 Ace   1   The Planet of the Double Sun. (s/P)
2) 1967 Ace   2   The Sunless World. (s/P)
3) 1967 Ace   3   Space War. (s/P)
4) 1967 Ace   4   Twin Worlds. (s/P)
5) 1968 Ace   5   Doomsday on Ajiat. (s/P)

SER: Professor Jameson Space Adventure.

FPS: "The Death's Head Meteor," Air Wonder Stories, January, 1930.

***   ***   ***   ***   ***

Neil Ronald Jones--born May 29, 1909 at Fulton, New York--Fulton, New York.

Son of Clarence E. & Etta (Davis) Jones--Rita Gwendoline Rees: June 19, 1945-September 28, 1964--no children.

Unemployment Insurance Claims Examiner, New York State.

Mr. Jones supplied the following comments on his work:
"Most of my work come under one of three categories: 1) The Professor Jameson Series; 2) Tales of the 24th Century; 3) Tales of the 26th Century. The latter two are historical in nature, as characters and events from one story often tie in with those of another. My story, 'The Citadel in Space,' is from the 26th Century Series, as is my first professional sale, 'The Death's Head Meteor.' On the other hand, 'Hermit of Saturn's Ring," which was reprinted by Don Wollheim in his Flight Into Space anthology, is from the earlier series. A good many readers mention my Durna Rangue stories as a definite series. Possibly, but these tales interwork into both historical series. For in the 26th Century we find that the cult has banded together with space pirates, and has conquered the earth (as related in the above-mentioned 'Citadel in Space').

"As for my Professor Jameson series, there are now thirty written stories, of which 23 have seen publication. Don Wollheim terms the series the longest-lived in sf history: 'The Jameson Satellite' first appeared in 1931, while the 22nd and 23rd stories appeared for the first time early this year, making a total span of 37 years. The Professor has been discontinued several times during this period, but he always seems to bob back to the top again eventually. When Ace began reprinting the earlier stories, I wrote the last three ('The Satellite Sun," 'Hidden World,' and 'The Metal Menace'), and began the 31st ('The Sun Dwellers'). The series is just what it is and can be nothing more. There are no human characteristics or situations, only novel phenomena, plenty of adventure, and action on strange worlds. There is no final conclusion to the series: why should there be when its entire theme deals with infinity?"

RAYMOND F. JONES

1)	1951	FPCI	The Toymaker. (s)
2)	1951	Gnome	Renaissance. (RPv)
3)	1951	Galaxy	The Alien. (P)
4)	1952	Shasta	This Island Earth.
5)	1952	Winston	Son of the Stars.
6)	1953	Winston	Planet of Light.
7)	1956	Avalon	The Secret People. (RPv)
8)	1958	Winston	The Year When Stardust Fell.
7A)	1959	Beacon	The Deviates. (P)
9)	1962	Avalon	The Cybernetic Brains. (RP)
2A)	1963	Pyramid	Man of Two Worlds. (P)
10)	1964	Belmont	The Non-Statistical Man. (P)
11)	1965	Whitman	Voyage to the Bottom of the Sea.

FKP: "Test of the Gods,"   Astounding, September, 1941.

WIP: 1969 Belmont   Syn. (P)

Raymond F. Jones was born in 1915.

M. K. JOSEPH

1)   1967 Gollancz   The Hole in the Zero. (RP)

FPS: 1958 Gollancz   I'll Soldier No More.
FSF: 1967 Gollancz   The Hole in the Zero.

***   ***   ***   ***   ***

Michael Kennedy Joseph--born July 9, 1914 at Chingford, Essex, England--B.A., Auckland University College, 1933; M.A., Auckland University College, 1934; B.A., Merton College, Oxford University, 1938; B.Litt., Merton College, 1939; M.A., Merton College, 1946--Auckland, New Zealand.

Son of George Frederick & Ernestine (Kennedy) Joseph--Mary Julia Antonovich: August 23, 1947--Anthony Joseph; Charles Joseph; Barbara Joseph; Peter Joseph; Nicholas Joseph.

Lecturer in English, University of Auckland, 1935-1936, 1946-1959; Associate Professor of English, 1960-1968; Professor, 1969-DATE.

M. K. JOSEPH (continued)

Mr. Joseph answered the editors' questions in this way:

"The current state of science fiction--interesting but a bit pretentious. It's good to see sf that has imagination and style; yet I'm old fashioned enough to feel a pull towards 'hard-line' sf (even though I'm too scientifically illiterate to write it).

"Where is it headed? No further, I hope, in the direction of avant-garde and general campiness. Delany or Aldiss I like (though I still prefer a book like Dune), whereas it seems to me that Dangerous Visions is fifty percent failure, and that William Burroughs shows a fundamental contempt for the form. Space Odyssey, yes; Barbarella, no.

"Why I began to write. Although I've enjoyed sf since about the age of eight, I still feel that it's a highly professional field to enter, and that my own novel was a bit cheeky. I mightn't have attempted it if it hadn't been for a suggestion from my publishers. But I like and value sf for the same reason that I like and value The Faerie Queen, The Tempest, Paradise Lost or The Ancient Mariner--because the tradition of romance gives an extra dimension which is missing from strict realism.

"The Hole in the Zero began with an idea from Satan's journey through chaos in Paradise Lost, Book II. The general idea was to do something like this in sf terms, and thus to make a story--all novel-writing comes back in the end to storytelling. The 'chaos' of the book developed into a set of simple exercises on cause and effect, free will and determinism.

"I can't, of course, judge its success as a novel; but it's my first novel (out of three) to reach an American edition, as well as translation rights (Danish and French). I'd like to try another, but write slowly, in the intervals of a very fulltime job. At present I'm completing an edition of Frankenstein, to be published by Oxford University Press late this year."

MacKINLAY KANTOR

1)   1961 Bantam   If the South Had Won the Civil War. (P)

MacKinlay Kantor was born in 1904. A complete biography may be found in Who's Who in America.

COLIN KAPP

1)   1964 Berkley   Transfinite Man. (P)
1A) 1965 Corgi   The Dark Mind. (P)

FKP: "Life Plan,   New Worlds, November, 1958.

HERBERT KASTLE

1) 1964 Gold Medal	The Reassembled Man. (P)	
FPS: "The Slow Draw,"	Thrilling Western, 1955.	
FSF: "The York Problem,"	If, February, 1955.	

***   ***   ***   ***   ***

Herbert David Kastle --born July 11, 1924 at Brooklyn, New York--B.A., Washington Square College of Arts and Sciences, 1949; M.A., New York University, 1950--Peekskill, New York.

Son of Meyer & Eva (Katz) Kastle--Laura: 1949/divorced--Rhona Deborah Kastle (16); Matthew Lloyd Kastle (11).

Free-Lance Writer--Member: Writers Guild of America, West.

DAY KEENE

1) 1960 Gold Medal	with Leonard Pruyn (q.v.) World Without Women. (P)
FKP: "Dead Man's Shoes,"	Weird Tales, March, 1950

JOSEPH E. KELLEAM

1)	1956 Ace	Overlords from Space. (P)
2)	1960 Avalon	The Little Men.
3)	1960 Avalon	Hunters of Space.
4)	1966 Avalon	When the Red King Awoke.
FPS:	"Rust,"	Astounding, October, 1939.

***   ***   ***   ***   ***

Joseph Everidge Kelleam--born February 11, 1913 at Boswell, Oklahoma--attended Oklahoma University; Southwestern Technical College; B.S., Central State College, 1936; graduate study at Central State College, 1936--Garvin, Oklahoma.

Son of Dr. Edwin A. & Ophelia (Everidge) Kelleam--Alta Tolle: October 6, 1934--Aljo Kelleam Gregg (29); Edwina Kelleam (16).

JOSEPH E. KELLEAM (continued)

Has been with the United States Army Engineers; was a Contract Officer with the United States Air Force; currently a retired ranch owner--Member: Science Fiction Writers of America; Oklahoma Poetry Writers; Sigma Tau Delta; Pi Kappa Phi.

Mr. Kelleam's family was among the first five or six to settle in southeast Oklahoma.

LEO P. KELLEY

1) 1967 Belmont   The Counterfeits. (P)
2) 1968 Belmont   Odyssey to Earthdeath. (P)

NOTE: Due to a typographical error, the byline on #1 was "Leo F. Kelley."

FPS: "Dreamtown, U.S.A." If, February, 1955.

WIP: Dell   Mythmaster. (P)
        Lancer   Weapon 7. (P)
        Berkley   Coins. (P)
        Belmont   The Accidental Earth. (P)

***   ***   ***   ***   ***

Leo Patrick Kelley--born September 10, 1928 at Wilkes Barre, Pennsylvania--B.A., The New School for Social Research, 1957--New York, New York.

Son of Leo A. & Regina (Caffrey) Kelley--unmarried.

Employed (Copywriter to Advertising Manager) by McGraw-Hill Book Company, 1959-1969; Free-Lance Writer, June, 1969-DATE--Member: Science Fiction Writers of America; Mystery Writers of America; National Fantasy Fan Federation; Mensa.

ROBERT KELLY

1) 1967 Doubleday   The Scorpions.

***   ***   ***   ***   ***

Robert Kelly (i)--born September 24, 1935 at Brooklyn, New York--A.B., City College of New York, 1955; graduate study at Columbia University, 1955-1958--Annandale-on-Hudson, New York.

ROBERT KELLY (continued)

Son of Samuel Jason & Margaret (Kane) Kelly--(1) Joan Lasker: August 27, 1955/1969; (2) Helen Belinkaya: April 17, 1969--no children.

Lecturer in English, Wagner College, 1960-1961; Assistant Professor of English, Bard College, 1961-1969; Associate Professor, 1969-DATE; Assistant Professor of English, State University of New York at Buffalo, 1964; Visiting Lecturer in Modern Poetry, Tufts University, 1966; Conductor, Fiction Workshop, New York Writers Conference, 1967; Founder-Editor, Chelsea Review, 1958-1960; Co-Editor, Trobar, 1960-1965; Editor, Matter, 1963-DATE; Contributing Editor, Caterpillar, 1968-DATE--Member: Phi Beta Kappa.

Mr. Kelly writes:
"It should be noted that I'm not a writer of sf as such (splendid though that field may be). Of my 16 or 17 books, only The Scorpions has been taken as sf. I'm a poet, and most of my books are, accordingly, books of poems."

---

*JAMES KENNAWAY

1)	1963 Longmans Pan	The Mind Benders. (H-P)
FPS:	1956 Putnam	Tunes of Glory.
FSF:	1963 Longmans Pan	The Mind Benders. (H-P)

***   ***   ***   ***   ***   ***

James Ewing Peebles--born June 5, 1928 at Perthshire, Scotland--attended Trinity College, Oxford University--London, England.

Son of Charles Gray & Marjory Helen Peebles--Susan: 1951--Emma Peebles (15); Jane Peebles (13); Guy Peebles (12); David Peebles (9).

Editor, Longmans, Green, 1951-1957; Free-Lance Writer, 1957-1968--Member: Royal Institution; Chelsea Arts Club; Raffles Club, Chelsea.

Mr. Kennaway was killed in an automobile accident the evening of December 21, 1968.

DANIEL KEYES

1)	1966 Harcourt	Flowers of Algernon. (RP)
2)	1968 Harcourt	The Touch.
FPS:	"Precedent," Marvel Science Fiction, May, 1952.	

***   ***   ***   ***   ***   ***

DANIEL KEYES (continued)

Daniel Keyes--born August 9, 1927 at Brooklyn, New York--A.B., Brooklyn College, 1950; A.M., Brooklyn College, 1961--Hugo Award, Best Short Fiction, 1960, "Flowers for Algernon;" Nebula Award, Best Novel, 1966, Flowers for Algernon; Elected to Science Fiction Hall of Fame, 1969, "Flowers for Algernon"--Athens, Ohio.

Son of William & Betty (Alicke) Keyes--Aurea Vazquez: October 14, 1952-- Hillary Ann Keyes (9); Leslie Joan Keyes (5).

Associate Editor, Marvel Science Fiction, February, 1951-November, 1951; Instructor in English, Wayne State University, 1962-1966; Lecturer in English, Ohio University, 1966-DATE; Free-Lance Writer--Member: Science Fiction Writers of America; P.E.N.; Modern Language Association.

---

*NOEL KEYES

1) 1963 Pap Lib   Contact. (@/P)

FPS: "Black Eyes and Truculence," Cavalier, September, 1961 (as David N. Keightley).
FSF: 1963 Pap Lib   Contact. (@/P)

***   ***   ***   ***   ***

David Noel Keightley--born October 25, 1932 at London, England--B.A., Amherst College, 1953; M.A., New York University, 1956; Ph.D. (Chinese History), Columbia University, 1969--New York, New York.

Son of Mr. & Mrs. Walter A. Keightley--married August 20, 1965--Steven Traylor Keightley (1).

Free-Lance Writer, 1960-1962; Graduate Student, 1962-1969.

---

*JOHN KIPPAX

1) 1968 Macdonald   1   with Dan Morgan (q.v.)
                          Thunder of Stars.

FKP: "Dimple," Science Fantasy, December, 1954; "Trojan Hearse," New Worlds, December, 1954 (with Dan Morgan)(simultaneous)

WIP: 2   Deadly Harvest. (with Dan Morgan)

John Kippax is a penname of John Hynam.

JAY KAY KLEIN

1)	1961 Klein	Convention Annual #1--Pittcon, (nf/P)
2)	1963 Klein	Convention Annual #2--Chicon III. (nf/P)
3)	1964 Klein	Convention Annual #3--Discon. (nf/P)
4)	1968 Klein	Convention Annual #4--Tricon. (nf/P)

FPS: "The Towering Problem," QST, October, 1962.
FPP: 1961 Klein   Convention Annual #1--Pittcon. (nf/P)

***   ***   ***   ***   ***

Jay Kay Klein--born July 28, 1931 at Philadelphia, Pennsylvania--B.A. (Cum Laude), Syracuse University, 1953; graduate study in English at Syracuse University, 1955-1959--New York Press Association Scholarship; New York War Veterans Scholarship--North Syracuse, New York.

Son of Louis & Florence Klein-unmarried.

Has been an assistant editor for a water works association; a Teaching Assistant in the English Department of Syracuse University; a Technical Writer of United States Military Handbooks on radar systems and missile complexes; currently an Advertising Specialist with General Electric in charge of national advertising with authorized GE semiconductor distributors--Member: Science Fiction Writers of America; First Fandom; National Fantasy Fan Federation; Philadelphia Science Fiction Association; Queens Science Fiction League; Eastern Science Fiction Association.

Mr. Klein's first science fiction short story, "On Conquered Earth," was published in If, December, 1967.

MARY CONWAY KLOOR

1)   1963 Vantage   My Beloved Troshanus.

Mary Conway Kloor could not be located.

DAMON KNIGHT

1)	1955 Lion	Hell's Pavement. (P)
2)	1956 Advent	In Search of Wonder. (nf/RHe)
3)	1959 Zenith	The People Maker. (P)
4)	1959 Ace	Masters of Evolution. (P)
5)	1961 Ace	The Sun Saboteurs. (P)
6)	1961 S&S	Far Out. (s/RP)

DAMON KNIGHT (continued)

7)	1962 S&S	A Century of Science Fiction. (@/RP)
1A)	1962 Berkley	Analogue Men. (P)
8)	1963 Lancer	First Flight: Maiden Voyages in Space and Time. (@/P)
9)	1963 Berkley	In Deep. (s/P/RH)
10)	1964 Doubleday	Beyond the Barrier. (RP)
11)	1964 Delacorte	A Century of Great Short Science Fiction Novels. (@/RP)
12)	1964 Gold Medal	Tomorrow x 4. (@/P)
13)	1965 Doubleday	The Dark Side. (@/RP)
14)	1965 Harper	Beyond Tomorrow. (@/RP)
15)	1965 Pop Lib	The Shape of Things. (@/P)
16)	1965 Ace	Off Center. (s/P)
17)	1965 Ace	The Rithian Terror. (P)
18)	1965 Bantam	13 French Science-Fiction Stories. (@/P)
3A)	1965 Berkley	A for Anything. (P)
19)	1965 Berkley	Mind Switch. (P/RHv)
20)	1966 Doubleday	Cities of Wonder. (@/RP)
21)	1966 Berkley	Orbit 1. (@/P/RH)
22)	1966 Doubleday	Turning On. (s/RP)
23)	1966 Doubleday	Nebula Award Stories 1965. (@/RP)
19A)	1966 Whiting	The Other Foot. (RP)
24)	1967 Advent	In Search of Wonder. (2/e/RP)
25)	1967 Doubleday	Three Novels. (s/RP)
26)	1967 Berkley	Orbit 2. (@/P/RH)
27)	1967 Lancer	Science Fiction Inventions. (@/P)
28)	1967 Harper	Worlds to Come. (@/RP)
29)	1968 Putnam	Orbit 3. (@/RP)
30)	1968 S&S	One Hundred Years of Science Fiction. (@)
31)	1968 Belmont	The Metal Smile. (@/P)
32)	1968 S&S	Toward Infinity: Nine Science Fiction Tales. (s)
33)	1968 Putnam	Orbit 4. (@/RP)

FPS: "Resilience," Stirring Science Stories, February, 1941.

WIP: 1969 Putnam Orbit 5. (@/RP)
 1969 Putnam Orbit 6. (@)

***   ***   ***   ***   ***

Damon Francis Knight--born September 20, 1922 at Baker, Oregon--Hugo Award, Best Critic, 1956--Madeira Beach, Florida.

Son of Frederick S. & Leola (Damon) Knight--(2) Kate Wilhelm: February, 1963--1) Valerie Knight (15); Christopher Knight (13); Leslie Knight (Daughter 8); 2) Jonathan Knight (2).

DAMON KNIGHT (continued)

Editor, Worlds Beyond, December, 1950-February, 1951 (all issues); If, October, 1958-February, 1959; Book Editor, Science Fiction Adventures, February, 1953-May, 1954; The Magazine of Fantasy and Science Fiction, April, 1959-September, 1960; Free-Lance Writer and Editor--Member: Science Fiction Writers of America (Founding President, 1965-1967).

Director, Milford Science Fiction Writers' Conference, 1956-DATE. Founding Editor, Science Fiction Writers of America Bulletin, July, 1965-June, 1967.

NORMAN L. KNIGHT

1) 1967 Doubleday   with James Blish (q.v.)
                         A Torrent of Faces. (RP)

FPS: "Frontier of the Unknown," Astounding, July, 1937.

***   ***   ***   ***   ***

Norman Louis Knight--born September 21, 1895 at St. Joseph, Missouri--B.S. (in Chemical Engineering), George Washington University, 1925--Achievement Award, United States Department of Agriculture, 1962--Silver Spring, Maryland.

Son of Louis Ruthven & Mary Elizabeth (Stauber) Knight--Marie Sarah Yenn: June 4, 1921--Paula Marie Knight Hendrickson (46).

Assistant Observer, Observer, and Code Translator, United States Weather Bureau, 1919-1925; Pesticide Chemist, United States Food and Drug Administration and the Pesticide Regulation Division, United States Department of Agriculture, 1925-1963; currently retired--Member: Science Fiction Writers of America.

Concerning his book, Mr. Knight writes:
   "I wrote the parts pertaining to the Tritons, at Jim's request, since I invented them. Also the chapter, 'A Walk in the Paradise Garden.' The rest is Jim's handiwork; he also edited and improved my sections."

----

*ZENO KOOMOTER

1) 1964 Vantage   Visitor from Planet Phlox.

Zeno Koomoter is a penname of Joseph Marnell.

DEAN R. KOONTZ

1) 1968 Ace   Star Quest. (P)

FPS: "The Kittens," Readers and Writers.
FSF: "Soft Come the Dragons," The Mazagine of Fantasy and Science Fiction, August, 1967.

WIP: 1969 Ace   The Fall of the Dream Machine. (P)
        1969 Ace   Fear That Man. (P)

"Have finished and placed with agent seven more books, four of which are science fiction. Am especially interested in one titled The Dark Symphony, an sf book structured like a 19th century symphony, complete with movements, tempo changes, and carefully structured moods. Am working with Vaughn Bodé on a series of multi-media books that will employ fiction and artwork in such a way that the art will be more than mere illustration."

***   ***   ***   ***   ***

Dean Ray Koontz--born July 9, 1945 at Everett, Pennsylvania--holds a Bachelor's Degree--Atlantic Monthly Creative Writing Award--Harrisburg, Pennsylvania.

Son of Ray & Florence Koontz--Gerda: October 15, 1966--no children.

Was an English teacher under the Applachian Program, and in a suburban school district; Free-Lance Writer, January, 1969-DATE--Member: Science Fiction Writers of America.

MICHAEL KURLAND

                    with Chester Anderson (q.v.)
1) 1964 Pyramid   Ten Years to Doomsday. (P)

FPS: 1964 Pyramid   Ten Years to Doomsday. (P/with Chester Anderson)

WIP: 1969 Pyramid   The Unicorn Girl. (P)
        1969 Pyramid   Transmission Error. (P)
        Berkley   The Reticent Listener. (P)

***   ***   ***   ***   ***

MICHAEL KURLAND (continued)

Michael J. Kurland (u)--born March 1, 1938 at Brooklyn, New York--attended Hiram College; University of Maryland (Germany); Columbia University--New York, New York.

Son of Jack & Stephanie (Yacht) Kurland--unmarried.

Free-Lance Writer--Member: Science Fiction Writers of America.

R. A. LAFFERTY

1)	1968 Ace	Past Master. (P/RH)
2)	1968 Berkley	The Reefs of Earth. (P)
3)	1968 Ace	Space Chantey. (P)

FPS: "The Wagons," New Mexico Quarterly Review, Spring, 1959.
FSF: "Day of the Glacier," Science Fiction, January, 1960.

WIP: 1969 Ace   Fourth Mansions. (P)

***   ***   ***   ***   ***

Raphael Aloysius Lafferty--born November 7, 1914 at Neola, Iowa--irregular college and correspondence courses--Tulsa, Oklahoma.

Son of Hugh David & Julia Mary (Burke) Lafferty--unmarried.

"Worked in electrical business most of my life"--Member: Science Fiction Writers of America.

Mr. Lafferty was raised in Oklahoma, and began writing in 1958.

ALLEN KIM LANG

1) 1966 Chilton   Wild and Outside.

FSF: "Machine of Klamugra," Planet Stories, November, 1950.

***   ***   ***   ***   ***

ALLEN KIM LANG (continued)

Allen Kim Lang--born July 31, 1928 at Fort Wayne, Indiana--attended Indiana University; Roosevelt University--Chicago, Illinois.

Son of Frank J. & Ona J. (Allen) Lang--Alberta R. Miller-- no children.

Blood Bank Supervisor, Michael Reese Research Foundation Blood Center--Member: Science Fiction Writers of America; Mystery Writers of America; Fellowship of Reconciliation.

GEORGE LANGELAAN

1)   1964 Mayflower   Out of Time. (P)

KEITH LAUMER

1)	1962 Ace		Worlds of the Imperium. (P/RH)
2)	1963 Berkley		A Trace of Memory. (P)
3)	1963 Ace	1	Envoy to New Worlds. (s/P)
4)	1964 S&S		The Great Time Machine Hoax. (RP)
5)	1965 Berkley		A Plague of Demons. (P)
6)	1965 Doubleday	2	Galactic Diplomat. (s/RP)
7)	1965 Berkley		The Other Side of Time. (P/RH)
8)	1966 Berkley		The Time Bender. (P)
9)	1966 Doubleday	3	Retief's War. (RP)
11)	1966 Berkley		Catastrophe Planet. (P)
12)	1966 Berkley		The Monitors. (P/RH)
13)	1967 Doubleday		Nine by Laumer. (s/RP)
14)	1967 Pyramid	-1	The Invaders. (s/P)
15)	1967 Berkley		Galactic Odyssey. (P/RH)
16)	1967 Pyramid	-2	Enemies from Beyond. (s/P)
18)	1968 Doubleday		The Day Before Forever and Thunderhead. (RP)
19)	1968 Berkley		Greylorn. (s/P/RHv)
20)	1968 Berkley	+5	"The Afrit Affair." (P)
21)	1968 Berkley	+6	"The Drowned Queen." (P)
22)	1968 Berkley		Assignment in Nowhere. (P)
23)	1968 Berkley	+7	"The Gold Bomb." (P)
19A)	1968 Dobson		The Other Sky. (s)
24)	1968 Doubleday	4	Retief and the Warlords.
25)	1968 Berkley		It's a Mad, Mad, Mad Galaxy. (s/P)

with Rosel George Brown

~~10)~~ ~~1966~~ Doubleday   Earthblood. (RP)

KEITH LAUMER (continued)

			with Gordon R. Dickson (q.v.)
17)	1967 Doubleday		Planet Run. (RP)
			as *Anthony LeBaron
14A)	1968 Corgi		The Meteor Men. (s/P)

SER: 1) Retief; 2) The Invaders; 3) The Avengers.
UNNUMBERED SERIES: #14A--The Invaders (British).

FPS: "Greylorn," Amazing, April, 1959.

WIP:	1969 Doubleday	5	Retief: Ambassador to Space. (s)
	1969 Putnam		The Long Twilight.
	Berkley		The Time Trap. (P)
	Berkley		The Glass Tree. (P)
	Berkley		Star Treasure. (P)
	Berkley		The House in November. (P)
	Berkley		The Shape Changer. (P)
	Berkley		Night of Delusions. (P)
	Doubleday		Once There Was a Giant. (s)
	Doubleday	6	Retief of the CDT.

***   ***   ***   ***   ***

John Keith Laumer--born June 9, 1925 at Syracuse, New York--attended University of Stockholm, 1948; B.Sc., University of Illinois, 1950; B.Sc. in Architecture, University of Illinois, 1952--Brooksville, Florida.

Son of Major & Mrs. William F. Laumer--Janice Perkinson: February, 1949/ September, 1968--Tom Wright (25); Virginia Kathleen Laumer (19); Janice Antoinette Laumer (17); Sabrina Dian Laumer (13).

Has been an Officer in the United States Air Force; Vice Consul, United States Foreign Service, 1956-1958 (in Burma); Free-Lance Writer, 1958-DATE-- Member: Science Fiction Writers of America.

The following excerpts are taken from a letter of Mr. Laumer:
"..... As to the current state of sf, it is enjoying unprecedented economic prosperity, with many major publishers getting into the act. Its scope is broadening at the same time that the limitations of 'mainstream' fiction are disappearing; thus, sf is merging with the mainstream--or possibly the mainstream is merging with so-called sf. 'Science Fiction' is, of course, a terrible piece of nomenclature. It reflects the primitive preoccupation with technological developments that were the chief evidence that the future was happening, back in the 20's. Remember, people like Hugo Gernsback grew up in a world without airplanes, radio, etc.;phones, phonographs, automobiles were rare. As for jets, TV, space technology, they were assumed to be five hundred years ahead. Naturally they were awed and fascinated by the transformation.

KEITH LAUMER (continued)

"Today we've gotten into the rhythm of change. We are no longer hung up on the idea that some ICS educated dropout is going to invent a time machine in his basement. We are exploring the new horizons of human experience opened up, or to be opened up, by the changes that have come or are coming. The emphasis on the human condition, human accomodation to a widening universe, is the concern of modern 'sf.' The 'New Wave' seems to be a term that can be applied to (a) any story you like, or (b) any story you don't like, depending on whether you consider yourself a New Wave fan. The only actual earmark I can sometimes detect in a group of alleged New Wave stories is a preoccupation with stylistic devices, as opposed to story values.

"I began writing by sitting down at the typewriter one day, while in Rangoon, Burma (and suffering from amoebic dysentery), and typing out the kind of story I wanted to read ("Greylorn"). As for my contribution to the development of the genre, I doubt if I have made one. I am probably too 'reactionary' to have influenced its course; by reactionary, I mean that I have been well content to accept the conventions of literature as I found them, and work within the framework, devoting my ingenuity to devising stories and characters and dialogue, and getting across (I hope) a few ideas which I consider important."

HENRY L. LAWRENCE

1)   1960 Macdonald   Children of Light. (RP)

Henry Lionel Lawrence.

DECIMA LEACH

1)   1962 Stockwell   The Garthians.

URSULA K. LE GUIN

1)   1966 Ace   Rocannon's World. (P)
2)   1966 Ace   Planet of Exile. (P)
3)   1967 Ace   City of Illusions. (P)
4)   1968 Parnassus   A Wizard of Earthsea.

FPS: "April in Paris," Fantastic, September, 1962.

WIP: 1969 Ace   The Left Hand of Darkness. (P/RH)

***   ***   ***   ***   ***

URSULA K. LE GUIN (continued)

Ursula LeGuin--born October 21, 1929 at Berkeley, California--B.A., Radcliffe College, 1951; M.A., Columbia University, 1952--London, England/Portland, Oregon.

Daughter of Alfred L. & Theodora (Kracaw) Kroeber--C. A. Le'Guin: December 22, 1953--Elisabeth Le Guin (1957); Caroline Le Guin (1959); Theodore Le Guin (1964).

Free-Lance Writer--Member: Science Fiction Writers of America; Phi Beta Kappa.

In response to a question, Mrs. Le Guin writes:
"Why do I write science fiction? In part, because my gift and inclination is for what comes out of profound fantasy when it is controlled by disciplined intelligence. I think that the imagination is as singularly human a faculty as rational intelligence, and that its uses are as various, and as necessary to our happiness as individuals and our viability as a species. I think that the imaginative faculty should be developed and trained just as intelligence is. The best and pleasantest school for such an eduction of the imagination is probably the practice, or the appreciation, of an imaginative art."

FRITZ LEIBER

1)	1947 Arkham		Night's Black Agents. (s/RPa)
2)	1950 Pellegrini		Gather, Darkness. (RP)
3)	1953 Lion		Conjure Wife. (P)
4)	1953 Abelard		The Green Millenium. (RP)
5)	1957 Gnome	0	Two Sought Adventure. (s)
6)	1957 Galaxy		Destiny Times Three. (P)
7)	1961 Ace		The Big Time (P)
8)	1961 Ace		The Mind Spider. (s/P)
9)	1961 Ballantine		The Silver Eggheads. (P)
10)	1962 Ballantine		Shadows With Eyes. (s/P)
11)	1964 Ballantine		The Wanderer. (P/RH)
12)	1964 Ace		Ships to the Stars. (P)
13)	1964 Ballantine		A Pail of Air. (s/P)
14)	1966 Ballantine		Tarzan and the Valley of Gold. (P)
15)	1966 Ballantine		The Night of the Wolf. (s/P)
16)	1968 Ace	1	The Swords of Lankhmar. (P)
17)	1968 Ace	2	Swords Against Wizardry. (P)
18)	1968 Hart-Davis		The Secret Songs. (s)
19)	1968 Ace	3	Swords in the Mist. (s/P)

SER: Fafhrd and the Grey Mouser.

FPS: "Two Sought Adventure," Unknown, August, 1939.

FRITZ LEIBER (continued)

WIP: 1969 Ace   Night Monsters. (s/P)
        1969 Walker   A Spectre Is Haunting Texas.
                                       further volumes in the Fafhrd series.

***   ***   ***   ***   ***

Fritz Reuter Leiber--born December 24, 1910 at Chicago, Illinois--Ph.B., University of Chicago, 1932--Hugo Award, Best Novel, 1958, The Big Time; 1965, The Wanderer; Best Novelette, 1968, "Gonna Roll the Bones;" Nebula Award, Best Novelette, 1967, "Gonna Roll the Bones;" Guest of Honor, 9th World Science Fiction Convention (Nolacon), 1951--Venice, California.

Son of Fritz & Virginia (Bronson) Leiber--Jonquil Stephens: January 16, 1936- September 3, 1969--Justin Leiber (July 8, 1938).

Free-Lance Writer--Member: Science Fiction Writers of America.

PETER LESLIE

1)	1966 Consul		Hell for Tomorrow. (P)	
3)	1966 4 Square	5	The Finger in the Sky Affair. (P)	
4)	1966	7	The Radioactive Camel Affair. (P)	
6)	1967 4 Square	10	The Diving Dames Affair. (P)	
7)	1967 4 Square	-4	The Cornish Pixie Affair. (P)	
8)	1967 Corgi		The Mogul Men. (P)	
9)	1968 4 Square	+4	The Frighteners. (P)	
10)	1968 4 Square	14	The Splintered Sunglasses Affair. (P)	
11)	1968 Corgi		The Night of the Trilobites. (P)	
12)	1968 4 Square	17	The Unfair Fare Affair. (P)	

                                          as *Patrick Macnee
2)   1966 Hodder   Deadline. (P)
5)   1967 Hodder   Dead Duck. (P)

SER: 1) The Man From U.N.C.L.E.; 2) The Girl From U.N.C.L.E.; 3) Daktari.
UNNUMBERED SERIES: #1--Danger Man (English), Secret Agent (American); #2, 5-- The Avengers; #11, 13--The Invaders.

NOTE: #4, 6, 10, 12 were reprinted in the United States with these series numbers; 7, 9, 16, and 18, respectively.

FPS: 1962 McGibbon   The Book of Bilk.
FSF: 1968 Corgi   The Night of the Trilobites. (P)

PETER LESLIE (continued)

WIP: 1969 Corgi   The Autumn Accelerator. (P)
      1969 Mayflower   The Plastic Magicians. (P)

***   ***   ***   ***   ***

Peter Leslie (u)--born February 5, 1922 at Launceston, Cornwall, England--attended The Queen's University, Belfast--Vence, France.

Son of Kenneth Chapelow & Doris Ellen Leslie--Helene Bond: November 27, 1954-deceased--Tanya Karen Leslie (November 16, 1956).

"At various times a journalist, publicist, jazz musician, draughtsman, actor, dancer, press censor, designer of record covers, typographer, magazine editor, interior decorator, columnist on showbiz, designer of film titles, radio and television broadcaster and interviewer; have also worked for Reuters, Daily Mirror, Daily Express's, Daily Herald, Odhams Press, British Broadcasting Corporation"; Free-Lance Writer--Member: Capricorn Club; Vintage Sports Car Club; Lancia Motor Club.

MILTON LESSER

1) 1952 Winston   Earthbound.
2) 1953 Beechhurst   Looking Forward. (@)
3) 1953 Winston   The Star Seekers.
4) 1959 Ace   Recruit for Andromeda. (P)
5) 1961 Holt   Stadium Beyond the Stars.
6) 1961 Holt   Spacemen, Go Home.
7) 1965 Belmont   Secret of the Black Planet. (P)

FKP: "All Heroes Are Hated," Amazing, November, 1950; "Who's That Knocking at My Door?" Amazing, November, 1950 (simultaneous).

Milton Lesser was born in 1928. A complete biography may be found in Contemporary Authors.

REX DEAN LEVIE

1) 1965 Ace   The Insect Warriors. (P)

IRWIN LEWIS

1) 1964 Avon   The Day They Invaded New York. (P)
2) 1967 Avon   The Day New York Trembled. (P)

FKP: "To Invade New York..."   Analog, August, 1963.

Irwin Lewis is a member of Science Fiction Writers of America.

ROY LEWIS

1) 1960 Hutchinson   What We Did to Father. (RPv)
1A) 1963 Penguin   The Evolution Man. (P)

FPS: "Birmingham in 1975,"   Birmingham Post, 1933.
FPP/FSP: 1931 Lewis   An Un-Natural History of Monsters. (poem)
FSF: To   The Adelphi, 1936

***   ***   ***   ***   ***

Ernest Michael Roy Lewis--born November 6, 1913 at Felixstowe, England--B.A., University College, Oxford University, 1934; graduate study at University of London, 1935-1936--Richmond, Surrey, England.

Son of Ernest I. & Susannah (Edmonds) Lewis--Christine Tew: 1938--Christine Miranda Lewis; Elizabeth Rachel Lewis.

Features Writer, Scope, 1946-1948; Assistant Editor, London Economist, 1952-1961; Assistant Foreign Editor, London Times, 1961-DATE--Member: London Library; Saville Club.

From a letter of Mr. Lewis:
    "....As regards your request that I should explain my views on science fiction: I must say that I don't think I am a writer in this field, my book Evolution Man, being something between a parable and a fantasy; though it was, I admit, published as sf, which may have indeed disappointed some readers.
    "However, I enjoy a measure of science fiction in my reading, and I might try to write some one day. (I am aging, and having to earn a living by journalism, you will understand.) My feeling is that science fiction should try to explore the effect of technological development or scientific discovery on human personality, and/or on human institutions as we know them; I am not very interested in 'Far Future' galaxy empire building, much of which extends into spacemanship (I think) only the American idea of life and politics as a perpetual cops vs. robbers story--which we effete Europeans think a bit simple. Please don't take offense!

ROY LEWIS (continued)

"It seems to me there is a case for setting up fictional 'models' of people and institutions under extraordinary impacts--i.e., you feed into a given known situation one strange event, which enables you to study reactions, or illuminate our limitations; and this is a kind of simplified drawing of what is happening to us, as the result of inventions and discoveries, all the time. I like this--but not apocalyptic visions, like Ray Bradbury's, which do not have for me any frame of reference to present human society. I feel, with renaissance man, that Man is the measure of All Things--so I must have present day society, and the personalities within it, as my module.

"Actually this is asking a terrific lot if you want to write sf credibly. What author now living can portray an American group of people, a Russian group, a Chinese group, A European group (mixed: English, French, German), and an African group to test the impact of a visitor from Mars, to take a simple case--and why should a visitor from Mars, as usually happens in these stories, spend his time in New York or London? I have travelled all over the world, except South America, and I affirm, as an Earthling, that he just would NOT. But so much science fiction, which should be global in its scenery and characterization, is parochial.

"Of course, the other thing you can do, either for imagination's sake, or satirically, is to destroy the world with the Bomb, and construct a new society-- but this is either to create a Utopia or an Erewhon, which isn't really new, or to produce a kind of bastard anthropology. Either way, you don't really deal in human emotions.

"I think imaginative writing does deal in human emotions; that's what it's for. We can read up on sociological reports, case histories, or marketing reports for the other measurements of life. What we want in novels is people, real people, and a sort of story--something a little more of a pattern, more complete than our lives are....I don't, as you see, believe in fiction producing Truth about humanity directly, only by interpretation, for which I find both plot and character vital to each other.

"When a man like Williamson writes a fantasy about animals, like Tarka the Otter, in fact he is writing about trans-bodied humanity--the virtues of effort and survival, love and sacrifice--not about animals at all, about whose consciousness we know nothing. And so it goes with the rest of fantasy, in my opinion; it is simply a way of studying human beings in an unfamiliar framework--but they must be human, very deeply so. This is where so much science fiction gives us only cardboard figurines, and rather bogus 'miracle' type science, and very inexact technology.

"Now you, as an expert, may not agree with any of this; I have friends devoted to sf who would not do so. But this is how I, as one reader, react; and I first read The War of the Worlds, and was bemused by it, in 1925, aetat. 12 or so. The people were real Victorians--my great aunt who lived with us was a Wellsian character, of 1898 vintage. So it was distressingly real."

TONY LICATA

1) 1965 Three Star   Great Science-Fiction. (@/P)

A. M. LIGHTNER

1) 1963 Putnam   The Rock of Three Planets.
2) 1965 Putnam   The Planet Poachers.
3) 1965 Norton   Doctor to the Galaxy.
4) 1965 Norton   The Galactic Troubadours.
5) 1966 Norton   The Space Plague.
6) 1967 Norton   The Space Olympics.
7) 1968 Putnam   The Space Ark.

FPS: "A New Game,"   Boys' Life, 1959.

WIP: 1969 Norton   Day of the Drones.

***   ***   ***   ***   ***

Alice Martha Lightner--born October 11, 1904 at Detroit, Michigan--B.A., Vassar College, 1927--New York, New York.

Daughter of Clarence & Frances Lightner--Ernest Joachim Hopf: 1935--Christopher Hopf (January 28, 1942).

Free-Lance Writer--Member: Science Fiction Writers of America; Authors Guild; Lepidopterists Society; New York Entomological Society; Audubon Society.

Miss Lightner mentions:
   "Day of the Drones was originally written for the adult field. It is the first novel I ever wrote, but failed to find a publisher until one of my juvenile editors happened to see it. She was enthusiastic and asked me to revise it as a juvenile. Now even before publication it has received a nibble from the film industry. In the 10 years since it was first written, the subject matter (race relations) has come to the fore."

ERIC M. LIVESEY

1) 1964 Digit   The Desolate Land. (P)

HAROLD LIVINGSTON

1) 1960 Ballantine   The Climacticon. (P)

Harold Livingston was born in 1924. A complete biography may be found in Contemporary Authors.

CHARLES R. LONG

1) 1957 Avalon   The Infinite Brain.
2) 1963 Avalon   The Eternal Man.

Charles Russell Long was born in 1904. A complete biography may be found in Contemporary Authors.

FRANK BELKNAP LONG

1) 1926 Cook   The Man from Genoa and Other Poems. (s)
2) 1935 Dragon-Fly   The Goblin Tower. (Poem/RP)
3) 1946 Arkham   The Hounds of Tindalos. (s/RPa/RPav)
4) 1949 Fell   John Carstairs, Space Detective. (s/RP)
5) 1957 Ace   Space Station #1. (P)
6) 1960 Chariot   Woman from Another Planet. (P)
7) 1961 Belmont   The Horror Expert. (P)
8) ?1962 Chariot   The Mating Center. (P)
9) 1962 Pyramid   Mars Is My Destination. (P)
10) 1963 Belmont   It Was the Day of the Robot. (P/RH)
11) 1963 Arkham   The Horror from the Hills.
12) 1963 Avalon   Three Steps Spaceward.
1A) 1964 Belmont   The Dark Beasts. (s/a/P)
13) 1964 Avalon   The Martian Visitors.
14) 1964 Avalon   Mission to a Star.
15) 1964 Belmont   Odd Science Fiction. (11/s/P)
15A) 1965 Digit   The Horror from the Hills. (11/s/P)
16) 1966 Belmont   This Strange Tomorrow. (P)
17) 1966 Belmont   Lest Earth Be Conquered. (P)
18) 1966 Lancer   So Dark a Heritage. (P)
19) 1967 Belmont   Journey Into Darkness. (P)
20) 1968 Belmont   ....And Others Shall Be Born. (P)

FRANK BELKNAP LONG (continued)

NOTE: Mr. Long mentions that the two Chariot books and the New Collectors paperbound reprint of The Goblin Tower were extensively mutilated.

FPS:	"The Desert Lich,"	Weird Tales, November, 1924.	
WIP:	1969 Tower	The Three Faces of Time. (P)	
	1969 Belmont	an untitled novel. (P)	
	1970 Arkham	The Rim of the Unknown. (s)	
		Two additional science-fantasy novels.	

***   ***   ***   ***   ***

Frank Belknap Long--born April 27, 1903 at New York, New York--attended New York University, 1920-1922; Columbia University, c. 1925--New York, New York.

Son of Dr. Frank & May (Doty) Long--Lyda Arco: August 9, 1959--no children.

Associate Editor, Satellite Science Fiction, February, 1959-May, 1959; Short Stories, c. 1959-1960; Mike Shayne Mystery Magazine, -1966; The Saint Mystery Magazine; Fantastic Universe; Free-Lance Writer and Lecturer--Member: Science Fiction Writers of America.

Mr. Long writes:
"A brief note as to my ancestral background--this sort of thing usually accompanies bibliographical listings, so I might as well make the historical record complete. A direct maternal ancestor, Edward Doty, was the only non-Puritanic rebel on the Mayflower, a young lad who was indentured to an English family. He was the first man to fight a duel on the American continent, was put in stocks, and had, I believe, about thirteen children. My paternal grandfather, a building contractor, erected the pedestal of the Statue of Liberty, and was superintendent at the statue for a number of years. I still have an obituary cutting from The New York Times--'Liberty's guardian dead.' I am of New England ancestry on my mother's side, English and Pennsylvanian Dutch on my father's."

In response to questions, Mr. Long also remarked:
"Yes, I was probably H. P. Lovecraft's closest friend for a number of years--certainly one of his two or three closest friends. He was frequently a guest at our home, and I visited him several times in Providence. The correspondence I exchanged with him would fill several large volumes. August Derleth has been pleading with me for several years now to write a much longer Lovecraft article than the brief one which appeared in Marginalia--even a book about Howard--but the pressure of my own work has prevented me from doing so. Eventually, however, I may decide to undertake such a venture. It's still very much in the lap of the gods. It would require so much thought and leisure that I've been hesitant to attempt it, particularly since leisure is something I seem forever to be courting in vain."

RICHARD L. LOUGHLIN

with Lilian M. Popp (q.v.)
1) 1961 Globe   Journeys in Science Fiction. (@)

- -

ROBERT A. W. LOWNDES

1) 1953 Winston   The Mystery of the Third Mine.
3) 1961 Avalon   Believers' World.
4) 1961 Ace   The Puzzle Planet.

                           with James Blish (q.v.)
2) 1959 Avalon   The Duplicated Man. (RP)

FPS: "To Edgar Allan Poe,"   Fantastic Novels, September, 1940 (poem)

***   ***   ***   ***   ***

Robert Augustine Ward Lowndes--born September 4, 1916 at Bridgeport, Connecticut--attended Stamford Community College, 1936--Hoboken, New Jersey.

Son of Harry Irving & Fannie R. (Stevens) Lowndes--Dorothy Barbara: August 14, 1948--Peter Michael Rogalin (26).

Editor, Future Fiction, April, 1941-April, 1960; Science Fiction Quarterly, Winter, 1941/1942-February, 1958; Science Fiction, April, 1943-May, 1960; Dynamic Science Fiction, December, 1952-January, 1954 (all issues); The Magazine of Horror, August, 1963-DATE; Startling Mystery Stories, Summer, 1966-DATE; Famous Science Fiction, Winter, 1966/1967-DATE; Weird Terror Tales, Winter, 1969/1970-DATE; Member: Science Fiction Writers of America; Hydra Club; Baker Street Irregulars; Praed Street Irregulars; The James Branch Cabell Society.

- -

EDMUND LUDLOW

1) 1965 Exposition   The Coming of the Unselves.

Edmund Ludlow was born in 1898.

- -

RICHARD A. LUPOFF

1) 1965 Canaveral   Edgar Rice Burroughs: Master of Adventure. (nf/RP)
2) 1967 Lancer   One Million Centuries. (P)

NOTE: The paperbound edition of #1 is revised.

FPS: Miscellaneous sports reporting circa 1949-1950.
FSF: 1965 Canaveral   Edgar Rice Burroughs: Master of Adventure. (nf/RP)

WIP: 1969 Arlington   All in Color for a Dime. (nf/with Don Thompson)
                       With the Bentfin Boomer Boys on Little Old
                             New Alabama.

***   ***   ***   ***   ***

Richard Allen Lupoff--born February 21, 1935 at Brooklyn, New York--B.A.,
University of Miami (Florida), 1956--Hugo Award, Best Amateur Publication, 1963,
Xero--Poughkeepsie, New York.

Son of Sol J. & Sylvia Lupoff-Patricia Loring: August 27, 1958--Kenneth Bruce
Lupoff (1961); Katherine Eve Lupoff (1964); Thomas Daniel Lupoff (1968).

Editor, Canaveral Press, 1963-1965--Member: Science Fiction Writers of America.

JOHN LYMINGTON

1) 1959 Hodder   The Night of the Big Heat. (RP)
2) 1960 Hodder   The Giant Stumbles. (RP)
3) 1960 Hodder   The Grey Ones. (RP)
4) 1961 Hodder   The Coming of the Strangers. (RP)
5) 1962 Hodder   A Sword Above the Night. (RP)
6) 1963 Hodder   The Sleep Eaters. (RP)
7) 1963 Hodder   The Screaming Face. (RP)
8) 1964 Corgi   The Night Spiders. (P/RH)
9) 1964 Hodder   Froomb! (RP)
10) 1965 Hodder   The Green Drift.
11) 1965 Hodder   The Star Witches. (RP)
12) 1967 Hodder   Ten Million Years to Friday.

---

*C. C. MacAPP

1) 1968 Pap Lib   Omha Abides. (P)

FSF: "A Pride of Islands,"   If, May, 1960.

WIP: 1969 Dell   Secret of the Sunless World. (P/as Carroll Capps)
      1969 Avon   Worlds of The Well. (P)

***   ***   ***   ***   ***

Carroll M. Capps (u)--San Francisco, California.

Mr. Capps is retired--Member: Science Fiction Writers of America.

RICHARD MACGREGOR

1) 1963 Digit   The Deadly Sin. (P)
2) 1963 Digit   Horror in the Night. (P)
3) 1963 Digit   The Creeping Plague. (P)
4) 1964 Digit   The First of the Last. (P)

R. W. MACKELWORTH

1) 1968 Hale   Firemantle. (RPv)

FPS: "I, the Judge,"   New Worlds, May, 1963.
FPP: "The Statue,"   New Worlds, January, 1963.

WIP:
1A) 1969 Pap Lib   The Diabols. (P)
    1969   Tiltangle.

***   ***   ***   ***   ***

Ronald Walter Mackelworth--born April 7, 1930 at London, England--five sales awards in insurance--Leeds, Yorkshire, England.

Son of William & Lillian Mackelworth--Sheila: June 1, 1957--David William Mackelworth (September 13, 1960); Siona Elizabeth Mackelworth (December 28, 1963).

R. W. MACKELWORTH (continued)

Spent two years in Military Intelligence; one year with Thomas Cooks; "remaining career in insurance: sales, sales administration, management;" also Free-Lance Writer--Member: Bramhope Art Club; Raynes Park Rugby Union Club; Insurance Institute Great Britain National Trust.

Mr. Mackelworth mentions that his father was a Director of Beans Express and later a hotelier, and that he has three brothers, two of which are in insurance.

He also adds:
   "I started writing short stories about five years ago, but wished I had started earlier, since I've always loved description. Eventually I began when I found I had some time free from the necessity of earning a living from insurance. I wrote at six in the morning or twelve at night when I was short of time. Writing is something of a vice with me, and I do not think I will ever be able to stop.
   "I chose sf because it has the greatest potential for the imaginative plot and freedom of style. It can combine poetry with the pace of a thriller, and it has the whole future in which to expand. Indeed, its possibilities are infinite. At the present time it is breaking free from its old problems, and discarding the 'cardboard' characterisation and scientific 'mumbo jumbo' which spoiled the earlier stories. We even write about women as well as space heroes now!
   "I admire authors such as Ballard and Wyndham, as well as the younger authors. There are a whole list of others from Bradley to Pohl I have read with relish, and I think the numbers indicate the strength of sf. My one hate in modern sf is the attempt, in a few short stories, to anticipate the pornography of the future--they will have enough to contend with!"

Mr. Mackelworth also mentions that he intends to complete a novel per year from this point on.

KATHERINE MacLEAN

1) 1962 Avon   The Diploids. (s/P)

                     with Charles V. De Vet (q.v.)
2) 1962 Ace   Cosmic Checkmate. (P)

FPS: "Adding Molasses to the Table," to a small business magazine, 1946.
FSF: "Defense Mechanism," Astounding, October, 1949.

***   ***   ***   ***   ***

Katherine Ann MacLean--born January 22, 1925 at Montclaire, New Jersey--B.A., Barnard College, 1950; also graduate study in Psychology--South Portland, Maine.

KATHERINE MacLEAN (continued)

Daughter of Gordon & Ruth (Crawford) MacLean--(1) Charles Dye: 1951/1953; (2) David Mason: 1956/1963--Christopher Dennis Mason.

"Tried the usual roster of all the different kinds of jobs I could get into without committing my time for life: Nurse's Aide, Store Detective, Pollster, Econ Graph-Analyst, Antibiotic Lab Researcher, Food Factory Quality Controller, Office Manager, Payroll Bookkeeper, College Teacher, Reporter"--Member: Science Fiction Writers of America; Mensa; National Audibon Society.

Mis MacLean is currently organizing the Free University of Portland, Maine.

ANGUS MacLEOD

1) 1958 Dobson   The Body's Guest.
2) 1962 Roy   The Eighth Seal.

FPS: a short story published in 1935.
FSF: 1958 Dobson   The Body's Guest.

WIP: Beelzebub's Road. (s)

***   ***   ***   ***   ***

Angus MacLeod--born September 13, 1906 at Wester Ross, Scotland--attended Edinburgh College of Art, 1924-1929; qualified as Teacher of Technical Subjects and Art, University of Aberdeen, 1937--Gatehouse of Fleet, Kirkudbright, Scotland.

Son of Colin & Katherine (MacRae) Macleod--Odwen Peat: July 26, 1947-- no children.

Free-Lance Writer and Artist, 1929-1935; Art Teacher, Kendal Grammar School, Westmoreland, 1940-1941; from 1945 taught at Hove County School for Boys, Sussex; Redden Court School, Essex; currently Free-Lance Writer--Member: Society of Authors; P.E.N.

Mr. MacLeod has had several radio plays broadcasted in England and Europe.

PAUL MacTYRE

1)	1962 Hodder		Midge. (RPv)
2)	1963 Hodder		Fish on a Hook.
1A)	1963 Ace		Doomsday, 1999. (P)
3)	1964 Hodder		Bar Sinister.

Paul MacTyre is a probable pseudonym.

------

*LARRY MADDOCK

3)	1966 Ace	1	The Flying Saucer Gambit. (P)
4)	1967 Ace	2	The Golden Goddess Gambit. (P)
5)	1967 Ace	3	The Emerald Elephant Gambit. (P)

with Julie Anne Jardine (q.v.) as
*Howard L. Cory

1)	1966 Ace	The Sword of Lankor. (P)
2)	1966 Ace	The Mind Monsters. (P)

SER: The Agent of T.E.R.R.A.

FPS: "The Disembodied Man," Imagination, April, 1954.

WIP:	1969 Ace	4	The Time Trap Gambit. (P)
	1969 Belmont		Volar the Mighty. (P)

*** *** *** *** ***

Jack Owen Jardine--born October 10, 1931 at Eaton Rapids, Michigan--attended college for 2 years--Tempe, Arizona.

Son of John W. & Blanche M. Jardine--(1) Julie Anne Harihor: 1958/February 2, 1967; (2) Marilyn: January 9, 1968--Sabra Jardine (10).

Has worked as a newspaper reporter, radio announcer, men's magazine editor, TV technician, salesman; currently Creative Director of two Arizona radio stations; Free-Lance Writer--Member: Science Fiction Writers of America.

Mr. Maddock notes:
   "The 'Cory' penname evolved from the stage name of my former wife ('Corrie Howard'), with an incidental 'L.' for Larry

------

ROBERT MAGIDOFF

1) 1964 Allen   Russian Science Fiction. (@)
2) 1968 NYU Press   Russian Science Fiction, Series II. (@)

FPS: 1949 Doubleday In Anger and Pity. (nf)
FSF: 1964 Allen   Russian Science Fiction. (@)

WIP: 1969 NYU Press Russian Science Fiction, Series III. (@)

***   ***   ***   ***   ***

Robert Magidoff--born December 26, 1905 at Kiev, Russia--B.A., University of Wisconsin, 1932; Ph.D., University of Michigan, 1963--New York, New York.

Son of Charles & Jennie Magidoff--Nila Shevko: October 14, 1937--no children.

Foreign Correspondent, Associated Press and National Broadcasting Company, 1935-1949; Lecturer in Russian, University of Michigan, 1958-1961; Assistant Professor of Russian, New York University, 1961-1962; Associate Professor, 1962-1964; Professor and Chairman of the Slavic Department, 1965-DATE--Member: Modern Language Association; American Association of University Professors; American Association of Teachers of Slavic and East European Languages.

Dr. Magidoff writes:
"American sf is more readable, more imaginative than Russian. The latter is still interesting to the American reader, though, because it offers insight into directions with which US science fiction writers have a limited preoccupation: socio-economic relationships and the psychological results thereof; and the evolution of a 'new type' of man."

----

*CHARLES ERIC MAINE

1) 1953 Hodder   Spaceways. (RP)
2) 1955 Hodder   Timeliner. (RP)
3) 1955 Hodder   Crisis 2000. (RP)
4) 1956 Hodder   Escapement.
5) 1957 Hodder   The Isotope Man. (RP)
6) 1957 Hodder   High Vacuum. (RP)
7) 1958 Hodder   The Tide Went Out. (RP)
8) 1958 Ace   World Without Men. (P)
4A) 1958 Lippincott   The Man Who Couldn't Sleep.
9) 1959 Hodder   Count-Down. (RP/RPv)
9A) 1959 Ballantine   Fire Past the Future. (P)
10) 1960 Hodder   Subterfuge. (RP)
11) 1960 Hodder   Calculated Risk. (RP)

*CHARLES ERIC MAINE (continued)

12)	1960 Avalon	He Owned the World. (RP)	
12A)	1961 Hodder	The Man Who Owned the World. (RP)	
13)	1961 Hodder	The Mind of Mr. Soames. (RP)	
14)	1962 Hodder	The Darkest of Nights. (RP/RPv)	
15)	1964 Hodder	Never Let Up.	
16)	1966 Hodder	B.E.A.S.T. (RP)	
14A)	1968 Gold Medal	Survival Margin. (P)	

Charles Eric Maine, penname of David McIlwain, was born in 1921. He could not be located.

ALEXANDER MALEC

1) 1967 Doubleday   Extrapolasis. (s/RP)

Alexander B. Malec is a member of Science Fiction Writers of America.

MARYA MANNES

1)   1968 Doubleday   They.

FSF: 1968 Doubleday   They.

***   ***   ***   ***   ***

Marya Mannes--born November 14, 1904 at New York, New York--George Polk Memorial Award for Magazine Criticism, 1958; L.H.D., Hood College, 1960; Achievement Award, Federation of Jewish Women's Organizations, 1961; Award of Honor, Theta Sigma Phi, 1962--Sagaponack, New York.

Daughter of David & Clara (Damrosch) Mannes-- 1) Jo Mielziner: 1926; 2) Richard Blow: February, 1937; 3) Christopher Clarkson: April 2, 1948--2) David J. Blow.

Staff Writer, The Reporter, 1952-1963; Moderator of her own TV program, "I Speak for Myself," 1959; Free-Lance Writer and Editor; lecturer and TV personality--Member: Authors League; Dramatists Guild; Newspaper Guild; American Federation of Television and Radio Artists.

ROGER MANSFIELD

1) 1968 Pergamon   The Starlight Corridor: Modern Science Fiction
                    Short Stories and Poems. (@/RP)

ROGER MANSFIELD (continued)

FPS: 1964 Oxford   Everyman Will Shout. (@)
FSF: 1968 Pergamon   The Starlight Corridor: Modern Science Fiction Short Stories and Poems. (@/RP)

WIP: an article on the role of science fiction in English teaching, to be published in A Symposium on English Teaching by Blackie & Son.

***   ***   ***   ***   ***

Roger Ernest Mansfield--born November 27, 1939 at Cambridge, England--attended City of Worcester Training College, 1958-1960--Wimbledon, London, England.

Son of Ernest Walter & Ruby May (Welch) Mansfield--married May 26, 1962--Kim Mansfield (6); Kerry Mansfield (3); Conrad Mansfield (0).

Teacher of English, Inner London Education Authority, 1960-DATE--Member: Society of Authors.

ROBERT E. MARGROFF

with *Piers Anthony (q.v.)
1) 1968 Ace   The Ring. (P)

FPS: "Monster Tracks,"   If, October, 1964.

WIP: The Rumpleskin Brat. (with *Piers Anthony)

***   ***   ***   ***   ***

Robert Ervien Margroff--born March 5, 1930 at Elgin, Iowa--Elgin, Iowa.

Son of Ervien & Lulu Margroff--unmarried.

"Tried operating a linotype machine and a number of other things; writing career is (hopefully) started"--Member: Science Fiction Writers of America.

Mr. Margroff comes from a farm background, and still lives on the farm owned by his parents at the time of his birth. His first published story was bought after he won second prize in the annual National Fantasy Fan Federation Fiction Contest.

LEO MARGULIES

4)	1958 Gold Medal	Three Times Infinity. (@/P)
5)	1959 Crest	Three from Out There. (@/P)
6)	1960 Crest	Get Out of My Sky. (@/P)
7)	1961 Pyramid	The Unexpected. (@/P)
8)	1961 Pyramid	The Ghoul Keepers. (@/P)
9)	1963 Pyramid	Three in One. (@/P)
10)	1964 Pyramid	Weird Tales. (@/P)
11)	1965 Pyramid	Worlds of Weird. (@/P)

with Oscar J. Friend.

1)	1949 Merlin	From Off This World. (@)
2)	1949 Merlin	My Best Science Fiction Story. (@/RPa)
3)	1954 Merlin	The Giant Anthology of Science Fiction. (@/RPav)
3A)	1958 Crest	Race to the Stars. (@/a/P)

FPS: unknown.

***   ***   ***   ***   ***

Leo Margulies--born 1900 at Brooklyn, New York--attended Columbia University--New York, New York.

Son of Jacob & Esther (Goldberg) Margulies--Cylvia Kleinman: December, 1937.

Editorial Director, Thrilling Publications (Captain Future, Thrilling Wonder, Startling Stories, Fantastic Stories Quarterly, Strange Stories, and variously more than 45 other magazines), c. 1932-c. 1952; Publisher, Fantastic Universe, June/July, 1953-August, 1956; Editorial Director, May, 1954-August, 1956; Publisher and Editorial Director, The Saint Mystery Magazine, c. 1953-c. 1956; Publisher, Mike Shayne Mystery Magazine, September, 1956-DATE; Satellite Science Fiction, October, 1956-May, 1959 (all issues); Editor, February, 1957; Publisher, The Man from U.N.C.L.E. Magazine, 1966-1968 (all issues); Shell Scott Mystery Magazine, 1966 (all issues); The Girl from U.N.C.L.E. Magazine, c. 1967 (all issues); variously employed by 20th Century-Fox Productions; Free-Lance Editor--Member: Overseas Press Club.

DAVID S. MARTIN

1)	1967 Stockwell	No Lack of Space.

DOUGLAS R. MASON

3)	1966 Doubleday	From Carthage Then I Came. (RPv)
3A)	1967 Pap Lib	Eight Against Utopia. (P)
6)	1968 Hale	Landfall Is a State of Mind.
7)	1968 Hale	Ring of Violence. (RP)
8)	1968 Hale	The Tower of Rizwan.

DOUGLAS R. MASON (continued)

as *John Rankine

1)	1966 Nelson	1	The Blockage of Sinitron. (s)
2)	1966 Dobson	2	Interstellar Two-Five. (RP)
4)	1968 Dobson		Never the Same Door.
5)	1968 Dobson	3	One Is One. (RP)

FPS: "Two's Company," in   New Writings in SF 1, edited by John Carnell, Dobson, 1964 (as *John Rankine).

WIP: 1969 Hale   The Janus Syndrome.
     1969 Dobson   Moons of Triopus. (RP/as *John Rankine)
     1969 Dobson   Binary Z. (as *John Rankine)
                    4   Darkside. (as *John Rankine)
                        Horizon Alpha.
                    5   The Plantos Illusion. (as *John Rankine)
                    6   The Garamas Affair. (as *John Rankine)
     1970 Ballantine   Matrix. (P)
                        Time Knot.

***   ***   ***   ***   ***

Douglas Rankine Mason--born September 26, 1918 at Hawarden, County of Flint, England--B.A., Manchester University, 1947; Diploma in Teaching, Manchester University, 1948--Wallasey, Cheshire, England.

Son of Russell & Bertha (Greenwood) Mason--Mary Norma Eucline Cooper: May, 1945--Keith Mason (21); Patricia Mason (18); John Mason (12); Elaine Rosemary Mason (8).

Headmaster, Somerville Junior School, 1954-1966; St. George's Junior School, Wallasey, 1966-DATE.

Mr. Mason began writing five years ago, and in the ensuing time has sold one million, one hundred thousand words.

DAVID I. MASSON

1) 1968 Faber   The Caltraps of Time. (s)

FPS: "Traveller's Rest," New Worlds, September, 1965.

***   ***   ***   ***   ***

DAVID I. MASSON (continued)

David I. Masson (u)--born 1915 at Edinburgh, Scotland--attended Oxford University--Leeds, England.

Mr. Masson is married and has children.

Rare Book Librarian.

RICHARD MATHESON

1)	1954 Chamberlain	Born of Man and Woman. (s/RPav)
2)	1954 Gold Medal	I Am Legend. (P)
1A)	1955 Bantam	Third from the Sun. (s/a/P)
3)	1956 Gold Medal	The Shrinking Man. (P)
4)	1957 Bantam	The Shores of Space. (s/P)
5)	1958 Lippincott	A Stir of Echoes. (RP)
6)	1961 Dell	Shock. (s/P)
7)	1964 Dell	Shock II. (s/P)
8)	1966 Dell	Shock III. (s/P)

FPS: "Born of Man and Woman," The Magazine of Fantasy and Science Fiction, Summer, 1950

***   ***   ***   ***   ***

Richard Burton Matheson--born February 20, 1926 at Allendale, New Jersey--Bachelor of Journalism, University of Missouri, 1949--Hugo Award, Best Motion Picture, 1958, "The Incredible Shrinking Man;" Guest of Honor, 16th World Science Fiction Convention (Solacon), 1958--Woodland Hills, California.

Son of Bertolf & Fanny (Mathiesen) Matheson--Ruth Ann Woodson: July 1, 1952--Richard Matheson (15); Alison Matheson (12); Christian Matheson (10); Adopted Child: Bettina (19).

"Since 1955, I have been primarily a television and screen writer, although I have attempted to produce some short stories and novels at the same time."--Member: Writers Guild of America, West.

ARTHUR S. MATTES

1)	1963 Regency	Soul Mates.
FPP:	1963 Regency	Soul Mates.

***   ***   ***   ***   ***

ARTHUR S. MATTES (continued)

Arthur S. Mattes--born July 10, 1901 at Creamery, Pennsylvania--Port Arthur, Texas.

Son of Alvin B. & Kate H. (Scholl) Mattes--Edna Irene Scholl: July 1, 1930--no children.

Commercial Wireless Telegraph Operator, 1926-1966; currently retired--Member: several radio operators' clubs.

Mr. Mattes has been a ham radio operator since 1924; his current call letters are W5JE.

JACQUELIN ROLLIT McAULEY

1) 1964 Exposition   The Cloud.

Jacquelin Rollit McAuley was born in 1925.

ANNE McCAFFREY

1) 1967 Ballantine   Restoree. (P/RH)
2) 1968 Ballantine   1   Dragonflight. (P/RH)

FPS: "Freedom of the Race," Science Fiction +, October, 1953.

WIP: 1969 Ballantine   Decision at Doona. (P)
      1969 Walker   The Ship Who Sang.
      1970   Bitter Talent.
      1970   2   Dragonquest.

***   ***   ***   ***   ***

Anne Inez McCaffrey--born April 1, 1926 at Cambridge, Massachusetts--B.A., Radcliffe College, 1947--Hugo Award, Best Novella, 1968, "Weyr Search;" Nebula Award, Best Novella, 1968, "Dragonrider"--Sea Cliff, New York.

Daughter of George Herbert & Anne Dorothy (McElroy) McCaffrey--H. Wright Johnson: January 14, 1950--Alec Johnson (August 29, 1952); Todd Johnson (April 27, 1956); Georgeanne Johnson (August 27, 1959).

ANNE McCAFFREY (continued)

"Worked as copywriter/layout artist for Liberty Music Shops, and as a copywriter for Helena Rubenstein; summer stock with Lambertville Music Circus, 1949; studied voice and drama nine years in US and Germany; directed opera and operetta professionally in Wilmington, Delaware; staged and directed the American Premier of Carl Orff's 'Ludus De Nato Infante Mirificus,' Delaware, 1963;" Free-Lance Writer--Member: Science Fiction Writers of America (Secretary/Treasurer 1968-1970); Mystery Writers of America.

DAVID McDANIEL

1)	1966 Ace	4	The Dagger Affair.	(P)
2)	1966 Ace	6	The Vampire Affair.	(P)
3)	1967 Ace	8	The Monster Wheel Affair.	(P)
4)	1967 Ace		The Arsenal Out of Time.	(P)
5)	1967 Ace	13	The Rainbow Affair.	(P)
6)	1968 Ace	15	The Utopia Affair.	(P)

SER: 1) The Man From U.N.C.L.E.; 2) The Prisoner.

WIP:	1969 Ace	17	The Hollow Crown Affair.	(P)
	1969 Ace	-2	Number Two.	(P)

David E. McDaniel is a member of Science Fiction Writers of America.

---

*J. T. McINTOSH

1)	1953 Doubleday	World Out of Mind.	(RP)
2)	1954 Doubleday	Born Leader.	(RPv)
3)	1954 Doubleday	One in Three Hundred.	(RP)
4)	1955 Doubleday	The Fittest.	(RPv)
4A)	1956 Crest	Rule of the Pagbeasts.	(P)
2A)	1958 Avon	Worlds Apart.	(P)
5)	1961 Ace	200 Years to Christmas.	(P)
6)	1963 Pyramid	The Million Cities.	(P)
7)	1964 Digit	The Noman Way.	(P)
8)	1965 Digit	Out of Chaos.	(P)
9)	1967 Joseph	Time for a Change.	(RPv)
9A)	1968 Avon	Snow White and the Giants.	(P)
10)	1968 Joseph	Six Gates from Limbo.	(RP)

*J. T. McINTOSH (continued)

FPS: "The Curfew Tolls," Astounding, December, 1950.

WIP: Cuckoo in the Mind.

***   ***   ***   ***   ***

James Murdoch Macgregor--born February 14, 1925 at Paisley, Scotland--attended Robert Gordon's College, 1936-1941; M.A. (Honors), University of Aberdeen, 1947-- Aberdeen, Scotland.

Son of Murdoch & Marion (Dracup) Macgregor--Margaret Murray: July 28, 1960-- no children.

Has been professional musician and school teacher; Sub-Editor, Aberdeen Press and Journal, 1964-DATE; Free-Lance Writer.

Mr. McIntosh sent the following letter:
"What I feel inclined to say about sf doesn't fit into the categories you set down. However, it is the most lasting impression of my experience in writing and trying to sell sf stories, so here it is.
"It is disappointing that editors and publishers continue to exclude more humanistic works by labelling them 'not science fiction.' In theory, sf should be the freest of all fields in that in sf anything is possible. But if an author who has set his story in a science fiction framework becomes particularly interested in the characters, and works the story out in terms of human relationships rather that pseudo-science, he is liable to find the story unpublishable.
"I have several times run up against this barrier. While we all agree that there is no point in writing stories in which sf gimmicks are merely stuck onto a story which doesn't need them, I find it sad that it's so often not possible (if the book is to be published, that is) to leave out the trappings of sf in concentrating on the people, the story, the solution, the moral. It's even sadder to have to record that several times when a story has been rejected as 'not sf' I've been able, merely by sticking in a few paragraphs of pseudo-scientific gobbledegook, to turn the story miraculously into sf and sell it.
"With my latest book, Cuckoo in the Mind, I have again run into this trouble. There are no machines, the time is the present, and the sole fantasy element is that the hero is able to flit from mind to mind. The story has been worked out as general fiction once this one element is accepted. The result is that publishers looking on the book as sf say 'not sf', and the publishers looking on it as a straightforward novel are thrown by the fantasy. I don't put this forward as a hard-luck story. But it's surely wrong that if I inserted a mad professor with a mind-switching device into what was meant to be a serious story, the book would at once become sf and would find a publisher right away."

MABEL L. McKINNEY

1) 1962 Carlton   The Adventures of Nicknames Incorporated.

DEAN McLAUGHLIN

1) 1962 Pyramid   Dome World. (P)
2) 1963 Pyramid   The Fury from Earth. (P)
3) 1965 Lancer   The Man Who Wanted Stars. (P)

FPS: "For Those Who Follow After," Astounding, July, 1951.

***   ***   ***   ***   ***

Dean Benjamin McLaughlin, Jr.--born July 22, 1931 at Ann Arbor, Michigan--B.A., University of Michigan, 1953--Ann Arbor, Michigan.

Son of Dean Benjamin & Laura (Hill) McLaughlin--no children.

Free-Lance Writer--Member: Science Fiction Writers of America.

SHEPHERD MEAD

1) 1949 Farrar   The Magnificent MacInnes.
2) 1951 Doubleday   Tessie, the Hound of Channel 1.
3) 1954 S&S   The Big Ball of Wax. (RP)
4) 1966 S&S   The Carefully Considered Rape of the World.

FPS: 1949 Farrar   The Magnificent MacInnes.

***   ***   ***   ***   ***

Edward Shepherd Mead--born April 26, 1914 at St. Louis, Missouri--B.A., Washington University, 1936--Epalinges, Switzerland.

Son of Edward & Sarah (Woodward) Mead--Annabelle Pettibone: September 18, 1943--Sally Ann Mead (23); Shepherd Mead (20); Edward Mead (17).

Employed with Benton & Bowles, Inc., New York, 1936-1956 (Vice-President, 1951-1956); Consultant, S. H. Benson Ltd., London, 1958-1962; Free-Lance Writer--Member: Phi Beta Kappa.

"I'm a satirist, and sf can be a powerful vehicle for satire, saying things about our own civilization and our own time more strongly--in certain cases--than they can be said otherwise. It was why I used the device in the books listed above."

S. P. MEEK

1) 1935 Morrow   The Monkeys Have No Tails in Zamboanga.
2) ?1945 Utopian   Arctic Bride. (P)
3) 1961 Avalon   The Drums of Tapajos.
4) 1961 Avalon   Troyana.

FPS: "Taming Poachers,"   Field and Stream, September, 1928.
FSF: "The Murgatroyd Experiment," Amazing Stories Quarterly, Winter, 1929.

***   ***   ***   ***   ***

Sterner St. Paul Meek--born April 8, 1894 at Chicago, Illinois--Sc.A., University of Chicago, 1914; S.B., University of Alabama, 1915; graduate study at University of Wisconsin, 1916; Massachusetts Institute of Technology, 1921-1923--Delray Beach, Florida.

Son of John Washington & Ella (Sterner) Meek--Edna Brundage Nobel: July 12, 1927--Nobel Stafford Meek (39).

Chemist, United States Army, 1917-1947 (retiring with rank of Colonel); Free-Lance Writer--Member: North American Committee, Christian Children's League; Phi Beta Kappa; Pi Tau Phi.

Col. Meek writes:
    "When I switched from magazine work (largely science fiction) to book writing (mainly juvenile horse and dog stories), for all practical purposes I dropped out of sf, and have not really kept up with it. I am not especially familiar with the modern version, and would prefer not to express an opinion on its merits, much less pontificate about it. I was in at the early days, I feel I made some contribution to it, and the mere fact that two of my old magazine serials were disentombed and reprinted in 1961 seems to indicate that my work was not wholly without merit. More I will not say."

DAVID MELTZER

1) 1968 Essex   1   The Agency. (P)
2) 1968 Essex   2   The Agent. (P)
3) 1968 Essex   3   How Many Blocks in the Pile? (P)

SER: 1) Agency Trilogy; 2) Brain-Plant Tetralogy

FPS: "Kick Me Deadly,"   Dazzle Magazine, 1957.
FSF: "And All That Jazz,"   Showcase Magazine, 1961.

DAVID MELTZER (continued)

WIP:	1968 Essex	-1	Lovely. (P)
	1969 Essex	-2	Healer. (P)
	1969 Essex	-3	Out. (P)
	1969 Essex	-4	Glue Factory. (P)

***   ***   ***   ***   ***

David Meltzer--born February 17, 1937 at Rochester, New York--Mill Valley, California.

Son of Louis & Rosemunde (Lovelace) Meltzer--Christina Howcroft: April 1, 1957--Jennifer Love Meltzer (July 7, 1961); Margaret Joy Meltzer (June 13, 1963); Amanda Rose Meltzer (June 2, 1965).

"Primarily known in the field of poetry; connected with the San Francisco poetry movement of the late 50's; also involved with music (two albums available on Vanguard Records);" Free-Lance Writer--Member: Science Fiction Writers of America.

A. J. MERAK

1)	1954 Panther	Dark Andromeda. (H-P)
2)	1959 Badger SF	No Dawn and No Horizon. (P/RH)
3)	1959 Badger SF	The Dark Millenium. (P/RH)
4)	1959 Badger SN	Dark Conflict. (P)
5)	1960 Badger SF	Barrier Unknown. (P/RH)
6)	1960 Badger SF	Hydrosphere. (P/RH)

A. J. Merak seems to be a real name, but no proof has been encountered to date verifying his existence.

JUDITH MERRIL

1)	1950 Bantam	Shot in the Dark. (@/P)
2)	1950 Doubleday	Shadow on the Hearth. (RP)
3)	1952 Random	Beyond Human Ken. (@/RPa)
6)	1954 Random	Beyond the Barriers of Time and Space. (@)
7)	1954 Lion	Human? (@/P)
8)	1955 Lion	Galaxy of Ghouls. (@/P)
9)	1956 Gnome Dell	S-F: The Year's Greatest Science-Fiction and Fantasy. (@/H-P)
10)	1957 Gnome	S-F: '57. (@/H-P)

JUDITH MERRIL (continued)

10A)	1957 Dell	S-F: The Year's Greatest Science-Fiction and Fantasy Second Annual Volume. (@/H-P)
11)	1958 Gnome	SF: '58. (@/H-P)
11A)	1958 Dell	S-F: The Year's Greatest Science-Fiction and Fantasy Third Annual Volume. (@/H-P)
12)	1959 Gnome	SF: '59. (@/H-P)
12A)	1959 Dell	The Year's Greatest Science-Fiction and Fantasy Fourth Annual Volume. (@/H-P)
8A)	1959 Pyramid	Off the Beaten Orbit. (@/P)
13)	1960 S&S	5th Annual Edition the Year's Best S-F. (@/RP)
14)	1960 Pyramid	Out of Bounds. (s/P)
15)	1960 Pyramid	The Tomorrow People. (P)
16)	1961 S&S	6th Annual Edition the Year's Best S-F. (@/RP)
17)	1962 S&S	7th Annual Edition the Year's Best S-F. (@/RP/RPv)
	1963 Mayflower	The Best of Sci-Fi No. 1. (@/P)
18)	1963 S&S	8th Annual Edition the Year's Best S-F. (@/RP)
	1964 Mayflower	The Best of Sci-Fi No. 2. (@/P)
19)	1964 S&S	9th Annual Edition the Year's Best S-F. (@/RP/RPv)
20)	1965 Delacorte	10th Annual Edition the Year's Best S-F. (@/RP)
17A)	1965 Mayflower	The Best of Sci-Fi No. 4. (@/P)
21)	1966 Delacorte	11th Annual Edition the Year's Best S-F. (@/RP)
19A)	1966 Mayflower	The Best of Sci-Fi No. 5. (@/P)
22)	1967 Delacorte	SF: The Best of the Best. (@/RP)
23)	1968 Gollancz	Daughters of Earth. (s)
24)	1968 Doubleday	England Swings SF. (@)
25)	1968 Delacorte	SF 12. (@/RP)

with Cyril M. Kornbluth as *Cyril Judd

4)	1952 S&S	Gunner Cade. (RP)
5)	1952 Abelard	Outpost Mars. (RP/RPv)
5A)	1961 Beacon	Sin in Space. (P)

FKP:	"That Only a Mother,"	Astounding, June, 1948.
WIP:	1969 Delacorte	SF 13. (@)

Judith Merril, formerly Josephine Judith Zissman, was born in 1923. She was Book Editor, The Magazine of Fantasy and Science Fiction, May, 1965-May, 1969.

NORM METCALF

1)	1968 Stark		The Index of Science Fiction Magazines 1951-1965. (nf/P)

ROY MEYERS

1)	1967 Ballantine	1	Dolphin Boy. (P/RHv)
1A)	1968 Whiting	1	Dolphin Rider.
2)	1968 Ballantine	2	Daughters of the Dolphin. (P)
FPS:	1945 Blackfriars Press		The Man They Couldn't Kill. (P)
FSF:	1967 Ballantine		Dolphin Boy. (P/RHv)
WIP:	1969 Ballantine	3	Destiny and the Dolphins. (P)

***   ***   ***   ***   ***

Roy Lethbridge Meyers--born November 17, 1910 at Hounslow, Middlesex, England--attended University College; medical education at St. Bartholomew's Hospital; Licentiate of the Royal College of Physicians (London), 1939; Member of the Royal College of Surgeons (England), 1940--Stogumber, Taunton, Somerset, England.

Son of Percy F. C. & Maud Meyers--Dr. Mary Leasor: February 14, 1941--C. J. L. Meyers (24).

Has been a House Physician, Mill Hill Hospital, London; House Surgeon, Wellhouse Hospital, London; Deputy Commissioner of Medical Service, Southwest Region; Chairman of M.S.S. Medical Boards; currently practicing General Medicine together with his wife--Member: Science Fiction Writers of America; British Medical Association.

CHARLES A. MILES

1)	1961 Vantage	Argosy: The Imaginery Memoirs of an Astronaut.

Charles A. Miles could not be located.

JOSEPH MILLARD

1)	1964 Monarch	The Gods Hate Kansas. (P)
FPS:	a story, title unknown, to	Portal, 1927.
FSF:	"Crash on Viar,"	Thrilling Wonder, February, 1941.

JOSEPH MILLARD

WIP:	*A Plague of Angels*. (P)
	Gilkerson's Hell. (P)

***   ***   ***   ***   ***

Joseph John Millard--born January 14, 1908 at Canby, Minnesota--graduate from Pioneer School of Business, 1926--Bridgeport, Connecticut.

Son of Frank Earnest & Alice (Lake) Millard--Lee Harrington: February 14, 1931--Michael Harrington Millard (29).

Has worked as an editor and advertising agent; Free-Lance Writer.

Mr. Millard comments:
    "I'm just getting back to my first love, sf, after cruelly deserting it for richer fields. I see it as poised on the brink of a real boom, sparked by such successes as *Planet of the Apes* and *2001*. When technology outstripped the imagination of sf writers, it was a blessing in disguise. It forced us to abandon bug-eyed monsters and pseudo-science doubletalk, and concentrate on people and their ageless problems. This will bring a steadily-widening readership, and, in turn, a wider market to attract more writers of the Clarke, Heinlein, Bradbury, Asimov, Vonnegut type. The hard-core fans are great but, unfortunately, just not numerous enough."

WALTER M. MILLER, JR.

1) 1959 Lippincott   *A Canticle for Leibowitz*. (RP)
2) 1962 Ballantine   *Conditionally Human*. (s/P/RH)
3) 1965 Ballantine   *The View from the Stars*. (s/P/RH)

FPS: "MacDougal's Wife,"   *American Mercury*, 1950.
FSF: "Secret of the Death Dome," *Amazing*, January, 1951.

***   ***   ***   ***   ***

Walter Michael Miller, Jr.--born January 23, 1923 at New Smyrna Beach, Florida--attended University of Tennessee, 1940-1942; University of Texas, 1947-1949--Hugo Award, Best Novelette, 1955, "The Darfstellar;" Best Novel, 1961, *A Canticle for Leibowitz*--Daytona Beach, Florida.

Son of Walter Michael & Ruth Adrian (Jones) Miller--Anna Louise Becker: May 1, 1945--Margaret Jean Miller (June 4, 1945); Walter Michael Miller III (September 11, 1947); Cathryn Augusta Miller (September 27, 1949); Alys Elaine Miller (November 9, 1951).

ALFRED L. MILLIGAN

1) 1965 Pan Press The Strange Flight of Frank Shapar.

FPP: 1965 Pan Press The Strange Flight of Frank Shaper.

*** *** *** *** ***

Alfred Lee Milligan--born August 26, 1893 at Attica, Indiana--Indianapolis, Indiana.

Son of Alfred A. & Charlotte Milligan--Beulah: November 10, 1926-1943--Beulah Milligan Fox (41); Charles Milligan (39); Arthur Milligan (35).

Actor, 1913-1914; with Medical Service of United States Army during World War I; has since been with the Railway Mail Service, and was an Assistant Postmaster and Clerk for 34 years at Attica, Indiana; currently retired--Member: AMORC Rosicrucians; The Lemurian Fellowship; The Order of the Essenes; Self-Realization Fellowship; Astara Foundation.

ROBERT P. MILLS

1) 1960 Doubleday The Best from Fantasy and Science Fiction Ninth Series. (@/RP)
2) 1960 Doubleday A Decade of Fantasy and Science Fiction. (@/RP)
3) 1961 Doubleday The Best from Fantasy and Science Fiction Tenth Series. (@/RP)
4) 1962 Doubleday The Best from Fantasy and Science Fiction Eleventh Series. (@/RP)
5) 1963 Dial The Worlds of Science Fiction. (@/RP)

FPS: "The Last Shall Be First," The Magazine of Fantasy and Science Fiction, August, 1958.

*** *** *** *** ***

Robert Park Mills--born 1920 at Missoula, Montana--B.A., Rutgers University, 1942--New York, New York.

Mr. Mills has been married and divorced--Alison Mills; Frederic Mills.

Managing Editor, The Magazine of Fantasy and Science Fiction, Fall, 1949-August, 1958; Editor, September, 1958-March, 1962; Consulting Editor, April, 1962-February, 1963; December, 1964-December, 1966; Editor, Venture Science Fiction, January, 1957-July, 1958; Manager, Robert P. Mills, Ltd., Literary Agency, September, 1959-DATE--Member: Science Fiction Writers of America.

NAOMI MITCHISON

1)	1962 Gollancz	Memoirs of a Spacewoman. (RP)
FSF:	1962 Gollancz	Memoirs of a Spacewoman.

***   ***   ***   ***   ***

Naomi Margaret Mitchison--born November 1, 1897 at Edinburgh, Scotland--Palmes de L'Academie Francaise--Campbeltown, Argyll, Scotland.

Daughter of John Scott & Louisa Kathleen (Trotter) Haldane--G. R. Mitchison (now Lord Mitchison): 1916--Dénis Antony Mitchison; Murdoch Mitchison; Lois Mitchison Godfrey; Avrion Mitchison; Valentine Mitchison Arnold.

Free-Lance Writer; Highland farmer; politician (left-wing)--Member: Matshego Regiment, Bakgatla Tribe, Botswana (Tribal Advisor, 1963); Highland and Island Advisory Council; Argyll Education Committee.

Mrs. Mitchison has travelled extensively, particularly in India and Africa. Her name in Botswana is Mmalinchwe.

NICHOLAS MONSARRAT

1)	1962 Sloane	The Time Before This. (RP)

Nicholas John Turney Monsarrat was born in 1910. He received the Heinemann Foundation Prize for Literature, 1954. A complete biography may be found in Contemporary Authors.

MICHAEL MOORCOCK

1)	1963 Spearman	1	The Stealer of Souls. (s/RP)
2)	1965 Compact		The Sundered Worlds. (P)
6)	1965 Compact		The Fireclown. (P)
7)	1965 Compact		The Best of New Worlds. (@/P)
8)	1965 Jenkins	2	Stormbringer. (RP)
10)	1966 Compact		The Twilight Man. (P)
11)	1967 Panther		The Best SF Stories from New Worlds. (@/P)
12)	1967 Lancer	-1	The Jewel in the Skull. (P)
13)	1967 Ace		The Wrecks of Time. (P)
14)	1968 Panther		Best Stories from New Worlds II. (@/P)
15)	1968 Lancer	-2	Sorcerer's Amulet. (P)
16)	1968 Avon		The Final Programme. (P/RH)
17)	1968 Panther		Best SF Stories from New World 3. (@/P)

MICHAEL MOORCOCK (continued)

18)	1968 Whiting		The Traps of Time. (@/RP)
19)	1968 Lancer	-3	Sword of the Dawn. (P)
15A)	1968 Mayflower	-2	The Mad God's Amulet. (P)

as *Edward P. Bradbury

3)	1965 Compact	+1	Warriors of Mars. (P)
4)	1965 Compact	+2	Blades of Mars. (P)
5)	1965 Compact	+3	The Barbarians of Mars. (P)

as *James Colvin

9)	1966 Compact		The Deep Fix. (s/P)

SER: 1) Elric; 2) History of the Runestaff.

NOTES: The Wrecks of Time originally appeared under the name James Colvin. All the stories contained in The Deep Fix are by Moorcock, although "Peace on Earth" is a collaboration with Barrington Bayley, appearing originally under the combined pseudonym of Michael Barrington.

FPS: a series on Edgar Rice Burroughs to Tarzan Adventures, 1957.
FSF: "Sojan the Swordsman," Tarzan Adventures, May, 1957.

WIP:	1969 Lancer	-4	The Secret of the Runestaff. (P)
20A)	1969 Mayflower		The Runestaff. (P)
6A)	1969 Pap Lib		The Winds of Limbo. (P)
	1969 Sphere		The Ice Schooner. (P)
	1969 Allison		Behold the Man. (RP)
	1969 Hart-Davis		The Time Dweller. (@)
	1969 Panther		Best SF Stories from New Worlds IV. (@/P)
	1969 Ace		The Black Corridor. (P)
	1970 Panther		Best SF Stories from New Worlds V. (@/P)
	1970 Allison		A Cure for Cancer.
	1970 Dell		The Eternal Champion. (P)
	a serial for		The Illustrated Weekly of India entitled "The Distant Suns."

***   ***   ***   ***   ***

Michael John Moorcock--born December 18, 1939 at Mitcham, Surrey, England--Nebula Award, Best Novella, 1967, "Behold the Man;" British Fantasy Award, 1967--London, England.

Son of Arthur & June (Taylor) Moorcock--Hilary Denham Bailey: September 29, 1962--Sophie Elizabeth Moorcock (September 3, 1963); Katherine Helen Moorcock (September 5, 1964).

MICHAEL MOORCOCK (continued)

Editor, <u>Tarzan Adventures</u>, 1957-1958; "Sexton Blake Library," 1958-1961; <u>New Worlds</u>, May/June, 1964-DATE; worked at miscellaneous journalism (criticism, poetry, etc.), 1956-1967; worked for the Liberal Party, 1962-- Member: Science Fiction Writers of America.

Mr. Moorcock states:
"I think the barriers between sf and ordinary modern fiction have already broken down. SF as a category form still exists--and will doubtless continue to exist. But the sf which no longer works <u>within</u> the conventions but merely <u>makes use</u> of some of the conventions can no longer easily be categorised save simply as 'modern fiction.' In much of my own work I write a completely personal story or novel, utilising what I have learned from writing sf but not producing what a purist would call 'true sf'--<u>The Final Programme</u> and <u>A Cure for Cancer</u> are examples. SF has been an invaluable training ground and provided considerable discipline to a number of writers--Ballard--Aldiss--Disch--Jones//Langdon--ed.// --Harrison (M. John)--etc., etc., whose current work is no longer what an enthusiastic reader of, say, <u>Galaxy</u>, would be willing to distinguish as sf, and yet which contains much of the freshness and many of the virtues of the best science fiction. I tend to hold the view (also expressed by Ballard) that magazine sf of the forties was a 'naive' form--a 'primitive' literary movement--and I tend to prefer the unsophisticated work that appeared in <u>Astounding</u>, <u>Planet</u>, <u>Super Science</u>, <u>Startling Stories</u>, etc. to the pseudo-sophisticated work that began to appear in <u>Galaxy</u> and the <u>Magazine of Fantasy and Science Fiction</u> in the early 50's."

C. L. MOORE

4)	1952 Gnome	<u>Judgment Night</u>. (RP)
8)	1953 Gnome	<u>Shambleau and Others</u>. (s/RP)
11)	1954 Gnome	<u>Northwest of Earth</u>. (s)
13)	1957 Doubleday	<u>Doomsday Morning</u>. (RP)
		with Henry Kuttner as *Henry Kuttner
1)	1950 Grosset	<u>Fury</u>. (RPv)
6)	1953 Ballantine	<u>Ahead of Time</u>. (s/H-P)
1A)	1959 Avon	<u>Destination: Infinity</u>. (P)
14)	1961 Ballantine	<u>Bypass to Otherness</u>. (s/P)
15)	1962 Ballantine	<u>Return to Otherness</u>. (s/P)
7A)	1963 Ballantine	<u>Mutant</u>. (P)
16)	1964 Ace	<u>Valley of the Flame</u>. (P)
18)	1965 Ace	<u>The Dark World</u>. (P)
9A)	1965 Ace	<u>The Well of the Worlds</u>. (P)
19)	1965 Ace	<u>The Time Axis</u>. (P)
20)	1965 Mayflower	<u>The Best of Kuttner 1</u>. (s/P)

C. L. MOORE (continued)

21)	1966 Mayflower	The Best of Kuttner 2. (s/P)

with Henry Kuttner as *Lewis Padgett

2)	1950 S&S	A Gnome There Was. (s/RPv)
3)	1951 Gnome	Tomorrow and Tomorrow and The Fairy Chessmen. (RPav)
5)	1952 Gnome	Robots Have No Tails. (s)
7)	1953 Gnome	Mutant. (RPv)
9)	1953 Galaxy	Well of the Worlds. (P)
2A)	1954 Bantam	Line to Tomorrow. (s/P)
3A)	1956 Galaxy	Chessboard Planet. (a/P)
3B)	1963 Consul	Tomorrow and Tomorrow. (a/P)
3C)	1963 Consul	The Far Reality. (a/P)

with *Lewis Padgett (Henry Kuttner)

10)	1954 Ace	Beyond Earth's Gates. (P)

with Henry Kuttner

12)	1955 Ballantine	No Boundaries. (s/H-P)
17)	1964 Ace	Earth's Last Citadel. (P)

FPS:	"Shambleau,"	Weird Tales, November, 1933.
WIP:	1969 Pap Lib	Jirel of Joiry. (P)

***   ***   ***   ***   ***

Catherine Lucile Moore--born January 24, 1911 at Indianapolis, Indiana--B.A., University of Southern California, 1956; M.A., 1964--Los Angeles, California.

Daughter of Otto N. & Maude (Jones) Moore--(1) Henry Kuttner: June 7, 1940-February 4, 1958; (2) Thomas Reggie: August 13, 1964--no children.

Secretary to the President, Fletcher Trust Company, Indianapolis, 1930-1940; Free-Lance Writer, 1933-1958; Instructor in Writing and Literature, University of Southern California, 1958-1961; Free-Lance Television Script Writer, 1958-1961--Member: Science Fiction Writers of America; Mystery Writers of America; Writers Guild of America, West; Phi Beta Kappa; Phi Kappa Phi.

WARD MOORE

1)	1947 Sloane	Greener Than You Think. (RPa)
2)	1953 Farrar	Bring the Jubilee. (RP)

WARD MOORE (continued)

3) 1962 Pyramid   with Avram Davidson (q.v.) *Joyleg*. (P)

FPS: unknown.
FSF: "Sword of Peace,"   *Amazing*, March, 1950.

***   **   ***   ***   ***

Ward Moore--born August 10, 1903 at Madison, New Jersey--Pacific Grove, California.

Son of Samuel & Stella (Lemlein) Moore--has been married--Frederica Moore (1924); Rebekah Moore (1927); David Moore (1943); Samuel Moore (1947); Benyamin Hanina Moore (1953); Hannah Moore (1955); Sara Moore (1965).

"What career? Too much, too good, too soon."

Mr. Moore is the Founder, Past President, Grand Exalted Master, SOCIETY UNALTERABLY OPPOSED TO ALL PROGRESS.

He mentions:
    "'Mais, je vous avouer, je ne pas couche avec une japonaisse.' (quoted from memory; spelling and grammer probably wrong.)"

Mr. Moore also states:
    "May I say as an aside that I deplore the segregation of imaginative writing under the phoney label of 'science fiction.' It was a sad day when Hugo Gernsback was plucked untimely from his mother's womb. (Any day would be untimely.) The surgery was fatal. 'Mainstream' survived, but 'science fiction' atrophied. The label has been an albatross around my neck."

DAN MORGAN

1) 1955 Hamilton   *Cee-Tee Man*. (H-P)
2) 1961 Digit   *The Uninhibited*. (P)
3) 1966 Compact   *The Richest Corpse in Show Business*. (P)
4) 1967 Corgi   1   *The New Minds*. (P)

                              with *John Kippax (q.v.)
5) 1968 Macdonald   -1   *Thunder of Stars*.

DAN MORGAN (continued)

FPS:	"Alien Analysis,"		New Worlds, January, 1952.	
WIP:	1969 Corgi	2	The Several Minds. (P)	
	Corgi	3	Mind Trap. (P)	
		-2	Deadly Harvest. (with *John Kippax)	

***   ***   ***   ***   ***

Dan Morgan--born December 24, 1925 at Holbeach, Lincoln, England--Spalding Lincoln, England.

Son of Cecil & Lilian Kate (Morley) Morgan--Jean: 1949/pending--Glenn Dan Morgan (May 18, 1951).

Has served with the Royal Army Medical Corps; Professional Guitarist for the past twenty years; Company Director, Gents Tailoring and Outfitting Business; Part-time Free-Lance Writer--Member: British Science Fiction Association.

SAM MOSKOWITZ

1)	1954 Asfo	The Immortal Storm. (nf)
2)	1954 McBride	Editor's Choice in Science Fiction. (@)
3)	1963 World	Explorers of the Infinite. (nf/RP)
4)	1963 Collier	The Coming of the Robots. (@/P)
5)	1963 Collier	Exploring Other Worlds. (@/P)
6)	1965 World	Seekers of Tomorrow. (nf/RP)
7)	1965 World	Modern Masterpieces of Science Fiction. (@/RPav)
7A)	1966 Macfadden	Doorway Into Time and Other Stories from Modern Masterpieces of Science Fiction. (@/a/P)
9)	1967 World	Masterpieces of Science Fiction. (@)
10)	1967 Sidgwick	A Sense of Wonder. (@)
7B)	1968 Macfadden	The Vortex Blasters and Other Stories from Modern Masterpieces of Science Fiction. (@/a/P)
12)	1968 World	Science Fiction by Gaslight. (@)
7C)	1968 Macfadden	Microscopic God and Other Stories from Modern Masterpieces of Science Fiction. (@/a/P)

SAM MOSKOWITZ (continued)

		with Roger Elwood (q.v.)
8)	1966 Holt	Strange Signposts. (@)
11)	1967 Tower	The Human Zero and Other Science-Fiction Masterpieces. (@/P)
13)	1968 Tower	The Time Curve. (@/P)
FKP:	"The Way Back,"	Comet, January, 1941.
WIP:	1969 Macfadden	Alien Earth and Other Stories. (@/P/with Roger Elwood)
	1969 Macfadden	Other Worlds, Other Times. (@/P/with Roger Elwood)
	1969 Pyramid	Great Untold Stories of Fantasy and Horror. (@/P/with Alden H. Norton)
	1969 Doubleday	The Man Who Called Himself Poe. (@)

Sam Moskowitz was born in 1920. He was Managing Editor, Science Fiction +, March, 1953-December, 1953 (all issues), and is currently a member of Science Fiction Writers of America. A complete biography may be found in Contemporary Authors.

WALTER MOUDY

1)	1964 Berkley	No Man on Earth. (P/RH)
FPS:	1964 Berkley	No Man on Earth. (P)

***   ***   ***   ***   ***

Walter Frank Moudy--born December 19, 1929 at Cassville, Missouri--A.B., University of Missouri, 1955; LL.D., University of Missouri, 1957--Order of the Coif--Kansas City, Missouri.

Son of Ernest & Maxine Moudy--Marguerite: 1952--Tony Moudy (15); Chris Moudy (14); Jenny Moudy (11).

Lawyer--Member: Science Fiction Writers of America; Phi Beta Kappa.

***JOHN E. MULLER

1)	1960 Badger SF	Space Void.	(P/RHv)
2)	1961 Badger SF	Search the Dark Stars.	(P)
3)	1961 Badger SF	Day of the Beasts.	(P/RH)
4)	1961 Badger SF	A 1000 Years On.	(P)
5)	1961 Badger SN	The Unpossessed.	(P)
6)	1961 Badger SF	The Ultimate Man.	(P)
7)	1961 Badger SF	The Uninvited.	(P)
8)	1961 Badger SF	The Mind Makers.	(P)
9)	1961 Badger SF	Crimson Planet.	(P/RH)
10)	1961 Badger SF	Alien.	(P)
11)	1961 Badger SF	The Venus Venture.	(P/RHv)
12)	1961 Badger SF	Forbidden Planet.	(P/RH)
13)	1962 Badger SF	Edge of Eternity.	(P)
14)	1962 Badger SN	The Return of Zeus.	(P)
15)	1962 Badger SF	Perilous Galaxy.	(P)
16)	1962 Badger SF	Uranium 235.	(P/RH)
17)	1962 Badger SF	The Man Who Conquered Time.	(P)
18)	1962 Badger SF	Orbit One.	(P/RHv)
19)	1962 Badger SN	The Eye of Karnak.	(P)
20)	1962 Badger SF	Micro Infinity.	(P)
21)	1962 Badger SF	Beyond Time.	(P/RHv)
22)	1962 Badger SF	Infinity Machine.	(P)
23)	1962 Badger SF	The Day the World Died.	(P)
24)	1962 Badger SN	The Vengeance of Siva.	(P)
25)	1962 Badger SF	Night of the Big Fire.	(P)
26)	1962 Badger SF	The X Machine.	(P)
27)	1962 Badger SF	In the Beginning.	(P)
28)	1963 Badger SF	Reactor XK9.	(P)
29)	1963 Badger SF	Special Mission.	(P)
30)	1964 Badger SF	Dark Continuum.	(P)
31)	1964 Badger SF	Mark of the Beast.	(P)
32)	1965 Badger SF	The Negative Ones.	(P)
33)	1965 Badger SN	The Exorcists.	(P)
34)	1965 Badger SF	The Man from Beyond.	(P/RH)
35)	1965 Badger SF	Beyond the Void.	(P)
36)	1965 Badger SN	Spectre of Darkness.	(P)
37)	?1966 Badger SN	Out of the Night.	(P)
38)	1966 Badger SF	Phenomena X.	(P)
39)	1966 Badger SF	Survival Project.	(P)
A)	1967 Arcadia	Moon Rocket.	

as Marston Johns

1A)	1965 Arcadia	Space Void.
11A)	1965 Arcadia	The Venus Venture.
21A)	1966 Arcadia	Beyond Time.

***JOHN E. MULLER (continued)

                                        as Mel Jay
18A) 1966 Arcadia   Orbit One.

John E. Muller is a house penname. Marston Johns and Mel Jay may be two of the real authors behind the Muller books, or quite possibly might be pseudonyms in their own right. They are treated here as if they were pennames of "John E. Muller."

H. WARNER MUNN

1)	1958 Grandon		The Werewolf of Ponkert.
2)	1966 Ace	1	King of the World's Edge. (P)
3)	1967 Ace	2	The Ship from Atlantis. (P)

FPS: "The Werewolf of Ponkert," Weird Tales, July, 1925.

WIP: 1969 Ace   3   Merlin's Ring. (P)
        ·Ace   The Melldrum Box. (s/P)
                             The Lost Legion.

***   ***   ***   ***   ***

Harold Warner Munn--born November 5, 1903 at Athol, Massachusetts--Tacoma, Washington.

Son of Edward E. & Jessie (Lemon) Munn--Malvena Bodway: January 14, 1930--John W. Munn (37); James E. Munn (32); Gerald D. Munn (26); Robin S. Munn (21).

Has worked as a toolmaker, brakeman (New York Central Railroad), deckhand on Hudson River boats, carpenter (built his own house), bakery route salesman, ice cream route salesman, Fuller Brush and vacuum cleaner salesman, planer man and rip saw operator in northwest lumber mills; writer (particularly of weird fiction) during the life of Weird Tales and Unknown; resumed writing in 1965--Member: Tacoma Writers Club.

Mr. Munn writes:
"I was once mentioned in Bernard de Voto's section in the Atlantic Monthly, as 'the only active student of witchcraft and demonology alive' at that time--'in Massachusetts.' I was pleased and flattered, being only a collector. Now I am more interested in historical fiction with a weird and fantasy slant, and probably most of my future writing will be either that type or science fiction with a sound historical basis. It is my belief that the surface of this earth, its interior and its seas, its future and its past, can yet contribute much to science fiction without the necessity of voyaging in imagination through space. I hope to be able to prove this."

---

*RAY NELSON

1)	1967 Ace	with Philip K. Dick (q.v.) The Ganymede Takeover. (P)
FSF:	"Turn Off the Sky,"	The Magazine of Fantasy and Science Fiction, August, 1963.

***   ***   ***   ***   ***

Radell Faraday Nelson--born October 3, 1931 at Schenectady, New York--B.A., University of Chicago, 1960; Computer Programmer Certificate, Automation Institute, Oakland, California, 1961--El Cerrito, California.

Son of Walter Huges & Marie (Reed) Nelson--Kirsten Enge: 1958--Walter Trygve Nelson (10).

Free-Lance Writer, 1960-DATE--Member: National Fantasy Fan Federation; Brotherhood of the Way.

Mr. Nelson writes:

"At the 1939 World's Fair in New York, I walked stunned through the future and decided how I would spend this lifetime. Took LSD in 1962, wandered around smiling until 1968, then swore off all drugs forever. Enough is enough!" Mr. Nelson also mentioned his previous reincarnations: 1) Oro ApoCrockidilapolis, Alexandria, Egypt, 1st Century AD; 2) Yoni McKarikan, Ireland, Early Middle Ages; 3) Jean de Toulouse, South France, Middle Middle Ages; 4) Lisha Borman, Germany, Late Middle Ages; 5) Jean Hassim, Paris, Turn-of-the-Century. Mr. Nelson is a well-known fan writer and cartoonist.

KRIS NEVILLE

1)	1964 Belmont	The Unearth People. (P)
2)	1966 Belmont	The Mutants. (P)
3)	1967 Belmont	Peril of the Starmen. (P)
4)	1967 Belmont	Special Delivery. (P)

FPS: "The Hand from the Stars," Super Science Stories, July, 1949.

WIP: Four novels, one with Barry Malzberg.

***   ***   ***   ***   ***

KRIS NEVILLE (continued)

Kris Ottman Neville--born May 9, 1925 at Carthage, Missouri--B.A., University of California at Los Angeles, 1950--Los Angeles, California.

Son of Gilbert Ottman & Ethel Mae (Peters) Neville--Lil Johnson: September 28, 1957--Lois Neville (25); Freddie Neville (23); Leonard Neville (21); Nieson Neville (6); Helen Neville (4).

After World War II, employed variously by the Conveyor Company, Rocketdyne; employed by the Epoxylite Corporation, 1955-1966, 1967, 1968-DATE. He is currently working on a book covering the uses for plastics in medical applications and in artificial internal organs--Member: Science Fiction Writers of America.

BERNARD NEWMAN

1) 1962 Hale   The Blue Ants. (RP)

JULIUS P. NEWTON

1) 1963 Digit   The Forgotten Race. (P/RH)

LARRY NIVEN

1) 1966 Ballantine   World of Ptavvs. (P/RH)
2) 1968 Ballantine   Neutron Star. (s/P/RH)
3) 1968 Ballantine   A Gift from Earth. (P)

FPS: "The Coldest Place,"   If, December, 1964.

WIP: 1969 Ballantine   The Shape of Space. (s/P)
        1970 Ballantine   Ringworld. (P)

***   ***   ***   ***   ***

LARRY NIVEN (continued)

Laurence Van Cott Niven--born April 30, 1938 at Los Angeles, California--B.A., Washburn University, 1962; graduate study at University of California at Los Angeles, 1962-1963--Hugo Award, Best Short Story, 1967, "Neutron Star"--Los Angeles, California.

Son of Waldemar Van Cott & Lucy Estelle/Washington/(Doheny) Niven--Marilyn Wisowaty: September 6, 1969.

Free-Lance Writer--Member: Science Fiction Writers of America; Los Angeles Science Fiction Society.

GUIDO NIZZI

1)	1946 Exposition	The Victor.
2)	1947 Field	The Paralyzed Kingdom and Other Stories. (s)
3)	1964 Vantage	The Paralyzing Rays Vs. the Nuclears.
4)	1968 Carlton	The Daring Trip to the Moon.
FPP:	1946 Exposition	The Victor.

***　　　　***　　　　***　　　　***　　　　***

Guido Nizzi--born May 7, 1900 at Fiumalbo, Modena, Italy--studied for the Priesthood--has won various philatelic awards--Albuquerque, New Mexico.

Son of Carlo & Gaetana (Cesare) Nizzi--unmarried.

Theater Manager--Member: Albuquerque Philatelic Society.

The Nizzi family can be traced back to the 16th Century Italy.

WILLIAM F. NOLAN

1)	1952 Nolan	The Ray Bradbury Review. (nf/@)
2)	1963 Pap Lib	Impact-20. (s/P)
3)	1965 Avon	Man Against Tomorrow. (@/P)
4)	1965 Sherbourne	The Pseudo-People. (@/RP)
4A)	1966 Souvenir	Almost Human. (@)
6)	1968 Avon	Three to the Highest Power. (@/P)

WILLIAM F. NOLAN (continued)

		with George Clayton Johnson (q.v.)
5)	1967 Delacorte	Logan's Run. (RP)
FPS:	1969 Sherbourne	A Wilderness of Stars. (@)
	1970 Bantam	A Sea of Space. (@/P)
		A second collection of his shorter works.

***   ***   ***   ***   ***

William Francis Nolan--born March 6, 1928 at Kansas City, Missouri--attended Kansas City Art Institute, 1946-1947; San Diego State College, 1947-1948; Los Angeles City College, 1953--Los Angeles, California.

Son of Michael Cahill & Bernadette M. (Kelly) Nolan--engaged.

Managing Editor, Gamma, 1963-1964; Science Fiction Book Reviewer, Los Angeles Times, 1964-DATE; Free-Lance Writer and Editor--Member: Science Fiction Writers of America.

Mr. Nolan writes:
  "I've been involved in every possible aspect of the science fiction business: as fan (beginning in high school in the mid-40's back in Kansas City, my home town); as a short story writer for the pro magazines; as co-chairman of a science fiction convention (the Westercon in 1952 in San Diego); as fanzine editor and publisher; as book reviewer; as pro mag editor; as anthology editor; as novelist; as TV and screen writer//for The Twilight Zone and One Step Beyond--ed.//; as bibliographer and indexer; and as a science fiction historian and biographer.
  "I've had great fun with science fiction, shared close friendships with Charles Beaumont, Ray Bradbury, Chad Oliver, Richard Matheson, Ray Russell, Charles E. Fritch, Forry Ackerman, Ron Goulart, and Robert Sheckley, among writers in the genre. Science fiction writers are wide, wacky, wonderful people to know, and they never bore you; at least not the people I've known.
  "I've seen many changes in the sf field, from the early days of the 40's, through the 'golden' births of F&SF, Galaxy, If; through the days when 40-some mags crowded the stands; through the 'monsters from Mars' movie stage; to the mature brillance of 2001; the New Wave of sf; on to the present maturity of the field. Like its best writers, it is never boring; things are always happening in sf: it is a vital, alive area to write in, edit in, work in. I've worked in many fields as a pro writer, having placed some 400 items and nearly 20 books in a variety of markers: from Sports Illustrated to Prairie Schooner, but I have never really left sf. I find the old life and joy still waiting for me when I turn back to the genre for a book or a story.

WILLIAM F. NOLAN (continued)

"There are things about sf I don't like, but this is not the time or place to discuss them. Suffice to say that sf has provided me with a stimulating base, good friends, some fine reading, and much pleasure down the years. I'm proud that my work has formed part of its history."

---

*JOHN NORMAN

1)	1966 Ballantine	1	Tarnsman of Gor.	(P/RH)
2)	1967 Ballantine	2	Outlaw of Gor.	(P)
3)	1968 Ballantine	3	Priest-Kings of Gor.	(P)

SER: Gor

FPS: "a radio script to a station in Lincoln, Nebraska for ten dollars when, as I recall, I was in high school."
FSF: 1966 Ballantine   1   Tarnsman of Gor. (P)

WIP: 1969 Ballantine   4   Nomads of Gor. (P)

***   ***   ***   ***   ***

John Frederick Lange, Jr.--born June 3, 1931 at Chicago, Illinois--B.A., University of Nebraska; M.A., University of Southern California; Ph.D. (Philosophy), Princeton University--has received several academic awards--Great Neck, New York.

Son of John Frederick & Almyra D. (Taylor) Lange--Bernice L. Green: January 14, 1956--John Lange (12); David Lange (2); Jennifer Lange (1).

"I have worked as a radio announcer and continuity writer; I have also written some film scripts for the University of Nebraska, and have been a story analyst at Warner Brothers Motion Pictures; I have also worked as a technical editor and special materials writer for Rocketdyne, a Division of North American Aviation specializing in the production of rocket engines. Primarily, however, I am a teacher of philosophy, and currently hold a post at Queens College of the City University of New York."--Member: Science Fiction Writers of America.

Mr. Norman is no relation of the John Lange who writes paperback suspense novels.

ALDEN H. NORTON

1)	1966 Award	Award Science Fiction Reader. (@/P)
2)	1967 Berkley	Horror Times Ten. (@/P)
3)	1968 Berkley	Masters of Horrow. (@/P)

FPS:	"Ten Minutes to Death,"	Detective Fiction Weekly, early 1930's.
FSF:	1966 Award	Award Science Fiction Reader. (@/P)

WIP:	1969 Berkley	Hauntings and Horrors: Ten Grisly Tales. (@/P)
	1969 Pyramid	Futures Unlimited. (@/P)
	19<u>69</u> Pyramid	Great Untold Stories of Fantasy and Horror.
		(@/P/with Sam Moskowitz)

***   ***   ***   ***   ***

Alden Holmes Norton--born July 23, 1903 at Lynn, Massachusetts-Ph.B., Brown University, 1925--New York, New York.

Son of Charles A. & Katherine (White) Norton--Margaret Acheson: October 12, 1943-- no children.

Editor, Astonishing Stories, November, 1941-April, 1943; Super Science Stories, November, 1941-May, 1943; currently in Releases and Foreign Sales, Popular Publications, Inc.

----

*ANDRE NORTON

1)	1951 Harcourt		Huon of the Horn. (RP)
2)	1952 Harcourt		Star Man's Son. (RPv)
3)	1953 World		Space Service. (@)
4)	1953 Harcourt		Star Rangers. (RPv)
2A)	1954 Ace		Daybreak--2250 A.D. (P)
5)	1954 World		Space Pioneers. (@)
6)	1954 World		The Stars Are Ours! (RP)
4A)	1955 Ace		The Last Planet. (P)
8)	1955 Harcourt		Star Guard. (RP)
9)	1956 World		Space Police. (@)
11)	1956 Ace		The Crossroads of Time. (P)
12)	1957 World		Star Born. (RP)
13)	1957 Harcourt		Sea Siege. (RP)
14)	1958 Harcourt		Star Gate. (RP)
15)	1958 Harcourt	1	The Time Traders. (RP)
17)	1959 Harcourt	-1	The Beast Master. (RPa)

*ANDRE NORTON (continued)

18)	1959 Ace		Secret of the Lost Race.	(P)
19)	1959 World	2	Galactic Derelict.	(RP)
20)	1960 World		Storm Over Warlock.	(RP)
21)	1960 Ace		The Sioux Spaceman.	(P)
22)	1961 Ace		Star Hunter.	(P)
23)	1961 Harcourt		Catseye.	(RP)
24)	1962 Ace		Eye of the Monster.	(P)
25)	1962 World	3	The Defiant Agents.	(RP)
26)	1962 Harcourt	-2	Lord of Thunder.	(RP)
27)	1963 World	4	Key Out of Time.	(RP)
28)	1963 Ace	+1	Witch World.	(P)
29)	1963 Harcourt	01	Judgment on Janus.	(RP)
30)	1964 World		Ordeal in Otherwhere.	(RP)
31)	1964 Ace	+2	Web of the Witch World.	(P)
32)	1964 Harcourt		Night of Masks.	(RP)
33)	1965 Ace	+3	Three Against the Witch World.	(P)
34)	1965 Harcourt		The X Factor.	(RP)
35)	1965 Viking		Quest Crosstime.	(RP)
36)	1965 Ace	+4	Year of the Unicorn.	(P)
37)	1965 World	/1	Steel Magic.	(RPv)
38)	1966 Viking		Moon of Three Rings.	(RP)
39)	1966 Harcourt	02	Victory on Janus.	(RP)
40)	1967 World	/2	Octagon Magic.	
37A)	1967 Scholastic	/1	Gray Magic.	(P)
41)	1967 Ace	+5	Warlock of the Witch World.	(P)
42)	1967 Harcourt		Operation Time Search.	(RP)
43)	1968 World	/3	Fur Magic.	
44)	1968 Viking	=1	The Zero Stone.	(RP)
45)	1968 Ace		Star Hunter and Voodoo Planet.	(P)
46)	1968 Ace	+6	Sorceress of the Witch World.	(P)
47)	1968 Harcourt		Dark Piper.	(RP)

as *Andrew North

7)	1955 Gnome	*1	Sargasso of Space.	(RP)
10)	1956 Gnome	*2	Plague Ship.	(RP)
16)	1959 Ace	*3	Voodoo Planet.	(P)

SER: 1) Time Agent; 3) Witch World

FPS: 1934 Appleton   Prince Commands.
FSF: "The People of the Crater," Fantasy Book, #1 (1947) (as *Andrew North).

*ANDRE NORTON (continued)

WIP: 1969 Viking =2 Uncharted Stars.
     1969 Harcourt   Postmarked the Stars.

*** *** *** *** ***

Alice Mary Norton--born 1912 at Cleveland, Ohio--attended Western Reserve University, 1930-1932--Award from Dutch Government, 1946; Ohiana Library Honorable Mention; Headliner Award, Theta Sigma Phi, 1963; Boys' Clubs of America Certificate, 1965--Maitland, Florida.

Daughter of Adalbert Freely & Bertha (Stemm) Norton--unmarried.

Children's Librarian, Cleveland Public Library, 1932-1950; Editor for Gnome Press, 1950-1958; Free-Lance Writer, 1958-DATE--Member: Science Fiction Writers of America; Women's National Book Association; Theta Sigma Phi.

Miss Norton writes:
"My first book was accepted and published when I was quite young, so I have had a long writing career. I began writing when I was in high school, and had written three full books before the third was published. I then went back and revised my first book, and that was the second title I had published. Until 1950, sf was very difficult to sell in the book field. I worked in the adventure-spy-historical-mystery areas. I really broke into the field as a writer after having edited some sf anthologies for World--I had written early books on the subject, but had not discovered any publishers interested in them until that date.

"SF appeals to me, as I have always enjoyed reading it, and it is a purely imaginative exercise--though one does have to do a lot of research reading for every book. For me swords and sorcery has the greatest appeal--and it is the most fun to write.

"Most of my contributions in the field have been for teenagers; my one rule is that one must never simplify, for to do so is an insult to the readers' intelligence--most sf readers tend to be in the upper third of their classes in school.

"I know very little about the new wave--it does not interest me for pleasure reading, and so I read very little of it. My favorite authors are de Camp, Anderson, Laumer, McCaffrey, Beam Piper, Cordwainer Smith, and Schmitz."

VICTOR NORWOOD

1) 1951 Scion   The Untamed. (P)
2) 1951 Scion   The Caves of Death. (P)
3) 1951 Scion   The Temple of the Dead. (P)

VICTOR NORWOOD (continued)

4)	1952 Scion	The Skull of Kanaima. (P)	
5)	1952 Scion	The Island of Creeping Death. (P)	
6)	1953 Scion	Drums Along the Amazon. (P)	
7)	1953 Scion	Cry of the Beast. (P)	
8)	1962 Badger SF	Night of the Black Horror. (P)	

Victor George Charles Norwood is an English professional writer.

ALAN E. NOURSE

1)	1954 Winston	Trouble on Titan. (RP)
2)	1955 Ace	A Man Obsessed. (P/RHe)
3)	1957 McKay	Rocket to Limbo. (RP)
4)	1959 McKay	Scavengers in Space. (RP)
6)	1960 McKay	Star Surgeon.
7)	1961 McKay	Tiger by the Tail. (s/RP/RPv)
8)	1962 McKay	Raiders from the Rings. (RP)
9)	1963 McKay	The Counterfeit Man. (s/RP)
7A)	1964 Corgi	Beyond Infinity. (s/P)
10)	1965 McKay	The Universe Between. (RP)
11)	1965 McKay	Psi High and Others. (s/RP)
12)	1968 McKay	The Mercy Men. (2/e)

with J. A. Meyer

5) 1959 Ace   The Invaders Are Coming. (P)

FPS: "High Threshold,"   Astounding, March, 1951.

*** *** *** *** ***

Alan Edward Nourse--born August 11, 1928 at Des Moines, Iowa--B.S., Rutgers University, 1951; M.D., University of Pennsylvania, 1955; Internship, Virginia Mason Hospital, Seattle, Washington, 1955-1956--Boys' Clubs of America Junior Book Award, 1963--North Bend, Washington.

Son of Benjamin Chamberlain & Grace (Ogg) Nourse--Ann Jane Morton: June 10, 1952--Benjamin Nourse (11); Rebecca Nourse (9); Jonathan Nourse (8); Christopher Nourse (6).

ALAN E. NOURSE (continued)

General Practitioner of Medicine and Partner, North Bend Medical Clinic, 1958-1964; Free-Lance Writer, 1964-DATE; Agent/Owner, Tradewinds Travel Bureau, Fall City, Washington, 1967-DATE--Member: Science Fiction Writers of America (President, 1968-1969); American Medical Association; Alpha Kappa Kappa.

Dr. Nourse writes:
"Regarding my opinion of the current state of science fiction, I feel that the traditional form of technological-oriented, hard-science-based science fiction is gradually passing from the scene, being replaced by soft-science (i.e., psychology, sociology, political science, etc.) based science fiction more concerned with human values on the one hand and science-disoriented romantic fantasy on the other hand....both representing humanistic rather than mechanistic or materialistic fiction; in particular, I feel that science fiction is becoming a highly romantic fiction in spite of the many superficially ultra-realistic or obscurely abstract faces it presents, and my impression is strong that most of the present trend-setting science fiction writers are at heart humanists and romantics. 'New Wave' is an altogether too vague term to be applied to the field with meaning, since at present it can be defined in any number of ways, and is generally defined by the individual using the term in whatever way he chooses. This has lead to a great deal of totally meaningless argument and dissention. There is certainly a discernable move, both conscious and unconscious, on the part of many leading sf writers to approach general fiction under the guise of science fiction, using science fictional techniques and frameworks. I find nothing objectional about this, and indeed feel it is, if anything, the 'trend,' but realize that many contemporaries working in the field would not agree with me. I also see in the increasing concentration on the novel form and length supportive evidence of my impression. SF writers are more than ever concerned with saying something relevant about the condition of Man, and find shorter lengths too restrictive or conducive to stories that seem empty or superficial.

"I do not believe that I have had any particularly significant impact on the development of the genre, although I feel that most of my best work, from the beginning, has been concerned with humanistic questions, human problems and exploration of human capabilities rather than with hard-science or technological problems. I think this has been well received because of the very acceptable medical-humanistic orientation of much of my sf work. I doubt that this has set any trends as such, but it has perhaps been in keeping with a general growing interest in humanistic sf that began long before the present more marked changes became apparent."

CHARLES NUETZEL

2) 1965 Book Co   If This Goes On. (@/P)
3) 1966 Greenleaf   Queen of Blood. (P)

CHARLES NUETZEL (continued)

			as *Charles English
1)	1964 Scorpion		Lovers: 2075. (P)

FPS:	To	Cocktail, 1960.
FSF:	"A Very Cultured Taste,"	Jade #1, 1960 (published without byline).

WIP:	1969 Powell		Swordmen of Vistar. (P)
	1969 Powell		Images of Tomorrow. (1/s/P)
	1969 Powell	1	Warriors of Noomas. (P)
	1969 Powell	2	Raiders of Noomas. (P)
	1969 Powell		Jungle, Jungle. (P)
	1969 Powell		Slaves of Lomooro. (P/as *Albert Augustus, Jr.)
	1969 Powell		Adapt or Die. (P)

***　　　***　　　***　　　***　　　***

Charles Alexander Nuetzel--born November 10, 1934 at San Francisco, California--attended Valley State College, one term--Thousand Oaks, California.

Son of Albert A. & Betty (Stockberger) Nuetzel--Brigitte Marianne Winter: October 13, 1962--no children.

"One-time would-be professional singer of pop music. The normal run-through of jobs of little importance, including some work in the motion picture industry for Studio Film Service, Pacific Title, General Film Labs. Have sold some 100+ short manuscripts under various pennames, as well as over 70 paperback novels. Was Publisher/Packager of eight books (my own); currently Packager, with total control, of Powell Sci-Fi, a paperback line publishing one sf title a month;" Free-Lance Writer, 1960-DATE--Member: Science Fiction Writers of America.

Mr. Nuetzel provided the following background material on his life--it has been edited slightly to conform with our usage and space requirements:
  "Met Ray Bradbury in a second hand book store, and consequently learned about fandom (and met Forrest J. Ackerman//Mr. Nuetzel's agent--ed.//). In my fan years became a very close friend of E. Everett Evans, and still have many manuscripts inscribed by him to 'my no. 1 fan.' Though his help and that of his wife, Thelma, I learned something about writing: a story should have a sub-plot. I did for a while publish a fanzine better forgotten. Was a great Edgar Rice Burroughs fan, and have what was called by Miss Jennings (ERB's secretary) the last books he autographed: no other proof but the shaky hand-writing. I'm told that my grandfather, editor of a local newspaper at the time ERB had his Tarzana ranch, knew him casually; again, no proof.
  "My father, now semi-retired//died June 18, 1969--ed.//, was a commercial artist all his life, working for the motion picture industry. To please his son, he did sf covers in the fifties for several magazines, including F&SF, Amazing, and Fantastic. All of which might seem to have little to do with myself as a writer. Not so!

CHARLES NUETZEL (continued)

"As Forry Ackerman is now saying (probably to please me): 'Ray Bradbury burned his first two million words; Charles Nuetzel <u>sold</u> his.' To which I silently add: maybe I should have burned mine too.

"But the point is that a writer can do one of several things: write just for the fun of it, and never even try to get published; write and write and write until you're good enough to get published in the good markets (burning all the crud, like Bradbury did); or write and write until you're just good enough to be published in the lowest crummy market possible, and keep writing as fast as you can, learning on the job. My father taught me that an artist can sit up in an attic and paint for himself--and starve--or he can use what talents and abilities and tricks he has, and direct them to a commercial market to make a living.

"Thus: my first year of professional writing was done in the following manner: I took a title, put it on the top third of the page, picked a penname, and then wrote until the story was finished. Most of the time I never read what I wrote, but sent it to Forry Ackerman, who suffered through something like a hundred manuscripts that first year. Needless to say, he didn't make much money as my agent, even though he did give me a pretty fair sale record for a first year pro writer. I was told by Forry not to bother with sci-fi. Thus the stories were on subjects I'd sooner say nothing about. I used over a dozen pennames.

"Thus: being a great lover of the way Edgar Rice Burroughs made his money (to say nothing about the man who created Perry Mason), and lovingly calling them 'hacks,' I consider myself a professional 'hack,' and wish to God I could be as much of a 'hack' as the two above-mentioned writers. Not that I expect this to happen--but we all have our dreams.

"Every science fiction writer and fan has heard Ray Bradbury say over and over again: 'Write, write, write, until you get all the bad words out of your system.... don't slant....write about what you hate and love violently....' A quote, in Mr. Bradbury's defense, deriving from my very weak memory. And while I very much admire the Ray Bradbury type of artist-writer, I disagree with him on one basic point: do slant and do write to sell as much as possible, and most importantly, attempt not only to write all the bad words out of your system, but also all the bad plots. You can use pennames to hide behind when the writing and/or subject matter is such that you don't wish to take credit for it. Save your own name for things you wish to think of as 'quality.'

"My own preferences in science fiction are for the adventure-romance (i.e., ERB) and social satire; this is fairly evident in my two recent books, <u>Swordmen of Vistar</u> and <u>Images of Tomorrow</u>, each of which shows a totally different side of my writing nature.

"I am very strong on the first few words of a story. 'The beautiful mountain' is not at all as interesting as 'If the beautiful....' Words like 'if' and 'but' are far more 'grabbing' than words like 'the,' 'a,' etc. I also believe of course that the immediately following words (right through to the end of the story) have importance. What they say must contain plot, sub-plot, theme, conflict--in other words, a damned good story. But those first words should cause the reader to start reading, should get him interested in what follows. And then it is the responsibility of the author to keep him hooked, until hopefully the reader will throw down the finished book, and say, 'God, that's one hell of a story!'

CHARLES NUETZEL (continued)

"My future plans are very simple: to be successful and to make a lot of money. I'd like to do more than simply write and package books for publishers--I have nothing at all against cutting out the middle man, and pocketing the remainder. I enjoy seeing books filled with words that came off my typewriter--for a few moments, at least. I enjoy seeing translations of my work. Like many writers, I have a big ego in that direction. It's gratifying to be told that there's someone out there who likes what you write. The other day Robert Bloch dropped me a short note in which he was kind enough to say that he spent an enjoyable rainy Sunday afternoon reading Swordmen of Vistar: that's the kind of boost writers need more of."

CLAUDE NUNES

1) 1966 Ace   Inherit the Earth. (P)

FPS: "The Problem,"   Science Fantasy, April, 1962
                        (with Rhoda Nunes)

***   ***   ***   ***   ***

Claude Nunes--born April 14, 1924 at Johannesburg, South Africa--Bachelor of Commerce Degree; Qualified as a Cost and Works Accountant (A.C.W.A.)--Johannesburg, South Africa.

Son of Manuel & Patricia Ina Rose (Ellis) Nunes--Rhoda: March 2, 1959--Michael Manuel Nunes (6); David Owen Nunes (2); Andrew Jonathan Nunes (0)

"Have worked since school days at the Chamber of Mines of South Africa, first as a Clerk in the Accounts Department, now as a Statistician"--Member: Association of Cost and Works Accountants.

Mr. Nunes writes:
"Most of my work has been in collaboration with my wife Rhoda....even Inherit the Earth, an adaptation of the short story of the same name, was partly written by her. She declined to have it published jointly, as she considered her share (about 10% in this case) too small. We have written two other sf novels, both of which were favorably reviewed by Ace Books, who have encouraged us to rewrite them. However, laziness in our besetting sin, and although one of them is well advanced again, the other is still in the planning stage. I have been a keen reader of the genre since about the age of 9, and have copies of Astounding reaching back to 1933. I still find science fiction my major literary interest."

P. T. OLEMY

1) 1968 Flagship   The Clones. (P)

P. T. Olemy is a possible pseudonym.

CHAD OLIVER

1) 1952 Winston   Mists of Dawn.
2) 1954 Ballantine Shadows in the Sun. (H-P)
3) 1955 Ballantine Another Kind. (s/H-P)
4) 1957 Doubleday   The Winds of Time. (RP)
5) 1960 Ballantine Unearthly Neighbors. (P)

FPS: "The Boy Next Door," The Magazine of Fantasy and Science Fiction
                            June, 1951.
FPP: "The Land of Lost Content," Super Science Stories, November, 1950.

WIP: The Shores of Another Sea.

***   ***   ***   ***   ***

Symmes Chadwick Oliver--born March 30, 1928 at Cincinnati, Ohio--B.A., University of Texas, 1951; M.A., University of Texas, 1952; Ph.D., University of California at Los Angeles, 1961--Spur Award, Best Western Novel, 1967, The Wolf Is My Brother--Austin, Texas.

Son of Dr. & Mrs. S. F. Oliver--Betty Jane Jenkins: 1952--Kim Oliver (13); Glen Oliver (1).

Professor and Chairman of the Department of Anthropology, University of Texas--Member: Science Fiction Writers of America; Western Writers of America; American Anthropological Association; African Studies Association; Texas Institute of Letters.

BEN ORKOW

1) 1962 Signet   When Time Stood Still. (P)

FPS: "Milgrim's Progress," a play, produced 1924.
FSF: 1962 Signet   When Time Stood Still. (P)

***   ***   ***   ***   ***

BEN ORKOW (continued)

Ben Harrison Orkow--born January 9, 1896 in Russia--privately educated to the equivalent of a university degree--Van Nuys, California.

Son of Abe & Anita Orkow--(3) Ruby: April 14, 1932--Miriam Orkow Biro (1933).

Free-Lance Writer and Playwright--Member: Writers Guild of America; Dramatists' Guild.

Mr. Orkow is the author of a number of plays produced on Broadway; among his credits are sixteen screen plays for major movie studios, and 20 television dramas. He came to the United States in 1906.

----

*DEAN OWEN

1)	1960 Monarch	The Brides of Dracula. (P)
2)	1960 Monarch	Konga. (P)
3)	1961 Monarch	Reptilicus. (P)
4)	1962 Ace	End of the World. (P)

Dean Owen is a penname of Dudley Dean McGaughy.

MABLY OWEN

with A. S. Williams-Ellis (q.v.)

1)	1960 Blackie	Out of This World 1. (@)
2)	1961 Blackie	Out of This World 2. (@)
3)	1962 Blackie	Out of This World 3. (@)
4)	1964 Blackie	Out of This World 4. (@)
5)	1965 Blackie	Out of This World 5. (@)
6)	1966 Blackie	Worlds Apart. (@)
7)	1967 Blackie	Out of This World 6. (@)
8)	1968 Blackie	Out of This World 7. (@)
FPS:	1960 Blackie	Out of This World 1. (@/with A. S. Williams-Ellis)
WIP:	1969 Blackie	Out of This World 8. (@/with A. S. Williams-Ellis)

***   ***   ***   ***   ***

MABLY OWEN (continued)

Mably Ceredig Owen--born March 17, 1912 at Heath, Glamorgan, South Wales--Honours Degree in English, Swansea University College, 1934--Frank Treharne James Welsh Prize, 1932; Glamorgan County Welsh Exhibition, 1932--Bangor, Caernarvon, North Wales.

Son of Edward & Sarah Owen--Daphne: September, 1942--no children.

Has been a Schoolmaster in North and South Wales; Lecturer in English, Normal College of Education, Bangor, North Wales, 1964-DATE--Member: Schools Council Committees.

MARK OWINGS

1)	1966 Anthem	with Jack L. Chalker (q.v.) The Index to the Science-Fantasy Publishers. (nf/P)
2)	1967 Mirage	(with Jack L. Chalker) (q.v.) The Necronomicon: A Study. (nf/P)
FPP:	1966 Anthem	The Index to the Science-Fantasy Publishers. (nf/P/with Jack L. Chalker)
WIP:	1970 Mirage	The Index to the Science-Fantasy Publishers III. (nf/with Jack L. Chalker)

***   ***   ***   ***   ***

Mark Samuel Owings--born January 3, 1945 at Baltimore, Maryland--attended Johns Hopkins University, two years--New York, New York.

Son of Henry Townsend & Elizabeth Theresa (Smith) Owings--unmarried.

Has been a pricing clerk; laborer (unloading boxcars, among others); Assistant Bookkeeper, Eastern Life Insurance Company, 1967-DATE.

WILLIAM J. PALMER

1) 1968 Vantage   The Curious Culture of the Planet Loretta.

WILLIAM J. PALMER (continued)

FPS: 1941
FSP: 1968 Vantage   The Curious Culture of the Planet Loretta.

***   ***   ***   ***   ***

William J. Palmer (u)--born August 20, 1890 at Le Roy, Minnesota--attended University of Minnesota; A.B., University of Southern California; J.D. University of Southern California--Oakland, California.

Son of George W. & Mary (Grattan) Palmer--Margaret Willis: July 22, 1915-- two children.

Judge, Superior Court of California for Los Angeles County, 1932-1963; Editor-in-Chief, Civil California Jury Instructions, 20 years; Criminal California Jury Instructions, 15 years; Free-Lance Writer and Composer (seven musical compositions published); currently retired--Member: Conference of California Judges; Los Angeles Bar Association; California State Bar; Hollywood Masonic Club (Honorary Life Member); Westwood Camera Club; Sierra Club; American Society of Composers, Authors and Publishers.

EDGAR PANGBORN

1) 1953 Doubleday   West of the Sun. (RP)
2) 1954 Doubleday   A Mirror for Observers. (RP)
3) 1964 St. Martin's   Davy. (RP)
4) 1966 S&S   The Judgment of Eve. (RP)

FPS: 1930 Dutton   A-100. (as *Bruce Harrison)
FSF: "Angel's Egg,"   Galaxy, June, 1951.

***   ***   ***   ***   ***

Edgar Pangborn--born February 25, 1909 at New York, New York--attended Harvard University, 1924-1926; New England Conservatory of Music--International Fantasy Award, 1954, A Mirror for Observers--Woodstock, New York.

Son of Harry Leroy & Georgia (Wood) Pangborn--unmarried.

Free-Lance Writer--Member: Authors Guild.

ALEXEI PANSHIN

1)	1968 Advent		Heinlein in Dimension. (nf)	
2)	1968 Ace		Rite of Passage. (P/RH)	
3)	1968 Ace	1	Star Well. (P)	
4)	1968 Ace	2	The Thurb Revolution. (P)	

SER: Anthony Villers.

FPS: "A Piece of Pie," Seventeen, November, 1960.
FSF: "Down to the Worlds of Men," If, July, 1963.

WIP:	1969 Ace	3	Masque World. (P)
	1969 Ace		The Farthest Star. (P)
			Science Fiction: A Critical Introduction (nf)
	Ace	4	The Universal Phantograph. (P)

***   ***   ***   ***   ***

Alexei Panshin (i)--born August 14, 1940 at Lansing, Michigan--B.A., Michigan State, 1965; M.A., University of Chicago, 1966--Hugo Award, Best Fan Writer, 1967; Nebula Award, Best Novel, 1968, Rite of Passage-- Brooklyn, New York.

Son of Alexis John & Lucie (Padgett) Panshin --unmarried.

Free-Lance Writer--Member: Science Fiction Writers of America (Editor, Science Fiction Writers of America Bulletin, August 1968-DATE).

Mr. Panshin's father was born in Russia; his mother's family is English-American, dating in this country from 1620.

J. PARKER-RICH

1) 1968 Gollancz   The Hendon Fungus.

EMIL PETAJA

1)	1965 Ace		Alpha Yes, Terra No! (P)
2)	1965 Ace		The Caves of Mars. (P)
3)	1966 Ace	1	Saga of Lost Earths. (P)

EMIL PETAJA (continued)

4)	1966 Ace	2	The Star Mill.	(P)
5)	1967 Ace	3	The Stolen Sun.	(P)
6)	1967 Ace	-1	Lord of the Green Planet.	(P)
7)	1967 Ace	4	Tramontane.	(P)
8)	1968 Ace		The Prism.	(P)
9)	1968 Ace	-2	Doom of the Green Planet.	(P)
10)	1968 Dell		The Time Twister.	(P)
11)	1968 Bokanalia		And Flights of Angels.	(nf/@/P)

SER: Kalevala.

FSF: "Time Will Tell,"   Amazing, June, 1942.

WIP: 1969 Dell   Path Beyond the Stars. (P)
     1969 Berkley   The Nets of Space. (P)
     1969 Ace   5   an untitled concluding novel in the
                                      Kalevala Series. (P)

***　　***　　***　　***　　***

Emil Theodore Petaja--born April 12, 1915 at Milltown, Montana--attended Montana State University, 1935-1937--minor poetry and photography awards--San Francisco, California.

Son of John & Hanna Petaja--unmarried.

Spent fifteen years as a professional photographer; also has worked for Technicolor Printing, Hollywood; has owned two portrait studios; currently Free-Lance Writer--Member: Science Fiction Writers of America; Mystery Writers of America; First Fandom.

Mr. Petaja is the founder and Chairman of the Bokanalia Memorial Foundation, dedicated to the perpetuation of the memory of the late artist, Hannes Bok. To this end, the Foundation is planning (and has published) a series of portfolios and anthologies featuring previously unpublished work by Bok, together with comments, biographies, and memorial articles, poetry, and fiction by Petaja and others.

Emil Petaja is of Finnish descent: his interest in Finnish folklore and legends is evident in the majority of his works, particularly the Kalevala Series. He provides the following short comment: "Due to the lamentable habit of eating, my writing was relegated to secondary consideration until six years ago; having purchased some property with a small income attached, I went back to my lifelong love with modest success after nearly thirty years!"

CHAPMAN PINCHER

1) 1965 Weidenfeld   Not Without a Bang. (RP)
2) 1967 Weidenfeld   The Giant Killer.

***   ***   ***   ***   ***

Henry Chapman Pincher--born March 29, 1914 at Ambala, Punjab, India--attended University of London, 1932-1936--London, England.

Son of Richard Chapman & Helen (Foster) Pincher.

Free-Lance Writer.

CHARLES PLATT

1) 1967 Berkley   Garbage World. (P)

FPS: "One of Those Days,"   Science Fantasy, December, 1964/January, 1965.

WIP: The City Dwellers.

***   ***   ***   ***   ***

Charles Platt (u)--born October 25, 1944 at Hertfordshire, England--attended college; First Class Diploma in Graphic Design--London, England.

Son of Michael & Elaine Bertha (Hubbard) Platt--has been married--no children.

"Organist in pop group; Free-Lance Photographer; Designer of New Worlds magazine; Free-Lance Designer of book jackets; Writer of sex books for Gold Star Publications, London;" Mr. Platt has also been an Associate Editor of New Worlds.

FREDERIK POHL

1) 1952 Permabook   Beyond the End of Time. (@/P)
2) 1953 Ballantine   Star Science Fiction Stories. (@/H-P)

FREDERIK POHL (continued)

4)	1953 Permabook	Shadow of Tomorrow.	(@/P)
5)	1953 Ballantine	Star Science Fiction Stories #2.	(@/H-P)
6)	1953 Columbia	Science Fiction Stories.	(@)
7)	1954 Ballantine	Star Science Fiction Stories #3.	(@/H-P)
9)	1954 Ballantine	Star Short Novels.	(@/H-P)
10)	1954 Hanover	Assignment in Tomorrow.	(@)
14)	1956 Ballantine	Alternating Currents.	(s/H-P)
16)	1957 Ballantine	Slave Ship.	(H-P)
17)	1957 Ballantine	The Case Against Tomorrow.	(s/P)
18)	1958 Ballantine	Star Science Fiction Stories #4.	(@/P)
20)	1959 Ballantine	Star Science Fiction Stories #5.	(@/P)
21)	1959 Ballantine	Tomorrow Times Seven.	(s/P)
23)	1959 Ballantine	Star Science Fiction Stories #6.	(@/P)
24)	1960 Doubleday	Star of Stars.	(@/RP)
25)	1960 Ballantine	The Man Who Ate the World.	(s/P)
26)	1961 Gnome	Drunkard's Walk.	(RP)
27)	1961 Ballantine	Turn Left at Thursday.	(s/P)
28)	1962 Doubleday	Time Waits for Winthrop and Four Other Short Novels.	(@)
29)	1962 Doubleday	The Expert Dreamers.	(@/RP)
31)	1963 Ballantine	The Abominable Earthman.	(s/P)
32)	1964 Doubleday	The Seventh Galaxy Reader.	(@/RP)
34)	1965 Doubleday	The Eighth Galaxy Reader.	(@/RP)
35)	1965 Ballantine	A Plague of Pythons.	(P/RH)
37)	1966 Doubleday	The Ninth Galaxy Reader.	(@/RP)
38)	1966 Ballantine	Digits and Dastards.	(s/P/RH)
39)	1966 Doubleday	The If Reader of Science Fiction.	(@/RP)
40)	1966 Whiting	Star Fourteen.	(@/RP)
41)	1966 Gollancz	A Frederik Pohl Omnibus.	(s)
42)	1967 Doubleday	The Tenth Galaxy Reader.	(@)
43)	1968 Doubleday	The Second If Reader of Science Fiction.	(@)

with Cyril M. Kornbluth

3)	1953 Ballantine	The Space Merchants.	(H-P)
8)	1954 Ballantine	Search the Sky.	(H-P)
12)	1955 Ballantine	Gladiator-at-Law.	(H-P)
22)	1959 Ballantine	Wolfbane.	(s/P/RH)
30)	1962 Ballantine	The Wonder Effect.	(s/P/RH)

with Jack Williamson (q.v.)

11)	1954 Gnome	1	Undersea Quest.
15)	1956 Gnome	2	Undersea Fleet.
19)	1958 Gnome	3	Undersea City.

FREDERIK POHL (continued)

33)	1964 Ballantine	The Reefs of Space. (P/RH)
36)	1965 Ballantine	Starchild. (P/RH)
13)	1955 S&S	with Lester del Rey (q.v.) as *Edson McCann Preferred Risk. (RP)

FPS: "Elegy to a Dead Planet: Luna," Amazing, October, 1937
(poem/as *Elton V. Andrews)

WIP:	1969 Trident	The Age of the Pussyfoot. (RP)
	1969 Ballantine	Rogue Star. (P/with Jack Williamson)
	1969 Doubleday	The Eleventh Galaxy Reader. (@)

*** *** *** *** ***

Frederik Pohl--born November 26, 1919 at New York, New York--Hugo Award, Best Professional Magazine, 1966, 1967, 1968, If; Invisible Little Man Award for Outstanding Service to the Field of Science Fiction, 1964; E. E. Smith Memorial Award, 1966--Red Bank, New Jersey.

Son of Fred George & Anna Jane (Mason) Pohl--Carol Metcalf Ulf: September 15, 1952--Ann Pohl; Karen Pohl; Frederik Pohl III (deceased); Frederik Pohl IV; Kathy Pohl.

Editor, Astonishing Stories, February, 1940-September, 1941; Assistant Editor, November, 1941-April, 1943; Editor, Super Science Stories, March, 1940-August, 1941; Assistant Editor, November, 1941-May, 1943; Editor, Star Science Fiction, January, 1958 (only issue); Feature Editor, If, July,1959-January, 1961; Managing Editor, May, 1961-July, 1962; Editor, September, 1962-May, 1969; Editor Emeritus, July, 1969-DATE; Managing Editor, Galaxy, June, 1961-June, 1962; Editor, August, 1962-May, 1969; Editor Emeritus, July, 1969-DATE; Editor, Worlds of Tomorrow, April, 1963-May, 1967; International Science Fiction, November, 1967-June, 1968; Managing Editor, Worlds of Fantasy, #1 (1968); Editor, Book Department, and Assistant Circulation Manager, Popular Science, 1946-1949; Literary Agent, 1949-1953; Free-Lance Writer--Member: Science Fiction Writers of America; Hydra Club; American Federation of Television and Radio Artists; New York Academy of Sciences; American Astronautical Society

---

LILIAN M. POPP

1)	1961 Globe	with Richard L. Loughlin (q.v.) Journeys in Science Fiction. (@)

J. L. POWERS

1) 1960 Badger SF Black Abyss. (P/RH)

J. L. Powers is a possible pseudonym.

JOE POYER

1) 1968 Doubleday Operation Malacca.

FPS: "TB in Cattle," Science News Letter, November, 1962.
FSF: "Mission 'Red Clash,'" Analog, December, 1965.

WIP: 1969 Doubleday North Cape.

***   ***   ***   ***   ***

Joseph J. Poyer (i)--born November 30, 1939 at Battle Creek, Michigan--graduated from college--Orange, California.

Mr. Poyer is married and has two children.

Manager, Interdisciplinary Communications, BioScience Planning Inc.--Member: Science Fiction Writers of America.

LEONARD PRUYN

with Day Keene (q.v.)
1) 1960 Gold Medal World Without Women. (P)

FKP: "In Time of Sorrow," Authentic, February, 1954.

TOM PURDOM

1) 1964 Ace I Want the Stars. (P)
2) 1966 Ace The Tree Lord of Imeten. (P)
3) 1967 Ace Five Against Arlane. (P)

TOM PURDOM (continued)

FPS:	"Grieve for a Man,"	<u>Fantastic Universe</u>, August, 1957.
FPP:	"A Matter of Privacy,"	<u>Science Fiction Quarterly</u>, August, 1957 (simultaneous).
WIP:	19<u>69</u> Berkley	<u>Reduction in Arms</u>. (P)
	19<u>70</u> Ace	<u>The Barons of Behavior</u>. (P)

***   ***   ***   ***   ***

Thomas Edward Purdom--born April 19, 1936 at New Haven, Connecticut--attended Lafayette College, 1952-1954--<u>New Republic</u> Young Writers Contest Award, 1958, "In Praise of Science Fiction"--Philadelphia, Pennsylvania.

Son of Orlando Jackson & Inez (Tigna) Purdom--Sara Wescoat: November 19, 1960--Christopher William Purdom (April 9, 1964).

"From 1954-1968 I worked at various clerical/sales jobs//with United Airlines, 1957-1968--ed.//; beginning in 1963, my last employer let me work part time. Since March, 1968, I've worked part time (20 hours a week) for the University of Pennsylvania as a science writer doing public relations writing for research in medicine, biology and the behavioral sciences;"Free-Lance Writer, 1963-DATE --Member: Science Fiction Writers of America; Philadelphia Science Fiction Society (President, 1962-1964); American Civil Liberties Union; Central Philadelphia Reform Democrats; West Philadelphia Independent Democrats.

"Hobbies, passions, enthusiasms: the city of Philadelphia (I came here in 1954 because it was the closest big city when I quit school, fell in love with it, and have lived here ever since); city planning; science and society; arms control, disarmament, nuclear policy, and military policy in general; politics; wines; etc."

Mr. Purdom writes:
"I think a lot of really good, exciting, interesting science fiction is being written these days--as much as when I first started reading the stuff in 1950. I began reading sf when I pulled a copy of <u>Adventures in Time and Space</u> off a library shelf in Tampa, Florida. I had already gotten interested in space travel through Ley's <u>Rockets</u>//<u>Rockets, Missiles and Space Travel</u>--ed.//, and that led me to the sf anthologies. I was a very intense reader--and a real space travel fanatic--for about five years, and then some of the interest waned, as it seems to do with most people. I've always thought those five years were a big event in my life, however, and that the time I spent reading three or four magazines and a couple of sf books per month was well spent. And I'm happy I still find enough sf to keep me reading the stuff. Even if you get tired of it after a while, anybody who goes through a period like that will be a lot richer in many different ways for the rest of his life. Most of my close friends have

TOM PURDOM (continued)

several things in common: they are all people engaged in some kind of professional or scholarly occupation, they all have wide-ranging, lively minds that are interested in virtually every subject a human being can be interested in, and they all have read sf intensely for at least one period in their lives, and still read it now and then. I tend to feel there's some connection.

"I don't know what contribution I've made to the field, but I know the contribution I would like to make: I would like to write stories that will make my readers feel the way I felt when I first entered the field--and still feel, for that matter, whenever I find something I really like."

---

*JOHN RACKHAM

1)	1954 Pearson		Space Puppet. (P)
2)	1954 Pearson		Master Weed. (P)
3)	1954 Pearson		Jupiter Equilateral. (P)
4)	1955 Pearson		Alien Virus. (P)
5)	1963 Digit		The Touch of Evil. (P)
6)	1964 Cape		Watch on Peter.
7)	1965 Ace		We, the Venusians. (P)
8)	1966 Ace		Danger from Vega. (P)
10)	1966 Ace		The Beasts of Kohl. (P)
11)	1966 Ace		Time to Live. (P/RH)
12)	1967 Ace		The Double Invaders. (P)
14)	1968 Ace		Alien Sea. (P)
16)	1968 Ace		The Proxima Project. (P)

as John T. Phillifent

9)	1966 Ace	5	The Mad Scientist Affair. (P)
13)	1967 Four Square	13	The Corfu Affair. (P)
15)	1968 Four Square	15	The Power-Cube Affair. (P)

SER: The Man From U.N.C.L.E.

NOTE: The Mad Scientist Affair was #8 in the British series; The Power-Cube Affair #19 in the American.

FPS: 1954 Pearson   Space Puppet. (P)

WIP: 1969 Ace   Ipomoea. (P)
      1969 Ace   Jewels of Jeopardy. (P)

***   ***   ***   ***   ***

*JOHN RACKHAM (continued)

John Thomas Phillifent--born November 10, 1916 at Durham, England--attended college--London, England.

Son of John T. & Mary Ann (Rackham) Phillifent--(1) Barbara Mary: /1946; (2) Joyce Isabel: January 1, 1947-- 2) Sarah Joan Phillifent (September, 1952); Katharine Anne Phillifent (February, 1954).

With Royal Navy, 1935-1947; currently Free-Lance Writer--Member: Science Fiction Writers of America; Mensa (British Original); Regional Planning Association.

LUAN RANZETTA

1) 1962 Digit   The Uncharted Planet. (P)
2) 1962 Digit   The Maru Invasion. (P)
3) 1962 Digit   The World in Reverse. (P)
4) 1963 Digit   Night of the Death Rain. (P)
5) 1964 Digit   The Yellow Inferno. (P)

RICK RAPHAEL

1) 1965 Gollancz   The Thirst Quenchers. (RP)
2) 1966 S&S   Code Three. (RP)

FSF: "A Filbert Is a Nut,"   Astounding, November, 1959.

WIP: two novels.

***   ***   ***   ***   ***

Rick Raphael--born February 20, 1919 at New York, New York--B.A., University of New Mexico, 1952--Washington, District of Columbia.

Son of Louis N. & Viola (Felix) Raphael--Elizabeth Van Schaick--Christopher M. Raphael; Patricia Raphael; Teresa Raphael; Melanie Raphael; Karen Raphael; Stephanie Raphael.

With United States Army, 1936-1947 (retired with rank of Captain); for 20 years a political and science writer for newspapers, radio, and television; Staff Member, Senator Frank Church, United States Senate, 1964-DATE.

ROBERT RAY

1)	1957 Jenkins	The Strange World of Planet X.
2)	1964 Digit	No Stars for Us. (P)
3)	1968 Panther	The Seedy. (P)

FKP: "If Tomorrow Be Lost,"   Fantastic Adventures, June, 1950.

F. G. RAYER

1)	1946 Grafton	Worlds at War. (P)
2)	1949 Grafton	Realm of the Alien. (P)
3)	1950 Tempest	Fearful Barrier. (P)
4)	1951 Home	Tomorrow Sometimes Comes. (RP)
5)	1953 Pearson	The Star Seekers. (P)
6)	1964 Digit	The Iron and the Anger. (P/RH)
7)	1964 Digit	Cardinal of the Stars. (P/RHv)
7A)	1964 Arcadia	Journey to the Stars.

FPS: 1942
FSF: "Juggernaut,"   Link House Publications, 1944.

***　　　***　　　***　　　***　　　***

Francis George Rayer--born June 6, 1921 at Worcestershire, England--Upton-on-Severn, Worcester, England.

Son of Harry & Florence Nellie (Shepherd) Rayer--Tessa Elizabeth Platt: February 23, 1957--William Francis Rayer (October 12, 1961); Quintin George Rayer (February 23, 1965).

Self-employed Technical Journalist and Equipment Designer--Associate: Institution of Electronic and Radio Engineers.

Mr. Rayer's radio call letters are G30GR.

WILLIAM READY

1)   1968 Regnery   The Tolkien Relation. (nf/RPv)

WILLIAM READY (continued)

WIP:
1A)   1969 Pap Lib   Understanding Tolkien and the Lord of the Rings.
                                (nf/P)

William Bernard Ready was born in 1914. A complete biography may be found in Who's Who in America

----

CLIFFORD C. REED

1)   1962 Digit   Martian Enterprise. (P)

FPS: "Jean-Gene-Jeanne,"   Authentic, November, 1954 (#51).

***   ***   ***   ***   ***

Clifford Cecil Reed--born May 13, 1911 at Durban, South Africa--London, England.

Son of Clifford & Marion Phyllis Reed--Dorothy Mary: October 8, 1948--Jeremy Clifford Reed (January 21, 1943).

Has been a salesman, civil servant (South African), accountant; now with a housing association registered as a charity--Member: Chartered Institute of Secretaries.

MICHAEL D. RESNICK

1)   1967 Grant   1   The Goddess of Ganymede. (RP)
2)   1968 Pap Lib   2   Pursuit on Ganymede. (P)

FPS: Unknown.
FSF: 1967 Grant   The Goddess of Ganymede. (RP)

WIP: 19<u>69</u> Lancer   -1   The Day of the Mutant: The Redbeard's Book.
                                  (P)
      Lancer   -2   Twilight of the Mutant: The Blind Baron's
                                  Book. (P)
      Lancer   -3   The Long Night of the Mutant: The Antihero's
                                  Book. (P)

***   ***   ***   ***   ***

MICHAEL D. RESNICK (continued)

Michael D. Resnick (i)--born March 5, 1942 at Chicago, Illinois--attended University of Chicago, 1959-1961--Libertyville, Illinois.

Son of William & Gertrude Resnick--Carol Cain: October 2, 1961--Laura Resnick (August 17, 1962).

Editor-in Chief, National Features Syndicate; Publisher, Oligarch Press, 1969-DATE; Free-Lance Writer (100+ book credits).

Mr. Resnick is interested in Edgar Rice Burroughs fandom, having written a sequel to Llana of Gathol entitled "The Forgotten Sea of Mars" (published in ERB-dom Magazine); he also breeds collies on the side.

----

*MACK REYNOLDS

2)	1963 Pyramid	The Earth War. (P)
3)	1965 Ace	Planetary Agent X. (P)
4)	1966 4 Square	Time Gladiator. (P)
5)	1966 Belmont	Of Godlike Power. (P)
6)	1966 Ace	Dawnman Planet. (P)
7)	1966 4 Square	Space Pioneer. (P)
8)	1967 Ace	The Rival Rigelians. (P)
9)	1967 Ace	Computer War. (P)
10)	1967 Belmont	After Some Tomorrow. (P)
5A)	1968 Belmont	Earth Unaware. (P)
11)	1968 Ace	Mercenary from Tomorrow. (P)
12)	1968 Ace	Code Duello. (P)
13)	1968 Whitman	Star Trek: Mission to Horatius.

with Fredric Brown (q.v.)
1) 1953 Shasta — Science Fiction Carnival. (@/RPa)

FPS: "What Is Courage," Esquire, December, 1946.
FSF: "Last Warning," Planet Stories (magazine folded before story could be published).
FSP: "Isolationist," Fantastic Adventures, April, 1950.

WIP: 1969 Ace — The Space Barbarians. (P)
1969 Belmont — The Cosmic Eye. (P)
Mack Reynolds' Looking Backward: From the Year 2000.

***   ***   ***   ***   ***

*MACK REYNOLDS (continued)

Dallas McCord Reynolds--born November 11, 1917 at Corcoran, California--graduated from Marine Officer's Cadet School--San Miguel de Allende, Guanajuato, Mexico.

Son of Verne LaRue & Pauline (McCord) Reynolds--Helen Jeanette Wooley: September, 1947--Emil Reynolds; LaVerne Reynolds Land; Dallas Mack Reynolds.

Editor, Catskill Mountain Star and Oneonta News for brief periods in the 1930's; Supervisor for IBM, 1937-1940; Lecturer for the Socialist Labor Party; Foreign Editor, Rogue, 1955-1965; Free-Lance Writer, 1965-DATE--Member: Science Fiction Writers of America.

Mr. Reynolds mentions that "my father was twice candidate for President of the U.S., 1928 and 1932. He didn't make it."

Mr. Reynolds also provided the following statement:
"I am of the opinion that science fiction is going through a period of growth unprecedented, and that this growth will continue as a new generation comes of age. It is not growth so much in the magazine field as in the paperback and hardcover; but the genre as a whole has never seen such opportunities for good science fiction. The advent of the field in the television and film industries will undoubtedly result in large numbers of new readers. Science fiction is in the air!
"The 'New Wave' is not for me. I like stories to be entertaining as well as thought-provoking, and to leave me with something 'new'. And despite its name, the New Wave is incapable of doing this for me.
"I think writers should write about things they know. When I write yarns laid in the center of the Sahara, Moscow, or even Borneo, for that matter, the reader can be assured that I've been on the scene. I am unschooled in the physical sciences, and hence avoid them. My special field is political economy, and most of my stories deal with extrapolations in socioeconomics (concerning which I have very strong opinions, although they are not connected with any particular organization or movement). I'm of the opinion that the world is going through an unprecedented period of revolution in all fields--not just science fiction or socioeconomics--and I'm all in favor of it."

LEIGH RICHMOND

with Walt Richmond (q.v.)

1) 1967 Ace   Shock Wave. (P)
2) 1967 Ace   The Lost Millenium. (P)

LEIGH RICHMOND (continued)

FPS: "Prologue to an Analogue," Analog, June, 1961.

***   ***   ***   ***   ***

Leigh Tucker Richmond (u)--Claremont, New Hampshire.

Married Walter F. Richmond.

Has been a reporter/photographer, editor, and managing editor for various newspapers throughout the country.

WALT RICHMOND

with Leigh Richmond (q.v.)
1) 1967 Ace   Shock Wave. (P)
2) 1967 Ace   The Lost Millenium. (P)

FPS: "Where I Wasn't Going," Analog, October-November, 1963 (with Leigh Richmond).

***   ***   ***   ***   ***

Walter F. Richmond (u)--Claremont, New Hampshire.

Married Leigh ?Tucker.

Doing basic research in physics.

JANE ROBERTS

1) 1963 Ace   The Rebellers. (P)

FPS: "The Red Wagon," The Magazine of Fantasy and Science Fiction, December, 1956.

***   ***   ***   ***   ***

Jane Roberts--born May 8, 1929 at Albany, New York--attended Skidmore College, 1947-1950--Elmira, New York.

JANE ROBERTS (continued)

Daughter of D. H. & Marie (Burdo) Roberts--Robert F. Butts: December, 1954--no children.

Free-Lance Writer and Poet.

KEITH ROBERTS

1)	1966 Berkley	The Furies. (P/RH)
2)	1968 Hart-Davis	Pavane. (RP)

FPS: either "Anita," Science Fantasy, September/October, 1964;
or "Escapism," Science Fantasy, September/October, 1964.

WIP: 19<u>69</u> Hart-Davis   The Inner Wheel.

***   ***   ***   ***   ***

Keith John Kingston Roberts--born September 20, 1935 at Kettering, Northamptonshire, England--attended Northampton School of Art--Henley-on-Thames, Oxford, England.

Unmarried.

Associate Editor, Science Fantasy, 1965-February 1966; Managing Editor, SF Impulse, March, 1966-February, 1967 (all issues); Free-Lance Writer and Illustrator; Agency Visualizer.

LIONEL ROBERTS

1)	1959 Badger SF	Dawn of the Mutants. (P)
2)	1959 Badger SF	Time Echo. (P/RHv)
3)	1960 Badger SF	Cyclops in the Sky. (P)
4)	1960 Badger SF	The In-World. (P/RH)
5)	1960 Badger SF	The Face of X. (P/RHv)
6)	1961 Badger SN	The Last Valkyrie. (P)
7)	1961 Badger SF	The Synthetic Ones. (P)
8)	1961 Badger SN	Flame Goddess. (P)

as *Robert Lionel

2A)	1964 Arcadia	Time Echo.
5A)	1965 Arcadia	The Face of X.

Lionel Roberts (and Robert Lionel) are probably exclusive pennames of R. Lionel Fanthorpe (q.v.).

GENE RODDENBERRY

1) 1968 Ballantine   with Stephen E. Whitfield (q.v.)
                        The Making of Star Trek. (nf/P)

FPS: a television play   to the Kaiser Aluminum Hour, 1953.
FSF: "The Secret Weapon of 117," a television play, Chevron Theater, 1954.

***   ***   ***   ***   ***

Eugene Wesley Roddenberry--born August 21, 1921 at El Paso, Texas--attended Los Angeles City College, three years; Miami University, one year; Columbia University, two years--Writers Guild of America Award, Best Script, 1958; Golden Reels Award, 1962, 1966; 24th World Science Fiction Convention (Tricon) Special Award, 1966; Hugo Award, Best Dramatic Presentation, 1967, "The Menagerie" (appeared on Star Trek); National Association for the Advancement of Colored People Brotherhood Award, 1967; Photoplay Magazine Gold Medal Award, 1968--Hollywood, California.

Son of Eugene Edward & Caroline Glen (Golemon) Roddenberry--Eileen Anita Rexroat: June 20, 1942/July, 1969--Darleen Anita Roddenberry (April 4, 1948); Dawn Alison Roddenberry (August 31, 1953).

Producer, Star Trek, 1966-1968; Executive Producer, 1968-1969--Member: Writers Guild of America; Science Fiction Writers of America.

ALVA ROGERS

1) 1964 Advent   A Requiem for Astounding. (nf/RP)

***   ***   ***   ***   ***

Alva Rogers (u)--born January 17, 1923 at Silver City, New Mexico--attended San Diego State College--Castro Valley, California.

Son of Alva & Anne Rogers--married June 15, 1947--David Rogers (21); William Rogers (18); Adrienne Rogers (11).

Member: First Fandom (Vice-President, West Coast); Elves', Gnomes', and Little Men's Science Fiction, Chowder, and Marching Society (Secretary).

Mr. Rogers was Co-Chairman of the 26th World Science Fiction Convention (Baycon), 1968.

BRUCE W. RONALD

1) 1965 Ace   Our Man in Space. (P)

Bruce W. Ronald could not be located.

ALBERT ROOT

1) 1967 Vantage   Tomorrow's Harvest; Or, Death Takes a
                                Holiday.

FPP: 1967 Vantage   Tomorrow's Harvest; Or, Death Takes
                                Holiday.

***   ***   ***   ***   ***

Albert Waldo Root--born June 19, 1891 at Ireland, Indiana--attended college for two years--Birdseye, Indiana.

Son of John Wetzel & Flora Belle (Corn) Root--Maude Ariel Dugan: December 30, 1916-July 21, 1968--Mary Root Bolden (51); Lillian Root Colber (49).

Has been a cost analyzer, poultry raiser, and hatcheryman.

MORDECAI ROSHWALD

1) 1959 Heinemann   Level Seven. (RP)
2) 1962 Heinemann   A Small Armageddon. (RP)

FPS: "The Development of Sciences and Moral Progress," Actes du Septieme
                                Congres International d'Histoire des
                                Sciences, Jerusalem, 1953.
FSF: 1959 Heinemann   Level Seven.

***   ***   ***   ***   ***

Mordecai Marceli Roshwald--born May 26, 1921 at Drohobycz, Poland--M.A., Hebrew University of Jerusalem, 1942; Ph.D., Hebrew University of Jerusalem, 1947--invited to deliver papers at two international conferences: History and Philosophy of Science, Jerusalem, 1953; Political Science, Stockholm, 1955-- Minneapolis, Minnesota.

MORDECAI ROSHWALD (continued)

Son of Abraham & Sidonia (Feuer) Roshwald--Miriam Wyszynski: 1945--Aviel Roshwald (7).

Lecturer on Political Theory, Israel Institute of Public Administration, 1947-1951; Instructor of Political Theory, Hebrew University of Jerusalem, 1951-1955; Instructor in Philosophy and Political Theory, Brooklyn College, 1956-1957; on the faculty of University of Minnesota, 1957-DATE; Professor of Social Science, 1966-DATE; also Visiting Professor, Israel Institute of Technology, 1963-1964; University of Bath, 1966.

----

*JOSEPH ROSS

1) 1967 Doubleday   The Best of Amazing   (@/RP)

Joseph Wrocz was Managing Editor, Amazing, August, 1965-October, 1967; Fantastic, September, 1965-September, 1967.

RAYMOND GEORGE ROSS

1) 1964 Vantage   Beyond the Chains of Bondage.

JOANNA RUSS

1) 1968 Ace   Picnic on Paradise. (P)

FPS: "Nor Custom Stale,"   The Magazine of Fantasy and Science
                            Fiction, September, 1959.

***   ***   ***   ***   ***

Joanna Russ (i)--born February 22, 1937 at Bronx, New York--B.A., Cornell University, 1957; M.F.A. in Playwriting, Yale Drama School, 1960--One of Top Ten in Westinghouse Science Talent Search, 1953--Ithaca, New York.

Daughter of Everett & Bertha Russ--Albert Amateau: 1963/1966--no children.

Has held various editorial jobs; currently Instructor in English, Cornell University--Member: Science Fiction Writers of America; American Educational Theatre Association.

ERIC FRANK RUSSELL

1)	1948 Fantasy	Sinister Barrier. (RPa)
2)	1951 Fantasy	Dreadful Sanctuary. (RPa)
3)	1953 Bouregy	Sentinels from Space. (RPv)
4)	1954 Fantasy	Deep Space. (s/RPa)
3A)	1954 Ace	Sentinels of Space. (P)
5)	1956 Roy	Men, Martians, and Machines. (RP)
6)	1956 Avalon	Three to Conquer. (RP)
7)	1957 Avalon	Wasp. (RP)
8)	1958 Ace	Six Worlds Yonder. (s/P)
9)	1958 Ace	The Space Willies. (P/RHv)
9A)	1959 Dobson	Next of Kin. (RP)
10)	1961 Dobson	Far Stars. (s/RP)
11)	1962 Dobson	The Great Explosion. (RP)
12)	1962 Dobson	Dark Tides. (RP)
13)	1964 Dobson	With a Strange Device. (RP)
14)	1965 Lancer	The Mindwarpers. (P)
14)	1965 Dobson	Somewhere a Voice. (RP)

FKP: "The Saga of Pelican West," Astounding, February, 1937.

Eric Frank Russell was born in 1905. He received a Hugo Award, Best Short Story, 1955, "Allamagoosa," and currently is a member of Science Fiction Writers of America. A partial biography may be found in Seekers of Tomorrow.

FRED SABERHAGEN

1)	1964 Ace		The Golden People. (P)
2)	1965 Ace		The Water of Thought. (P)
3)	1967 Ballantine	1	Berserker. (s/P)
4)	1968 Ace		The Broken Lands. (P)

FPS: "Volume Paa-Pyx," Galaxy, February, 1961.

WIP: 1969 Ballantine 2 Brother Assassin. (P)

***   ***   ***   ***   ***

Fred Thomas Saberhagen--born May 18, 1930 at Chicago, Illinois--Chicago, Illinois.

Son of Frederick Augustus & Julia Agnes (Moynihan) Saberhagen--Joan Dorothy Spicci: June 29, 1968--Jill Ann Saberhagen (March 31, 1969).

FRED SABERHAGEN (continued)

Electronics Technician, Motorola, 1956-1962; Free-Lance Writer, 1962-1967; Writer, Encyclopedia Britannica, 1967-DATE--Member: Science Fiction Writers of America.

MARGARET ST. CLAIR

1)	1956 Ace	Agent of the Unknown. (P)
2)	1956 Ace	The Green Queen. (P)
3)	1960 Ace	The Games of Neith. (P)
4)	1963 Bantam	Sign of the Labrys. (P)
5)	1964 Ace	Message from the Eocene. (P)
6)	1964 Ace	Three Worlds of Futurity. (s/P)
7)	1967 Dell	The Dolphins of Altair. (P)
FPS:	"Current History,"	Detective Story, March, 1945.
FSF:	"Rocket to Limbo,"	Fantastic Adventures, November, 1946.
WIP:	1969 Dell	The Shadow People. (P)

***　　　　***　　　　***　　　　***　　　　***

Margaret St. Clair (u)--born in Kansas--M.A., University of California--El Sobrante, California.

Daughter of George A. & Eva M. Neeley--Eric St. Clair--no children.

Free-Lance Writer--Member: Dramatists Guild; Science Fiction Writers of America; Phi Beta Kappa.

Mrs. St. Clair writes:
"I think I am a short story writer by temperament, but they tend to be so evanescent and paid for so poorly that for the last several years I have been writing in the longer lengths almost exclusively. I should very much like to see a volume, or several volumes, of my short stories published.
"If my life sounds rather colorless, I think this is because I tend to be reticent. Actually, I have been absorbed in as many things as most writers, but I don't like having them noised abroad. My life has been interesting to me, at any rate. I have sometimes been unhappy, but I have almost never been bored.
"I suppose the strongest influences on my work have been Greek authors, English and Celtic folklore, and a few writers whose work I particularly admire (like Boccaccio). I like weather, soap bubbles, opals, champagne, some rock music, a good many perfumes, and fireworks."

WILLIAM SAMBROT

1) 1963 Permabook   <u>Island of Fear and Other Science Fiction Stories</u>. (s/P)

FPS: "The Strong Box,"   <u>Esquire</u>, 1951.
FSF: "Report to the People,"   <u>Bluebook</u>, October, 1953.

WIP: a second collection of short stories.

***   ***   ***   ***   ***

William Anthony Sambrot--born December 17, 1920 at Pittsburgh, Pennsylvania--attended University of Biarritz, 1945; University of California at Berkeley, 1947; University of California at San Francisco, 1947-1948--Freedom Foundation George Washington Gold Medal Award, 1951, "Of Those Who Came"--Napa, California.

Son of Anthony & Nancy (Ciccetti) Sambrot--Marina Dianda: January 19, 1948--Steven Sambrot (17); Shellie Sambrot (Daughter; 15).

Has been a bouncer in a night club, a physical education instructor, a brewery quality controller, a script consultant; currently Free-Lance Writer--Member: Science Fiction Writers of America; Authors Guild.

In August, the editors sent a series of follow-up letters to those writers whose entries were only partially complete. One such letter brought the following response:
    "In re your queries concerning my Neanderthal period; I haven't the faintest recollection of every having attended the U. of Biarritz--although I know I did for a short time in the winter of '45. I'd been stationed in Germany after the war (which I won for us virtually singlehandedly), and we were told we'd be there until the War with Tibet, in '60. Meanwhile, Switzerland or Biarritz were up for grabs. I took the U. at Biarritz. Screen documentaries. Many famous Hollywood writers and directors were lecturing (at least, they told us they were famous. They all were colonels). Utter confusion. I spent most of the time trying to get something to eat. On detached duty. No outfit. No one would feed me. I didn't even get my regular pay. I wasn't on anyone's list. One Sergeant even tried to claim I was a kraut. In Jan. '46 I learned my outfit was moving out--for the States. I rolled up my kit (one blanket, one pair of sox, three battered contraceptive devices), and simply left for Le Havre. I learned a lot though--I learned I should have gone to Switzerland."

WILLIAM SAMBROT (continued)

"Attended U.C. Berkeley under exactly similar circumstances: G.I. Bill. 50,000 ex-G.I.'s under one squad tent, listening to canned lectures. 1947. Decided to specialize; courses in journalism, short story, etc., offered at Cal. extension in San Francisco. Took these during '47, '48 at night, and worked in a brewery days. Learned a lot. Beer is beautiful before being pasteurized. Just dead water afterward. Made a big sale, thereby confounding prof who'd never made even one, and dropped out of school. No degree. Self taught. I also attended the Institute D'Allende, in Mexico, but that's even more confusing.

"Freedom Foundation awarded in 1951 for article in Kiwanis, 'Of Those Who Came.' Basis for Radio series on Mutual. Given award in March, '52 at Palace Hotel (SF). Others also present were Stanford University, Bank of America, and Standard Oil of Cal. Herbert Hoover was also there--a traumatic beginning for any writer--but all that was a long time ago, and not even worth recording. All I know is I should have stayed in the brewery. Who ever gave a rejection slip to a cool, tall beer?"

HANS STEFAN SANTESSON

1)	1960 Prentice	The Fantastic Universe Omnibus. (@/RP)
2)	1965 Pyramid	Rulers of Men. (@/P)
3)	1967 Award	Gods for Tomorrow. (@/P)
4)	1968 Lancer	Flying Saucers in Fact and Fiction. (@/P)
FPS:	1960 Prentice	The Fantastic Universe Omnibus. (@)
WIP:	1969 Belmont	The Gentle Invaders. (@/P)
	1969 Little	The Days After Tomorrow. (@)
	1969 Walker	Crime Prevention in the 30th Century. (@)
	1969 Lancer	The Mighty Barbarians-Great Swords and Sorcery Heroes. (@/P)

***   ***   ***   ***   ***

Hans Stefan Santesson--born July 8, 1914 at Paris, France--Edgar Award, Best Critic, 1963--New York, New York.

Son of Nils & Astrid (Medeus) Santesson--unmarried.

HANS STEFAN SANTESSON (continued)

Editor, <u>Unicorn Mystery Book Club</u>, 1945-1952; Editorial Director, <u>Fantastic Universe</u>, September, 1956-September, 1959; Editor, October, 1959-March, 1960; Editorial Director, <u>The Saint Mystery Magazine</u>, September, 1956-September, 1959; Editor, October, 1959-1967; Editor, <u>New Worlds</u> (US), March, 1960-July, 1960--Member: Science Fiction Writers of America; Mystery Writers of America (Member of the Board); Crime Writers' Association; Hydra Club (Executive Secretary); Society for the Investigation of the Unexplained (SITU)(President and Chairman of the Board); American Oriental Society; Booksellers League of New York; National Association of Book Editors (Chairman, Program Committee).

Mr. Santesson has been actively interested in Indo-Pakistani affairs, and in minority problems in this country since the early 1930's. He is particularly familiar with the increasing interest in Islam in the urban areas of the United States. A member of the American Oriental Society since the mid-thirties, he has spoken at several AOS Conferences since 1938, in more recent years on Indian literature at the turn of the century. He has written and lectured on both Indian literature and Muslim art, and is currently working on a paperback dealing with Mu.

---

*ROGER SARAC

1)	1965 Belmont	<u>The Throwbacks</u>. (P)	
FPS:	1962 Chilton	<u>Antarctica: Land of Frozen Time</u>.	
		(nf/as Roger A. Caras)	
FSF:	1965 Belmont	<u>The Throwbacks</u>. (P)	

***   ***   ***   ***   ***

Roger Andrew Caras--born May 24, 1928 at Methuen, Massachusetts--attended Western Reserve and Northeastern University, 1948-1950; B.A., University of Southern California, 1953--Jamaica, New York.

Son of Joseph J. & Bessie E. (Kasanoff) Caras--Jill Barclay: September 5, 1954--Pamela Jill Caras (August 8, 1956); Barclay Gordon Caras (July 20, 1959).

*ROGER SARC (continued)

Motion Picture Executive (successively Executive Assistant to the Vice-President; National Director of Merchandizing for the United States and Canada; Casting and Story Department Executive), Columbia Pictures, 1955-1965; Joint Vice-President, Polaris Productions, Inc., and Hawk Films, Ltd., 1965-1968 (during the filming of 2001: A Space Odyssey); Free-Lance Writer, 1968-DATE--Member: Writers Guild of America, West; Authors Guild; Outdoor Writers Association of America; Mensa.

RICHARD SAXON

1) ?1963 Consul?   The Stars Came Down. (P/RH)
2) ?1964 Consul?   The Hour of the Phoenix. (P/RHv)
3) 1964 Consul   Cosmic Crusade. (P/RHv)
4) ?1964 Consul?   Future for Sale. (P/RH)

                   as *Henry Richards
2A) 1965 Arcadia   The Hour of the Phoenix.

JAMES H. SCHMITZ

1) 1960 Gnome   Agent of Vega. (s/RP)
2) 1962 Torquil   A Tale of Two Clocks. (RP)
3) 1964 Ace   The Universe Against Her. (P)
4) 1965 Chilton   A Nice Day for Screaming and Other Tales
                       of the Hub. (s)
5) 1966 Chilton   The Witches of Karres. (RP)
6) 1968 Ace   The Demon Breed. (P)

FPS: "Greenface,"   Unknown Worlds, August, 1943.

***   ***   ***   ***   ***

James Henry Schmitz--born October 15, 1911 at Hamburg, Germany--attended Realgymnasium Obersekunda, Germany--Inglewood, California.

Son of Joseph H. & Catherine (Davis) Schmitz--Betty Chapman: 1957--no children.

Employed in Germany by International Harvester Company, 1932-1938; Self-employed (building automobile trailers), 1946-1949; Free-Lance Writer, 1949-DATE--Member: Science Fiction Writers of America; Authors Guild.

JAMES H. SCHMITZ (continued)

Mr. Schmitz moved to the United States in 1938.

LAWRENCE SCHOONOVER

1)	1962 Sloane	Central Passage. (RP)
FPS:	1946 Macmillian	The Burnished Blade.
FSF:	1962 Sloane	Central Passage.

***   ***   ***   ***   ***

Lawrence Lovell Schoonover--born March 6, 1906 at Anamosa, Iowa--Diploma, Shattuck School, 1923; attended University of Wisconsin, 1923-1926--Long Beach, New York.

Son of George Lawrence & Grace (Lovell) Schoonover--Gertrude Bonn: May 29, 1938--Judith Schoonover; Mary-Elizabeth Schoonover; Caroline Schoonover; Virginia Schoonover.

Reporter, Collier's Magazine, 1927-1928; Copywriter, Barton, Durstine & Osborn, 1928-1931; Advertising Manager, Underwood & Underwood, 1931-1941; Copy Chief, Gotham Advertising Company, 1943-1945; Account Executive, Batten, Barton, Durstine & Osborn, 1945-1947; Free-Lance Writer, 1947-DATE--Member: Chi Phi (cum laude; Charter Member).

F. H. P. SCHUCK

1)	1964 Vantage	The Phantom Caravan.
FPP:	1964 Vantage	The Phantom Caravan.

***   ***   ***   ***   ***

Frederick Hugh Paul Schuck--born January 18, 1916 at Brighton, Trinidad, West Indies--attended Northeastern University; Florida Southern College; various USAF Technical Schools--Lowry Award, 1967 (National Guard of Florida); Florida Commendation Ribbon, National Guard of Florida--Clearwater, Florida.

F. H. P. SCHUCK (continued)

Son of Joseph G. & Mary (Delger) Schuck--unmarried.

Has been a weather observer and forecaster, a licensed commercial pilot and instructor of multi-engine land planes, and has taught meteorology; currently a member of the 53rd Infantry Brigade Headquarters, Florida National Guard, Tampa, Florida--Member: Air Force Association; American Ordnance Association; International Oceanographic Society; American Museum of Natural History.

ALAN SCHWARTZ

1) 1967 Ace   The Wandering Tellurian. (P)

Alan Schwartz could not be located.

JACK SHARKEY

1) 1960 Ace   The Secret Martians. (P)
2) 1965 Ace   Ultimatum in 2050 A.D. (P)
3) 1965 Pyramid   The Addams Family. (P)

FPS: "The Case of the Frosty Fiend," A.D. Magazine, 1952.
FSF: "The Arm of Enmord,"   Fantastic, April, 1959.
FSP: "The Captain of His Soul," Fantastic, March, 1959;
      "The Obvious Solution,"   Fantastic, March, 1959 (simultaneous).

***   ***   ***   ***   ***

John Michael Sharkey--born May 6, 1931 at Chicago, Illinois--B.A., St. Mary's College, 1962--American Association of Industrial Editors Best Editorial, 1967, "Stop or I'll Shoot...Unless We're in a Hospital Zone"--Northbrook, Illinois.

Son of John Patrick & Mary (Luckey) Sharkey--Patricia Walsh: Bastille Day, 1962--Beth Sharkey (5); Carole Sharkey (4); Susan Sharkey (2); Michael Sharkey (0).

Editor, Good Hands Magazine, Allstate Insurance Corporation; Free-Lance Writer and Playwright--Member: Alpha Psi Omega.

JACK SHARKEY (continued)

"A good yarn is a good yarn. I consider myself a good yarn-spinner, not a literary great. If I can give a reader a pleasant hour or so, I'm succeeding in my vocation. (à propos to nothing: I can't believe Arthur C. Clarke approved the idiotic science bloopers in 2001--holding one's breath in space vacuum, indeed! (among other bloopers even worse!)"

BOB SHAW

1)	1967 Banner	Night Walk. (P)
2)	1968 Ace	The Two-Timers. (P/RH)
FPS:	"Aspect,"	Nebula, August, 1954.
WIP:	1969 Avon	The Shadow of Heaven. (P)
	1969 Ace	The Palace of Eternity. (P)

***   ***   ***   ***   ***

Robert Shaw (u)--born December 31, 1931 at Belfast, North Ireland--attended Belfast College of Technology--Belfast, North Ireland.

Son of Robert William & Elizabeth Shaw--Sarah: July 3, 1954--Alisa Claire Shaw (July 11, 1956); Robert Ian Shaw (June 15, 1962); Elizabeth Denise Shaw (December 18, 1964).

Constructional Draftsman, 1947-1969; Aircraft Draftsman, 1959-1960; in public relations, 1960-1966; Journalist, 1966-1969; Free-Lance Writer, January, 1969-DATE--Member: Science Fiction Writers of America.

FREDERICK L. SHAW, JR.

1)	1967 Ace		1	Envoy to the Dog Star. (P)
FPS:	1967 Ace			Envoy to the Dog Star. (P)
WIP:	1969 Ace		2	The Dog Star Manifesto. (P)

***   ***   ***   ***   ***

FREDERICK L. SHAW, JR. (continued)

Frederick Lincoln Shaw, Jr.--born July 3, 1928 at Providence, Rhode Island--B.A., University of California at Los Angeles, 1954; M.A. (Theater Arts), University of California at Los Angeles, 1960--Jamaica, New York.

Son of Frederick Lincoln & Lillian (Thomas) Shaw--married December 19, 1966--no children.

"Served a hitch in medical journalism (five years), rising to the position of Science Editor of Drug Topics; quit to found own publishing/printing firm and do free-lance writing"--Member: Science Fiction Writers of America; American Educational Theater Association; American Association for the Advancement of Science.

Mr. Shaw had five plays produced at UCLA, one being on a science fiction theme.

LARRY T. SHAW

1)	1963 Lancer	Great Science Fiction Adventures. (@/P)
2)	1966 Lancer	Terror! (@/P)
FKP:	"Simworthy's Circus,"	Worlds Beyond, December, 1950.

Lawrence T. Shaw has held the following positions: Associate Editor, If, May, 1953-March, 1954; Editor, Infinity, November, 1955-November, 1958 (all issues); Science Fiction Adventures, December, 1956-June, 1958 (all issues); Science Fiction Adventures (English), March, 1958-November, 1958; Lancer Books, c.1961-1968; Senior Editor, Dell Books, 1968-1969; Editor, Bee-Line Books, 1969; Editorial Director, Brandon House, 1969-DATE. Mr. Shaw is a member of Science Fiction Writers of America.

ROBERT SHECKLEY

1)	1954 Ballantine	Untouched by Human Hands. (H-P)
2)	1956 Ballantine	Citizen in Space. (s/H-P)
3)	1957 Bantam	Pilgrimage to Earth. (P)
4)	1958 Avalon	Immortality Delivered. (RPv)
4A)	1959 Bantam	Immortality, Inc. (P/RH)
5)	1960 Bantam	Store of Infinity. (s/P)

ROBERT SHECKLEY (continued)

6)	1960 Bantam	Notions: Unlimited. (s/P)
7)	1960 Signet	The Status Civilization. (P)
8)	1962 Bantam	Shards of Space. (s/P)
9)	1962 Signet	Journey Beyond Tomorrow. (P/RH)
10)	1966 Delacorte	Mindswap. (RP)
11)	1966 Ballantine	The 10th Victim. (P)
12)	1968 Dell	Dimension of Miracles. (P/RH)
13)	1968 Dell	The People Trap. (s/P)

FPS: "Final Examination,"   Imagination, May, 1952.

***   ***   ***   ***   ***

Robert Sheckley--born July 16, 1928 at New York, New York--B.A., New York University, 1951--New York, New York.

Son of David & Rachel (Feinberg) Sheckley--Ziva Kwitney: April 7, 1957--Alissa Sheckley (December 1, 1964).

Free-Lance Writer--Member: Writers Guild of America, East.

---

*LEE SHELDON

1)   1967 Avalon   Doomed Planet.

FPS: "Gunsmoke in Paradise,"   Lariat Story Magazine, January, 1945.
FSF: "Project Asteroid,"   Teens, February 27, 1966.

***   ***   ***   ***   ***

Wayne Cyril Lee--born July 2, 1917 at Lamar, Nebraska--correspondence course in composition from University of Nebraska--Lamar, Nebraska.

Son of David Elmer & Rosa (Deserlms) Lee--Pearl May Sheldon: March 17, 1948--Wayne Sheldon Lee (June 14, 1950); Charles Lester Lee (May 27, 1952).

Farmer until 1951; Rural Mail Carrier, 1951-DATE; Free-Lance Writer--Member: Western Writers of America; Christian Writers Guild; Nebraska Authors Guild.

GEORGE E. SHIRLEY

1)	1965 Vantage	A World Their Own.
2)	1967 Vantage	The Robot Rulers.
3)	1967 Vantage	A World Beyond.
FPP:	1965 Vantage	A World Their Own.
WIP:		Disaster for Sale.

***   ***   ***   ***   ***

George Ernest Shirley--born November 8, 1898 at Phelps, Missouri--attended Business School--Lincoln, Missouri.

Son of James E. & Lepha May Shirley--Mr. Shirley is married and has six children.

With United States Marines, 1918-1919; produce work and sales, 1920-1927; Professional Wrestler, 1925-1930; Rancher, 1928-1934; Senior Heating Engineer, Holland Furnace Company, 1935-1937; Branch Manager, 1937-1942; Real Estate Broker and Developer, 1944-DATE--Member: Disabled American Veterans.

ROBERT SILVERBERG

1)	1955 Crowell	Revolt on Alpha C. (RP)
2)	1957 Ace	The 13th Immortal. (P)
3)	1957 Ace	Master of Life and Death. (P)
5)	1958 Ace	Invaders from Earth. (P)
6)	1958 Gnome	Starman's Quest.
10)	1958 Ace	Stepsons of Terra. (P)
14)	1959 Ace	The Planet Killers. (P)
15)	1960 Holt	Lost Race of Mars. (RP)
16)	1961 Avalon	Collision Course. (RP)
17)	1962 Ace	The Seed of Earth. (P)
18)	1962 Ace	Next Stop the Stars. (s/P)
19)	1962 Lancer	Recalled to Life. (P)
20)	1963 Ace	The Silent Invaders. (P)
22)	1964 Pyramid	Regan's Planet. (P)
23)	1964 Belmont	Godling, Go Home! (s/P)
24)	1964 Holt	Time of the Great Freeze. (RP)
25)	1965 Chilton	To Worlds Beyond. (@)
26)	1965 Holt	Conquerors from the Darkness. (RP)

ROBERT SILVERBERG (continued)

27)	1966 Duell		Earthmen and Strangers. (@/P)
28)	1966 Ballantine		Needle in a Timestack. (s/P)
29)	1967 Holt		The Gate of Worlds.
30)	1967 Doubleday		The Time Hoppers. (RP)
31)	1967 Signet		Those Who Watch. (P)
32)	1967 Meredith		Voyagers in Time. (@)
33)	1967 Ballantine		To Open the Sky. (P)
34)	1967 Ballantine		Thorns. (P/RH)
35)	1967 Holt		Planet of Death.
36)	1968 Doubleday		Hawksbill Station.
37)	1968 Ballantine		The Masks of Time. (P)
38)	1968 Meredith		Men and Machines. (@)

with Randall Garrett (q.v.) as *Robert Randall

4)	1957 Gnome	1	The Shrouded Planet.
12)	1959 Gnome	2	The Dawning Light. (RP)

as *David Osborne

7)	1958 Avalon	Invisible Barriers.
11)	1958 Avalon	Aliens from Space.

as *Ivar Jorgenson

8)	1958 Avalon	Starhaven. (RP)

as *Calvin M. Knox

9)	1958 Ace	Lest We Forget Thee, Earth. (P)
13)	1959 Ace	The Plot Against Earth. (P)
21)	1964 Ace	One of Our Asteroids Is Missing. (P)

FPS:	"Fanmag Department,"	Science Fiction Adventures, December, 1953.

WIP:	1969 Avon	The Man in the Maze. (P)
36A)	1969 Sidgwick	The Anvil of Time.
	1969 Meredith	Tomorrow's Worlds. (@)
	1969 Holt	The Calibrated Alligator. (s)
	1969 Holt	Three Survived.
	1969 Ballantine	Dimension Thirteen. (s/P)
	1969 Ballantine	Up the Line. (P)
	1969 Doubleday	To Live Again.
	1969 Avon	Nightwings. (P)
	1969 Ballantine	The Dark Stars. (@/P)

***   ***   ***   ***   ***

ROBERT SILVERBERG (continued)

Robert Silverberg--born at New York, New York--A.B., Columbia College, 1956--Hugo Award, Most Promising New Author, 1956; Best Novella, 1969, "Nightwings"--New York, New York.

Son of Michael & Helen (Baim) Silverberg--Barbara H. Brown: August 26, 1956-- no children.

Associate Editor, Amazing Stories, January, 1969; Fantastic Stories, February-April, 1969 (never actually served); Free-Lance Writer and Editor--Member: Science Fiction Writers of America (President, 1967-1968); Hydra Club (Director, 1958-1963).

Statement of Mr. Silverberg:
"I thing that the state of science fiction has never been healthier, that we are in the midst of an incredibly fertile period, and that the trend will continue upward as new writers are attracted by the new freedoms of the medium. Until a few years ago most sf was fundamentally juvenile in style and content: simple sentences, avoidance of material likely to unsettle the reader's emotions (such as erotic material), etc. There were some honorable exceptions, of course. Now sf is catching up with the outer world, at least to the extent that literary techniques used by the best mainstream writers since the 1920's are now acceptable in science fiction books. One can write the slam-bang kind of sf if one pleases, but markets now exist for a rich, more moving kind of fiction. Almost nothing that I've written since 1966 could have found a publisher when I began writing professionally in 1953; and yet I'm by no means an extremely experimental writer, nor is my material radical in content.
"I view my current position in sf as that of a consolidator as much as an innovator. The 'new wave,' by which I mean chiefly the group of writers contributing to New Worlds, has imported into science fiction the experimental techniques of the avant-garde, leaning heavily on Joyce and Beckett; I find much of this fascinating as a reader, but feel no impulse to make use of those techniques in my own work. I think sf must be brought to a state of functional literacy before we go bounding off into avant-gardery. In my writing I have two chief goals: to attain the sort of stylistic proficiency that is demanded of any writer in non-category fiction, and to transform the standard material of science fiction through an emphasis on emotion, intensity of incident, and complexity of character. I think my most successful attempt in these efforts was The Masks of Time, though I'm pleased with the flamboyant imagery of Thorns and the stylistic level of the book version of The Man in the Maze. Much of my recent work has had a strong erotic content; I see this sf a useful corrective to the innocence of nearly all sf of the past, and I expect to keep mining this particular lode as long as it yields rich ore for me. It seems preposterous to me that there should even be a debate on the place of sex in science fiction. (Would there be a debate on the appropriateness of sex in one's life?) I don't intend to write

ROBERT SILVERBERG (continued)

pornography that is incidentally sf, not because of moral objections, but simply because it seems like a boring thing to do; but where I can employ erotic themes to heighten the sf element of a novel, I'll do so unhesitatingly. Again, I think I was most successful at this in <u>The Masks of Time</u>, and if I sound defensive about that book's sexual content, it's because I've been attacked for it several times by fans, and even by writers of the old guard.

"I believe that when the current revolutionary movement in sf has run its course, we'll emerge with a vastly more interesting literature than we've had before, and that present controversies will seem astonishing puerile to tomorrow's readers. I feel that sf will survive the injection of literacy that it's had lately, even if some old-line readers will be driven away by the transformation of their favorite genre, and I'm eager to be a part of the emerging new sf, standing as I do between the pulp-oriented writers of the past and the literature-oriented writers of the past few years."

CLIFFORD D. SIMAK

1)	1946	Crawford	<u>The Creator</u>. (P)
2)	1950	Gnome	<u>Cosmic Engineers</u>. (RP)
3)	1951	Galaxy	<u>Empire</u>. (P)
4)	1951	S&S	<u>Time and Again</u>. (RP/RPv)
5)	1952	Gnome	<u>City</u>. (RP)
4A)	1952	Dell	<u>First He Died</u>. (P)
6)	1953	S&S	<u>Ring Around the Sun</u>. (RP)
7)	1956	S&S	<u>Strangers in the Universe</u>. (s/RPa)
8)	1960	S&S	<u>The Worlds of Clifford Simak</u>. (s/RPa/RPav)
8A)	1961	Faber	<u>Aliens for Neighbours</u>. (s/a/RP)
9)	1961	Doubleday	<u>Time Is the Simplest Thing</u>. (RP)
10)	1961	Ace	<u>The Trouble with Tycho</u>. (P)
11)	1962	Doubleday	<u>All the Traps of Earth</u>. (s/RP/RPav)
12)	1962	Doubleday	<u>They Walked Like Men</u>. (RP)
8B)	1962	Avon	<u>Other Worlds of Clifford Simak</u>. (s/a/P)
13)	1963	Doubleday	<u>Way Station</u>. (RP)
11A)	1964	4 Square	<u>The Night of the Puudly</u>. (s/a/P)
14)	1964	Belmont	<u>Worlds Without End</u>. (s/P/RH)
15)	1965	Doubleday	<u>All Flesh Is Grass</u>. (RP)
16)	1967	Doubleday	<u>Why Call Them Back from Heaven?</u> (RP)
17)	1967	Faber	<u>Best Science Fiction Stories of Clifford Simak</u>. (s)
18)	1967	Putnam	<u>The Werewolf Principle</u>. (RP)
19)	1968	Putnam	<u>The Goblin Reservation</u>. (RP)
20)	1968	Ace	<u>So Bright the Vision</u>. (s/P)

CLIFFORD D. SIMAK (continued)

FPS: "The World of the Red Sun," Wonder Stories, December, 1931.

***   ***   ***   ***   ***

Clifford Donald Simak--born August 3, 1904 at Millville, Wisconsin--attended University of Wisconsin--International Fantasy Award, 1953, City; Hugo Award, Best Novelette, 1959, "The Big Front Yard;" Best Novel, 1964, Way Station; Award for Distinguished Service to Science, Minnesota Academy of Science-- Minnetonka, Minnesota.

Son of John Lewis & Margaret (Wiseman) Simak--Agnes Kuchenberg: April 13, 1929--Scott Simak (21); Shelley Simak (18).

With Minneapolis Star and Minneapolis Tribune, 1939-1949; News Editor, Minneapolis Star, 1949-1962; Editor and Co-ordinator, Minneapolis Tribune Science Reading Series, 1962-DATE--Member: Science Fiction Writers of America; Sigma Delta Chi; Minnesota Academy of Science.

Mr. Simak comments:
   "In my writing many of my stories have been placed in what may seem to be the mythical town of Millville. It is not. I was born in the township of Millville, Wis., in the southwestern corner of the state. My grandfather's farm house, where I was born, sits on the end of a high ridge, from which can be seen the confluence of the Wisconsin and Mississippi rivers. Millville itself is a wide place in the road in one of the deep hollows of that rugged country. When I last saw it, it had a gas station, an old-time country store, a church and school and a few residences. It probably has fewer buildings now. The rough, picturesque country in the area is the kind of land a man can easily fall in love with, and I have been in love with it all my life, although I only get to visit it occasionally. Bridgeport, which is used as a locale in Time and Again, is in the same part of Wisconsin. Willow Grove or Willow Bend, which I have also used, is an entirely mythical place."

And then he replies to the editors' questions:
   "I don't even pretend to know where the field is headed. I do think that the status of science fiction has improved. At one time it was sneered at as a pulp paper fiction even lower than westerns, whodunits, and love stories. It was thought of in the terms of ray guns and buy-eyed monsters. Today it is widely accepted as a legitimate literature.

CLIFFORD D. SIMAK (continued)

"It is hard for a man to stand off and view his own work objectively. It does seem to me that I, along with others, back in the late 30's and early 40's, may have made a contribution to naturalism in science fiction. The work done in that period relegated the mad scientist, the beastly alien invader, and many other old cliches to the past, and introduced believable characters and normal backgrounds. I recall that I wrote about Iowa farmers on Venus, a football team, an old soldier going to Mars for a reunion of the veterans of the Earth-Mars war. Other people did much the same thing. This was a revolution of considerable importance in the field, and to think that I may have had some small hand in it is gratifying.

"I have no opposition to the so-called new wave. It does pain me somewhat to see a small group of people, some of them good friends of mine, who proclaim that the new wave is the only way in which science fiction should be written. I think that the new wave does have something to offer to the field, but I do not think that it will dominate sf; at the moment it has less dominance, perhaps, than it had a couple of years ago. It has a viewpoint and a technique which will be taken into the field as a part of the overall pattern of writing and of thought, and in that way it will contribute. When it disappears as a separate entity, which I am sure it will do in time, it will leave the field richer and more significant. It will have contributed; it will not have taken over. After all, all literature is in a certain sense 'escape literature,' in which the reader can momentarily identify with another character than his own; and the good story line still remains the backbone of all writing."

HOWARD SIMPSON

1) 1968 Vantage — <u>West of the Moon</u>.

CURT SIODMAK

1) 1933 Little — <u>F. P. 1 Does Not Reply</u>.
2) 1943 Knopf — 1 <u>Donovan's Brain</u>. (RP)
3) 1953 Ballantine — <u>Riders to the Stars</u>. (H-P)
4) 1959 Crown — <u>Skyport</u>. (RP)
5) 1968 Putnam — 2 <u>Hauser's Memory</u>. (RP)

NOTE: #3 is a novelization of Mr. Siodmak's screenplay. Although he had no other connection with the novel, his byline appears on its cover, and it is, consequently, listed here.

CURT SIODMAK (continued)

FSF: "The Eggs from Lake Tanganyika," *Amazing*, July, 1926.

***   ***   ***   ***   ***

Curt Siodmak--born August 10, 1902 in Germany--Ph.D. (Mathematics), University of Zurich, 1927; postgraduate study at Technische Hochschule, Dresden and Stuttgart, 1929-1930--Bundespreis (German Oscar), 1964, *Feuerschiff* (Lightship)--Three Rivers, California.

Son of Irvin & Rose Siodmak--Henrietta: 1931--Geoffrey Siodmak (1933).

Employed in England at Gaumont British, 1933-1937; Free-Lance Writer and Screen Writer, and Motion Picture Director--Member: Science Fiction Writers of America; Writers Guild of America; Directors Guild.

Mr. Siodmak moved to the United States in 1937. Prior to that time, he wrote primarily in German (18 published novels). He has 35 motion picture credits in the United States, 18 in Europe.

JOHN T. SLADEK

1)	1968 Gollancz	The Reproductive System. (RPv)
2)	1968 Doubleday	with Thomas M. Disch (q.v.) as *Thom Demijohn Black Alice.

FKP: "The Way to a Man's Heart," *Bizarre*, January, 1966
(with Thomas M. Disch).

WIP:
1A)   1969 Ace   Mechasm. (P)

CORDELIA TITCOMB SMITH

1)   1964 Dell   Great Science Fiction Stories. (@/P)
1A)   1964 Mayflower   The Best of Sci-Fi 3. (@/P)

CORDELIA TITCOMB SMITH (continued)

FPS: 1947 — Paul Bunyan in Geauga County.
FSF: 1964 Dell — Great Science Fiction Stories. (@/P)

***   ***   ***   ***   ***

Cordelia Meda Titcomb Smith--born November 6, 1902 at Bath, Maine--B.L.S., Simmons College, 1926; Certificate in Library Work with Children, Western Reserve University, 1929-- Maumee, Ohio.

Daughter of Fred Evans & Katrina (Beals) Titcomb--James Ambler Smith: May 24, 1930-deceased--Sally Smith Fenton; Margaret Smith Inglis.

School and Children's Library Cataloger; currently Director of Young Adult Work, Lucas County Library, Ohio--Member: American Library Association; Pan Pacific and South East Asia Association; League of Women Voters; International Institute.

EVELYN E. SMITH

1) 1962 Avalon — The Perfect Planet. (RP)

FKP: "Tea Tray in the Sky," — Galaxy, September, 1952.

Evelyn E. Smith is a member of Science Fiction Writers of America.

GEORGE H(ENRY) SMITH

1) 1961 Epic   — 1976--Year of Terror. (P)
2) 1961 Epic   — Scourge of the Blood Cult. (P)
3) 1961 Pike   — The Coming of the Rats. (P)
6) 1963 Monarch — Doomsday Wing. (P)
7) 1964 Monarch — The Unending Night. (P)
9) 1965 Avalon   — The Forgotten Planet.
10) 1966 Belmont — The Four Day Weekend. (P)
11) 1967 Avalon   — Druids' World.

GEORGE H(ENRY) SMITH (continued)

with M. Jane Deer as *M. J. Deer
4) 1963 France   A Place Named Hell. (P)
5) 1963 France   Flames of Desire. (P)

as *Jerry Jason
8) 1965 Tempo   The Psycho Makers. (P)

FPS: "The Last Spring,"   Startling Stories, August, 1953.

WIP: 1969 Signet   Witch Queen of Lochlann. (P)
     1969 Ace   Kar Kaballa, King of the Gogs. (P)

***   ***   ***   ***   ***

George Henry Smith--born October 27, 1922 at Vicksburg, Mississippi--attended University of Southern California--Inglewood, California.

Son of George H. & Marie E. (Poche)/Cutter/Smith--M. Jane Deer: February 10, 1950--no children.

Free-Lance Writer--Member: Science Fiction Writers of America.

Mr. Smith comments on his career:
   "Although most of my writing has been outside the sf field, I started my professional career almost exclusively in sf, and most of my early short story sales were to science fiction pulps. Since then I've written and sold more material in other fields: men's magazines, non-fiction books dealing with the occult, political and biographical subjects."

JERRY SOHL

1) 1952 Rinehart   The Haploids. (RP)
2) 1953 Rinehart   The Transcendent Man. (RP)
3) 1953 Rinehart   Costigan's Needle. (RP)
4) 1954 Rinehart   The Altered Ego. (RP)
5) 1955 Rinehart   Point Ultimate. (RP)
6) 1956 Ace   The Mars Monopoly. (P)

JERRY SOHL (continued)

7)	1957 Rinehart	Prelude to Peril.
8)	1957 Avon	The Time Dissolver. (P)
9)	1959 Rinehart	The Odious Ones. (RP)
10)	1959 Ace	One Against Herculum. (P)
11)	1965 Gold Medal	Night Slaves. (P)

FPS: a short story to the Chicago Daily News, 1932.
FSF: "The 7th Order,"   Galaxy, March, 1952.

***   ***   ***   ***   ***

Gerald Allan Sohl--born December 2, 1913 at Los Angeles, California--Thousand Oaks, California.

Son of Fred J. & Florence (Wray) Sohl--Jean Gordon: October 28, 1943--Gerald Allan Sohl, Jr. (November 17, 1944); Martha Jane Sohl (December 26, 1947); Jennifer Sohl (December 3, 1949).

Was a Newspaperman before turning to writing: "Let Bob Tucker talk me into writing my first book, and have been unable to stop writing since"--Member: Science Fiction Writers of America; Mystery Writers of America; Writers Guild of America, West.

Mr. Sohl is currently collaborating with Theodore Sturgeon and George Clayton Johnson(qq.v.) in writing the screen version of Robert A. Heinlein's "The Green Hills of Earth."

NORMAN SPINRAD

1)	1966 Pap Lib	The Solarians. (P)
2)	1967 Belmont	Agent of Chaos. (P)
3)	1967 Doubleday	The Men in the Jungle. (RP)

FPS: "The Last of the Romany,"   Analog, May, 1963.

WIP: 1969 Walker   Bug Jack Barron. (H-P)
            Avon

***   ***   ***   ***   ***

Norman Richard Spinrad--born September 15, 1940 at New York, New York--B.S., City College of New York,--Los Angeles, California.

Son of Morris & Ray Spinrad--unmarried.

Has been a literary agent and television writer; currently Free-Lance Writer--Member: Science Fiction Writers of America (Chairman, Elections Committee, 1967); Writers Guild of America, West.

A. J. STEIGER

1) 1961 Phil Lib   The Moon Man.

Andrew Jacob Steiger was born in 1900. He could not be located. A complete biography may be found in Contemporary Authors.

HANK STINE

1) 1968 Essex   Season of the Witch. (P)

FPS: "A Love Called This Thing," Bait.
FSF: "Dark of Night," Baracuda. (as *Sibly Whyte).

WIP: 1969 Essex   Radio Waves. (P)

***   ***   ***   ***   ***   ***

Henry Eugene Stine--born April 13, 1945 at Sikeston, Missouri--Los Angeles, California.

Cristine Annette Kindred: June, 1966/April, 1968--Eden Rain Stine (September 21, 1966).

"I am a writer/film director/film editor/magazine editor"--Member: Science Fiction Writers of America.

"Reality fascinates me. I keep looking for it. Father in Service. Moved from town to town. I keep looking for something real."

"Structure has become my all consuming passion: not style or plot. I can handle them. But structure. Like a song is structured or a film. If something must be said about me let it be this: I'm a 'Citizens for Boysenberry Jam' fan."

GRAHAM BRICE STONE

1) 1955 Futurian   Index to the Australian Science Fiction
                                Magazines Part 1. (nf/P)
2) 1958 Futurian   Index to the Australian Science Fiction
                                Magazines Part 2. (nf/P)
3) 1964 Futurian   Australian Science Fiction Index, 1939-62.
                                (nf/P)
4) 1968 ASFA   Australian Science Fiction Index, 1925-67.
                                (nf/P)

GRAHAM BRICE STONE (continued)

FPS: c. 1948: "reviews, articles, journalistic work for various trade publications"

WIP: 1969   Index to British Science Fiction Magazines Part 1. (nf/P)
        1969   Index to British Science Fiction Magazines Part 2. (nf/P)

***   ***   ***   ***   ***

Graham Brice Stone--born January 7, 1926 at Norwood, South Australia, Australia--B.A., University of Sydney, 1962--Canberra City, Australian Capital Territory, Australia.

Son of Nelson Brice & Jeannie Campbell (McAnna) Stone--(1) Joy Anderson: 1956/1965; (2) Patricia Cowper: 1965--1) Timothy Nicholas Stone (April 19, 1961); 2) Dorinda Dawn Stone (August 17, 1968).

Librarian, Public Library of New South Wales, 1953-1963; National Library of Australia, 1963-DATE--Member: Library Association of Australia (Associate); Australian and New Zealand Association for the Advancement of Science; Futurian Society of Sydney (Life Member); Australian Science Fiction Association.

Mr. Stone writes:
   "I have been compiling data on science fiction books for many years. It is disgraceful that there is no general bibliography, which should have been done before any of the (mostly quite worthless) commentary and marginalia that has been produced. Forty years of associated activities, thousands of little magazines and trivial sheets, and no bibliography of science fiction books--and no complete and reliable magazine index either. My own efforts have been done out of desperation. I have reached the point where my information on books is close to being complete enough to think about publication, and I am almost persuaded to undertake it beginning in instalments, perhaps next year.
   "I deplore most of the activities supposedly in support of science fiction. I think it is significant that those involved allow themselves to be called 'fans,' a 'fan' being commonly understood as a half-wit who makes a nuisance of himself at a public entertainment: no one claiming to have a serious interest in any other subject would tolerate the word being applied to him. The development of private jargon, the habit of meaningless titles for publications, the general ignorance and lack of background that makes possible the association of 'fantasy' with science fiction, the general treating of the whole movement as a joke, have contributed to the weakness and lack of progress of the field."

----

*LESLIE F. STONE

1)	1930 Stellar	When The Sun Went Out. (P)
2)	1967 Avalon	Out of the Void.

FKP: "Men with Wings," Air Wonder, July, 1929.

Leslie F. Stone, penname of Mrs. William Silberberg, is most likely deceased.

LEON E. STOVER

with Harry Harrison (q.v.)
1) 1968 Doubleday   Apeman, Spaceman: Anthropological Science
                    Fiction. (@)

FPS: four articles on China and Southeast Asia to The American Oxford Encyclopedia, 1961.
FSF: 1968 Doubleday   Apeman, Spaceman: Anthropological Science
                      Fiction. (@/with Harry Harrison).

WIP: an untitled novel based around the building of Stonehenge circa 1500 B.C. (with Harry Harrison).

***   ***   ***   ***   ***

Leon Eugene Stover--born April 9, 1929 at Lewiston, Pennsylvania--B.A., Western Maryland College, 1950; graduate study in archaeology at University of New Mexico, 1950; graduate study in Chinese (advanced Mandarin) at Harvard University, 1951; M.A., Columbia University, 1952; Ph.D. (Anthropology), Columbia University, 1962--Chicago, Illinois.

Son of Dr. G. Franklin & Helen E. Stover--Takeko Kawai: October 12, 1956-- no children.

Science Editor, Amazing Stories, February, 1968-DATE; Fantastic Stories, March, 1968-DATE; Visiting Professor, Tokyo University, 1963-1965; Associate Professor of Anthropology, Illinois Institute of Technology, 1965-DATE--Member: Science Fiction Writers of America.

LEON E. STOVER (continued)

Dr. Stover writes:
"It might be fitting to mention that I have taught a course on SF ever since I came to IIT in 1965. The course is entitled ANTHRO 345--Science in Contemporary Culture. Readings in the literature of science fiction as a guide to the impact of the scientific estate. That's exactly the way the course appears in the IIT Bulletin."

THEODORE STURGEON

1)	1948	Prime	Without Sorcery. (s/RPav)
1A)	1948	Prime	It. (a/P)
2)	1950	Greenberg	The Dreaming Jewels. (RPv)
3)	1953	Farrar/Ballantine	More Than Human. (H-P)
4)	1953	Abelard	E Pluribus Unicorn. (s/RP)
5)	1955	Funk	A Way Home. (s/RP)
6)	1955	Ballantine	Caviar. (s/H-P)
5A)	1957	Joseph	Thunder and Roses. (s)
7)	1958	World	The King and Four Queens. (P)
2A)	1958	Pyramid	The Synthetic Man. (P)
8)	1958	Dell	The Cosmic Rape. (P)
9)	1958	Doubleday	A Touch of Strange. (s/RP)
10)	1959	Avon	Aliens 4. (s/P)
11)	1960	Pyramid	Venus Plus X. (P/RH)
12)	1960	Avon	Beyond. (s/P)
13)	1961	Ballantine	Some of Your Blood. (P)
1B)	1961	Ballantine	Not Without Sorcery. (s/a/P)
14)	1961	Pyramid	1 Voyage to the Bottom of the Sea. (P)
15)	1964	Pyramid	Sturgeon in Orbit. (s/P)
16)	1965	Gollancz	The Joyous Invasions.
17)	1965	Galaxy	...And My Fear is Great and Baby Is Three. (P)
18)	1966	Pyramid	Starshine. (s/P/RH)

FKP: "The Ether Breather," Astounding, September, 1939.

Theodore Hamilton Sturgeon (formerly Edward Hamilton Waldo) was born in 1918. He won The International Fantasy Award, 1954, More Than Human, and was Guest of Honor, 20th World Science Fiction Convention (Chicon III), 1962. Mr. Sturgeon was Feature Editor, If, March, 1961-March, 1964; Book Editor, Venture, January-July, 1958. A partial biography may be found in Seekers of Tomorrow.

EUNICE SUDAK

1)	1963 Lancer	The Raven. (P)
2)	1963 Lancer	X. (P)

JEAN SUTTON

with Jeff Sutton (q.v.)

1)	1968 Putnam	The Beyond.
2)	1968 Putnam	The Programmed Man.
FPS:	1968 Putnam	The Beyond. (with Jeff Sutton)
WIP:	1969 Putnam	Lord of the Stars. (with Jeff Sutton)

***   ***   ***   ***   ***

Eugenia Geneva Sutton--born July 5, 1917 at Denmark, Wisconsin--B.A., University of California at Los Angeles, 1940; M.A. (Education), San Diego State College, 1956--La Mesa, California.

Daughter of Christopher & Mary Honora (Baumgart) Hansen--Jefferson Howard Sutton: February 1, 1941--Christopher Sutton (23); Gale Sutton (17).

Secretary, San Diego City Council, 1948-1952; Currently Social Studies Teacher, Grossmont Union High School District--Member: Science Fiction Writers of America.

JEFF SUTTON

1)	1958 Ace	First on the Moon. (P)
2)	1959 Ace	Bombs in Orbit. (P)
3)	1960 Ace	Spacehive. (P)
4)	1963 Putnam	Apollo at Go. (RP)
5)	1963 Avalon	The Atom Conspiracy. (RP)
6)	1966 Putnam	Beyond Apollo.
7)	1967 Ace	H-Bomb Over America. (P)
10)	1968 Ace	The Man Who Saw Tomorrow. (P)

with Jean Sutton (q.v.)

8)	1968 Putnam	The Beyond.
9)	1968 Putnam	The Programmed Man.

JEFF SUTTON (continued)

FPS: "The Third Empire,"   Spaceway, February, 1955.

WIP: 1969 Putnam   Lord of the Stars. (with Jean Sutton)

***   ***   ***   ***   ***

Jefferson Howard Sutton--born July 25, 1913 at Los Angeles, California--B.A., San Diego State College, 1954; M.A. (Psychology), San Diego State College, 1955--La Mesa, California.

Son of Thomas S. & Sarah Elizabeth (King) Sutton--Eugenia Geneva Hansen: February 1, 1941--Chris Sutton (23); Gale Sutton (17).

Has been a news photographer and reporter; currently Editorial Consultant to Aerospace Industries; Free-Lance Writer--Member: Science Fiction Writers of America.

Mr. Sutton mentions that he started his newspaper career as the proverbial copy boy on a large metropolitan newspaper.

THOMAS BURNETT SWANN

1) 1966 Ace   Day of the Minotaur. (P)
2) 1967 Ace   The Weirwoods. (P)
3) 1968 Ace   The Dolphin and the Deep. (s/P)
4) 1968 Ace   Moondust. (P)

FPS: "Winged Victory,"   Fantastic Universe, July, 1958.

WIP: 1969 Ace   Where Is the Bird of Fire? (s/P)
                             The Goat Without Horns.

***   ***   ***   ***   ***

Thomas Burnett Swann, Jr.--born October 11, 1928 at Tampa, Florida--B.A., Duke University, 1950; M.A., University of Tennessee, 1955; Ph.D., University of Florida, 1960--Boca Raton, Florida.

Son of Thomas Burnett & Margaret (Gaines) Swann-unmarried.

THOMAS BURNETT SWANN (continued)

Assistant Professor of English, Florida Southern College, 1960-1962; Free-Lance Writer and Poet--Member: Science Fiction Writers of America; American Poetry Association; Modern Language Association; American Association of University Professors; Phi Beta Kappa; Phi Kappa Phi.

Dr. Swann writes:
 "I'm really not qualified to judge the current state of science fiction, since I don't get to read very much. As for fantasy, I think it has, and always will have, an important place, because the best of it is true, even if fanciful. It is our dreams verbalized, and who can live without dreams? Or deny their ultimate truth? My own contribution has been slight. I think of myself as writing domestic rather than epic fantasy--stories in which the focus is on the daily lives of a very small group of people or humanized beasts. Someone once called my stories too bland. I prefer to call them microcosmic."

LEO SZILARD

1)	1961 S&S		The Voice of the Dolphins. (s/RP)	

PAUL TABORI

1)	1959 Consul		The Survivors. (P)	
2)	1961 Pyramid		The Green Rain. (P)	
3)	1967 Pyramid	1	The Doomsday Brain. (P)	
4)	1967 Pyramid	2	The Invisible Eye. (P)	

SER: The Hunters.

FPS: c. 1922 (in Hungarian).
FSF: 1959 Consul   The Survivors. (P)

WIP: 1969 Pyramid.   The Cleft. (P)

***   ***   ***   ***   ***

Paul Tabori--born May 8, 1908 at Budapest, Hungary--Ph.D., Kaiser Friedrich Wilhelm University, 1930; Doctor of Economics and Political Science, Pazmany Peter University, 1932--Medal of the City of Paris, 1961; Special Award, Writers Guild of Great Britain, 1964; Special Award, International Writers Guild, 1967--London, England.

PAUL TABORI (continued)

Son of Cornelius & Elsa (Ziffer) Tabori--Katherine Elizabeth Barlay: February 16, 1933--Peter Tabori (38).

Mr. Tabori has served as a writer, correspondent, and editor for various Hungarian and British magazines and news agencies; also: Film Critic, <u>London Daily Mail</u>, 1942-1944; Contract Writer, Korda, 1943-1948; Director, Telewriters Ltd., 1951-1958; European Feature Editor, Reuters News Service; currently Director, Taden Productions Ltd.; Visiting Professor, Fairleigh Dickinson University, 1966; City College of New York, 1967; University of Illinois, 1969-1970--Member: P.E.N. (Chairman, Center for Writers-in-Exile, 1954-1957; Permanent International Delegate, 1957-1962; Member, Writers in Prison Committee, 1965-DATE; Member, Greenhoe Council, English P.E.N. Centre, 1967-DATE); Screenwriters' Guild (International Secretary, 1953-1966); International Writers Fund (Honorary Secretary, 1962-DATE).

The following remarks are taken from Mr. Tabori's letter:
"...As for the current state of science fiction, I am afraid I do not read enough of it to be a qualified judge; but it seems to me that the frontiers of general fiction and science fiction are being rapidly abolished, and that the distinction between the two is becoming increasingly blurred. I think the best science fiction is the sort which takes a fantastic or out-of-way idea and treats it with complete factual realism--exploring all possibilities to their logical end. I don't very much like Westerns, soap opera, or detective stories disguised as sf, and I believe (as in connection with every other form of writing) that excessive pre-occupation with form and experimentations for experimentation's sake is always a cover up for a lack of ideas, an absence of real content.

"I have written in three languages, beginning with Hungarian, then switching to German, and now for the last 33 years writing almost exclusively in English. I wrote a science fiction novel in my teens which was called <u>Death of Sleep</u>, and which envisaged a world in which sleep had been abolished. I wrote a number of short stories in all three languages, but I think that my own contribution to sf, if any, has been in science fiction satire, as a very humble follower of Swift and Orwell. I am, at the moment, working on a short study called 'Sex and Utopia,' which will be a brief analysis of the treatment of this problem in various classical and modern works of science fiction."

WILLIAM F. TEMPLE

1)	1949 Long		<u>Four-Sided Triangle</u>. (RP)
2)	1951 Long		<u>Dangerous Edge</u>.
3)	1955 Muller	1	<u>Martin Magnus, Planet Rover</u>.
4)	1955 Muller	2	<u>Martin Magnus on Venus</u>.

WILLIAM F. TEMPLE (continued)

5)	1956 Muller	3	Martin Magnus on Mars.	
6)	1962 Ace		The Automated Goliath.	(P)
7)	1962 Ace		The Three Suns of Amara.	(P)
8)	1963 Ace		Battle on Venus.	(P)
9)	1966 S&S		Shoot at the Moon.	(RP)
10)	1968 Macdonald		The Fleshpots of Sansato.	

FPS: "The Kosso," Thrills, 1935.
FSF: "Lunar Lilliput," Tales of Wonder, #2, 1938.

***   ***   ***   ***   ***

William Frederick Temple--born March 9, 1914 at London, England--attended Woolwich Polytechnic--Folkestone, Kent, England.

Son of William & Doris Temple--Joan: September 16, 1939--Anne Temple (28); Cliff Temple (21).

Stock Exchange Official (London) for twenty years--Member: Science Fiction Writers of America.

Prewar Editor, Journal of the British Interplanetary Society.

----

*WILLIAM TENN

1)	1953 S&S	Children of Wonder. (@/RPv)
1A)	1954 Permabook	Outsiders: Children of Wonder. (@/P)
2)	1955 Ballantine	Of All Possible Worlds. (s/H-P)
3)	1956 Ballantine	The Human Angle. (s/H-P)
4)	1958 Bantam	Time in Advance. (s/P/RH)
5)	1968 Belmont	A Lamp for Medusa. (P)
6)	1968 Ballantine	Of Men and Monsters. (P/RH)
7)	1968 Ballantine	The Seven Sexes. (s/P)
8)	1968 Ballantine	The Square Root of Man. (s/P)
9)	1968 Ballantine	The Wooden Star. (s/P)

FKP: "Alexander the Bait," Astounding, May, 1946.

William Tenn, penname of Philip J. Klass, was born in 1920. He was Consulting Editor, The Magazine of Fantasy and Science Fiction, September, 1958-December, 1958; and is currently an instructor at the university level.

WALTER S. TEVIS, JR.

1) 1963 Gold Medal   The Man Who Fell to Earth. (P)

FKP: "The Ifth of Oofth,"   Galaxy, April, 1957.

Walter S. Tevis could not be located.

ERIC THACKER

1) 1968 Cape   with A. Earnshaw (q.v.) Musrum.

---

*DAN THOMAS

1) 1968 Ballantine   The Seed. (P)

FPS: "Race to the Frozen Sea,"   True, May, 1952.
FSF: 1968 Ballantine   The Seed. (P)

***   ***   ***   ***   ***

Leonard M. Sanders, Jr. (u)--born January 15, 1929 at Denver, Colorado--attended University of Oklahoma--Fort Worth, Texas.

Son of Mr. & Mrs. Leonard M. Sanders--married August 21, 1956.

Book Page Editor and Fine Arts Editor, Fort Worth Star Telegram--Member: Science Fiction Writers of America; Western Writers of America; Authors Guild; Texas Institute of Letters.

---

*MARTIN THOMAS

1) 1958 Fleetway   The Evil Eye. (P)
2) 1960 Fleetway   Bred to Kill. (P)
3) 1961 Fleetway   Assignment Doomsday. (P)
4) 1964 Digit   Beyond the Spectrum. (P)
5) 1965 Mayflower   Laird of Evil. (P/RH)

*MARTIN THOMAS (continued)

6)	1965 Mayflower	The Mind Killers. (P/RH)
7)	1965 Mayflower	Such Men Are Dangerous. (P)
8)	1966 Mayflower	Sorcerers of Set. (P)
9)	1966 Mayflower	The Hand of Cain. (P/RH)
11)	1968 Mayflower	Brainwashed. (P)

as ***Peter Saxon

10) 1968 Lancer   The Curse of Rathlaw. (P/RH)

FPS: a series of occult short stories, 1946-1947.

WIP: 1969 Baker   Dark Veils of Murder. (2/e)
      1969 Baker   Immortal Vendetta. (as ***Peter Saxon)

***   ***   ***   ***   ***   ***

Thomas Hector Martin--born June 29, 1913 at Bristol, Somerset, England--Bristol, Somerset, England.

Son of Charles & Helen Josephine (Butcher) Martin--unmarried.

Free-Lance newspaper contributor from age 17; also has been a commercial artist, and has done a cartoon strip; Free-Lance Writer, 1946-DATE.

Interests: reading philosophy and psychology, listening to good music, riding.

Mr. Thomas mentions that his father died on active service in Iraq in 1921, and was buried in Baghdad. During the First World War, he served on the western front and in Mesopotamia, and was twice mentioned in dispatches.

THEODORE L. THOMAS

with Kate Wilhelm (q.v.)
1) 1965 Berkley   The Clone. (P/RH)

FKP: "The Revisitor," Space, September, 1952; "Improbable Profession," Astounding, September, 1952 (as *Leonard Lockhard)(simultaneous).

WIP: Doubleday   The Year of the Cloud. (with Kate Wilhelm)

Theodore L. Thomas is a member of Science Fiction Writers of America.

TREBOR THORPE

1) 1960 Badger SN   Five Faces of Fear. (P)
2) 1960 Badger SF   Lightning World. (P)

Trebor Thorpe is probably an exclusive penname of R. Lionel Fanthorpe (q.v.).

PEL TORRO

1) 1960 Badger SF   Frozen Planet. (P)
2) 1960 Badger SF   World of the Gods. (P)
3) 1961 Badger SN   The Phantom Ones. (P)
4) 1962 Badger SN   The Legion of the Lost. (P)
5) 1963 Badger SN   The Strange Ones. (P)
6) 1963 Badger SF   Galaxy 666. (P/RH)
7) 1963 Badger SF   Formula 29X. (P)
8) 1963 Badger SF   Through the Barrier. (P)
9) 1963 Badger SN   The Timeless Ones. (P)
10) 1963 Badger SF   The Last Astronaut. (P)
11) 1963 Badger SN   The Face of Fear. (P)
12) 1964 Badger SF   The Return. (P/RHv)
13) 1964 Badger SF   Space No Barrier. (P)
14) 1965 Badger SF   Force 97X. (P)

WIP:
12A) 1969 Arcadia   Exiled in Space.
?7A) 1969 Tower   Beyond the Barrier of Space. (P)

Pel Torro is a probable pseudonym, R. Lionel Fanthorpe (q.v.) being the likely author or all or most of the works appearing under this name.

ROBERT TRALINS

1) 1966 Belmont   The Cosmozoids. (P)

FPS: 1948
FSF: 1966 Belmont   The Cosmozoids. (P)

***   ***   ***   ***   ***

Stanley Robert Tralins--born April 28, 1926 at Baltimore, Maryland--Miami Beach, Florida.

Son of Emanuel & Rose Tralins--Sonya: September 2, 1945--Myles Jay Tralins (21); Alan Harvy Tralins (18).

Free-Lance Writer--Member: Science Fiction Writers of America.

S. J. TREIBICH

			with Laurence M. Janifer (q.v.)
1)	1968 Ace	1	Target: Terra. (P)
FPS:	1966 Lancer		Haelstrom Manor. (P)
FSF:	"First Context,"		The Magazine of Fantasy and Science Fiction, August, 1965 (with Laurence M. Janifer).
WIP:	1969 Ace	2	The High Hex. (P/with Laurence M. Janifer)
	1969 Ace	3	The Wagered World. (P/with Laurence M. Janifer)

*** *** *** *** ***

Stephen John Treibich--born March 8, 1936--holds a Master's Degree--Provincetown, Maine.

Free-Lance Writer.

LOUIS TRIMBLE

1)	1968 Ace	Anthropol. (P)
FPS:	1938 Golden West	Sports of the World. (nf)
FSF:	"Probability,"	If, April, 1954.

*** *** *** *** ***

Louis Preston Trimble--born March 2, 1917 at Seattle, Washington--attended University of Washington, 1948-1949; B.A., Eastern Washington State College, 1950; Ed.M., 1953; graduate study at University of Washington, 1952-1953, 1955; University of Pennsylvania, 1955-1956--Graduate Fellowship, University of Pennsylvania, 1955-1956--Kirkland, Washington.

Son of Charles Louis & Rose Alice (Potter) Trimble--Jacquelyn Whitney: November 21, 1952--Victoria Rosemary Trimble (September 11, 1939).

Instructor in Spanish and English, Eastern Washington State College, 1950-1954; Instructor, University of Washington, 1956-1959; Assistant Professor of Humanities and Social Studies, 1959-1967; Associate Professor, 1967-DATE--Member: Science Fiction Writers of America; Western Writers of America (Executive Board, 1963-1964); American Oriental Society; Linguistic Society of America; Association for Machine Translation and Computational Linguistics.

E. C. TUBB

4)	1952 Hamilton	Alien Impact. (P)
5)	1952 Hamilton	Atom War on Mars. (P)
12)	1953 Panther	The Mutants Rebel. (P)
16)	1953 Paladin	Alien Life. (P)
19)	1953 Comyns	Venusian Adventure. (P)
23)	1954 Panther	World at Bay. (H-P)
24)	1954 Scion	City of No Return. (P)
25)	1954 Scion	Journey to Mars. (P)
26)	1954 Scion	The Stellar Legion. (P)
27)	1954 Scion	The Hell Planet. (P)
28)	1954 Scion	The Resurrected Man. (P)
31)	1955 Boardman	Alien Dust.
32)	1956 Ace	The Space-Born. (P)
30A)	1958 Ace	The Mechanical Monarch. (P)
33)	1964 Jenkins	Moon Base. (RP)
34)	1966 Hart-Davis	Ten from Tomorrow. (RP)
35)	1967 Hart-Davis	Death Is a Dream. (RP)
36)	1967 Ace	The Winds of Gath. (P/RHv)
36A)	1968 Hart-Davis	Gath.
37)	1968 Ace	C.O.D. Mars. (P)
38)	1968 Ace	Derai. (P/RH)

as ***King Lang

1)	1951 Curtis	Saturn Patrol. (P)

as ***Gill Hunt

2)	1952 Curtis	Planet Fall. (P)

as ***Brian Shaw

3)	1952 Curtis	Argentis. (P)

as ***Volsted Gridban

6)	1952 Scion	Alien Universe. (P)
7)	1952 Scion	Reverse Universe. (P)
8)	1953 Milestone	Planetoid Disposals Ltd. (P)
9)	1953 Scion	De Bracy's Drug. (P)
10)	1953 Milestone	Fugitive of Time. (P)

as *Charles Grey

11)	1953 Milestone	The Wall. (P)
13)	1953 Milestone	Dynasty of Doom. (P)
14)	1953 Milestone	Tormented City. (P)
15)	1953 Milestone	Space Hunger. (P)
17)	1953 Milestone	I Fight for Mars. (P)
21)	1954 Milestone	The Extra Man. (P)
29)	1954 Milestone	Hand of Havoc. (P)
30)	1954 Milestone	Enterprise 2115. (H-P)

E. C. TUBB (continued)

as *Carl Maddox
18)	1953 Pearson	Menace from the Past. (P)
20)	1954 Pearson	The Living World. (P)

as ***Roy Sheldon
22)	1954 Panther	The Metal Eater. (H-P)

FPS:	"No Short Cuts,"	New Worlds, Summer, 1951.
WIP:	1969 Pap Lib	S.T.A.R. Flight. (P)
	1969 Ace	Toyman. (P)
	1969 Ace	Kalin. (P)
	1969 Sidgwick	Second Chance.

***　　***　　***　　***　　***

Edwin Charles Tubb--born October 15, 1919 at London, England--Cytricon Literary Award, 1955; Five-time winner of Nebula Science Fiction Literary Award as year's best author--London, England.

Son of Edwin Margrie & Marie Francois (Bonzec) Tubb--Iris Kathleen Smith: 1944--Jennifer Tubb (20); Linda Tubb (14).

Editor, Authentic Science Fiction, February, 1956 (#66)-October, 1957 (#85); Free-Lance Writer--Member: Science Fiction Writers of America; British Science Fiction Association; Knight of St. Fantony (Grand Lord of the London Circle).

WILSON TUCKER

1)	1951 Rinehart	City in the Sea. (RPa)
2)	1952 Rinehart	The Long Loud Silence. (RP)
3)	1953 Rinehart	The Time Masters. (RP)
4)	1954 Rinehart	Wild Talent. (RP/RPv)
5)	1954 Rinehart	The Science Fiction Subtreasury. (s/RPv)
6)	1955 Rinehart	Time Bomb. (RPv)
4A)	1955 Bantam	The Man from Tomorrow. (P)
5A)	1955 Bantam	Time: X. (s/P)
6A)	1957 Avon	Tomorrow Plus X. (P)
7)	1958 Rinehart	The Lincoln Hunters. (RP)
8)	1960 Ace	To the Tombaugh Station. (P)

FKP: "Interstellar Way-Station," Super Science, May, 1941 (as *Bob Tucker).

WILSON TUCKER (continued)

Arthur Wilson Tucker was born in 1914. He was Editor and Publisher of <u>Science Fiction News Letter</u>, 1945-1953, and is currently a member of Science Fiction Writers of America. A complete biography may be found in <u>Contemporary Authors</u>.

----

*THEODORE TYLER

1)	1968 Doubleday	<u>The Man Whose Name Wouldn't Fit</u>.	(RP)
FPS:	1962 Macmillan	<u>Men Who Make Us Rich</u>. (nf/as Edward Ziegler)	
FSF:	1968 Doubleday	<u>The Man Whose Name Wouldn't Fit</u>.	

***   ***   ***   ***   ***

Edward William Ziegler--born July 12, 1932 at New York, New York--B.A., Duke University, 1955--Briarcliff Manor, New York.

Son of Vinton E. & Beatrice (Skelton) Ziegler--Sally McIntosh: June 15, 1957--Andrew Ziegler (10); Matthew Ziegler (8); Sally Ziegler (2).

Editor for <u>Reader's Digest</u>.

RENA VALE

1)	1965 Pap Lib	<u>Beyond the Sealed World</u>. (P)	
FKP:	"The Shining City,"	<u>Science Fiction Quarterly</u>, May, 1952.	
WIP:	1970 Pap Lib	<u>The X-Factor on Taurus 4</u>. (P)	

Rena Marie Vale was born in 1898. She is currently a member of Science Fiction Writers of America.

DAVE VAN ARNAM

2)	1967 Belmont	<u>Star Gladiator</u>. (P)
4)	1968 Belmont	<u>The Players of Hell</u>. (P)
1)	1967 Pyramid	with *Ron Archer (Ted White, q.v.) <u>Lost in Space</u>. (P)

DAVE VAN ARNAM (continued)

		with Ted White (q.v.)
3)	1968 Pyramid	Sideslip. (P)
WIP:	1969 Lancer	Star Barbarian. (P)
	1969 Ballantine	Starmind. (P)

David G. Van Arnam is a member of Science Fiction Writers of America.

JACK VANCE

1)	1950 Hillman	1	The Dying Earth. (P)
2)	1953 Toby Press		The Space Pirate. (P)
3)	1953 Winston		Vandals of the Void.
4)	1956 Ballantine		To Live Forever. (H-P)
5)	1957 Bouregy		Big Planet. (RP)
6)	1958 Ace		Slaves of the Klau. (P)
7)	1958 Bouregy		The Languages of Pao. (RP)
8)	1963 Ace		The Dragon Masters. (P/RH)
2A)	1963 Ace		The Five Gold Bands. (P)
9)	1964 Ace		Son of the Tree. (P)
10)	1964 Ace		The Houses of Iszm. (P)
11)	1964 Berkley	-1	The Star King. (P/RH)
12)	1964 Ballantine		Future Tense. (s/P)
13)	1964 Berkley	-2	The Killing Machine. (P/RH)
14)	1965 Pyramid		Space Opera. (P)
15)	1965 Ace		Monsters in Orbit. (P)
16)	1965 Ace		The World Between. (s/P)
17)	1966 Ace		The Brains of Earth. (P)
18)	1966 Ace		The Many Worlds of Magnus Ridolph. (s/P)
19)	1966 Ballantine		The Blue World. (P)
20)	1966 Ace	2	The Eyes of the Overworld. (P)
21)	1967 Ace		The Last Castle. (P)
22)	1967 Berkley	-3	The Palace of Love. (P/RH)
23)	1968 Ace	+1	City of the Chasch. (P)

SER: 3) Planet of Adventure or The Tschai Cycle.

FPS: "The World-Thinker," Thrilling Wonder Stories, Summer, 1945.

WIP:	1969 Ace	+2	Servants of the Wankh. (P)
	1969 Doubleday		Emphyrio.
	1969 Ace	+3	The Dirdir. (P)
	1970 Ace	+4	The Pnume.

***   ***   ***   ***   ***

JACK VANCE (continued)

John Holbrook Vance--born c. 1920 at San Francisco, California--attended University of California--Hugo Award, Best Short Fiction, 1963, "The Dragon Masters;" Best Novelette, 1967, "The Last Castle;" Nebula Award, Best Novella, 1966, "The Last Castle"--Oakland, California.

Son of Charles Albert & Edith Vance--Norma--John Holbrook Vance II (7).

Free-Lance Writer--Member: Science Fiction Writers of America.

Mr. Vance writes:
"I do considerable travelling: I'm now building a blue-water ketch to take us at least as far as the South Pacific." Mr. Vance spent his childhood on a ranch in the San Joaquin Valley.

---

*ZAARA VAN TUYL

1)	1967 Beacons	Skyways for Doorian.
FPP:	1966 Beacons	Breakthrough from Within. (nf)
FSP:	1967 Beacons	Skyways for Doorian.

***   ***   ***   ***   ***

Rosealthea Van Tuyl--born November 3, 1901 at Lynch, Nebraska--A.B. (Education), Fresno State College, 1932--Fresno, California.

Daughter of Charles & Leora (MacGinitie) Cornell--Harold Heuer Van Tuyl: October 27, 1919-1929--Andrew Van Tuyl (46); Barbara Van Tuyl Backer (44); Carol Van Tuyl Scott (42).

Grade school teacher until 1955; has also delved in real estate and farming; currently student of the occult.

A. E. van VOGT

1)	1946 Arkham		Slan. (RP)
2)	1946 Hadley	1	The Weapon Makers. (RP/RPv)
3)	1947 Fantasy		The Book of Ptath. (RP/RPv)
4)	1948 S&S	-1	The World of Null-A. (RP)

A. E. van VOGT (continued)

6)	1950 Fantasy		Masters of Time and The Changeling. (RPav)
7)	1950 Greenberg		The House That Stood Still. (RP/RPav)
8)	1950 S&S		The Voyage of the Space Beagle. (RP)
9)	1951 Greenberg	2	The Weapon Shops of Isher. (RP)
10)	1952 Pellegrini		Destination: Universe. (RP)
11)	1952 Pellegrini		Away and Beyond. (s/RP/RPa)
12)	1952 Gnome		The Mixed Men. (RPv)
13)	1953 Ace		Universe Maker. (P)
12A)	1955 Berkley		Mission to the Stars. (P)
2A)	1955 Ace		One Against Eternity. (P)
15)	1956 Ace	-2	The Pawns of Null-A. (P)
16)	1957 Shasta		Empire of the Atom. (RP)
17)	1958 S&S		The Mind Cage. (RP)
18)	1959 S&S		The War Against the Rull. (RP)
19)	1959 Ace		Siege of the Unseen. (P)
7A)	1960 Beacon		The Mating Cry. (a/P)
6A)	1960 Ace		Earth's Last Fortress. (a/P)
20)	1962 Ace		The Wizard of Linn. (P)
21)	1963 Doubleday		The Beast. (6C /e/RP)
3A)	1964 Pap Lib		Two Hundred Million A. D. (P)
22)	1964 Ace		The Twisted Men. (P/RHv)
23)	1965 Pap Lib		Monsters. (s/P)
22A)	1965 Doubleday		Rogue Ship. (RP)
15A)	1966 Berkley	2	The Players of Null-A. (P)
6B)	1967 Macfadden		Masters of Time. (a/P)
6C)	1967 Macfadden		The Changeling. (a/P)
25)	1967 Sidgwick		An A. E. van Vogt Omnibus. (3/14/21)
26)	1968 Ace		The Far-Out Worlds of A. E. van Vogt. (s/P)

with E. Mayne Hull (q.v.)

5)	1948 FPCI	Out of the Unknown. (s/RPe)
14)	1954 Fell	Planets for Sale. (RP)
24)	1966 Doubleday	The Winged Man. (RP)

NOTE: #6A is identical to #6B.

FKP: "Black Destroyer,"   Astounding, July, 1939.

WIP: 1969 Ace   The Silkie. (P)
        1969 Powell   Out of the Unknown. (S/e/P/with
                                    E. Mayne Hull)
        Ace   The Battle of Forever. (P)
        Ace   Quest for the Future. (P)
        Ace   The Other-Men. (P)

Alfred Elton van Vogt was born in 1912. He was Guest of Honor at 4th World Science Fiction Convention (Pacificon I), 1946, and is now a member of Science Fiction Writers of America. A partial biography may be found in Seekers of Tomorrow.

OTTO VIKING

1) 1964 Exposition   A World Intervenes.

Otto Viking was born in 1883.

KURT VONNEGUT, JR.

1) 1951 Scribner   Player Piano. (RP/RPv)
1A) 1956 Bantam   Utopia 14. (P)
2) 1960 Dell   The Sirens of Titan. (P/RH)
3) 1961 Fawcett   Canary in a Cat House. (P)
4) 1963 Holt   Cat's Cradle. (RP)

Kurt Vonnegut, Jr. was born in 1922. A complete biography may be found in Contemporary Authors.

JOHN VORHIES

1)   1967 Regnery   Pre-Empt. (RP)

FPS: 1967 Regnery   Pre-Empt. (RP)

WIP: The Mothers.

***   ***   ***   ***   ***

John Royal Harris Vorhies--born March 25, 1920 at Dallas, Texas--LL.B., University of Texas, 1944--Dallas, Texas.

Son of O.W. & Bessie Lu Vorhies--Jessie Alice Nettleton: October 7, 1944--John Royal Harris Vorhies, Jr. (23); Gordon Vorhies (21); Peter Vorhies (19); Bettie Lu Vorhies (16).

Free-Lance Writer.

TOM WADE

1) 1962 Digit   The World of Theda. (P)
2) 1963 Digit   The Voice from Baru. (P)

VICTOR WADEY

1) 1962 Digit   A Planet Named Terra. (P)
2) 1962 Digit   The United Planets. (P/RH)

---

*IAN WALLACE

1)   1967 Putnam   Croyd. (RP)
2)   1968 Putnam   Dr. Orpheus. (RP)

FSF: 1967 Putnam   Croyd.

WIP: 1969 Putnam   Deathstar Voyage.

***   ***   ***   ***   ***

"Ian Wallace"--holds a doctoral degree--New York, New York.

Dr. Wallace is married and has two sons.

"Psychologist, philosopher (clinics and a university); editor, author. Professional experience in USA, Canada, and Europe"--Member: Science Fiction Writers of America.

Hobbies: archaeology, astrophysics.

Dr. Wallace adds:
"Some readers will wish, perhaps, that I had given more details about myself. However, all these that I have given are personally most significant: my family, my education, one valued and pertinent affiliation, a statement of my side-and-background interests, the general nature of my career, and the bibliography. If I do not mention my age, perhaps it is vanity: I am either too old or too young to want it generally known. To protect the editors, I add that I have told them only what appears herein, so they have no convenient cross-checks; but also I vouch for the unembellished accuracy of these few points."

DAVE WALLIS

1)   1964 Dutton   Only Lovers Left Alive. (RP)

G. McDONALD WALLIS

1)	1961 Ace	Light of Lilith. (P)
2)	1963 Ace	Legend of Lost Earth. (P)

---

*HUGH WALTERS

1)	1957 Faber	Blast Off at Woomera. (RP)
1A)	1958 Criterion	Blast Off at 0300.
2)	1958 Faber	The Domes of Pico.
2A)	1959 Criterion	Menace from the Moon.
3)	1960 Faber	Operation Columbus.
3A)	1960 Criterion	First on the Moon. (RP)
4)	1961 Faber	Moon Base One.
4A)	1962 Criterion	Outpost on the Moon. (altered)
5)	1962 Faber	Expedition Venus.
6)	1963 Faber	Destination Mars.
7)	1964 Faber	Terror by Satellite.
8)	1965 Faber	Journey to Jupiter.
9)	1965 Faber	Mission to Mercury.
10)	1967 Faber	Spaceship to Saturn.
11)	1968 Faber	The Mohole Mystery.

FPS: 1957 Faber   Blast Off at Woomera. (RP)

WIP:
11A)	1969 Criterion	The Mohole Menace.
	1969 Faber	Nightmare on Neptune.

***   ***   ***   ***   ***

Walter Llewellyn Hughes--born June 15, 1910 at Bilston, Stafford, England--attended Aston College of Technology, 1955--Bilston, Stafford, England.

Son of W.M. & Kate (Latham) Hughes--Doris Higgens: April 18, 1933-deceased--Walter F. Hughes (34); Gillian D. Hughes (27).

Engineer and Managing Director, Bradsteds Ltd.; has been a Justice of the Peace; Free-Lance Writer--Member: British Interplanetary Society; Wolverhampton Astronomical Society; Associate Member: Institute of British Engineers.

TONY RUSSELL WAYMAN

1)   1967 Ace   World of the Sleeper. (P)

TONY RUSSELL WAYMAN (continued)

FPS: 1955
FSF: a series of Malaysian fantasy movies in 1959: "Jula Juli Bintang Tujoh;" "Siti Zubaidah;" "Aladin Burok;" "Pedang Hikmat;" "Wily Delilah." (as *Abdul Rahman).

WIP:
<u>Sheerluc, Champion of Earth</u>.
<u>To You Who Are Civilized</u>.
<u>Mixmaster</u>.
<u>Miss Anne</u>.
<u>Dunes of Pradai</u>.
<u>Ads Infinitum</u>.
<u>The Mutiny on the Borman</u>.

***   ***   ***   ***   ***

Tony Russell Wayman--born March 3, 1929 at Branksome, Dorset, England--Berkeley, California.

Son of Russell James & Amy Ivy (Whiteman) Wayman--Norah: October, 1950/May, 1969--no children.

"Became apprentice optometrist in 1945, joined Royal Navy 1946, served in Hong Kong and Singapore till 1954, went into advertising in Singapore till 1957, quit in disgust, wrote articles and features for Malaysian media, broadcast for Australian Broadcasting Commission, wrote stories, treatments, scenarios and shooting scripts for Malay movies, helped produce Indian-Malaysian and Indonesian-Malaysian movies, managed a snake show, did movie and stage PR work, etc."--Member: Science Fiction Writers of America; National Travel Club; Singapore Recreation Club; Cosmopolitan Club (Kuala Lumpur, Malaysia).

Mr. Wayman came to the United States in 1963.

Mr. Wayman writes:
"I don't particularly regard myself as a 'science fiction' or 'fantasy' writer. Nor, for that matter, do I regard myself as a writer of books necessarily. My philosophy is that the subject chooses its form, and when I have an idea, it might work out to a short story, an article, a novel, a play, a movie, or whatever. Incidentally, my novel <u>World of the Sleeper</u> was originally a Malay movie called 'Pedang Hikmat;' what I did was to supply a science fiction framework within which I could use the plot, though not the intent, of the original fantasy.
"There is very little 'speculative fiction' written or published, today or in any time, that might not as easily be mainstream writing, and none at all if one excludes the science-gadgetry yarns beloved of John Campbell."

TONY RUSSELL WAYMAN (continued)

"I was led into writing by (1) a natural aptitude for telling of the fantastic ('Diary of a Snail' at age 10); (2) an interested English teacher who turned me on at age 11 to LITERATURE; (3) a desire at 13 to be a newspaper columnist; (4) the winning of a short story competition at age 15; (5) the fascinations of Harry Stephen Keeler; (6) being put down at age 16 by John Creasey, a patron of the Boys' Club I was in; (7) being cursed with a facile talent for sales writing; (8) an inborn detestation for a honest day's work."

A. C. WEBB

1) 1967 Vantage   Farewell to the Bomb.

FPS: "Clue of the Missing Dog," Master Detective Stories, c. 1929.
FSF: "Double Lightning," Amazing Detective Stories, c. 1930.

WIP: The Witch of Endor.

***   ***   ***   ***   ***

Augustus Caesar Webb--born April 9, 1894 at Montgomery, Alabama--B.Ph., Brown University, 1918; attended Northwestern University, 1924--Lake Geneva, Wisconsin.

Son of Joshua & Martha (Jones) Webb--unmarried.

Pathologist, Provident Hospital, Chicago, Illinois, 1942-1945; Deputy Coroner and Pathologist, Cook County, Illinois, 1948-1960; has also been Assistant Professor of Pathology, Howard University; now retired--Member: Chicago Pathological Society; New York Academy of Science; American Association for the Advancement of Science.

MANLY WADE WELLMAN

1) 1932 Stellar   The Invading Asteroid. (P)
2) 1949 Crestwood   Sojarr of Titan. (P)
3) 1950 Pemberton   The Beasts from Beyond. (P)
4) 1951 Pemberton   Devil's Planet. (P)
5) 1957 Avalon   Twice in Time. (RP)
6) 1959 Avalon   Giants from Eternity.
7) 1959 Avalon   The Dark Destroyers. (RP)
8) 1961 Avalon   Island in the Sky.
9) 1963 Arkham   Who Fears the Devil? (s/RP)
10) 1968 Pop Lib   2 The Solar Invasion. (P)

MANLY WADE WELLMAN (continued)

SER: Captain Future.

FPS: "Back to the Beast," Weird Tales, November, 1927.

***   ***   ***   ***   ***   ***

Manly Wade Wellman--born May 21, 1903 at Kamundongo, Angola--A.B., University of Wichita, 1926; B. Litt., Columbia University, 1927--Ellery Queen Award, 1946, Star of a Warrior; Edgar Award, Best Non-Fiction Study of Crime, 1955, Dead and Gone: Classic Crimes of North Carolina--Chapel Hill, North Carolina.

Son of Frederick Creighton & Lydia (Isely) Wellman--Frances Obrist: June 14, 1930--Wade Wellman (November 13, 1939).

Worked as a reporter, reviewer, and feature writer for various Kansas newspapers, 1927-1934; Free-Lance Writer.

Mr. Wellman's brother is the late Paul I. Wellman, noted writer of Western fiction.

Mr. Wellman writes:
  "I wish I could say I had something sf in the works, but I'm pretty much caught up in history and fiction of the American past. As a matter of fact, the technical knowledge most sf writers have these days leaves me nowhere. I am no scientist, and my work in the field has been more flavored with fantasy than science. But good things are being written and read, and some of them are deservedly recognized as great. As man goes into space, we old gaffers see what we dreamed and dared to tell of our dreams--we see it coming true.
  "Back in the 1930's, the then New York World-Telegram had a symposium of scientists and one or two writers who were asked two questions. No. 1: when, if ever, do you think a successful manned landing will take place on the moon? My answer was 1975, a little late for when it will happen. No. 2: if guaranteed a 50-50 chance of safe return, would you make such a flight? I answered yes, because I reflected I'd be past 70, full of years, but probably still with some physical vigor and a mind lively enough to appreciate the experience; and if the odds came up no return, it might be a good, swift death."

BARRY WELLS

1) 1961 Ballantine   The Day the Earth Caught Fire. (P)

---

*BARTON WERPER

1)	1964 Gold Star	1	Tarzan and the Silver Globe. (P)
2)	1964 Gold Star	2	Tarzan and the Cave City. (P)
3)	1964 Gold Star	3	Tarzan and the Snake People. (P)
4)	1965 Gold Star	4	Tarzan and the Abominable Snowman. (P)
5)	1965 Gold Star	5	Tarzan and the Winged Invaders. (P)

SER: New Tarzan Series

Barton Werper is a penname of Peter T. Scott.

WALLACE WEST

1)	1959 Gnome	The Bird of Time. (RP)
2)	1960 Avalon	Lords of Atlantis. (RP)
3)	1961 Avalon	The Memory Bank. (RP)
4)	1962 Avalon	Outposts of Space.
5)	1963 Avalon	River of Time.
6)	1964 Avalon	The Time-Lockers.
7)	1967 Avalon	The Everlasting Exiles.

FPS: "Static,"   Sea Stories, September, 1926.

***   ***   ***   ***   ***

George Wallace West--born May 22, 1900 at Walnut Hills, Kentucky--A.B., Butler University, 1924; LL.B., Indiana Law School, 1924--Ferry, Michigan/ George Town, Exuma, Bahama Islands.

Son of William & Anna Pauline (Scott) West--Claudia M. Weyant: October, 1928-- no children.

Has been a farmer, barber, press telegrapher, journalist for United Press International, with the Publicity Department of Paramount Pictures, an editor of ROTO, Voice of Experience, Song Hits, Movie Mirror, with the Publicity Department of Columbia Broadcasting System, a news writer and commentator for American Broadcasting Network, National Broadcasting Network, Mutual Broadcasting Network; Air and Water Pollution Control Expert, American Petroleum Institute, 1947-1968; Consultant on Air Pollution, Air Pollution Control Administration, United States Public Health Service, Department of Health, Education & Welfare, 1968-DATE; also Free-Lance Writer--Member: Science Fiction Writers of America; National Fantasy Fan Federation.

DONALD E. WESTLAKE

1) 1968 Random   The Curious Facts Preceding My Execution and Other Fictions. (s)

FPS: "Or Give Me Death,"   Universe, November, 1954 (#8).

***   ***   ***   ***   ***

Donald Edwin Westlake--born July 12, 1933 at New York, New York--attended Champlain College; State University of New York--Edgar Award, Best First Novel, 1960, The Mercenaries; Best Novel, 1968, God Save the Mark--New York, New York.

Son of Albert Joseph & Lillian (Bounds) Westlake--(1) Nedra Henderson: August 10, 1957/1966; (2) Sandra Foley: April 9, 1967-1) Sean Alan Westlake (1959); Steven Albert Westlake (1961); Tod David Foley (1963; adopted 1969); 2) Paul Edwin Westlake (1969).

Associate Editor for a Literary Agency, 1958-1959; Free-Lance Writer, 1959-DATE --Member: Writers Guild of America, West.

Mr. Westlake mentions:
"That's it. I've been out of sf 8 years. It was too hidebound, conservative, and Campbell-ridden. Probably still is."

BERYL WHITAKER

1) 1967 Hale   Of Mice and Murder.
2) 1967 Hale   A Matter of Blood.
3) 1968 Hale   The Chained Crocodile.
4) 1968 Hale   The Man Who Wasn't There.

FPS: 1967 Hale   Of Mice and Murder.

NOTE: All the above novels are mysteries. The inclusion of Mrs. Whitaker was due to an error on the editors' part, and resulted primarily from their belief that her latest work was a science fiction novel. This illustrates, perhaps, the difficulties they have had with British bibliography, and the British book scene in general. Despite the fact that Mrs. Whitaker is not an sf writer, her listing is included in keeping with our general policy (see the Introduction) of making available any information received. As it turns out, this may be an act of anticipation, since Mrs. Whitaker states that her next novel will be a full-length sf work.

***   ***   ***   ***   ***

BERYL WHITAKER (continued)

Beryl Salusbury Whitaker--born August 8, 1916 at Manchester, England--West Crewkerne, Somerset, England.

Daughter of Charles & Rosamund Colman--(1) Humphrey Wilson: 1936/divorced; (2) Edward Levy: 1944/divorced; (3) Gerald Whitaker: 1950--1) Andrew Wilson (December 15, 1942); 2) Rory Levy (June 26, 1946); Tom Levy (June 2, 1947); 3) Rosamund Whitaker (April 13, 1951).

Free-Lance Writer--Member: Crime Writers Association.

Mrs. Whitaker mentions that her mother was a direct descendant of Mrs. Thrale (see Dr. Johnson), and that her father's father was a first cousin to Delius.

DAVID WHITAKER

1) 1964 Muller   Doctor Who in an Exciting Adventure with the Daleks. (RP)
2) 1966 Muller   Doctor Who and the Crusaders.

JAMES WHITE

1) 1957 Ace   The Secret Visitors. (P)
2) 1962 Ballantine   Hospital Station. (P)
3) 1962 Ace   Second Ending. (P)
4) 1963 Ballantine   Star Surgeon. (P)
5) 1964 Ballantine   Deadly Litter. (s/P)
6) 1965 Ace   The Escape Orbit. (P)
6A) 1964 4 Square   Open Prison. (P)
7) 1966 Ballantine   The Watch Below. (P/RH)
8) 1968 Whiting   All Judgment Fled.

FPS: "Assisted Passage,"   New Worlds, January, 1953.

WIP: 1969 Ballantine   The Aliens Among Us. (s/P)

***   ***   ***   ***   ***

James White--born April 7, 1928 at Belfast, North Ireland--Belfast, North Ireland.

Orphan--Margaret: May 17, 1955--Patricia White (12); Martin White (10); Peter White (7).

JAMES WHITE (continued)

Sartorial Consultant, 1942-1965; Assistant Publicity Director, SHORTS (an aircraft and missile company), 1965-DATE; also Free-Lance Writer--Member: Science Fiction Writers of America.

Mr. White began writing for fanzines (mainly Hyphen) in 1949, and now writes sf in his spare time.

---

*JAY C. WHITE

1)	1962 Vantage		A Cup of Life.

Jay C. White is a penname.

TED WHITE

2)	1965 Ace	1	Android Avenger. (P)
3)	1966 Lancer	-1	Phoenix Prime. (P)
4)	1966 Lancer	-2	Sorceress of Qar. (P)
6)	1967 Belmont		The Jewels of Elsewhen. (P)
7)	1967 West		The Secret of the Marauder Satellite.
9)	1968 Bantam		The Great Gold Steal. (P)
10)	1968 Pap Lib	2	The Spawn of the Death Machine. (P)
			with Terry Carr (q.v.) as *Norman Edwards
1)	1964 Monarch		Invasion from 2500. (P)
			as *Ron Archer with Dave Van Arnam (q.v.)
5)	1967 Pyramid		Lost in Space. (P)
			with Dave Van Arnam (q.v.)
8)	1968 Pyramid		Sideslip. (P)
FKP:	"Phoenix,"		Amazing, February, 1963 (with Marion Zimmer Bradley).
WIP:	1969 Crown		No Time Like Tomorrow.

Theodore Edward White is a member of Science Fiction Writers of America. Among the posts he has held are: Assistant Editor, The Magazine of Fantasy and Science Fiction, November, 1963-May, 1968; Managing Editor, Fantastic, April, 1969-DATE; Amazing, May, 1969-DATE. He won a Hugo Award, Best Fan Writer, 1968.

STEPHEN E. WHITFIELD

with Gene Roddenberry (q.v.)
1)   1968 Ballantine   The Making of Star Trek. (nf/P)

Stephen Edward Whitfield is a member of Science Fiction Writers of America.

KATE WILHELM

1)   1963 Berkley   The Mile-Long Spaceship. (s/P)
3)   1966 Dobson   Andover and the Android.
4)   1966 Doubleday   The Nevermore Affair. (RP)
5)   1967 Doubleday   The Killer Thing. (RP)
5A) 1967 Jenkins   The Killing Thing.
6)   1968 Doubleday   The Downstairs Room and Other Speculative
                              Fiction. (s)

with Theodore L. Thomas (q.v.)
2)   1965 Berkley   The Clone. (P/RH)

FPS: "The Pint-Size Genie,"   Fantastic, October, 1956.

WIP: 1969 Doubleday   Let the Fire Fall.
       Doubleday   The Plastic Abyss and Stranger in the House.
       Doubleday   The Year of the Cloud. (with Theodore L. Thomas)

***   ***   ***   ***   ***

Katie Wilhelm Knight--born June 8, 1928 at Toledo, Ohio--Nebula Award, Best Short Story, 1968, "The Planners"--Madeira Beach, Florida.

Daughter of Jesse & Ann Meredith--(1) Joseph B. Wilhelm: 1947/September, 1962; (2) Damon Knight: February, 1963--1) Douglas Wilhelm (19); Richard Wilhelm (15); 2) Jonathan Knight (3).

Free-Lance Writer--Member: Science Fiction Writers of America.

Co-Director, Milford Science Fiction Writers' Conference, 1963-DATE.

JOHN N. WILL

1)   1968 Carlton   My Blond Princess of Space.

CHARLES WILLEFORD

1) 1963 Belmont	The Machine in Ward Eleven. (P)

ERIC C. WILLIAMS

1) 1968 Hale	Time Injection.
2) 1968 Hale	Monkman Comes Down.

FPS: "The Garden of Paris," 1964.

WIP: 1969 Hale	To End All Telescopes.
	The Utopia Syndrome.

***   ***   ***   ***   ***

Eric C. Williams (u)--born July 22, 1918 at Peckham, London, England--Balcombe, Sussex, England.

Son of Charles John & Mabel Grace Williams--Mona Winifred: April 28, 1962--Rosemary Monica Williams (April 7, 1965).

Photographer, Civil Service, 1933-1940; Bookseller, 1947-1961; Engineers' Contract Clerk, 1961-1965; Shipper, 1965-DATE; Free-Lance Writer.

ROBERT MOORE WILLIAMS

1) 1955 Ace	The Chaos Fighters. (P)
2) 1955 Ace	Conquest of the Space Sea. (P)
3) 1957 Ace	Doomsday Eve. (P)
4) 1958 Ace	The Blue Atom. (P)
5) 1958 Ace	The Void Beyond and Other Stories. (s/P)
6) 1960 Ace	To the End of Time. (s/P)
7) 1960 Ace	World of the Masterminds. (P)
8) 1962 Ace	The Day They H-Bombed Los Angeles. (P)
9) 1962 Ace	The Darkness Before Tomorrow. (P)
10) 1962 Ace	King of the Fourth Planet. (P)
11) 1962 Avalon	Walk Up the Sky.
12) 1963 Ace	The Star Wasps. (P)

ROBERT MOORE WILLIAMS (continued)

13)	1963 Ace		Flight from Yesterday.	(P)
14)	1964 Ace		The Lunar Eye.	(P)
15)	1965 Ace		The Second Atlantis.	(P)
16)	1967 Lancer		Vigilante--21st Century.	(P)
17)	1967 Lancer	1	Zanthar of the Many Worlds.	(P)
18)	1968 Lancer	2	Zanthar at the Edge of Never.	(P)
19)	1968 Lancer		The Bell from Infinity.	(P)
20)	1968 Lancer	3	Zanthar at Moon's Madness.	(P)

FPS: "Zero As a Limit,"   Astounding, July, 1937 (as *Robert Moore).

WIP: 1969 Lancer   4   Zanthar at Trip's End. (P)
      1969 Dell   Beachhead Planet. (P)

***   ***   ***   ***   ***

Robert Moore Williams--born June 19, 1907 at Farmington, Missouri--B.A., University of Missouri--Valley Center, California.

Son of John Browning & Ida May (Moore) Williams--Margaret Jelley: 1938/1952--Susan Browning Williams (August 22, 1944).

Free-Lance Writer--Member: Science Fiction Writers of America.

Mr. Williams mentions that he is an eleventh generation descendent of Robert and Elizabeth Williams, who settled in Roxbury, Massachusetts, in 1638.

Mr. Williams provided the following essay "On Writing:
   "Writing a piece on writing I find very difficult. In truth, I find it more than usually difficult in this case simply because the letter requesting it referred to writing as a 'discipline.' Writing is one of the most difficult of the arts. I have scant sympathy for anyone who refers to it as a discipline. Certainly discipline is needed, but the usual meaning of this word cannot be used to describe writing. You don't discipline writing, it disciplines you. You don't write, you are written. You don't go to school to learn how to write, you bring it with you.
   "Probably both the psychologists and the professors of literature will disagree with me. I couldn't care less if they do. You don't learn how to write by listening to psychologists or to professors of literature. You learn to write by writing. Then, if the It so chooses, or if She so wills, and if you have brought something with you, perhaps you become a writer.

ROBERT MOORE WILLIAMS (continued)

"What is the <u>IT</u> and who is <u>She</u>? Dig the answers out of some of the world's great books, out of George Groddecks's <u>Book of the It</u>, out of Erich Neumann's <u>The Great Mother</u>, dig them out of Raynor C. Johnson's <u>Nurslings of Immortality</u>, dig them out of Robert Graves' <u>The White Goddess</u>. Most important, if you want to be a writer, dig them out of yourself. They're all in you. If you would find them, all you have to do is go looking, and when you find your answers, to face the consequences of discovery.

"After the rules of grammar and spelling are half-way learned, writing becomes a process of exploring your own emotional world and the history that is contained therein. This history is longer and deeper than most people realize, and the real roots of fiction writing lie in it. From it they emerge as vague impulses in the patterns of the archetypes, as hunches to go in this direction and to avoid that direction, to use this idea as a major theme and to avoid that one, to use the episode at the river crossing--which just 'happened' to pop into your mind--as part of your story. From the whole history of the human race--it's your history too, and it's all within you--you select those bits that you wish to use to tell your story.

"And this above all, this first and foremost, this the beginning and the ending, <u>that you love it</u>! Love <u>what</u>? The whole wide world and all that's in it, the lady of your choice, and the meaning of the word <u>story</u>. Where do you get this kind of Love? You bring it with you from a thousand lifetimes! How do you find out if you have it? You get a typewriter and start pointing it in some direction. If you don't have it, the knocks you get on the noggin will send you into some other activity. If you do have it, it will give you the ability to withstand those knocks. Whether you have it or don't have it, the knocks are coming. Love helps you rise above them.

"What I am talking about here is a particular kind of way of being in love. Since love is a flow toward the opposite sex (but is not necessarily restricted to sex, all the psychoanalysis on earth to the contrary!), if you are a boy type, it comes out as a way of seeing every woman not only as herself and as being worth loving for herself, but also as a representative of the Goddess of the entire feminine side of nature.

"Individual women have a way of being around for a time, then of going on. The Goddess was with you in the beginning, She will be with you in the ending: pour your love for Her into the story you are writing.

"If you are a girl type, you reverse this, of course.

"I have needed about thirty years of the hardest kind of work to dig this out of my inner world. I give it to you for free, but, speaking bluntly, I doubt if many of you will be able to use it. I suspect this is something that does not come down from the Olympian heights of schools of writing or from courses in literature in universities, but which you have to learn for yourself in the only way that matters, the hard way. Maybe not, though. It seems to me that the kids I see coming into the world today have talents and gifts that simply were not in the world when I was young. Perhaps they will not have to learn the hard way.

"My advice to writers everywhere is--<u>be in love</u>! And no matter what happens--<u>stay in love</u>!

ROBERT MOORE WILLIAMS (continued)

"I would give the same advice to plumbers and carpenters and to the wet-backs working in the orange grove across the road--except they don't seem to need it as much as writers. For writers, however, it is the essence and the secret of existence."

A. S. WILLIAMS-ELLIS

with Mably Owen (q.v.)

1)	1960 Blackie		Out of This World 1. (@)
2)	1961 Blackie		Out of This World 2. (@)
3)	1962 Blackie		Out of This World 3. (@)
4)	1964 Blackie		Out of This World 4. (@)
5)	1965 Blackie		Out of This World 5. (@)
6)	1966 Blackie		Worlds Apart. (@)
7)	1967 Blackie		Out of This World 6. (@)
8)	1968 Blackie		Out of This World 7. (@)

WIP: 19<u>69</u> Blackie   Out of This World 8. (@/with Mably Owen)

Mary Amabel Nassau Strachey Williams-Ellis was born in 1894. A complete biography may be found in Who's Who.

JACK WILLIAMSON

2)	1945 Utopian		Lady in Danger. (P)
3)	1947 Fantasy	1	The Legion of Space. (RP/RPa)
4)	1949 Fantasy		Darker Than You Think. (RP)
5)	1949 S&S		The Humanoids. (RP)
6)	1950 Avon		The Green Girl. (P)
8)	1950 Fantasy	2	The Cometeers. (RP)
9)	1950 Fantasy	3	One Against the Legion. (RPe)
10)	1951 S&S		Dragon's Island. (RP/RPv)
12)	1952 Fantasy		The Legion of Time. (RP/RPa/RPav)
14)	1955 Ace		Dome Around America. (P)
12A)	1961 Digit		After World's End. (a/P)
18)	1962 Ace		The Trial of Terra. (P)
19)	1964 Lancer		Golden Blood. (P)
21)	1964 Lancer		The Reign of Wizardry. (P)
10A)	1965 Tower		The Not-Men. (P)
23)	1967 Ace		Bright New Universe. (P/RH)

JACK WILLIAMSON (continued)

24)	1967 Pyramid	3A	One Against the Legion. (9/e/P)
7A)	1968 Lancer	-1	Seetee Ship. (P)
11A)	1968 Lancer	-2	Seetee Shock. (P)
25)	1968 Doubleday		Trapped in Space.

with Miles J. Breuer

1)   1930 Stellar   The Girl from Mars. (P)

as *Will Stewart

7)	1950 S&S	-2	Seetee Shock. (RPv)
11)	1951 Gnome	-1	Seetee Ship. (RPv)

with Frederik Pohl (q.v.)

13)	1954 Gnome	+1	Undersea Quest.
16)	1956 Gnome	+2	Undersea Fleet.
17)	1958 Gnome	+3	Undersea City.
20)	1964 Ballantine		The Reefs of Space. (P)
22)	1965 Ballantine		Starchild. (P/RH)

with James E. Gunn (q.v.)

15)   1955 Gnome   Star Bridge. (RP)

SER: 1) The Legion of Space

FPS: "The Metal Man,"   Amazing, December, 1928.

WIP: 1969 Ace   The Pandora Effect. (s/P)
       1969 Ballantine   Rogue Star. (P/with Frederik Pohl)
                             The Moon Children.
                             Science Fiction: Future History. (nf)

***   ***   ***   ***   ***

John Stewart Williamson--born April 29, 1908 at Bisbee, Arizona--B.A., East New Mexico University; M.A., East New Mexico University, 1957; Ph.D., University of Colorado, 1964--First Fandom Science Fiction Hall of Fame Award, 1969--Portales, New Mexico.

Son of Asa Lee & Lucy Betty (Hunt) Williamson--Blanche Slaten Harp: August 15, 1947--Stepchildren: Keigm H.; Adele H. Lovorn.

Weather Forecaster, United States Air Force, 1942-1945; Instructor, New Mexico Military Institute, 1957-1959; University of Colorado, 1960; Associate Professor of English, Eastern New Mexico University, 1960-1968; Professor, 1968-DATE--Member: Science Fiction Writers of America; Modern Language Association; National Council of Teachers of English; American Association of University Professors; Rotary Club.

JACK WILLIAMSON (continued)

Mr. Williamson originated the comic strip <u>Beyond Mars</u> for the <u>New York Sunday News</u>, and wrote the scripts for it (1953-1956).

"Comment from Jack Williamson:
  "I regret the feud over what's 'new' in science fiction, because good writing is too rare to be despised under any label. Good science fiction, to my taste, is any story that presents something new, significant, and therefore wonderful about human possibility in a way that evokes the 'willing suspension of disbelief.'
  "I think there's always a 'new thing.' To me, in 1927, it was my first copy of <u>Amazing Stories</u>, with Stribling's 'The Green Splotches' and Wells' 'Under the Knife' and Merritt's 'The People of the Pit' and Part II of Burroughs' 'The Land That Time Forgot.'
  "A few years later, some readers seemed to find something new in my own 'Legion of Space.' Another few years, and the 'new wave' was being made by such people as Heinlein and van Vogt in Campbell's <u>Astounding</u>.
  "A lot of the current 'new' looks to me like worthless stuff, neither wonderful nor believable nor really new. But some of it is fine. I'm still excited about Delany's <u>Einstein Intersection</u>, and I'm using Judy Merril's 11th 'best' collection as one of the texts for a science fiction course I teach.
  "About the future of science fiction, I think it will be determined pretty much by shifting attitudes toward science and progress. I think it will continue the great debate about such issues that it has carried on since Swift's <u>Gulliver's Travels</u>. Generally, I think the future of the genre is exciting. It has no troubles that new writers can't cure."

RAYMOND WILSON

with Alan Frank Barter (q.v.)
1) 1966 Macmillan   <u>Untravelled Worlds.</u> (@/P)

About Raymond Wilson:
  "Largely self-educated. Took an external degree in English at London University, c. 1950. I met him teaching at Dulwich College--he became Head of English there. In 1964 he went as a Lecturer to Southampton University Department of Education. In 1968 he was elected to a chair at Reading University, where he is now as Professor of Education. He has a wife and three children."
(Courtesy, Alan Frank Barter.)

RICHARD WILSON

1)	1955 Ballantine	The Girls from Planet 5. (H-P)
2)	1957 Ballantine	Those Idiots from Earth. (s/P)
3)	1960 Ace	And Then the Town Took Off. (P)
4)	1960 Ballantine	30-Day Wonder. (P)
5)	1962 Ballantine	Time Out for Tomorrow. (s/P)

FPS: "Murder from Mars," Astonishing Stories, April, 1940.
FPP: "Stepsons of Mars," Astonishing Stories, April, 1940 (with Cyril M. Kornbluth as *Ivar Towers)(simultaneous).

***   ***   ***   ***   ***

Richard Wilson--born September 23, 1920 at Huntington Station, New York--attended University of Chicago--Nebula Award, Best Novelet, 1968, "Mother to the World"--Syracuse, New York.

Son of Richard & Felicitas K. (Krause) Wilson--(2) Frances K. Daniels: September 1, 1967--Margot Owens (22); Richard David Wilson (16); James B. Daniels (13); Stephen W. Daniels (11).

Newsman: has served with Fairchild Publications, New York; Transradio Press, Chicago; Reuters Ltd., New York; Director, News Bureau, Syracuse University, 1964-DATE--Member: Science Fiction Writers of America; American College Public Relations Association; Syracuse Press Club.

RUSS WINTERBOTHAM

1)	1958 Avalon	The Space Egg. (RP)
2)	1962 Monarch	The Red Planet. (P)
4)	1963 Avalon	The Men from Arcturus. (RP)
5)	1964 Avalon	The Puppet Planet.
7)	1966 Avalon	The Lord of Nardos.

as *J. Harvey Bond
3) 1963 Avalon   The Other World. (RP)

as *Franklin Hadley
6) 1964 Monarch   Planet Big Zero. (P)

FPS: 1928 Haldeman   Lindbergh: Hero of the Air.' (nf)
FSF: "The Star That Would Not Behave," Astounding, August, 1935.

***   ***   ***   ***   ***

RUSS WINTERBOTHAM (continued)

Russell Robert Winterbotham--born August 1, 1904 at Salina, Kansas--B.A., University of Kansas, 1927--Bay Village, Ohio.

Son of Jonathan Harvey & Gertrude (Bond) Winterbotham--Nadine Schick: November 25, 1932--H. Ann Winterbotham Jones.

Was a Writer, Editor, and Reporter for various newspapers in Kansas, South Dakota, and Ohio; with Newspaper Enterprises Association, Cleveland, Ohio, 1943-1968; currently retired--Member: Science Fiction Writers of America; Mystery Writers of America; Western Writers of America; Sigma Delta Chi.

Mr. Winterbotham also wrote some 60 Big Little Books just prior to World War II; included among these were several borderline sf works, but because of the difficulties of compiling a list, the nature of the material, and the fact that several that were sold were never published due to the onset of the war (and Mr. Winterbotham does not know which ones), they are not included in his bibliography. The editors list, however, those whose titles are known: Maximo, the Amazing Superman; Superman Maximo and the Super-Machine; Superman Maximo and the Crystals of Doom; Hal Hardy and the Lost Land of Giants; Ghost Avenger (may never have been published); Mole the Diminishing Man (publication halted). Mr. Winterbotham also revised six Roy Rockwell books (originally published 1900-1913) for publication by Whitman (the parent company of Big Little Books) in 1939: Torn Away World; 5000 Miles Underground; Through Space to Mars; Voyage to Venus; Voyage to Saturn; Lost on the Moon.

Mr. Winterbotham writes:

"As noted above, I'm now retired, and devoting my entire time to loafing, with the exception of doing the script for one comic strip (a newspaper comic). The science fiction market doesn't seem to demand my talents, whatever they are, and I need the rest."

ARTHUR WISE

2)	1961 Gollancz	The Little Fishes. (RP)
4)	1962 Cassell	The Death's-Head.
5)	1968 Cavalier	The Day the Queen Flew to Scotland for the Grouse Shooting. (RP)
		as *John McArthur
1)	1960 Cassell	Days in the Hay.
3)	1962 Cassell	How Now Brown Cow.
FPS:	1960 Cassell	Days in the Hay. (as *John McArthur)
WIP:	1969 Weidenfeld	Leatherjacket.

***   ***   ***   ***   ***

ARTHUR WISE (continued)

Arthur Wise--born January 12, 1923 at York, England--Diploma in Speech and Drama, Central School of Speech and Drama, 1949; Diploma in Dramatic Art, University of London, 1949; Certificate, International Phonetics Association--York, England.

Son of Arthur & Edith Mary (Hobson) Wise--Lilian Nanette Gregg: September 6, 1947--John Christopher Wise (20); Susan Wise (18); Julie Wise (16).

Chief Examiner of spoken English, University of Durham, 1959-1969; University of London, 1963-1969; Consultant on technical weapons, 1950-DATE; Director, Swords of York, 1963-DATE; Free-Lance Writer, 1969-DATE--Member: Society of Authors; Society of Teachers of Speech and Drama; Association of University Teachers; York Society of Speakers; Society of Arms and Armour.

Mr. Wise mentions that he has just resigned his academic posts to write full-time: "This is, to quote Thurber, 'Like falling backwards on a bed of nails.'"

ROBERT A. WISE

1) 1961 Badger SF   12 to the Moon. (P)

Robert A. Wise is probably a real person.

ELLEN WOBIG

1)   1968 Ace   The Youth Monopoly. (P)

FPS: 1968 Ace   The Youth Monopoly. (P)

***   ***   ***   ***   ***

Ellen Wobig (u)--born April 18, 1911 at Janesville, Wisconsin--Beloit, Wisconsin.

Daughter of Mr. & Mrs. J. A. Forrest--Harold Wobig: September 4, 1940--Gerald C. Wobig (27); Harold A. Wobig (22).

Housewife.

DONALD A. WOLLHEIM

1)	1943 Pocket		The Pocketbook of Science Fiction. (@/P)
2)	1945 Viking		Portable Novels of Science. (@)
3)	1950 Fell		Flight Into Space. (@/RP)
4)	1951 Fell		Every Boy's Book of Science Fiction. (@)
5)	1953 McBride		Prize Science Fiction. (@)
5A)	1953 Weidenfeld		Prize Stories of Space and Time. (@)
6)	1954 Ace		The Ultimate Invader. (@/P)
7)	1954 Ace		Adventures in the Far Future. (@/P)
8)	1954 Ace		Tales of Outer Space. (@/P)
9)	1954 Winston		The Secret of Saturn's Rings. (RP)
10)	1955 Ace		Adventures on Other Planets. (@/P)
11)	1955 Hanover		Terror in the Modern Vein. (@/RPa/RPav)
12)	1955 Winston		The Secret of the Martian Moons. (RP)
13)	1956 Ace		The End of the World. (@/P)
14)	1956 World		One Against the Moon.
15)	1957 Ace		The Earth in Peril. (@/P)
18)	1958 Ace		Men on the Moon. (@/P)
19)	1959 Ace		The Macabre Reader. (@/P)
20)	1959 Ace		The Hidden Planet. (@/P)
21)	1959 Winston		The Secret of the Ninth Planet. (RP)
23)	1961 Ace		More Macabre. (@/P)
24)	1961 Doubleday	1	Mike Mars, Astronaut. (RP)
25)	1961 Doubleday	2	Mike Mars Flies the X-15. (RP)
11A)	1961 Digit		More Terror in the Modern Vein. (@/a/P)
26)	1961 Doubleday	3	Mike Mars at Cape Canaveral. (RPv)
27)	1961 Doubleday	4	Mike Mars in Orbit. (RP)
29)	1962 Doubleday	5	Mike Mars Flies the Dyna-Soar. (RP)
30)	1962 Doubleday	6	Mike Mars, South Pole Spaceman. (RP)
31)	1963 Doubleday	7	Mike Mars and the Mystery Satellite. (RP)
32)	1963 Ace		More Adventures on Other Planets. (@/P)
33)	1964 Doubleday	8	Mike Mars Around the Moon. (RP)
34)	1964 Ace		Swordsmen in the Sky. (@/P)
26A)	1966 Pap Lib	3	Mike Mars at Cape Kennedy. (P)
39)	1967 Phantagraph		Operation: Phantasy; The Best from the Phantagraph. (nf/@)

as *David Grinnell

16)	1957 Avalon		Across Time. (RP)
17)	1958 Avalon		Edge of Time. (RP)
22)	1959 Avalon		The Martian Missile. (RP)
28)	1961 Avalon	-1	Destiny's Orbit. (RP)

DONALD A. WOLLHEIM (continued)

		with Terry Carr (q.v.)
35)	1965 Ace	World's Best Science Fiction: 1965. (@/P)
36)	1966 Ace	World's Best Science Fiction: 1966. (@/P)
37)	1967 Ace	World's Best Science Fiction: 1967. (@/P)
40)	1968 Ace	World's Best Science Fiction: 1968. (@/P)

			as *David Grinnell with Lin Carter (q.v.)
38)	1967 Avalon	-2	Destination: Saturn. (RP)

FPS: "The Man from Ariel," Wonder Stories, January, 1934.

WIP:	1969 Avon	The Avon Fantasy Reader. (@/P/with George Ernsberger)
	1969 Avon	The Second Avon Fantasy Reader. (@/P/with George Ernsberger)
	1969 Ace	World's Best Science Fiction: 1969. (@/P/RH/with Terry Carr)
	1969 Powell	24 Dragon Eggs. (P)

***   ***   ***   ***   ***

Donald Allen Wollheim--born October 1, 1914 at New York, New York--B.A., New York University--Rego Park, New York.

Son of J. L. & Rose (Grinnell) Wollheim--Elsie Balter: June 25, 1943--Elizabeth Wollheim.

Editor, Stirring Science Stories, February, 1941-March, 1942 (all issues); Cosmic Stories, March, 1941-July, 1941 (all issues); Ace Magazines, 1942-1947; Avon Books, 1947-1952; Avon Fantasy Reader, #1 (1947)-#18 (1952); Out of This World Adventures, July, 1950-December, 1950 (all issues); 10 Story Fantasy, Spring, 1951 (only issue); Avon Science Fiction Reader, #1 (1951)-#3 (1952); Ace Books, 1952-1967; Editorial Consultant, Saturn, March, 1957-March, 1958 (all issues); Vice President, Editorial, Ace Books, 1967-DATE--Member: Science Fiction Writers of America; Mystery Writers of America; Aviation Space Writers Association; American Rocket Society; National Association of Book Editors; British Model Soldier Society; The Burroughs Bibliophiles; Miniature Figure Collectors of America.

RICHARD WORMSER

1)	1961 Dell	Thief of Baghdad. (P)
2)	1963 Avon	Pan Satyrus. (P)

Richard Edward Wormser was born in 1908.

-----

*LAN WRIGHT

1)	1957 Ace	Who Speaks of Conquest?	(P)
2)	1958 Ace	A Man Called Destiny.	(P)
3)	1963 Digit	Assignment Luther.	(P)
4)	1964 Ace	Exile from Xanadu.	(P)
5)	1964 Jenkins	Space Born.	
6)	1965 Ace	The Last Hope of Earth.	(P)
7)	1966 Compact	The Creeping Shroud.	(P)
8)	1968 Ace	The Pictures of Pavanne.	(P/RHv)
8A)	1968 Jenkins	A Planet Called Pavanne.	

FPS: "Operation Exodus," New Worlds, January, 1952.

***   ***   ***   ***   ***

Lionel Percy Wright--born July 8, 1923 at Watford, Hertfordshire, England--St. Albans, Hertfordshire, England.

Son of Percy Robert & Frances Ethel (Fothergill) Wright--Betty Foster: May 7, 1949--no children.

Various purchasing jobs with British Railways, twenty years; currently Chief Buyer, Haden Electrical Ltd., a major firm of electrical contractors; Free-Lance Writer--Member: Institute of Purchasing and Supply; Royal Society of Arts (Fellow).

Mr. Wright mentions that he has been a "keen cricketeer for 30 years--and still playing."

ROBERT F. YOUNG

1)	1965 S&S		The Worlds of Robert F. Young.	(s/RP)
2)	1968 H-W	1	A Glass of Stars.	(s)

FPS: "The Black Deep Thou Wingest," Startling Stories, June, 1953.

WIP: 1969   2 The Thousand Eyes of Night.
                3 Elegy.

***   ***   ***   ***   ***

ROBERT F. YOUNG (continued)

Robert Franklin Young--born June 8, 1915 at Silver Creek, New York--Silver Creek, New York.

Son of Franklin & Edna Young--Regina: October 7, 1941--Roberta Jean Young (26).

Employed in a non-ferous foundry; Free-Lance Writer--Member: Science Fiction Writers of America.

KARL ZEIGFREID

1)	195? Spencer	Beyond the Galaxy. (P)
2)	1953 Spencer	Chariot into Time. (P)
3)	1953 Spencer	Chaos in Arcturus. (P)
4)	1953 Spencer	The Uranium Seekers. (P)
5)	1954 Spencer	Dark Centauri. (P)
6)	1962 Badger SF	Walk Through Tomorrow. (P)
7)	1962 Badger SF	Android. (P)
8)	1962 Badger SN	Gods of Darkness. (P)
9)	1962 Badger SF	Zero Minus X. (P/RH)
10)	1962 Badger SF	Atomic Nemesis. (P)
11)	1963 Badger SF	Radar Alert. (P/RH)
12)	1963 Badger SF	Escape to Infinity. (P)
13)	1963 Badger SF	World of Tomorrow. (P/?RHv)
14)	1963 Badger SF	The World That Never Was. (P)
15)	1964 Badger SF	Projection Infinity. (P)
16)	1964 Badger SF	No Way Back. (P/RH)
?13A)	1964 Arcadia	World of the Future.
17)	1965 Badger SF	Barrier 346. (P/RH)
18)	?1966 Badger SF	Girl from Tomorrow. (P)

Karl Zeigfreid is a probable house penname.

ROGER ZELAZNY

1)	1966 Ace	This Immortal. (P/RH)
2)	1966 Ace	The Dream Master. (P/RH)
3)	1967 Ace	Four for Tomorrow. (s/P)

ROGER ZELAZNY (continued)

4)	1967 Doubleday	Lord of Light. (RP)
5)	1968 Doubleday	Nebula Award Stories Three. (@/RP)
FPS:	"Passion Play,"	Amazing, August, 1962.
FPP:	"Horseman!"	Fantastic, August, 1962 (simultaneous).
WIP:	1969 Ace	Isle of the Dead. (P)
	1969 Doubleday	Creatures of Light and Darkness.
	1969 Putnam	Damnation Alley.
	1970 Doubleday	Nine Princes in Amber.

***　　　***　　　***　　　***　　　***

Roger Joseph Zelazny--born May 13, 1937 at Euclid, Ohio--B.A., Western Reserve University, 1959; M.A. (in English and Comparative Literature), Columbia University, 1962--Hugo Award, Best Novel, 1966, ...And Call Me Conrad; 1968, Lord of Light; Nebula Award, Best Novelette, 1965, "The Doors of His Face, the Lamps of His Mouth;" Best Novella, "He Who Shapes"--Baltimore, Maryland.

Son of Joseph F. & Josephine (Sweet) Zelazny--(1) Sharon Steberl: December 5, 1964/June 27, 1966; (2) Judith Callahan: August 20, 1966--no children.

Social Insurance Specialist, Social Security Administration, Federal Government, 1962-1969; Free-Lance Writer, 1969-DATE--Member: Science Fiction Writers of America (Secretary/Treasurer, 1967-1968); National Fantasy Fan Federation.

CHLOE ZERWICK

		with Harrison Brown (q.v.)
1)	1968 Doubleday	The Cassiopeia Affair. (RP)
FPS:	unknown.	
FSF:	1968 Doubleday	The Cassiopeia Affair. (with Harrison Brown)

***　　　***　　　***　　　***　　　***

Chloe Zerwick--born February 13, 1923 at Cincinnati, Ohio--B.A., University of Chicago, 1943--New York, New York.

Daughter of Meyer and Corinne/Roth/Greenwold--(1) Jacob L. Fox, Jr.: 1943/1951; (2) M. B. Zerwick: 1959--1) Jay Fox (24); 2) Phoebe Zerwick (8).

Associate Editor, Common Cause, 1948-1950; American Exporter, 1953-1955; Free-Lance Writer.

ROSE A. ZIMBARDO

1) 1968 Notre Dame

with Neil D. Isaacs (q.v.)
Tolkien and the Critics. (nf/RP)

FPS: 1965 Yale
FSF: 1968 Notre Dame

Wycherley's Drama. (nf)
Tolkien and the Critics. (nf/with Neil D. Isaacs)

***　　　***　　　***　　　***　　　***

Rose Zimbardo (u)--born May 29, 1932 in the United States--A.B., Brooklyn College, 1956; M.A., Yale University, 1957; Ph.D., Yale University, 1960--Palo Alto, Calif.

Daughter of Albert J. & Angela (Lombardi) Abdelnour--Philip Zimbardo: July 13, 1957--Adam Zimbardo.

Assistant Professor of English, City College of New York, 1960-1968; Associate Professor, 1968-DATE.

ADDENDUM

POUL ANDERSON

Winner, Hugo Award, Best Novelette, 1969, "The Sharing of Flesh."

RON ARCHER

Ron Archer is a penname of Ted White (q.v.).

BEN BARZMAN

<u>Out of This World</u>=<u>Twinkle, Twinkle Little Star</u>=<u>Echo X</u>. First edition unknown, but probably <u>Out of This World</u> (February, 1960).

JOHN BRUNNER

Winner, Hugo Award, Best Novel, 1969, <u>Stand on Zanzibar</u>.

LIN CARTER

Mr. Carter's mother is Lucy (Vrooman) Carter.

ARTHUR C. CLARKE

Winner, Hugo Award, Best Drama, 1969, <u>2001: A Space Odyssey</u>.

STANTON A. COBLENTZ

add to bibliography:
1)   1929 Cosmopolitan   <u>The Wonder Stick</u>.

*LESTER del REY

alter #23 to read:
                                (with Paul W. Fairman)(q.v.)
23)   1966 Belmont   <u>The Scheme of Things</u>. (P)

The book was outlined by del Rey, but written by Fairman.

HARLAN ELLISON

Winner, Hugo Award, Best Short Story, 1969, "The Beast That Shouted Love at the Heart of the World."

PAUL W. FAIRMAN

add to bibliography:
                                with *Lester del Rey as *Lester del Rey
8)   1966 Belmont   <u>The Scheme of Things</u>. (P)

EDWARD L. FERMAN

Winner, Hugo Award, Best Professional Magazine, 1969, The Magazine of Fantasy and Science Fiction.

JOSEPH W. FERMAN

Winner, Hugo Award, Best Professional Magazine, 1969, The Magazine of Fantasy and Science Fiction.

RICHARD E. GEIS

Winner, Hugo Award, Best Fan Magazine, 1969, Psychotic/Science Fiction Review.

*WERPER, BARTON

Tarzan and the Snake People was written by Peg O'Neill Scott, presumably the wife of Peter T. Scott (q.v.).

J. F. BONE

1)	1962 Bantam	The Lani People.	(P)
FPS:	"Survival Type,"	Galaxy, March, 1957.	
WIP:		Gladiator.	

***   ***   ***   ***   ***

Jesse Franklin Bone--born June 15, 1916 at Tacoma, Washington--B.A., Washington State College, 1937; D.V.M., Washington State University, 1950; also holds a B.S. and an M.S.--Borden Scholarship Award, 1949; Alumni of the Year Award, Washington State University, 1963--Corvallis, Oregon.

Son of Homer T. & Eva K. Bone--(1) Jayne M.: January, 1942/September, 1946; (2) Felizitas M.: June, 1950--1) Janice Lee Bone (December 5, 1942); 2) Michael Jay Bone (November 11, 1951); David Franklin Bone (January 10, 1956).

On the faculty of Oregon State University from 1950; currently Professor of Veterinary Medicine--Member: Science Fiction Writers of America; Royal Society of Health; various professional organizations.

ERIC THACKER

1)	1966 McCarthy	Dongdeath and Jazzabeth. (poem)	
2)	1968 Cape	Musrum.	with A. Earnshaw (q.v.)
FPS:	1968 Cape	Musrum. (with A. Earnshaw)	
FPP:	1966 McCarthy	Dongdeath and Jazzabeth. (poem)	
WIP:	1970 Cape	Wintersol. (with A. Earnshaw)	

***   ***   ***   ***   ***

Eric Lee Thacker--born September 29, 1923 at Leeds, Yorkshire, England--attended Hartley Victoria Methodist College (Theological School), 1952-1955--Rawmarsh, Rotherham, England/Leeds, Yorkshire, England.

Son of George Ernest & Jane (Lee) Thacker--Doreen Mary Smith: August 11, 1956--Andrea Mary Thacker (February 8, 1960); Miles David Thacker (October 18, 1963); Clinton Roger Thacker and Deborah Clare Thacker (January 4, 1965).

With a department store, 1937-1938; shopfitters firm, 1938-1939; Billposter's Assistant, 1939; with an engraver's firm, 1939-1944; 1947-1952; Methodist Minister (variously in Derbyshire, Lancashire, Yorkshire, all in England, and in South India), 1955-DATE; Free-Lance Writer.

Rev. Thacker writes:
   "My writing activity has largely been in the areas of poetry and jazz criticism. No collection of poems has yet been published; individual poems have appeared in English and Indian magazines; and the long poem 'Dongdeath and Jazzabeth' was produced in mimeo, with linocub cover, non-professionally, by Cavan McCarthy, whose occasional magazine specializes in concrete poetry. ('Dongdeath' is not a concrete poem, but one which combines jazz imagery with mythology, real and invented, together with verbal techniques which employ the heavy use of puns and the occasional use of change and automatism.)
   "Musrum is not sf, but belongs, I suppose, to the 'super-genre.' It invents the category of the 'musroid,' which is virtually limitless in its possibilities, excluding only the self-containedly mundane. The book depends on the interaction of the verbal and the visual. Drawings are as important as text, and are numerous--drawn by both authors in their differing but related styles. 'Strong' humour is the pervading genius, sparked by extravagant paradox and violent shifts of meaning and imagery. Surrealism is perhaps the strongest influence. Both authors admire the best in sf, but are unaware of definite influence here.
   "My long friendship with Anthony Earnshaw is rooted in our common interest in jazz, and in the art and literature of the fantastic. We write largely for the sake of mutual entertainment."

JOHN HAY

1)	1968 Hodder	<u>The Invasion</u>.
FPS:	an article to the	<u>Australian Country Magazine</u>, 1956.
FSF:	1968 Hodder	<u>The Invasion</u>.
WIP:		<u>Sell Out</u>.
		<u>Bella</u>.

***   ***   ***   ***   ***

John Warwick Dalrymple-Hay--born August 16, 1928 at Sydney, Australia--Graduate, Australian School Pacific Administration--Deakin, Australian Capital Territory, Australia.

Son of Charles Stewart & Barbara Charlotte (Chambers) Dalrymple-Hay--Barbara Deirdre Moir: October 31, 1953--Heather Nancy Dalrymple-Hay (August 22, 1954); Ann Louise Dalrymple-Hay (June 28, 1956).

Patrol Officer, Territory of Papua and New Guinea, 1949-1950; Farmer (Cattle Breeder and Wool Classer), 1952-1968; Agricultural Journalist, 1956-DATE; TV Critic, 1965-1969; Columnist, <u>Canberra Times</u>, 1965-1968; Free-Lance Writer.

CHARLES BARREN

		with R. Cox Abel (q.v.)	
1)	1966 Library 33 Panther	*Trivana 1.* (H-P)	

FSF: 1966 Library 33/Panther *Trivana 1.* (H-P) (with R. Cox Abel)

***   ***   ***   ***

Charles Barren (u)--born December 21, 1913 at London, England--attended West Ham Technical College; Forest Training College--Ilford, Essex, England.

Son of Thomas Bearman and Ada Boone (Winfield) Barren--Vera Dace: November 21, 1936--Melvyn Barren; Stuart Barren; Dianne Barren.

Has been a warden of various youth and community centers; currently Lecturer in English and History, Barking Regional College of Technology (formerly South East Essex Technical College and School of Art), Dagenham, Essex, England.

ALVA ROGERS

Mr. Roger's full name is Alva C. Rogers.

RANDALL GARRETT

Mr. Garrett's full name is Gordon Randall Philip David Garrett.

MICHAEL KURLAND

Mr. Kurland's full name is Michael Joseph Kurland.

HARRY HARRISON

Mr. Harrison's full name is Harry Maxwell Harrison.

G.C. EDMONDSON

Mr. Edmondson was born in Washington State (exact place unknown); a former metals technician for a naval electronics laboratory, he is recently retired.

R. LIONEL FANTHORPE

2)	1957 Cobra SN	"Resurgam" (s/P)
3)	1957 Cobra SN	"Secret of the Snows" (s/P)
4)	1958 Badger SN	"The Flight of the Valkyries" (s/P)
5)	1958 Badger SF	*The Waiting World.* (P)
6)	1958 Badger SN	"Watchers of the Forest" (s/P)
8)	1958 Badger SN	"Call of the Werwolf" (s/P)
10)	1958 Badger SN	"The Death Note" (s/P)
12)	1959 Badger SN	"Mermaid Reef" (s/P)

R. LIONEL FANTHORPE (continued)

14)	1959 Badger SF	Alien from the Stars.	(P/RH)
16)	1959 Badger SN	"The Ghost Rider"	(s/P)
17)	1959 Badger SF	Hyperspace.	(P/RH)
20)	1960 Badger SF	Doomed World.	(P)
22)	1960 Badger SN	"The Man Who Couldn't Die"	(s/P)
23)	1960 Badger SN	Out of the Darkness.	(P)
24)	1960 Badger SF	Asteroid Man.	(P/RH)
31)	1960 Badger SN	"Werewolf at Large"	(s/P)
33)	1960 Badger SF	Hand of Doom	(P/RH)
35)	1960 Badger SN	"Whirlwind of Death"	(s/P)
40)	1961 Badger SF	Flame Mass.	(P)
41)	1961 Badger SN	"Fingers of Darkness"	(s/P)
45)	1961 Badger SN	"Face in the Dark"	(s/P)
52)	1961 Badger SN	"Devil from the Depths"	(s/P)
54)	1961 Badger SN	"Centurion's Vengeance"	(s/P)
56)	1961 Badger SN	The Golden Chalice.	(P)
57)	1961 Badger SN	"The Grip of Fear"	(s/P)
60)	1962 Badger SN	"Chariot of Apollo"	(s/P)
65)	1962 Badger SN	"Hell Has Wings"	(s/P)
69)	1962 Badger SN	"Graveyard of the Damned"	(s/P)
73)	1962 Badger SN	"The Darker Drink"	(s/P)
78)	1962 Badger SN	"Curse of the Totum"	(s/P)
79)	1962 Badger SF	Space Fury	(P/RH)
87)	1963 Badger SN	"Goddess of the Night"	(s/P)
91)	1963 Badger SN	"Twilight Ancestor"	(s/P)
95)	1963 Badger SN	"Sands of Eternity"	(s/P)
100)	1963 Badger SF	Negative Minus.	(P)
103)	1963 Badger SN	"Moon Wolf"	(s/P)
117)	1964 Badger SN	"Avenging Goddess"	(s/P)
121)	1964 Badger SN	"Death Has Two Faces"	(s/P)
125)	1964 Badger SN	"The Shrouded Abbot"	(s/P)
137)	1965 Badger SN	"Bitter Reflection"	(s/P)
138)	1965 Badger SF	Neuron World.	(P)
140)	1965 Badger SN	The Triple Man.	(P)
141)	1965 Badger SN	"Call of the Wild"	(s/P)
145)	1965 Badger SN	"Vision of the Damned"	(s/P)
149)	1965 Badger SN	"The Sealed Sarcophagus"	(s/P)
152)	1966 Badger SN	The Unconfined.	(P)
153)	1966 Badger SN	"Stranger in the Shadow"	(s/P)
157)	1966 Badger SN	"Curse of the Khan"	(s/P)
158)	1966 Badger SF	Watching World.	(P)

as *Lionel Roberts

1)	1954 Spencer	"The Incredulist"	(s/P)
7)	1958 Badger SN	"Guardians of the Tomb"	(s/P)
9)	1958 Badger SN	"The Golden Warrior"	(s/P)
18)	1959 Badger SF	Time Echo.	(P/RHv)
25)	1960 Badger SF	The In-World.	(P/RH)
27)	1960 Badger SF	The Face of X.	(P/RHv)

R. LIONEL FANTHORPE (continued)

39)	1961 Badger SN	The Last Valkyrie. (P)
43)	1961 Badger SF	The Synthetic Ones. (P)
50)	1961 Badger SN	Flame Goddess. (P)

as *Trebor Thorpe

11)	1958 Badger SN	"The Haunted Pool" (s/P)
21)	1960 Badger SN	Five Faces of Fear. (P)
26)	1960 Badger SF	Lightning World. (P/RH)
38)	1961 Badger SN	"Voodoo Hell Drums" (s/P)

as *Leo Brett

13)	1959 Badger SN	"The Drud" (s/P)
15)	1959 Badger SN	"The Return" (s/P)
28)	1960 Badger SF	Exit Humanity. (P/RH)
32)	1960 Badger SF	The Microscopic Ones. (P)
37)	1960 Badger SF	The Faceless Planet. (P)
44)	1961 Badger SF	March of the Robots. (P)
46)	1961 Badger SN	Black Infinity. (P)
47)	1961 Badger SF	Mind Force. (P)
61)	1962 Badger SN	Nightmare. (P)
68)	1962 Badger SN	Face in the Night. (P)
75)	1962 Badger SN	The Immortals. (P)
83)	1962 Badger SN	"The Frozen Tomb" (s/P)
86)	1963 Badger SN	They Never Come Back. (P)
94)	1963 Badger SN	The Forbidden. (P)
98)	1963 Badger SN	From Realms Beyond. (P)
99)	1963 Badger SN	"Phantom Crusader" (s/P)
110)	1963 Badger SF	The Alien Ones. (P/RH)
111	1963 Badger SF	Power Sphere. (P/RH)

as *Bron Fane

19)	1960 Badger SN	"The Crawling Fiend" (s/P)
29)	1960 Badger SF	Juggernaut. (P/RHv)
36)	1960 Badger SF	Last Man on Earth. (P)
48)	1961 Badger SF	Rodent Mutation. (P)
62)	1962 Badger SN	"Storm God's Fury" (s/P)
101)	1963 Badger SF	The Intruders. (P)
106)	1963 Badger SF	Somewhere Out There. (P/RH)
108)	1963 Badger SN	Softly by Moonlight. (P)
109)	1963 Badger SN	"The Thing from Sheol" (s/P)
116)	1964 Badger SN	Unknown Destiny. (P)
122)	1964 Badger SF	Nemesis. (P)
126)	1964 Badger SF	Suspension. (P)
128)	1964 Badger SN	The Macabre Ones. (P)
133)	1964 Badger SN	"The Walking Shadow" (s/P)
29A)	1965 Arcadia	Blue Juggernaut.
151)	1965 Badger SF	U.F.O. 517. (P)

R. LIONEL FANTHORPE (continued)

as *Pel Torro

30)	1960 Badger SF	Frozen Planet. (P)
34)	1960 Badger SF	World of the Gods. (P)
53)	1961 Badger SN	The Phantom Ones. (P)
82)	1962 Badger SN	Legion of the Lost. (P)
90)	1963 Badger SN	The Strange Ones. (P)
96)	1963 Badger SF	Galaxy 666. (P/RH)
97)	1963 Badger SF	Formula 29X. (P)
102)	1963 Badger SN	The Timeless Ones. (P)
104)	1963 Badger SF	Through the Barrier. (P)
107)	1963 Badger SF	The Last Astronaut. (P)
112)	1963 Badger SN	The Face of Fear. (P)
123)	1964 Badger SF	The Return. (P/RHv)
134)	1964 Badger SF	Space No Barrier. (P)
142)	1965 Badger SF	Force 97X. (P)
123A)	1969 Arcadia	Exiled in Space.
97A)	1969 Tower	Beyond the Barrier of Space. (P)

as ***John E. Muller

42)	1961 Badger SF	A 1,000 Years On. (P)
49)	1961 Badger SF	The Ultimate Man. (P)
51)	1961 Badger SF	The Uninvited. (P)
55)	1961 Badger SF	Crimson Planet. (P/RH)
58)	1961 Badger SF	The Venus Venture. (P/RHv)
59)	1962 Badger SN	The Return of Zeus. (P)
63)	1962 Badger SF	Perilous Galaxy. (P)
64)	1962 Badger SN	The Eye of Karnak. (P)
66)	1962 Badger SF	The Man Who Conquered Time. (P)
67)	1962 Badger SF	Orbit One. (P/RHv)
70)	1962 Badger SF	Micro Infinity. (P)
71)	1962 Badger SF	Beyond Time. (P/RHv)
72)	1962 Badger SN	Vengeance of Siva. (P)
74)	1962 Badger SF	The Day the World Died. (P)
76)	1962 Badger SF	The X-Machine. (P)
114)	1963 Badger SF	Reactor XK9. (P)
115)	1963 Badger SF	Special Mission. (P)
130)	1964 Badger SF	Dark Continuum. (P)
131)	1964 Badger SF	Mark of the Beast. (P)
136)	1965 Badger SN	The Exorcists. (P)
139)	1965 Badger SF	The Negative Ones. (P)
143)	1965 Badger SF	The Man from Beyond. (P/RH)
144)	1965 Badger SN	Spectre of Darkness. (P)
146)	1965 Badger SF	Beyond the Void. (P)
148)	1965 Badger SN	Out of the Night. (P)
154)	1966 Badger SF	Phenomena X. (P)
155)	1966 Badger SF	Survival Project. (P/RH)

R. LIONEL FANTHORPE (continued)

as ***Karl Zeigfreid

77)	1962 Badger SN	Gods of Darkness. (P)
80)	1962 Badger SF	Walk Through To-Morrow. (P)
81)	1962 Badger SF	Android. (P)
84)	1962 Badger SF	Atomic Nemesis. (P)
85)	1962 Badger SF	Zero Minus X. (P/RH)
88)	1963 Badger SF	Escape to Infinity. (P)
89)	1963 Badger SF	Radar Alert. (P/RH)
92)	1963 Badger SF	World of Tomorrow. (P/RHv)
93)	1963 Badger SF	The World That Never Was. (P)
127)	1964 Badger SF	Projection Infinity. (P)
135)	1964 Badger SF	No Way Back. (P/RH)
92A)	1964 Arcadia	World of the Future.
147)	1965 Badger SF	Barrier 346. (P/RH)
150)	1965 Badger SF	Girl from Tomorrow. (P)

as *Lee Barton

105)	1963 Badger SN	The Unseen. (P)
156)	1966 Badger SN	The Shadow Man. (P)

as *Olaf Trent

113)	1963 Badger SN	"Roman Twilight" (s/P)

as *Thornton Bell

118)	1964 Badger SF	Space Trap. (P/RH)
132)	1964 Badger SN	Chaos. (P)

as *Erle Barton

119)	1964 Badger SF	The Planet Seekers. (P)

as *Neil Thanet

120)	1964 Badger SN	Beyond the Veil. (P)
124)	1964 Badger SN	The Man Who Came Back. (P)

as *Phil Nobel

129)	1964 Badger SN	"The Hand from Gehenna" (s/P)

as *Robert Lionel

18A)	1964 Arcadia	Time Echo.
27A)	1965 Arcadia	The Face of X.

as ***Marston Johns

58A)	1965 Arcadia	The Venus Venture.
71A)	1966 Arcadia	Beyond Time.

R. LIONEL FANTHORPE (continued)

as *Mel Jay

67A) 1966 Arcadia   Orbit One. (RP)

NOTE: the following novels by "John E. Muller" remain unidentified: THE MIND MAKERS, FORBIDDEN PLANET, URANIUM 235, and INFINITY MACHINE.

FKP: "'Discovery'" Futuristic Science Stories, No. 7 (1952) (as *Lionel Roberts).

WIP: a new collection of Val Stearman/La Noire stories.

***   ***   ***   ***

Robert Lionel Fanthorpe--born February 9, 1935 at Dereham, Norfolk, England--attended Keswick College, Norwich, England, 1961-1963: attained Distinctions in Advanced Main Theology in English, and Merit in entire final examination; received Diploma, Electrical Development Association, 1958, for Public Speaking; Associate, College of Preceptors--Romford, Essex, England.

Son of Robert and Greta Christine (Garbutt) Fanthorpe--Patricia Alice Tooke: September 7, 1957--Stephanie Dawn Patricia Fanthorpe (July 25, 1964); Fiona Mary Patricia Alcibiadette Fanthorpe (May 16, 1966).

Schoolmaster, Dereham Secondary Modern School, 1958-1961, 1963-1967; Tutor for Further Education, Gamlingay Village College, 1967-1969; Group Industrial Training Officer, Phoenix Timber Company, Rainham, Essex, England, 1969-DATE; Free-Lance Writer, Associate Member: National Association of Schoolmasters; Former Member: Mensa; British Interplanetary Society.

APPENDICES

TITLE INDEX

Title	Author
An ABC of Science Fiction.	Tom Boardman, Jr.
An A. E. van Vogt Omnibus.	A. E. van Vogt
A for Andromeda.	John Elliot & Fred Hoyle
A for Anything.	Damon Knight
The A. G. Man.	William Hansman
Abandon Galaxy!	Bart Somers (Gardner F. Fox)
The Abominable Earthman.	Frederik Pohl
Across the Sea of Stars.	Arthur C. Clarke
Across Time.	David Grinnell (Donald A. Wollheim)
Adam Link--Robot.	Eando Binder (Otto O. Binder)
Adam M-1.	William C. Anderson
The Addams Family.	Jack Sharkey
Adventures in the Far Future.	Donald A. Wollheim
The Adventures of Nicknames Incorporated.	Mabel L. McKinney
Adventures on Other Planets.	Donald A. Wollheim
"The Afrit Affair".	Keith Laumer
After Doomsday.	Poul Anderson
After Some Tomorrow.	Mack Reynolds
After 12000 Years.	Stanton A. Coblentz
After World's End.	Jack Williamson
Aftermath.	George Corston
Against the Fall of Night.	Arthur C. Clarke
An Age.	Brian W. Aldiss
The Age of Ruin.	John M. Faucette
The Agency.	David Meltzer
The Agent.	David Meltzer
Agent of Chaos.	Norman Spinrad
Agent of the Terran Empire.	Poul Anderson
Agent of the Unknown.	Margaret St. Clair
Agent of Vega.	James H. Schmitz
Ahead of Time.	C. L. Moore & Henry Kuttner
The Airs of Earth.	Brian W. Aldiss
An Alfred Bester Omnibus.	Alfred Bester
The Alien.	L. P. Davies
The Alien.	Raymond F. Jones
Alien.	John E. Muller
Alien Dust.	E. C. Tubb
Alien from Arcturus.	Gordon R. Dickson
Alien from the Stars.	R. Lionel Fanthorpe
Alien Impact.	E. C. Tubb
Alien Life.	E. C. Tubb
The Alien Ones.	Leo Brett
Alien Sea.	John Rackham
Alien Skies.	Peter Dagmar
Alien Universe.	E. C. Tubb
Alien Virus.	John Rackham
The Alien Way.	Gordon R. Dickson
Alien World.	Adam Lukens (Diane Detzer)

Alien Worlds.	Roger Elwood
The Aliens.	Murray Leinster (Will F. Jenkins)
Aliens for Neighbours.	Clifford D. Simak
Aliens 4.	Theodore Sturgeon
Aliens from Space.	David Osborne (Robert Silverberg)
All About Venus.	Brian W. Aldiss
All Flesh Is Grass.	Clifford D. Simak
All Fools' Day.	Edmund Cooper
All Judgment Fled.	James White
All the Colors of Darkness.	Lloyd Biggle, Jr.
All the Traps of Earth.	Clifford D. Simak
The Alley God.	Philip Jose Farmer
Almost Human.	William F. Nolan
Alpha Centauri--Or Die!	Leigh Brackett
Alpha Yes, Terra No!	Emil Petaja
The Altar on Asconel.	John Brunner
The Altered Ego.	Jerry Sohl
The Alternate Martians.	A. Bertram Chandler
Alternating Currents.	Frederik Pohl
The Amsirs and the Iron Thorn.	Algis Budrys
The Analog Anthology.	John W. Campbell
Analog 5.	John W. Campbell
Analog 4.	John W. Campbell
Analog 1.	John W. Campbell
Analog 6.	John W. Campbell
Analog 3.	John W. Campbell
Analog 2.	John W. Campbell
Analogue Men.	Damon Knight
Anarchaos.	Curt Clark
And Flights of Angels.	Emil Petaja
...And My Fear is Great and Baby is Three.	Theodore Sturgeon
...And Others Shall Be Born.	Frank Belknap Long
...And Some Were Human.	Lester del Rey
And Then the Town Took Off.	Richard Wilson
Andover and the Android.	Kate Wilhelm
Android.	Karl Zeigfreid
Android Avenger.	Ted White
Andromeda Breakthrough.	Fred Hoyle & John Elliot
Angels and Spaceships.	Fredric Brown
The Angry Espers.	Lloyd Biggle, Jr.
Another Kind.	Chad Oliver
Anthropol.	Louis Trimble
Anton York, Immortal.	Eando Binder (Otto O. Binder)
The Anything Box.	Zenna Henderson
Anything You Can Do.	Randall Garrett
Apeman, Spaceman.	Harry Harrison & Leon E. Stover
Apollo at Go.	Jeff Sutton
Appointment in Space.	Ernest J. Blow
Arctic Bride.	S. P. Meek
Argentis.	Brian Shaw (E. C. Tubb)
Argosy.	Charles A. Miles

Army of the Undead.	Rafe Bernard
The Arsenal of Miracles.	Gardner F. Fox
The Arsenal Out of Time.	David McDaniel
An Arthur C. Clarke Omnibus.	Arthur C. Clarke
The Artificial Man.	L. P. Davies
Asimov's Mysteries.	Isaac Asimov
Aspects of Science Fiction.	Geoffrey Doherty
The Assassination Affair.	J. Hunter Holly
Assassins from Tomorrow.	Peter Heath
Assignment Doomsday.	Martin Thomas
Assignment in Eternity.	Robert A. Heinlein
Assignment in Nowhere.	Keith Laumer
Assignment in Tomorrow.	Frederik Pohl
Assignment Luther.	Lan Wright
Astera: The Planet That Committed Suicide.	
Asteroid Man.	Ray W. Johnson
The Astounding Science Fiction Anthology.	R. Lionel Fanthorpe
	John W. Campbell
Astounding Tales of Space and Time.	
The Astronauts Must Not Land.	John W. Campbell
Asylum Earth.	John Brunner
Atlan.	Bruce Elliott
The Atlantic Abomination.	Jane Gaskell
The Atom Conspiracy.	John Brunner
Atom War on Mars.	Jeff Sutton
Atomic Nemesis.	E. C. Tubb
Atoms and Evil.	Karl Zeigfreid
Attack from Atlantis.	Robert Bloch
Australian Science Fiction Index 1939-62.	Lester del Rey
	Graham Brice Stone
Australian Science Fiction Index 1925-67.	
The Automated Goliath.	Graham Brice Stone
The Avengers Battle the Earth-Wrecker.	William F. Temple
Award Science Fiction Reader.	Otto O. Binder
Away and Beyond.	Alden H. Norton
	A. E. van Vogt
B.E.A.S.T.	Charles Eric Maine
Babel-17.	Samuel R. Delany
Backdrop of Stars.	Harry Harrison
The Ballad of Beta-2.	Samuel R. Delany
Bar Sinister.	Paul MacTyre
The Barbarians of Mars.	Edward P. Bradbury (Michael Moorcock)
Barrier 346.	Karl Zeigfreid
Barrier Unknown.	A. J. Merak
Battle for the Stars.	Edmond Hamilton
Battle on Mercury.	Eric Van Lhin (Lester del Rey)
Battle on Venus.	William F. Temple
The Beast.	A. E. van Vogt
The Beast Master.	Andre Norton
The Beasts from Beyond.	Manly Wade Wellman
The Beasts of Kohl.	John Rackham

Bedlam Planet.	John Brunner
Behold the Stars.	Kenneth Bulmer
Believers' World.	Robert A. W. Lowndes
The Bell from Infinity.	Robert Moore Williams
Berserker.	Fred Saberhagen
Best Fantasy Stories.	Brian W. Aldiss
The Best from Fantasy and Science Fiction Ninth Series.	Robert P. Mills
The Best from Fantasy and Science Fiction Tenth Series.	Robert P. Mills
The Best from Fantasy and Science Fiction Eleventh Series.	Robert P. Mills
The Best from Fantasy and Science Fiction Twelfth Series.	Avram Davidson
The Best from Fantasy and Science Fiction Thirteenth Series.	Avram Davidson
The Best from Fantasy and Science Fiction Fourteenth Series.	Avram Davidson
The Best from Fantasy and Science Fiction Fifteenth Series.	Edward L. Ferman
The Best from Fantasy and Science Fiction Sixteenth Series.	Edward L. Ferman
The Best from Fantasy and Science Fiction Seventeenth Series.	Edward L. Ferman
The Best from New Worlds.	John Carnell
The Best of Amazing.	Joseph Ross
The Best of Kuttner 1.	C. L. Moore & Henry Kuttner
The Best of Kuttner 2.	C. L. Moore & Henry Kuttner
The Best of New Worlds.	Michael Moorcock
The Best of Sci-Fi No. 1.	Judith Merril
The Best of Sci-Fi No. 2.	Judith Merril
The Best of Sci-Fi No. 3.	Cordelia Titcomb Smith
The Best of Sci-Fi No. 4.	Judith Merril
The Best of Sci-Fi No. 5.	Judith Merril
Best SF: Science Fiction Stories.	Edmund Crispin
Best SF Two.	Edmund Crispin
Best SF Three.	Edmund Crispin
Best SF Four.	Edmund Crispin
Best SF Five.	Edmund Crispin
Best SF Six.	Edmund Crispin
Best SF: 1967.	Brian W. Aldiss & Harry Harrison
The Best SF Stories from New Worlds.	Michael Moorcock
The Best SF Stories from New Worlds 3.	Michael Moorcock
The Best Science Fiction Stories and Novels: 1955.	T. E. Dikty
The Best Science Fiction Stories and Novels: 1956.	T. E. Dikty
The Best Science Fiction Stories and Novels Ninth Series.	T. E. Dikty
Best Science Fiction Stories of Brian W. Aldiss.	Brian W. Aldiss
Best Science Fiction Stories of Clifford Simak.	Clifford D. Simak

Best Science Fiction Stories of James Blish. — James Blish
The Best Science Fiction Stories: 1950. — T. E. Dikty & Everett F. Bleiler
The Best Science Fiction Stories: 1954. — T. E. Dikty & Everett F. Bleiler
The Best Science Fiction Stories: 1951. — T. E. Dikty & Everett F. Bleiler
The Best Science Fiction Stories: 1953. — T. E. Dikty & Everett F. Bleiler
The Best Science Fiction Stories: 1952. — T. E. Dikty & Everett F. Bleiler
The Best Science Fiction Stories: 1949. — T. E. Dikty & Everett F. Bleiler
The Best Stories from New Worlds. II. — Michael Moorcock
Best Tales of Terror. — Edmund Crispin
Best Tales of Terror Two. — Edmund Crispin
Between Planets. — Robert A. Heinlein
Beyond. — Theodore Sturgeon
The Beyond. — Jean & Jeff Sutton
Beyond Apollo. — Jeff Sutton
Beyond Earth's Gates. — C. L. Moore & Lewis Padgett (Henry Kuttner)
Beyond Human Ken. — Judith Merril
Beyond Infinity. — Alan E. Nourse
Beyond the Barrier. — Damon Knight
Beyond the Barriers of Time and Space. — Judith Merril
Beyond the Black Enigma. — Bart Somers (Gardner F. Fox)
Beyond the Chains of Bondage. — Raymond George Ross
Beyond the Curtain of Dark. — Peter Haining
Beyond the End of Time. — Frederik Pohl
Beyond the Galactic Rim. — A. Bertram Chandler
Beyond the Galaxy. — Karl Zeigfreid
Beyond the Moon. — Edmond Hamilton
Beyond the Sealed World. — Rena Vale
Beyond the Silver Sky. — Kenneth Bulmer
Beyond the Spectrum. — Martin Thomas
Beyond the Void. — John E. Muller
Beyond This Horizon. — Robert A. Heinlein
Beyond Time. — Marston Johns (John E. Muller)
Beyond Tomorrow. — Damon Knight
Bibliography of Adventure. — Bradford M. Day
The Big Ball of Wax. — Shepherd Mead
The Big Jump. — Leigh Brackett
Big Planet. — Jack Vance
The Big Time. — Fritz Leiber
Bill, the Galactic Hero. — Harry Harrison
Billenium. — J. G. Ballard
The Bird of Time. — Wallace West
The Bird, the Ghoul, and in the Name of My Friend. — Robert Easson
Black Abyss. — J. L. Powers
Black Alice. — Thom Demijohn (Thomas M. Disch & John T. Sladek)

The Black Cloud.	Fred Hoyle
Black Easter.	James Blish
The Black Galaxy.	Murray Leinster (Will F. Jenkins)
Black Infinity.	Leo Brett
The Black Star Passes.	John W. Campbell
Blades of Mars.	Edward P. Bradbury (Michael Moorcock)
Blast Off at 0300.	Hugh Walters
Blast Off at Woomera.	Hugh Walters
The Blockade of Sinitron.	John Rankine (Douglas R. Mason)
Blood Runs Cold.	Robert Bloch
Bloodworld.	Laurence M. Janifer
The Bloody Sun.	Marion Zimmer Bradley
The Blue Ants.	Bernard Newman
The Blue Atom.	Robert Moore Williams
The Blue Barbarians.	Stanton A. Coblentz
Blue Juggernaut.	Bron Fane
The Blue World.	Jack Vance
Bodyguard.	H. L. Gold
The Body Snatchers.	Jack Finney
The Body's Guest.	Angus MacLeod
Bogey Men.	Robert Bloch
Bombs in Orbit.	Jeff Sutton
The Book of Ptath.	A. E. van Vogt
Born in Space.	Cyril Donson
Born Leader.	J. T. McIntosh
Born of Man and Woman.	Richard Matheson
Born Under Mars.	John Brunner
Bow Down to Nul.	Brian W. Aldiss
Boy Beneath the Sea.	Arthur C. Clarke
The Brain-Stealers.	Murray Leinster (Will F. Jenkins)
Brain Twister.	Mark Phillips (Randall Garrett & Laurence M. Janifer)
Brain Wave.	Poul Anderson
The Brains of Earth.	Jack Vance
Brainwashed.	Martin Thomas
Brak the Barbarian.	John Jakes
Breakthrough.	Richard Cowper
Breakthrough.	John Iggulden
Bred to Kill.	Martin Thomas
The Brides of Dracula.	Dean Owen
Bridge to Yesterday.	E. L. Arch
Brigands of the Moon.	John W. Campbell
Bright New Universe.	Jack Williamson
The Brightfount Diaries.	Brian W. Aldiss
Bring Back Yesterday.	A. Bertram Chandler
Bring the Jubilee.	Ward Moore
The Brink.	John Brunner
The Broken Lands.	Fred Saberhagen
Budrys' Inferno.	Algis Budrys
The Burning World.	J. G. Ballard
The Butterfly Kid.	Chester Anderson
Bypass to Otherness.	C. L. Moore & Henry Kuttner

C.O.D. Mars.	E. C. Tubb
Cache from Outer Space.	Philip Jose Farmer
Calculated Risk.	Charles Eric Maine
The Caltraps of Time.	David I. Masson
Camp Concentration.	Thomas M. Disch
Canary in a Cat House.	Kurt Vonnegut, Jr.
The Canopy of Time.	Brian W. Aldiss
A Canticle for Leibowitz.	Walter M. Miller, Jr.
Captives of the Flame.	Samuel R. Delany
Cardinal of the Stars.	F. G. Rayer
The Carefully Considered Rape of the World.	Shepherd Mead
The Carnelian Cube.	L. Sprague de Camp & Fletcher Pratt
The Case Against Tomorrow.	Frederik Pohl
A Case of Conscience.	James Blish
The Cassiopeia Affair.	Harrison Brown & Chloe Zerwick
Castaways' World.	John Brunner
The Castle of Iron.	L. Sprague de Camp & Fletcher Pratt
Catastrophe Planet.	Keith Laumer
Catch a Falling Star.	John Brunner
Cat's Cradle.	Kurt Vonnegut, Jr.
Catseye.	Andre Norton
The Caves of Death.	Victor Norwood
The Caves of Mars.	Emil Petaja
The Caves of Steel.	Isaac Asimov
Caviar.	Theodore Sturgeon
Cee-Tee Man.	Dan Morgan
The Celestial Blueprint.	Philip Jose Farmer
Central Passage.	Lawrence Schoonover
A Century of Great Short Science Fiction Novels.	Damon Knight
A Century of Science Fiction.	Damon Knight
Chain Reaction.	Christopher Hodder-Williams
The Chained Crocodile.	Beryl Whitaker
Challenge.	H. K. Bulmer
Chamber of Horrors.	Robert Bloch
The Change.	George C. Foster
The Changeling.	A. E. van Vogt
The Changeling Worlds.	Kenneth Bulmer
Chaos.	Thornton Bell
The Chaos Fighters.	Robert Moore Williams
Chaos in Arcturus.	Karl Zeigfreid
Chariot into Time.	Karl Zeigfreid
The Checklist of Fantastic Literature in Paperbound Books.	Bradford M. Day
A Checklist of Fantastic Magazines.	Bradford M. Day
A Checklist of Science Fiction Anthologies.	Walter R. Cole
Checkpoint Lambda.	Murray Leinster (Will F. Jenkins)
Chessboard Planet.	Lewis Padgett (C. L. Moore & Henry Kuttner)

Childhood's End.	Arthur C. Clarke
Children of Light.	Henry L. Lawrence
Children of Wonder.	William Tenn
Chocky.	John Wyndham (John Beynon Harris)
The Chrysalids.	John Wyndham (John Beynon Harris)
Chthon.	Piers Anthony
The Circus of Doctor Lao.	Charles G. Finney
The Circus of Dr. Lao and Other Improbable Stories.	Ray Bradbury
Cities of the Dead.	Peter Edgar
Cities of Wonder.	Damon Knight
Citizen in Space.	Robert Sheckley
Citizen of the Galaxy.	Robert A. Heinlein
City.	Clifford D. Simak
The City.	Jane Gaskell
The City and the Stars.	Arthur C. Clarke
City at World's End.	Edmond Hamilton
City in the Sea.	Wilson Tucker
City of a Thousand Suns.	Samuel R. Delany
The City of Gold and Lead.	John Christopher
City of Illusions.	Ursula K. Le Guin
City of No Return.	E. C. Tubb
City of the Chasch.	Jack Vance
City on the Moon.	Murray Leinster (Will F. Jenkins)
City Under the Sea.	Kenneth Bulmer
Clans of the Alphane Moon.	Philip K. Dick
Claret, Sandwiches and Sin.	Madelaine Duke
A Clash of Cymbals.	James Blish
Clash of Star-Kings.	Avram Davidson
Claws of the Night.	Vern Hansen
The Climacticon.	Harold Livingston
The Cloak of Aesir.	John W. Campbell
The Clock of Time.	Jack Finney
A Clockwork Orange.	Anthony Burgess
The Clone.	Theodore L. Thomas & Kate Wilhelm
The Clones.	P. T. Olemy
Close to Critical.	Hal Clement
The Closed Worlds.	Edmond Hamilton
The Cloud.	Jacquelin Rollit McAuley
Cloud on Silver.	John Christopher
Code Duello.	Mack Reynolds
Code Three.	Rick Raphael
The Coils of Time.	A. Bertram Chandler
Collected Editorials from Analog.	John W. Campbell
Collision Course.	Robert Silverberg
Colonial Survey.	Murray Leinster (Will F. Jenkins)
The Colors of Space.	Marion Zimmer Bradley
Colossus.	D. F. Jones
The Cometeers.	Jack Williamson
The Coming of the Rats.	George H. Smith
The Coming of the Robots.	Sam Moskowitz
The Coming of the Strangers.	John Lymington

The Coming of the Terrans.	Leigh Brackett
The Coming of the Unselves.	Edmund Ludlow
The Complete Checklist of Science-Fiction Magazines.	Bradford M. Day
Computer War.	Mack Reynolds
Conan.	Lin Carter, L. Sprague de Camp & Robert E. Howard
Conan of the Isles.	Lin Carter & L. Sprague de Camp
The Conan Reader.	L. Sprague de Camp
Conan the Adventurer.	L. Sprague de Camp & Robert E. Howard
Conan the Avenger.	L. Sprague de Camp, Robert E. Howard & Bjorn Nyberg
Conan the Freebooter.	L. Sprague de Camp & Robert E. Howard
Conan the Usurper.	L. Sprague de Camp & Robert E. Howard
Conan the Wanderer.	Lin Carter, L. Sprague de Camp & Robert E. Howard
Conditionally Human.	Walter M. Miller, Jr.
Conjure Wife.	Fritz Leiber
Connoisseur's Science Fiction.	Tom Boardman, Jr.
Conquerors from the Darkness.	Robert Silverberg
Conquest of Life.	Adam Lukens (Diane Detzer)
Conquest of the Space Sea.	Robert Moore Williams
Consider Her Ways.	John Wyndham (John Beynon Harris)
Contact.	Noel Keyes
The Continent Makers.	L. Sprague de Camp
Contraband from Outer Space.	A. Bertram Chandler
Convention Annual #4--Tricon.	Jay Kay Klein
Convention Annual #1--Pittcon.	Jay Kay Klein
Convention Annual #3--Discon.	Jay Kay Klein
Convention Annual #2--Chicon III.	Jay Kay Klein
The Corfu Affair.	John T. Phillifent (John Rackham)
The Cornish Pixie Affair.	Peter Leslie
Corpus Earthling.	Louis Charbonneau
The Corridors of Time.	Poul Anderson
Cosmic Checkmate.	Charles V. De Vet & Katherine MacLean
Cosmic Crusade.	Richard Saxon
Cosmic Engineers.	Clifford D. Simak
Cosmic Manhunt.	L. Sprague de Camp
Cosmic Puppets.	Philip K. Dick
The Cosmic Rape.	Theodore Sturgeon
The Cosmozoids.	Robert Tralins
Costigan's Needle.	Jerry Sohl
Count-Down.	Charles Eric Maine
Counter-Clock World.	Philip K. Dick
The Counterfeit Man.	Alan E. Nourse
Counterfeit World.	Daniel F. Galouye
The Counterfeits.	Leo P. Kelley
The Crack in Space.	Philip K. Dick
The Craft of Terror.	Peter Haining
Crashing Suns.	Edmond Hamilton

The Creator.	Clifford D. Simak
Creatures of the Abyss.	Murray Leinster (Will F. Jenkins)
Creatures of the Mist.	Vern Hansen
The Creeping Plague.	Richard Macgregor
The Creeping Shroud.	Lan Wright
The Crimson Capsule.	Stanton A. Coblentz
Crimson Planet.	John E. Muller
Crisis on Cheiron.	Juanita Coulson
Crisis 2000.	Charles Eric Maine
The Crossroads of Time.	Andre Norton
Crown of Infinity.	John M. Faucette
Croyd.	Ian Wallace
Cry of the Beast.	Victor Norwood
Crypotozoic!	Brian W. Aldiss
The Crystal World.	J. G. Ballard
A Cup of Life.	Jay C. White
A Cupful of Space.	Mildred Clingerman
The Curious Culture of the Planet Loretta.	William J. Palmer
The Curious Facts Preceding My Execution.	Donald E. Westlake
The Curious Masters.	Margot Bennett
The Currents of Space.	Isaac Asimov
The Curse of Rathlaw.	Peter Saxon (Martin Thomas)
The Cybernetic Brains.	Raymond F. Jones
Cybernetic Controller.	H. K. Bulmer & A. V. Clarke
Cycle of Fire.	Hal Clement
Cycle of Nemesis.	Kenneth Bulmer
Cyclops in the Sky.	Lionel Roberts
D-99.	H. B. Fyfe
The Dagger Affair.	David McDaniel
The Dakota Project.	Jack Beeching
Danger from Vega.	John Rackham
Danger Planet.	Brett Sterling (Edmond Hamilton)
Dangerous Edge.	William F. Temple
Dangerous Visions.	Harlan Ellison
Dare.	Philip Jose Farmer
The Daring Trip to the Moon.	Guido Nizzi
Dark Andromeda.	A. J. Merak
The Dark Beasts.	Frank Belknap Long
Dark Carnival.	Ray Bradbury
Dark Centauri.	Karl Zeigfreid
Dark Conflict.	A. J. Merak
Dark Continuum.	John E. Muller
Dark December.	Alfred Coppel
The Dark Destroyers.	Manly Wade Wellman
The Dark Enemy.	J. Hunter Holly
The Dark Intruder and Other Stories.	Marion Zimmer Bradley
The Dark Light-Years.	Brian W. Aldiss
The Dark Millenium.	A. J. Merak
The Dark Mind.	Colin Kapp
Dark Piper.	Andre Norton
The Dark Planet.	J. Hunter Holly

The Dark Side.	Damon Knight
The Dark Side of Earth.	Alfred Bester
Dark Tides.	Eric Frank Russell
Dark Universe.	Daniel F. Galouye
The Dark World.	C. L. Moore & Henry Kuttner
Darker Than You Think.	Jack Williamson
The Darkest of Nights.	Charles Eric Maine
The Darkness Before Tomorrow.	Robert Moore Williams
Daughters of Earth.	Judith Merril
Daughters of the Dolphin.	Roy Meyers
David Starr, Space Ranger.	Paul French (Isaac Asimov)
Davy.	Edgar Pangborn
Dawn of the Mutants.	Lionel Roberts
Dawning Light.	Robert Randall (Randall Garrett & Robert Silverberg)
Dawnman Planet.	Mack Reynolds
The Day After Romorrow.	Robert A. Heinlein
The Day Before Forever and Thunderhead.	Keith Laumer
The Day It Rained Forever.	Ray Bradbury
The Day New York Trembled.	Irwin Lewis
The Day New York Went Dry.	Charles Einstein
The Day of Forever.	J. G. Ballard
Day of the Beasts.	John E. Muller
Day of the Giants.	Lester del Rey
Day of the Minotaur.	Thomas Burnett Swann
The Day of the Star Cities.	John Brunner
The Day of the Triffids.	John Wyndham (John Beynon Harris)
The Day of Timestop.	Philip Jose Farmer
The Day the Earth Caught Fire.	Barry Wells
The Day the Earth Froze.	Gerald Hatch
The Day the Machines Stopped.	Christopher Anvil
The Day the Oceans Overflowed.	Charles L. Fontenay
The Day the Queen Flew to Scotland for the Grouse Shooting.	Arthur Wise
The Day the World Died.	John E. Muller
The Day the World Stopped.	Stanton A. Coblentz
The Day They H-Bombed Los Angeles.	Robert Moore Williams
The Day They Invaded New York.	Ray Bradbury
Daybreak--2250 A.D.	Andre Norton
Daymares.	Fredric Brown
Days in the Hay.	John McArthur (Arthur Wise)
Dead Duck.	Patrick Macnee (Peter Leslie)
Deadline.	Patrick Macnee (Peter Leslie)
Deadly Image.	Edmund Cooper
Deadly Litter.	James White
The Deadly Sin.	Richard Macgregor
Deals with the Devil.	Allen DeGraeff & Basil Davenport
Death Is a Dream.	E. C. Tubb
The Death of Grass.	John Christopher
The Death's-Head.	Arthur Wise
The Deathstones.	E. L. Arch
Deathworld.	Harry Harrison

Deathworld 3.	Harry Harrison
Deathworld 2.	Harry Harrison
De Bracy's Drug.	Volsted Gridban (E. C. Tubb)
A Decade of Fantasy and Science Fiction.	Robert P. Mills
The Deep Fix.	James Colvin (Michael Moorcock)
The Deep Range.	Arthur C. Clarke
The Deep Reaches of Space.	A. Bertram Chandler
Deep Space.	Eric Frank Russell
Defiance.	Kenneth Bulmer
The Defiant Agents.	Andre Norton
Delusion World.	Gordon R. Dickson
The Demolished Man.	Alfred Bester
The Demon Breed.	James H. Schmitz
The Demons.	Kenneth Bulmer
Demons' World.	Kenneth Bulmer
Derai.	E. C. Tubb
The Desolate Land.	Eric M. Livesey
Destination: Infinity.	C. L. Moore & Henry Kuttner
Destination Mars.	Hugh Walters
Destination: Saturn.	Lin Carter & David Grinnell (Donald A. Wollheim)
Destination: Universe.	A. E. van Vogt
Destination: Void.	Frank Herbert
Destiny Times Three.	Fritz Leiber
Destiny's Orbit.	David Grinnell (Donald A. Wollheim)
Destroy the U.S.A.	Will F. Jenkins
The Deviates.	Raymond F. Jones
The Devil His Due.	Douglas A. Hill
Devil's Planet.	Manly Wade Wellman
Devil's Scrapbook.	Jerome Bixby
Digits and Dastards.	Frederik Pohl
Dimension of Miracles.	Robert Sheckley
The Diploids.	Katherine MacLean
The Disaster Area.	J. G. Ballard
Divide and Rule.	L. Sprague de Camp
The Diving Dames Affair.	Peter Leslie
Do Androids Dream of Electric Sheep?	Philip K. Dick
Dr. Bloodmoney.	Philip K. Dick
Dr. Caligari's Black Book.	Peter Haining
Dr. Futurity.	Philip K. Dick
Doctor Mirabilis.	James Blish
Dr. Orpheus.	Theodore Sturgeon
Doctor to the Galaxy.	A. M. Lightner
Doctor to the Stars.	Murray Leinster (Will F. Jenkins)
Doctor Who and the Crusaders.	David Whitaker
Doctor Who in an Exciting Adventure with the Daleks.	David Whitaker
The Dolphin and the Deep.	Thomas Burnett Swann
Dolphin Boy.	Roy Meyers
Dolphin Island.	Arthur C. Clarke
Dolphin Rider.	Roy Meyers
The Dolphins of Altair.	Margaret St. Clair
The Dome.	Gonner Jones

Dome Around America.   Jack Williamson
Dome World.   Dean McLaughlin
The Domes of Pico.   Hugh Walters
Donovan's Brain.   Curt Siodmak
Doom of the Green Planet.   Emil Petaja
Doomed Planet.   Lee Sheldon
Doomed World.   R. Lionel Fanthorpe
The Doomsday Brain.   Paul Tabori
Doomsday Eve.   Robert Moore Williams
The Doomsday Men.   Kenneth Bulmer
Doomsday Morning.   C. L. Moore
Doomsday, 1999.   Paul MacTyre
Doomsday on Ajiat.   Neil R. Jones
Doomsday Wing.   George H. Smith
Doomsman.   Harlan Ellison
Doomstar.   Edmond Hamilton
The Door into Summer.   Robert A. Heinlein
The Door Through Space.   Marion Zimmer Bradley
Doorway into Time.   Sam Moskowitz
The Double Invaders.   John Rackham
The Double-Minded Man.   E. L. Arch
Double Star.   Robert A. Heinlein
Down to Earth.   Louis Charbonneau
The Downstairs Room.   Kate Wilhelm
Dracula.   Otto O. Binder & Craig Tennis
Dragon in the Sea.   Frank Herbert
The Dragon Masters.   Jack Vance
Dragonflight.   Anne McCaffrey
Dragon's Island.   Jack Williamson
Dreadful Sanctuary.   Eric Frank Russell
The Dream Master.   Roger Zelazny
The Dreaming Earth.   John Brunner
The Dreaming Jewels.   Theodore Sturgeon
The Drought.   J. G. Ballard
"The Drowned Queen".   Keith Laumer
The Drowned World.   J. G. Ballard
The Drowned World and The Wind from Nowhere.   J. G. Ballard
The Druid Stone.   Simon Majors (Gardner F. Fox)
Druids' World.   George H. Smith
Drums Along the Amazon.   Victor Norwood
The Drums of Tapajos.   S. P. Meek
Drunkard's Walk.   Frederik Pohl
Dune.   Frank Herbert
The Duplicated Man.   James Blish & Robert A. W. Lowndes
The Duplicators.   Murray Leinster (Will F. Jenkins)
The Dying Earth.   Jack Vance
Dynasty of Doom.   Charles Grey (E. C. Tubb)

E. C. Tubb-An Evaluation.   Phil Harbottle
E Pluribus Unicorn.   Theodore Sturgeon
ESPer.   James Blish
The Earth Gods Are Coming.   Kenneth Bulmer

The Earth in Peril.	Donald A. Wollheim
The Earth Is Mine.	Luther Cox
Earth Is Room Enough.	Isaac Asimov
Earth Unaware.	Mack Reynolds
The Earth War.	Mack Reynolds
Earthblood.	Keith Laumer & Rosel George Brown
Earthbound.	Milton Lesser
Earthlight.	Arthur C. Clarke
Earthman, Come Home.	James Blish
Earthman, Go Home!	Poul Anderson
Earthman, Go Home!	Harlan Ellison
Earthman's Burden.	Poul Anderson & Gordon R. Dickson
Earthmen and Strangers.	Robert Silverberg
Earth's Last Citadel.	C. L. Moore & Henry Kuttner
Earth's Last Fortress.	A. E. van Vogt
Earth's Long Shadow.	Kenneth Bulmer
Earthworks.	Brian W. Aldiss
Echo in the Skull.	John Brunner
Echo Round His Bones.	Thomas M. Disch
Echo X.	Ben Barzman
Edgar Rice Burroughs Biblio.	Bradford M. Day
Edgar Rice Burroughs: Master of Adventure.	Richard A. Lupoff
Edge of Eternity.	John E. Muller
The Edge of Things.	William E. Barrett
Edge of Time.	David Grinnell (Donald A. Wollheim)
The Edge of Tomorrow.	Howard Fast
Editor's Choice in Science Fiction.	Sam Moskowitz
Eevalu.	Adam Lukens (Diane Detzer)
The Egg-Shaped Thing.	Christopher Hodder-Williams
Eight Against Utopia.	Douglas R. Mason
8th Annual Edition the Year's Best S-F.	Judith Merril
The Eighth Galaxy Reader.	Frederik Pohl
The Eighth Seal.	Angus MacLeod
The Eighth Stage of Fandom.	Robert Bloch
The Einstein Intersection.	Samuel R. Delany
Element 79.	Fred Hoyle
11th Annual Edition the Year's Best S-F.	Judith Merril
The Eleventh Commandment.	Lester del Rey
Elidor.	Alan Garner
Ellison Wonderland.	Harlan Ellison
The Emerald Elephant Gambit.	Larry Maddock
Empire.	Clifford D. Simak
Empire of Chaos.	H. K. Bulmer
Empire of the Atom.	A. E. van Vogt
Empire Star.	Samuel R. Delany
Empress of Outer Space.	A. Bertram Chandler
Encounter.	J. Hunter Holly
Encounter in Space.	H. K. Bulmer
Encounters with Aliens.	George W. Earley
The End of Eternity.	Isaac Asimov

End of the World.	Dean Owen
The End of the World.	Donald A. Wollheim
The Endless Orgy.	Richard E. Geis
Endless Shadow.	John Brunner
Enemies from Beyond.	Keith Laumer
The Enemy of My Enemy.	Avram Davidson
The Enemy Stars.	Poul Anderson
England Swings SF.	Judith Merril
Enigma from Tantalus.	John Brunner
Ensign Flandry.	Poul Anderson
Enslaved Brains.	Eando Binder (Otto O. Binder & Earl Andrew Binder)
Enterprise 2115.	Charles Grey (E. C. Tubb)
Envoy to New Worlds.	Keith Laumer
Envoy to the Dog Star.	Frederick L. Shaw, Jr.
Equator.	Brian W. Aldiss
Escape Across the Cosmos.	Gardner F. Fox
The Escape Orbit.	James White
Escape to Earth.	Ivan Howard
Escape to Infinity.	Karl Zeigfreid
Escapement.	Charles Eric Maine
The Eskimo Invasion.	Hayden Howard
The Eternal Man.	Charles R. Long
The Ethical Engineer.	Harry Harrison
The Everlasting Exiles.	Wallace West
Every Boy's Book of Outer Space Stories.	T. E. Dikty
Every Boy's Book of Science Fiction.	Donald A. Wollheim
The Evil Eye.	Martin Thomas
The Evil People.	Peter Haining
The Evolution Man.	Roy Lewis
Exile and Other Tales of Fantasy.	M. A. Cummings
Exile from Xanadu.	Lan Wright
Exit Humanity.	Leo Brett
The Exorcists.	John E. Muller
Expedition to Earth.	Arthur C. Clarke
Expedition Venus.	Hugh Walters
The Expert Dreamers.	Frederik Pohl
Explorers of the Infinite.	Sam Moskowitz
Exploring Other Worlds.	Sam Moskowitz
The Extra Man.	Charles Grey (E. C. Tubb)
Extrapolasis.	Alexander Malec
Eye in the Sky.	Philip K. Dick
The Eye of Karnak.	John E. Muller
Eye of the Monster.	Andre Norton
The Eyes of Heisenberg.	Frank Herbert
The Eyes of the Overworld.	Jack Vance
F.P. 1 Does Not Reply.	Curt Siodmak
Face in the Night.	Leo Brett
The Face of Fear.	Pel Torro
The Face of X.	Robert Lionel (Lionel Roberts)
The Faceless Planet.	Leo Brett
Fahrenheit 451.	Ray Bradbury

Falcons of Narabedla.	Marion Zimmer Bradley
A Fall of Moondust.	Arthur C. Clarke
Fallen Star.	James Blish
The Falling Torch.	Algis Budrys
False Fatherland.	A. Bertram Chandler
False Night.	Algis Budrys
Famous Monster Tales.	Allen De Graeff & Basil Davenport
The Fantastic Swordsmen.	L. Sprague de Camp
The Fantastic Universe Omnibus.	Hans Stefan Santesson
Fantastic Voyage.	Isaac Asimov
Far Out.	Damon Knight
The Far-Out Worlds of A. E. van Vogt	A. E. van Vogt
The Far Reality.	Lewis Padgett (C. L. Moore & Henry Kuttner)
Far Stars.	Eric Frank Russell
A Far Sunset.	Edmund Cooper
Farewell, Earth's Bliss.	D. G. Compton
Farewell Fantastic Venus!	Brian W. Aldiss
Farewell to the Bomb.	A. C. Webb
Farmer in the Sky.	Robert A. Heinlein
Farnham's Freehold.	Robert A. Heinlein
The Farthest Reaches.	Joseph Elder
The Fatal Eggs and Other Soviet Satire.	Mirra Ginsburg
The Fatal Fire.	Kenneth Bulmer
Father of Lies.	John Brunner
Fearful Barrier.	F. G. Rayer
Fee, Fei, Fo, Fum.	John Aylesworth
Fiends.	R. Lionel Fanthorpe
5th Annual Edition the Year's Best S-F.	Judith Merril
The Fifth Galaxy Reader.	H. L. Gold
Fifth Planet.	Fred Hoyle & Geoffrey Hoyle
50 Short Science Fiction Tales.	Isaac Asimov & Groff Conklin
Fight for Life.	Murray Leinster (Will F. Jenkins)
The Final Programme.	Michael Moorcock
A Fine and Private Place.	Peter S. Beagle
The Finger in the Sky Affair.	Peter Leslie
Fire Past the Future.	Charles Eric Maine
Fireball at the Lake.	Jay Groves
The Fireclown.	Michael Moorcock
Firemantle.	R. W. Mackelworth
The First Astounding Science Fiction Anthology.	John W. Campbell
First Flight.	Damon Knight
First He Died.	Clifford D. Simak
The First Immortals.	E. L. Arch
The First of the Last.	Richard Macgregor
First on Mars.	Rex Gordon
First on the Moon.	Jeff Sutton
First on the Moon.	Hugh Walters
First Through Time.	Rex Gordon
First to the Stars.	Rex Gordon
Fish on a Hook.	Paul MacTyre

A Fistful of Digits.	Christopher Hodder-Williams
The Fittest.	J. T. McIntosh
Five Against Arlane.	Tom Purdom
Five Faces of Fear.	Trebor Thorpe
Five Galaxy Short Novels.	H. L. Gold
The Five Gold Bands.	Jack Vance
Five Tales from Tomorrow.	T. E. Dikty
Five to Twelve.	Edmund Cooper
Five Weeks in a Balloon.	Gardner F. Fox
Flame Goddess.	Lionel Roberts
Flame Mass.	R. Lionel Fanthorpe
The Flame of Iridar.	Lin Carter
Flames of Desire.	M. J. Deer (George H. Smith)
Flandry of Terra.	Poul Anderson
Flesh.	Philip Jose Farmer
The Fleshpots of Sansato.	William F. Temple
Flight from Yesterday.	Robert Moore Williams
Flight from Youth.	William E. Barrett
Flight into Space.	Donald A. Wollheim
Flight into Yesterday.	Charles L. Harness
Flowers for Algernon.	Daniel Keyes
The Flying Eyes.	J. Hunter Holly
Flying High.	Dewey C. Brookins
The Flying Saucer Gambit.	Larry Maddock
Flying Saucers in Fact and Fiction.	Hans Stefan Santesson
The Fools of Time.	William E. Barrett
The Forbidden.	Leo Brett
Forbidden Planet.	John E. Muller
Force 97X.	Pel Torro
The Forgetful Robot.	Paul W. Fairman
The Forgotten Planet.	Murray Leinster (Will F. Jenkins)
The Forgotten Planet.	George H. Smith
The Forgotten Race.	Julius P. Newton
Formula 29X.	Pel Torro
The Fortec Conspiracy.	Edmond G. Addeo & Richard M. Garvin
Foundation.	Isaac Asimov
Foundation and Empire.	Isaac Asimov
The Foundation Trilogy.	Isaac Asimov
Four Came Back.	Martin Caidin
The Four Day Weekend.	George H. Smith
The Four-Dimensional Nightmare.	J. G. Ballard
Four for Tomorrow.	Roger Zelazny
Four from Planet 5.	Murray Leinster (Will F. Jenkins)
Four-Sided Triangle.	William F. Temple
The Fourth Galaxy Reader.	H. L. Gold
The Fox, the Dog, and the Griffin.	Poul Anderson & Christian Molbech
A Frederik Pohl Omnibus.	Frederik Pohl
The Frighteners.	Peter Leslie
From Carthage Then I Came.	Douglas R. Mason
From Frankenstein to Andromeda.	James Goldie Brown
From Off This World.	Leo Margulies & Oscar J. Friend
From Outer Space.	Hal Clement

From Outer Space.	Mildred E. Danforth
From Realms Beyond.	Leo Brett
From the Land of Fear.	Harlan Ellison
From the Oceans, from the Stars.	Arthur C. Clarke
From Unknown Worlds.	John W. Campbell
Frontiers in Space.	T. E. Dikty & Everett F. Bleiler
Froomb!	John Lymington
Frozen Planet.	Pel Torro
The Frozen Year.	James Blish
Fugitive of the Stars.	Edmond Hamilton
Fugitive of Time.	Volsted Gridban (E. C. Tubb)
Full Circle.	Bruce Ariss
Fur Magic.	Andre Norton
The Furies.	Keith Roberts
The Furious Future.	Algis Budrys
Fury.	C. L. Moore & Henry Kuttner
The Fury from Earth.	Dean McLaughlin
The Fury Out of Time.	Lloyd Biggle, Jr.
Future for Sale.	Richard Saxon
Future Imperfect.	James E. Gunn
The Future Makers.	Peter Haining
Future Perfect.	H. Bruce Franklin
Future Tense.	Richard A. Curtis
Future Tense.	Jack Vance
Gadget City.	I. O. Evans
The Galactic Breed.	Leigh Brackett
Galactic Cluster.	James Blish
Galactic Derelict.	Andre Norton
Galactic Diplomat.	Keith Laumer
Galactic Intrigue.	H. K. Bulmer
Galactic Odyssey.	Keith Laumer
The Galactic Troubadours.	A. M. Lightner
Galaxies Like Grains of Sand.	Brian W. Aldiss
Galaxy of Ghouls.	Judith Merril
The Galaxy Reader of Science Fiction.	H. L. Gold
The Galaxy Science Fiction Omnibus.	H. L. Gold
Galaxy 666.	Pel Torro
The Game-Players of Titan.	Philip K. Dick
The Games of Neith.	Margaret St. Clair
The Gantry Episode.	June Drummond
The Ganymede Takeover.	Philip K. Dick & Ray Nelson
The Garamas Affair.	John Rankine (Douglas R. Mason)
Garbage World.	Charles Platt
The Garthians.	Decima Leach
The Gate of Time.	Philip Jose Farmer
The Gate of Worlds.	Robert Silverberg
The Gates of Creation.	Philip Jose Farmer
Gateway to Elsewhere.	Murray Leinster (Will F. Jenkins)
Gateway to the Stars.	John Carnell
Gateway to Tomorrow.	John Carnell.
Gath.	E. C. Tubb

Gather, Darkness.	Fritz Leiber
The Genetic General.	Gordon R. Dickson
The Genocides.	Thomas M. Disch
Gentleman Junkie.	Harlan Ellison
The Gentlewomen of Evil.	Peter Haining
Get Off My World!	Murray Leinster (Will F. Jenkins)
Get Out of My Sky.	Leo Margulies
The Ghosts of Manacle.	Charles G. Finney
The Giant Anthology of Science Fiction.	Leo Margulies & Oscar J. Friend
The Giant Killer.	Chapman Pincher
The Giant Stumbles.	John Lymington
Giants from Eternity.	Manly Wade Wellman
A Gift from Mars.	Jack Williamson & Miles J. Breuer
Girl from Tomorrow.	Karl Zeigfreid
The Girls from Planet 5.	Richard Wilson
Gladiator-at-Law.	Frederik Pohl & C. M. Kornbluth
The Glass Cage.	Adam Lukens (Diane Detzer)
A Glass of Stars.	Robert F. Young
Glide Path.	Arthur C. Clarke
Glory Planet.	A. Bertram Chandler
Glory Road.	Robert A. Heinlein
The Glory That Was.	L. Sprague de Camp
A Gnome There Was.	Lewis Padgett (C. L. Moore & Henry Kuttner)
The Goblin Reservation.	Clifford D. Simak
The Goblin Tower.	L. Sprague de Camp
The Goblin Tower.	Frank Belknap Long
The God Machine.	Martin Caidin
The Goddess of Ganymede.	Michael D. Resnick
Godling, Go Home!	Robert Silverberg
Gods for Tomorrow.	Hans Stefan Santesson
The Gods Hate Kansas.	Joseph Millard
Gods of Darkness.	Karl Zeigfreid
"The Gold Bomb".	Keith Laumer
A Golden Anniversary Bibliography of Edgar Rice Burroughs. .	Hardy Heins
The Golden Apples of the Sun.	Ray Bradbury
Golden Blood.	Jack Williamson
The Golden Chalice.	R. Lionel Fanthorpe
The Golden Goddess Gambit.	Larry Maddock
The Golden People.	Fred Saberhagen
The Gooney Bird.	William C. Anderson
The Gray Aliens.	J. Hunter Holly
Gray Magic.	Andre Norton
The Great Explosion.	Eric Frank Russell
The Great Gold Steal.	Ted White
The Great Leap Backwards.	Robert Green
Great Science-Fiction.	Tony Licata
Great Science Fiction About Doctors.	Noah D. Fabricant & Groff Conklin
Great Science Fiction Adventures.	Larry T. Shaw
Great Science Fiction Stories.	Cornelia Titcomb Smith
Great Science Fiction Stories About Mars.	T. E. Dikty

Great Science Fiction Stories About the Moon.	T. E. Dikty
Great Stories of Science Fiction.	Murray Leinster (Will F. Jenkins)
The Great Time Machine Hoax.	Keith Laumer
The Green Brain.	Frank Herbert
The Green Drift.	John Lymington
The Green Girl.	Jack Williamson
The Green Hills of Earth.	Robert A. Heinlein
The Green Millenium.	Fritz Leiber
The Green Odyssey.	Philip Jose Farmer
The Green Planet.	J. Hunter Holly
The Green Queen.	Margaret St. Clair
The Green Rain.	Paul Tabori
Greener Than You Think.	Ward Moore
The Greks Bring Gifts.	Murray Leinster (Will F. Jenkins)
The Grey Ones.	John Lymington
Greybeard.	Brian W. Aldiss
Greylorn.	Keith Laumer
The Grip of Fear.	Vern Hansen
Guardians of Time.	Poul Anderson
A Gun For Dinosaur.	L. Sprague de Camp
Gunner Cade.	Cyril Judd (Judith Merril & Cyril M. Kornbluth)
H-Bomb Over America.	Jeff Sutton
The Halo Highway.	Rafe Bernard
The Hamelin Plague.	A. Bertram Chandler
The Hand of Cain.	Martin Thomas
Hand of Doom.	R. Lionel Fanthorpe
Hand of Havoc.	Charles Grey (E. C. Tubb)
The Hand of Zei.	L. Sprague de Camp
A Handful of Darkness.	Philip K. Dick
The Haploids.	Jerry Sohl
The Haunted Stars.	Edmond Hamilton
Hauser's Memory.	Curt Siodmak
Have Space Suit--Will Travel.	Robert A. Heinlein
Hawksbill Station.	Robert Silverberg
He Owned the World.	Charles Eric Maine
The Heaven Makers.	Frank Herbert
Heinlein in Dimension.	Alexei Panshin
A Heinlein Triad.	Robert A. Heinlein
Helen.	E. V. Cunningham (Howard Fast)
Hell for Tomorrow.	Peter Leslie
The Hell of Mirrors.	Peter Haining
The Hell Planet.	E. C. Tubb
Hell's Pavement.	Damon Knight
The Hendon Fungus.	J. Parker-Rich
The Hidden Planet.	Donald A. Wollheim
Hidden World.	Stanton A. Coblentz
The High Crusade.	Poul Anderson
High Vacuum.	Charles Eric Maine
The Hole in the Zero.	M. K. Joseph
Home Is the Martian.	Philip Kent (H. K. Bulmer)
Honeymoon in Hell.	Fredric Brown
The Horn of Time.	Poul Anderson
The Horror Expert.	Frank Belknap Long

The Horror from the Hills.	Frank Belknap Long
Horror in the Night.	Richard Macgregor
The Horror on the Asteroid.	Edmond Hamilton
Horror-7.	Robert Bloch
Horror Times Ten.	Alden H. Norton
Hospital Station.	James White
Hothouse.	Brian W. Aldiss
The Hounds of Tindalos.	Frank Belknap Long
The Hour of the Phoenix.	Richard Saxon
The House of the Hatchet.	Robert Bloch
The House That Stood Still.	A. E. van Vogt
The Houses of Iszm.	Jack Vance
How Many Blocks on the Pile?	David Meltzer
How Now Brown Cow.	John McArthur (Arthur Wise)
The Hugo Winners.	Isaac Asimov
Human?	Judith Merril
Human and Other Beings.	Allen De Graeff
The Human Angle.	William Tenn
The Human Zero.	Roger Elwood & Sam Moskowitz
The Humanoids.	Jack Williamson
The 100th Millenium.	John Brunner
Hunter and the Trap.	Howard Fast
The Hunter Out of Time.	Gardner F. Fox
Hunters of Space.	Joseph E. Kelleam
Huon of the Horn.	Andre Norton
Hydrosphere.	A. J. Merak
Hyper-Drive.	Matthew Grant
Hyperspace.	R. Lionel Fanthorpe
I Am Legend.	Richard Matheson
I Fight for Mars.	Charles Grey (E. C. Tubb)
I Have No Mouth, and I Must Scream.	Harlan Ellison
I Love Galesburg in the Springtime.	Jack Finney
I, Robot.	Isaac Asimov
I Speak for Earth.	Keith Woodcott (John Brunner)
I, the Machine.	Paul W. Fairman
I Want the Stars.	Tom Purdom
Iceworld.	Hal Clement
The If Reader of Science Fiction.	Frederik Pohl
If the South Had Won the Civil War.	MacKinlay Kantor
If This Goes On.	Charles Nuetzel
The Illustrated Man.	Ray Bradbury
The Image of the Beast.	Philip Jose Farmer
Imagination Unlimited.	T. E. Dikty & Everett F. Bleiler
The Immortal Storm.	Sam Moskowitz
Immortality Delivered.	Robert Sheckley
Immortality, Inc.	Robert Sheckley
The Immortals.	Leo Brett '
The Immortals.	James E. Gunn
Impact-20.	William F. Nolan
Implosion.	D. F. Jones
Impossible?	Laurence M. Janifer
The Impossible Man.	J. G. Ballard
The Impossibles.	Mark Phillips (Randall Garrett & Laurence M. Janifer)

In Deep.	Damon Knight
In Memoriam: Clark Ashton Smith.	Jack L. Chalker
In Search of Wonder.	Damon Knight
In the Beginning.	John E. Muller
The In-World.	Lionel Roberts
The Incomplete Enchanter.	L. Sprague de Camp & Fletcher Pratt
The Incredible Planet.	John W. Campbell
The Index of Science Fiction Magazines 1951-1965.	Norm Metcalf
Index to the Australian Science Fiction Magazines Part 1.	Graham Brice Stone
Index to the Australian Science Fiction Magazines Part 2.	Graham Brice Stone
The Index to the Science-Fantasy Publishers.	Jack L. Chalker & Mark Owings
An Index to the Weird and Fantastica in Magazines.	Bradford M. Day
The Infinite Brain.	Charles R. Long
The Infinite Moment.	John Wyndham (John Beynon Harris)
The Infinite Worlds of Maybe.	Lester del Rey
Infinity Machine.	John E. Muller
Inherit the Earth.	Claude Nunes
The Insect Warriors.	Rex Dean Levie
The Inseperables.	Russell Braddon
Inside Outside.	Philip Jose Farmer
The Interpreter.	Brian W. Aldiss
Interstellar Two-Five.	John Rankine (Douglas R. Mason)
Into Plutonian Depths.	Stanton A. Coblentz
Into the Alternate Universe.	A. Bertram Chandler
Into the Slave Nebula.	John Brunner
Introducing SF.	Brian W. Aldiss
The Intruders.	Bron Fane
Invader on My Back.	Philip E. High
The Invaders.	Keith Laumer
The Invaders Are Coming.	Alan E. Nourse & J. A. Meyer
Invaders from Earth.	Robert Silverberg
Invaders from the Infinite.	John W. Campbell
Invaders of Space.	Murray Leinster (Will F. Jenkins)
The Invading Asteroid.	Manly Wade Wellman
The Invasion.	John Hay
Invasion from 2500.	Norman Edwards (Terry Carr & Ted White)
Invasion of the Robots.	Roger Elwood
Invisible Barriers.	David Osborne (Robert Silverberg)
The Invisible Eye.	Paul Tabori
Invisible Men.	Allen De Graeff & Basil Davenport
The Iron and the Anger.	F. G. Rayer
The Iron Thorn.	Algis Budrys
An Isaac Asimov Omnibus.	Isaac Asimov
Island in the Sky.	Manly Wade Wellman
The Island of Creeping Death.	Victor Norwood

Island of Fear.	William Sambrot
Islands in the Sky.	Arthur C. Clarke
Islands of Space.	John W. Campbell
The Isotope Man.	Charles Eric Maine
The Issue at Hand.	William Atheling, Jr. (James Blish)
It.	Theodore Sturgeon
It Was the Day of the Robot.	Frank Belknap Long
It's a Mad, Mad, Mad Galaxy.	Keith Laumer
Jack of Eagles.	James Blish
The Jewel in the Skull.	Michael Moorcock
The Jewels of Aptor.	Samuel R. Delany
The Jewels of Elsewhen.	Ted White
Jinn and Jitters.	John Carnell
Jizzle.	John Wyndham (John Beynon Harris)
John Carstairs, Space Detective.	Frank Belknap Long
John Russell Fearn--An Evaluation.	Phil Harbottle
A John Wyndham Omnibus.	John Wyndham (John Beynon Harris)
Journey Beyond Tomorrow.	Robert Sheckley
Journey into Darkness.	Frank Belknap Long
Journey into Space.	Charles Chilton
Journey to Jupiter.	Hugh Walters
Journey to Mars.	E. C. Tubb
Journey to the Stars.	F. G. Rayer
Journeys in Science Fiction.	Richard L. Loughlin & Lilian M. Popp
The Joy Makers.	James E. Gunn
Joyleg.	Avram Davidson & Ward Moore
The Joyous Invasions.	Theodore Sturgeon
Judgment Night.	C. L. Moore
The Judgment of Eve.	Edgar Pangborn
Judgment on Janus.	Andre Norton
Juggernaut.	Bron Fane
Jules Verne and His Work.	I. O. Evans
Jules Verne: Master of Science Fiction.	I. O. Evans
Jupiter Equilateral.	John Rackham
The Kar-Chee Reign.	Avram Davidson
Key Out of Time.	Andre Norton
The Key to Irunium.	Kenneth Bulmer
The Key to Venudine.	Kenneth Bulmer
The Killer Thing.	Kate Wilhelm
The Killing Machine.	Jack Vance
The Killing Thing.	Kate Wilhelm
The King and Four Queens.	Theodore Sturgeon
King Kull.	Lin Carter & Robert E. Howard
King of the Fourth Planet.	Robert Moore Williams
King of the World's Edge.	H. Warner Munn
King's Daughter.	Jane Gaskell
Kings of Infinite Space.	Nigel Balchin
Konga.	Dean Owen
The Kraken Wakes.	John Wyndham (John Beynon Harris)

The Ladder in the Sky.	Keith Woodcott (John Brunner)
Ladies' Day and This Crowded Earth.	Robert Bloch
Lady in Danger.	Jack Williamson
Laird of Evil.	Martin Thomas
Lambda 1 and Other Stories.	John Carnell
A Lamp for Medusa.	William Tenn
The Lampton Dreamers.	L. P. Davies
Land Beyond the Map.	Kenneth Bulmer
Land of the Giants.	Murray Leinster (Will F. Jenkins)
The Land of Unreason.	L. Sprague de Camp & Fletcher Pratt
Landfall Is a State of Mind.	Douglas R. Mason
The Languages of Pao.	Jack Vance
The Lani People.	J. F. Bone
The Last Astronaut.	Pel Torro
The Last Castle.	Jack Vance
Last Door to Aiya.	Mirra Ginsburg
The Last Fathom.	Martin Caidin
The Last Hope of Earth.	Lan Wright
The Last Leap.	Daniel F. Galouye
Last Man on Earth.	Bron Fane
The Last of the Great Race.	Stanton A. Coblentz
The Last Planet.	Andre Norton
The Last Spaceship.	Murray Leinster (Will F. Jenkins)
The Last Starship from Earth.	John Boyd
The Last Unicorn.	Peter S. Beagle
The Last Valkyrie.	Lionel Roberts
Legend of Lost Earth.	G. McDonald Wallis
Legends for the Dark.	Peter Haining
The Legion of Space.	Jack Williamson
The Legion of the Lost.	Pel Torro
The Legion of Time.	Jack Williamson
Lest Darkness Fall.	L. Sprague de Camp
Lest Earth Be Conquered.	Frank Belknap Long
Lest We Forget Thee, Earth.	Calvin M. Knox (Robert Silverberg)
Let the Spacemen Beware!	Poul Anderson
Level Seven.	Mordecai Roshwald
A Life for the Stars.	James Blish
The Light Benders.	Jonathan Chance
Light of Lilith.	G. McDonald Wallis
Light of Mars.	Paul Charkin
Lightning World.	Trebor Thorpe
The Lights in the Sky Are Stars.	Fredric Brown
The Lincoln Hunters.	Wilson Tucker
Line to Tomorrow.	Lewis Padgett (C. L. Moore & Henry Kuttner)
The Lion of Commare and Against The Fall of Night.	Arthur C. Clarke
Listen! The Stars!	John Brunner
The Little Fishes.	Arthur Wise
The Little Men.	Joseph E. Kelleam
The Little People.	John Christopher

The Living Demons.	Robert Bloch
The Living Gem.	Paul Charkin
Living Way Out.	Wyman Guin
The Living World.	Carl Maddox (E. C. Tubb)
The Lizard Lords.	Stanton A. Coblentz
The Loafers of Refuge.	Joseph L. Green
Logan's Run.	George Clayton Johnson & William F. Nolan
The Long Afternoon of Earth.	Brian W. Aldiss
The Long Loud Silence.	Wilson Tucker
The Long Result.	John Brunner
The Long Tomorrow.	Leigh Brackett
The Long Winter.	John Christopher
Looking Forward.	Milton Lesser
Lord of Light.	Roger Zelazny
The Lord of Nardos.	Russ Winterbotham
Lord of the Green Planet.	Emil Petaja
Lord of Thunder.	Andre Norton
Lord of Tranerica.	Stanton A. Coblentz
Lords of Atlantis.	Wallace West
Lords of Creation.	Eando Binder (Otto O. Binder)
Lords of the Psychon.	Daniel F. Galouye
Lords of the Starship.	Mark S. Geston
The Lost Comet.	Stanton A. Coblentz
Lost in Space.	Ron Archer (Ted White) & Dave Van Arnam
Lost Legacy.	Robert A. Heinlein
The Lost Millenium.	Leigh Richmond & Walt Richmond
The Lost Ones.	Ian Cameron
The Lost Perception.	Daniel F. Galouye
Lost Race of Mars.	Robert Silverberg
Love Ain't Nothing But Sex Misspelled.	Harlan Ellison
Love in Time.	Johnson Harris (John Beynon Harris)
The Lovers.	Philip Jose Farmer
Lovers: 2075.	Charles English (Charles Nuetzel)
Lucky Starr and the Big Sun of Mercury.	Paul French (Isaac Asimov)
Lucky Starr and the Moons of Jupiter.	Paul French (Isaac Asimov)
Lucky Starr and the Oceans of Venus.	Paul French (Isaac Asimov)
Lucky Starr and the Pirates of the Asteroids.	Paul French (Isaac Asimov)
Lucky Starr and the Rings of Saturn.	Paul French (Isaac Asimov)
The Lunar Eye.	Robert Moore Williams.
The Macabre Ones.	Bron Fane
The Macabre Reader.	Donald A. Wollheim
The Machine in Ward Eleven.	Charles Willeford
The Machineries of Joy.	Ray Bradbury
The Mad God's Amulet.	Michael Moorcock
The Mad Metropolis	Philip E. High

The Mad Scientist Affair	John T. Phillifent (John Rackham)
The Magnificent MacInnes.	Shepherd Mead
The Main Experiment.	Christopher Hodder-Williams
Make Room! Make Room!	Harry Harrison
The Maker of Universes.	Philip Jose Farmer
The Making of Star Trek.	Gene Roddenberry & Stephen E. Whitfield
The Male Response.	Brian W. Aldiss
Man Against Tomorrow.	William F. Nolan
A Man Called Destiny.	Lan Wright
The Man from Beyond.	John E. Muller
The Man from Genoa.	Frank Belknap Long
The Man from P.I.G.	Harry Harrison
The Man from Tomorrow.	Wilson Tucker
The Man in the High Castle.	Philip K. Dick
A Man Obsessed.	Alan E. Nourse
A Man of Double Deed.	Leonard Daventry
Man of Earth.	Algis Budrys
Man of Two Worlds.	Raymond F. Jones
The Man Who Ate the World.	Frederik Pohl
The Man Who Conquered Time.	John E. Muller
The Man Who Couldn't Sleep.	Charles Eric Maine
The Man Who Fell to Earth.	Walter S. Tevis, Jr.
The Man Who Japed.	Philip K. Dick
The Man Who Owned the World.	Charles Eric Maine
The Man Who Saw Tomorrow.	Jeff Sutton
The Man Who Sold the Moon.	Robert A. Heinlein
The Man Who Upset the Universe	Isaac Asimov
The Man Who Wanted Stars.	Dean McLaughlin
The Man Who Wasn't There.	Beryl Whitaker
The Man Whose Name Wouldn't Fit.	Theodore Tyler
The Man with Three Eyes.	E. L. Arch
Mankind on the Run.	Gordon R. Dickson
Mankind Under the Leash.	Thomas M. Disch
The Many Worlds of Magnus Ridolph.	Jack Vance
March of the Robots.	Leo Brett
Mark of the Beast.	John E. Muller
Marooned.	Martin Caidin
Marooned on Mars.	Lester del Rey
Mars Is My Destination.	Frank Belknap Long
The Mars Monopoly.	Jerry Sohl
The Martian Chronicles.	Ray Bradbury
Martian Enterprise.	Clifford C. Reed
The Martian Missile.	David Grinnell (Donald A. Wollheim)
The Martian Sphinx.	Keith Woodcott (John Brunner)
Martian Time-Slip.	Philip K. Dick
The Martian Visitors.	Frank Belknap Long
The Martian Way.	Isaac Asimov
Martians, Go Home.	Fredric Brown
Martin Magnus on Mars.	William F. Temple
Martin Magnus on Venus.	William F. Temple
Martin Magnus, Planet Rover.	William F. Temple
The Maru Invasion.	Luan Ranzetta
The Masks of Time.	Robert Silverberg

Master of Life and Death.	Robert Silverberg
Master of Space.	Arthur C. Clarke
Master Weed.	John Rackham
Masterpieces of Science Fiction.	Sam Moskowitz
Masters' Choice.	Laurence M. Janifer
Masters of Evolution.	Damon Knight
Masters of Horror.	Alden H. Norton
Masters of the Maze.	Avram Davidson
The Masters of Time.	A. E. van Vogt
Masters of Time and The Changeling.	A. E. van Vogt
The Mating Center.	Frank Belknap Long
The Mating Cry.	A. E. van Vogt
A Matter of Blood.	Beryl Whitaker
Mayday Orbit.	Poul Anderson
The Mechanical Monarch.	E. C. Tubb
A Medicine for Melancholy.	Ray Bradbury
Meeting at Infinity.	John Brunner
Memoirs of a Spacewoman.	Naomi Mitchison
The Memory Bank.	Wallace West
Men and Machines.	Robert Silverberg
The Men from Arcturus.	Russ Winterbotham
The Men in the Jungle.	Norman Spinrad
Men Into Space.	Murray Leinster (Will F. Jenkins)
Men, Martians, and Machines.	Eric Frank Russell
Men on the Moon.	Donald A. Wollheim
Men Who Die Twice.	Peter Heath
The Menace from Earth.	Robert A. Heinlein
Menace from the Moon.	Hugh Walters
Menace from the Past.	Carl Maddox (E. C. Tubb)
Mercenary from Tomorrow.	Mack Reynolds
Mercy Island.	Etta Bowden & Phil Bowden
The Mercy Men.	Alan E. Nourse
Message from the Eocene.	Margaret St. Clair
The Metal Eater.	Roy Sheldon (E. C. Tubb)
The Metal Smile.	Damon Knight
The Meteor Men.	Anthony Le Baron (Keith Laumer)
Methuselah's Children.	Robert A. Heinlein
Micro Infinity.	John E. Muller
Microscopic God.	Sam Moskowitz
The Microscopic Ones.	Leo Brett
Midge.	Paul MacTyre
The Midnight People.	Peter Haining
The Midwich Cuckoos.	John Wyndham (John Beynon Harris)
The Mightiest Machine.	John W. Campbell
Mike Mars and the Mystery Satellite.	Donald A. Wollheim
Mike Mars Around the Moon.	Donald A. Wollheim
Mike Mars, Astronaut.	Donald A. Wollheim
Mike Mars at Cape Canaveral.	Donald A. Wollheim
Mike Mars at Cape Kennedy.	Donald A. Wollheim
Mike Mars Flies the Dyna-Soar.	Donald A. Wollheim
Mike Mars Flies the X-15.	Donald A. Wollheim
Mike Mars in Orbit.	Donald A. Wollheim
Mike Mars, South Pole Spaceman.	Donald A. Wollheim
The Mile-Long Spaceship.	Kate Wilhelm
The Million Cities.	J. T. McIntosh

The Million Year Hunt.	Kenneth Bulmer
The Mind Benders.	James Kennaway
The Mind Brothers.	Peter Heath
The Mind Cage.	A. E. van Vogt
Mind Force.	Leo Brett
The Mind Killers.	Martin Thomas
The Mind Makers.	John E. Muller
The Mind Masters.	Arthur C. Clarke
The Mind Monsters.	Howard L. Cory (Julie Ann Jardine & Larry Maddock)
The Mind of Mr. Soames.	Charles Eric Maine
Mind Partner and Eight Other Novelets.	H. L. Gold
The Mind Spider.	Fritz Leiber
Mind Switch.	Damon Knight
The Mind Thing.	Fredric Brown
The Mind Traders.	J. Hunter Holly
Mindswap.	Robert Sheckley
The Mindwarpers.	Eric Frank Russell
Miners in the Sky.	Murray Leinster (Will F. Jenkins)
Mirage on Lovecraft.	Jack L. Chalker
A Mirror for Observers.	Edgar Pangborn
Mirror Image.	Bruce Duncan
Mission of Gravity.	Hal Clement
Mission to a Star.	Frank Belknap Long
Mission to Mercury.	Hugh Walters
Mission to the Heart Stars.	James Blish
Mission to the Moon.	Lester del Rey
Mission to the Stars.	Philip Kent (H. K. Bulmer)
Mission to the Stars.	A. E. van Vogt
Mission to Universe.	Gordon R. Dickson
Mists of Dawn.	Chad Oliver
The Mixed Men.	A. E. van Vogt
Modern Masterpieces of Science Fiction.	Sam Moskowitz
Modern Science Fiction: Its Meaning and Its Future.	R. Bretnor
The Mogul Men.	Peter Leslie
The Mohole Mystery.	Hugh Walters
The Monitors.	Keith Laumer
Monkman Comes Down.	Eric C. Williams
The Monster from World's End.	Murray Leinster (Will F. Jenkins)
The Monster Wheel Affair.	David McDaniel
Monsters.	A. E. van Vogt
Monsters and Such.	Murray Leinster (Will F. Jenkins)
Monsters in Orbit.	Jack Vance
The Monsters of Juntonheim.	Edmond Hamilton
Moon Base.	E. C. Tubb
Moon Base One.	Hugh Walters
The Moon Is a Harsh Mistress.	Robert A. Heinlein
The Moon Is Hell!	John W. Campbell
The Moon Man.	A. J. Steiger
The Moon of Gomrath.	Alan Garner

Moon of Mutiny.	Lester del Rey
Moon of Three Rings.	Andre Norton
The Moon People.	Stanton A. Coblentz
Moon Rocket.	John E. Muller
Moondust.	Thomas Burnett Swann
Moonspin.	Elmer J. Carpenter
More Adventures on Other Planets.	Donald A. Wollheim
More Macabre.	Donald A. Wollheim
More Nightmares.	Robert Bloch
More Penguin Science Fiction.	Brian W. Aldiss
More Terror in the Modern Vein.	Donald A. Wollheim
More Than Human.	Theodore Sturgeon
Mortals and Monsters.	Lester del Rey
The Multi-Man.	Phil Harbottle
Murder in the Clinic.	Edmond Hamilton
Murder Madness.	Will F. Jenkins
The Murder of the U.S.A.	Will F. Jenkins
Murder with Menaces.	Vern Hansen
A Murray Leinster Omnibus.	Murray Leinster (Will F. Jenkins)
Musrum.	A. Earnshaw & Eric Thacker
Mutant.	C. L. Moore & Henry Kuttner
The Mutant Weapon.	Murray Leinster (Will F. Jenkins)
The Mutants.	Kris Neville
The Mutants Rebel.	E. C. Tubb
Mutiny in Space.	Avram Davidson
My Beloved Troshanus.	Mary Conway Kloor
My Best Science Fiction Story.	Leo Margulies & Oscar J. Friend
My Blond Princess of Space.	John N. Will
The Mystery of the Third Mine.	Robert A. W. Lowndes
The Naked Lunch.	William Burroughs
The Naked Sun.	Isaac Asimov
Naked to the Stars.	Gordon R. Dickson
Natives of Space.	Hal Clement
Nebula Alert.	A. Bertram Chandler
Nebula Award Stories 1965.	Damon Knight
Nebula Award Stories Three.	Roger Zelazny
Nebula Award Stories Two.	Brian W. Aldiss & Harry Harrison
Necromancer.	Gordon R. Dickson
The Necronomicon: A Study.	Jack C. Chalker & Mark Owings
Needle.	Hal Clement
Needle in a Timestack.	Robert Silverberg
Negative Minus.	R. Lionel Fanthorpe
The Negative Ones.	John E. Muller
Nemesis.	Bron Fane
The Nemesis from Terra.	Leigh Brackett
Nerves.	Lester del Rey
Neuron World.	R. Lionel Fanthorpe
Neutron Star.	Larry Niven
Never Let Up.	Charles Eric Maine
Never the Same Door.	John Rankine (Douglas R. Mason)

Title	Author
The Nevermore Affair.	Kate Wilhelm
New Dreams This Morning.	James Blish
The New H. P. Lovecraft Bibliography.	Jack L. Chalker
New Maps of Hell.	Kingsley Amis
The New Minds.	Dan Morgan
New Worlds of Fantasy.	Terry Carr
New Writings in SF 1.	John Carnell
New Writings in SF 2.	John Carnell
New Writings in SF 3.	John Carnell
New Writings in SF 4.	John Carnell
New Writings in SF 5.	John Carnell
New Writings in SF 6.	John Carnell
New Writings in SF 7.	John Carnell
New Writings in SF 8.	John Carnell
New Writings in SF 9.	John Carnell
New Writings in SF 10.	John Carnell
New Writings in SF 11.	John Carnell
New Writings in SF 12.	John Carnell
New Writings in SF 13.	John Carnell
News from Elsewhere.	Edmund Cooper
Next Door to the Sun.	Stanton A. Coblentz
Next of Kin.	Eric Frank Russell
Next Stop, Mars!	David Edwards
Next Stop the Stars.	Robert Silverberg
A Nice Day for Screaming.	James H. Schmitz
Night of Light.	Philip Jose Farmer
Night of Masks.	Andre Norton
Night of the Big Fire.	John E. Muller
Night of the Big Heat.	John Lymington
Night of the Black Horror.	Victor Norwood
Night of the Death Rain.	Luan Ranzetta
The Night of the Puddly.	Clifford D. Simak
The Night of the Trilobites.	Peter Leslie
The Night of the Wolf.	Fritz Leiber
The Night Shapes.	James Blish
Night Slaves.	Jerry Sohl
The Night Spiders.	John Lymington
Night Walk.	Bob Shaw
The Night Walker.	Robert Bloch
Nightmare.	Leo Brett
Nightmares.	Robert Bloch
Nightmares and Geezenstacks.	Fredric Brown
Night's Black Agents.	Fritz Leiber
The Nine Billion Names of God.	Arthur C. Clarke
Nine by Laumer.	Keith Laumer
Nine Tomorrows.	Isaac Asimov
1976--Year of Terror.	George H. Smith
9th Annual Edition the Year's Best S-F.	Judith Merril
The Ninth Galaxy Reader.	Frederik Pohl
No Blade of Grass.	John Christopher
No Boundaries.	C. L. Moore & Henry Kuttner
No Dawn and No Horizon.	A. J. Merak
No Future in It.	John Brunner

No Lack of Space.	David S. Martin
No Limits.	Joseph W. Ferman
No Man Friday.	Rex Gordon
No Man on Earth.	Walter Moudy
No Man's World.	Kenneth Bulmer
No Man's World.	Martin Caidin
No Other Gods But Me.	John Brunner
No Place Like Earth.	John Carnell
No Place on Earth.	Louis Charbonneau
No Room for Man.	Gordon R. Dickson
No Stars for Us.	Robert Ray
No Time Like Tomorrow.	Brian W. Aldiss
No Truce with Terra.	Philip E. High
No Way Back.	Karl Zeigfreid
No World of Their Own.	Poul Anderson
The Noman Way.	J. T. McIntosh
The Non-Statistical Man.	Raymond F. Jones
Non-Stop.	Brian W. Aldiss
Northwest of Earth.	C. L. Moore
Not Before Time.	John Brunner
The Not-Men.	Jack Williamson
Not Without a Bang.	Chapman Pincher
Not Without Sorcery.	Theodore Sturgeon
Notions: Unlimited.	Robert Sheckley
Nova.	Samuel P. Delany
Nova Express.	William Burroughs
Novelets of Science Fiction.	Ivan Howard
Now Then!	John Brunner
Now Wait for Last Year.	Philip K. Dick
Octagon Magic.	Andre Norton
The October Country.	Ray Bradbury
October the First Is Too Late.	Fred Hoyle
Odd Science Fiction.	Frank Belknap Long
The Odious Ones.	Jerry Sohl
Odyssey to Earthdeath.	Leo P. Kelley
Of All Possible Worlds.	William Tenn
Of Earth Foretold.	Kenneth Bulmer
Of Godlike Power.	Mack Reynolds
Of Men and Monsters.	William Tenn
Of Mice and Murder.	Beryl Whitaker
Off Center.	Damon Knight
Off the Beaten Orbit.	Judith Merril
The Off-Worlders.	John Baxter
The Old China Hands.	Charles G. Finney
The Old Die Rich.	H. L. Gold
The Old Man of Mow.	Alan Garner
Omha Abides.	C. C. MacApp
Omnivore.	Piers Anthony
Once and Future Tales from the Magazine of Fantasy and Science Fiction.	Edward L. Ferman
Once in Time.	Peter Dagmar
One Against Eternity.	A. E. van Vogt
One Against Herculum.	Jerry Sohl
One Against the Legion.	Jack Williamson

One Against the Moon.	Donald A. Wollheim
One Hundred and Two H Bombs.	Thomas M. Disch
One Hundred Years of Science Fiction.	Damon Knight
One in Three Hundred.	J. T. McIntosh
One Is One.	John Rankine (Douglas R. Mason)
One Million Centuries.	Richard A. Lupoff
One of Our Asteroids is Missing.	Calvin M. Knox (Robert Silverberg)
Only Lovers Left Alive.	Dave Wallis
Open Prison.	James White
The Opener of the Way.	Robert Bloch
Operation Columbus.	Hugh Walters
Operation Malacca.	Joe Poyer
Operation: Outer Space.	Murray Leinster (Will F. Jenkins)
Operation: Phantasy.	Donald A. Wollheim
Operation Space.	John Ball
Operation Springboard.	John Ball
Operation Terror.	Murray Leinster (Will F. Jenkins)
Operation Time Search.	Andre Norton
Or All the Seas with Oysters.	Avram Davidson
Orbit One.	Mel Jay (John E. Muller)
Orbit 1.	Damon Knight
Orbit 2.	Damon Knight
Orbit 3.	Damon Knight
Orbit 4.	Damon Knight
Orbit Unlimited.	Poul Anderson
Ordeal in Otherwhere.	Andre Norton
Orphans of the Sky.	Robert A. Heinlein
Ossian's Ride.	Fred Hoyle
The Other Foot.	Damon Knight
The Other Side of Here.	Murray Leinster (Will F. Jenkins)
The Other Side of Night.	Paul Charkin
The Other Side of Nowhere.	Murray Leinster (Will F. Jenkins)
The Other Side of the Sky.	Arthur C. Clarke
The Other Side of Time.	Keith Laumer
The Other Sky.	Keith Laumer
The Other World.	J. Harvey Bond (Russ Winterbotham)
Other Worlds of Clifford Simak.	Clifford D. Simak
Our Man in Space.	Bruce W. Ronald
Out of Bounds.	Judith Merril
Out of Chaos.	J. T. McIntosh
Out of My Mind.	John Brunner.
Out of the Darkness.	R. Lionel Fanthorpe
Out of the Dead City.	Samuel R. Delany
Out of the Deeps.	John Wyndham (John Beynon Harris)
Out of the Night.	John E. Muller
Out of the Sun.	Ben Bova
Out of the Unknown.	E. Mayne Hull & A. E. van Vogt
Out of the Void.	Leslie F. Stone
Out of This World.	Ben Barzman

Out of This World.
Out of This World 1.
Out of This World 2.
Out of This World 3.
Out of This World 4.
Out of This World 5.
Out of This World 6.
Out of This World 7.

Out of Time.
Outlaw of Gor.
Outpost Mars.

Outpost of Jupiter.
Outpost on the Moon.
Outposts of Space.
Outside the Universe.
Outsiders: Children of Wonder.
The Outward Urge.

The Overloaded Man.
Overlords from Space.
The Owl Service.

The Pacific Book of Australian Science Fiction.
Pagan Passions.

A Pail of Air.
Paingod and Other Delusions.
The Palace of Love.
Pan Satyrus.
Pandemonium on the Potomac.
The Paper Dolls.
The Paradox Men.
The Paralyzed Kingdom.
The Paralyzing Rays vs. the Nuclears.
Passport to Eternity.
Past and Future and The Last Generation.
Past Master.
Past the End of the Pavement.
The Past Through Tomorrow.
Pavane.
The Paw of God.
The Pawns of Null-A.
The Peacemakers.
Pebble in the Sky.
Pendulum.
Penelope.

Murray Leinster (Will F. Jenkins)
Mably Owen & Anabel Williams-Ellis
Mably Owen & Anabel Williams-Ellis
Mably Owen & Anabel Williams-Ellis
Mably Owen & Anabel Williams-Ellis
Mably Owen & Anabel Williams-Ellis
Mably Owen & Anabel Williams-Ellis
Mably Owen & Anabel Williams-Ellis
George Langelaan
John Norman
Cyril Judd (Judith Merril & Cyril M. Kornbluth)
Lester del Rey
Hugh Walters
Wallace West
Edmond Hamilton
William Tenn
John Wyndham & Lucas Parkes (John Beynon Harris)
J. G. Ballard
Joseph E. Kelleam
Alan Garner

John Baxter
Randall Garrett & Larry M. Harris (Laurence M. Janifer)
Fritz Leiber
Harlan Ellison
Jack Vance
Richard Wormser
William C. Anderson
L. P. Davies
Charles L. Harness
Guido Nizzi
Guido Nizzi
J. G. Ballard

Bradford M. Day
R. A. Lafferty
Charles G. Finney
Robert A. Heinlein
Keith Roberts
Rex Gordon
A. E. van Vogt
Curtis W. Casewit
Isaac Asimov
John Christopher
William C. Anderson

343

Penguin Science Fiction.	Brian W. Aldiss
The Penultimate Truth.	Philip K. Dick
The People Maker.	Damon Knight
People Minus X.	Raymond Z. Gallun
The People: No Different Flesh.	Zenna Henderson
People of the Talisman.	Leigh Brackett
The People Trap.	Robert Sheckley
The Perfect Planet.	Evelyn E. Smith
Peril from Space.	Karl Maras (H. K. Bulmer)
Peril of the Starmen.	Kris Neville
Perilous Galaxy.	John E. Muller
The Phantom Caravan.	F. H. P. Schuck
The Phantom Ones.	Pel Torro
Phenomena X.	John E. Muller
The Philosophical Corps.	Everett B. Cole
Phoenix.	Richard Cowper
Phoenix Prime.	Ted White
Phyllis.	E. V. Cunningham (Howard Fast)
Picnic on Paradise.	Joanna Russ
The Pictures of Pavanne.	Lan Wright
A Piece of Martin Cann.	Laurence M. Janifer
Pilgrimage: The Book of the People.	Zenna Henderson
Pilgrimage to Earth.	Robert Sheckley
The Pirates of Zan.	Murray Leinster (Will F. Jenkins)
Pity About Earth.	Ernest Hill
A Place Named Hell.	M. J. Deer (George H. Smith & M. Jane Deer)
Plague from Space.	Harry Harrison
A Plague of Demons.	Keith Laumer
A Plague of Pythons.	Frederik Pohl
Plague Ship.	Andrew North (Andre Norton)
Plan for Conquest.	A. A. Glynn
Planet Big Zero.	Franklin Hadley (Russ Winterbotham)
A Planet Called Krishna.	L. Sprague de Camp
A Planet Called Pavanne.	Lan Wright
The Planet Explorer.	Murray Leinster (Will F. Jenkins)
Planet Fall.	Gill Hunt (E. C. Tubb)
Planet in Peril.	John Christopher
The Planet Killers.	Robert Silverberg
A Planet Named Terra.	Victor Wadey
Planet of Death.	E. L. Arch
Planet of Death.	Robert Silverberg
Planet of Exile.	Ursula K. Le Guin
Planet of Fear.	Diane Detzer
Planet of Light.	Raymond F. Jones
Planet of No Return.	Poul Anderson
The Planet of the Blind.	Paul Corey
Planet of the Damned.	Harry Harrison
The Planet of the Double Sun.	Neil R. Jones
A Planet of Your Own.	John Brunner
The Planet of Youth.	Stanton A. Coblentz
The Planet Plane.	John Beynon (John Beynon Harris)

The Planet Poachers.	A. M. Lightner
Planet Run.	Gordon R. Dickson & Keith Laumer
The Planet Savers.	Marion Zimmer Bradley
The Planet Seekers.	Erle Barton
The Planet Strappers.	Raymond Z. Gallun
Planetary Agent X.	Mack Reynolds
The Planeteers.	John W. Campbell
Planetoid Disposals, Ltd.	Volsted Gridban (E. C. Tubb)
Planets for Sale.	E. Mayne Hull & A. E. van Vogt
The Plantos Illusion.	John Rankine (Douglas R. Mason)
Player Piano.	Kurt Vonnegut, Jr.
The Players of Hell.	Dave Van Arnam
The Players of Null-A.	A. E. van Vogt
Pleasant Dreams: Nightmares.	Robert Bloch
The Plot Against Earth.	Calvin M. Knox (Robert Silverberg)
The Pocketbook of Science Fiction.	Donald A. Wollheim
Podkayne of Mars.	Robert A. Heinlein
Point Ultimate.	Jerry Sohl
Police Your Planet.	Eric Van Lhin (Lester del Rey)
The Pool of Fire.	John Christopher
Portable Novels of Science.	Donald A. Wollheim
The Possessors.	John Christopher
The Power-Cube Affair.	John T. Phillifent (John Rackham)
Power Sphere.	Leo Brett
Pre-Empt.	John Vorhies
Preferred Risk.	Edson McCann (Lester del Rey & Frederik Pohl)
Prelude to Mars.	Arthur C. Clarke
Prelude to Peril.	Jerry Sohl
Prelude to Space.	Arthur C. Clarke
Priest-Kings of Gor.	John Norman
The Primal Urge.	Brian W. Aldiss
The Prism.	Emil Petaja
Prisoners of Space.	Lester del Rey (Paul W. Fairman)
A Private Cosmos.	Philip Jose Farmer
Prize Science Fiction.	Donald A. Wollheim
Prize Stories of Space and Time.	Donald A. Wollheim
The Prodical Sun.	Philip E. High
The Productions of Time.	John Brunner
The Programmed Man.	Jean & Jeff Sutton
Project Barrier.	Daniel F. Galouye
Project Jupiter.	Fredric Brown
Project 12.	Thomas E. Grouling
Projection Infinity.	Karl Zeigfreid
Prologue to Analog.	John W. Campbell
The Proxima Project.	John Rackham
The Pseudo-People.	William F. Nolan
Psi High and Others.	Alan E. Nourse
The Psionic Menace.	Keith Woodcott (John Brunner)
Psychedelic-40.	Louis Charbonneau
The Psycho Makers.	Jerry Jason (George H. Smith)
Psychogeist.	L. P. Davies

The Puppet Masters.	Robert A. Heinlein
The Puppet Planet.	Russ Winterbotham
Pursuit on Ganymede.	Michael D. Resnick
The Puzzle Planet.	Robert A. W. Lowndes
The Quality of Mercy.	D. G. Compton
Queen of Blood.	Charles Nuetzel
Queen Victoria's Bomb.	Ronald Clark
Quest Crosstime.	Andre Norton
Quicksand.	John Brunner
R Is for Rocket.	Ray Bradbury
Race to the Stars.	Leo Margulies & Oscar J. Friend
Radar Alert.	Karl Zeigfreid
The Radioactive Camel Affair.	Peter Leslie
The Ragged Edge.	John Christopher
Raiders from the Rings.	Alan E. Nourse
The Rainbow Affair.	David McDaniel
The Ranger Boys in Space.	Hal Clement
Rare Science Fiction.	Ivan Howard
The Rat Race.	Alfred Bester
The Raven.	Eunice Sudak
The Ray Bradbury Review.	William F. Nolan
Reach for Tomorrow.	Arthur C. Clarke
Reactor XK9.	John E. Muller
Reality Forbidden.	Philip E. High
Realm of the Alien.	F. G. Rayer
The Reassembled Man.	Herbert Kastle
The Rebel of Rhada.	Robert Cham Gilman (Alfred Coppel)
The Rebellers.	Jane Roberts
The Rebellious Stars.	Isaac Asimov
Rebels of the Red Planet.	Charles L. Fontenay
Re-Birth.	John Wyndham (John Beynon Harris)
Recalled to Life.	Robert Silverberg
Recruit for Andromeda.	Milton Lesser
The Red Planet.	Charles Chilton
Red Planet.	Robert A. Heinlein
The Red Planet.	Russ Winterbotham
The Reefs of Earth.	R. A. Lafferty
The Reefs of Space.	Frederik Pohl & Jack Williamson
Regan's Planet.	Robert Silverberg
The Reign of Wizardry.	Jack Williamson
Renaissance.	Raymond F. Jones
Rendezvous on a Lost World.	A. Bertram Chandler
The Repairmen of Cyclops.	John Brunner
Report on Probability A.	Brian W. Aldiss
The Reproductive System.	John T. Sladek
Reptilicus.	Dean Owen
A Requiem for Astounding.	Alva Rogers
Rest in Agony.	Paul W. Fairman
The Rest of the Robots.	Isaac Asimov
Restoree.	Anne McCaffrey
The Resurrected Man.	E. C. Tubb

Retief and the Warlords.	Keith Laumer
Retief's War.	Keith Laumer
The Return.	Pel Torro
The Return of Conan.	L. Sprague de Camp & Bjorn Nyberg
Return of the Starships.	Jorge de Reyna (Diane Detzer)
The Return of Zeus.	John E. Muller
Return to Otherness.	C. L. Moore & Henry Kuttner
Reverse Universe.	Volsted Gridban (E. C. Tubb)
Revolt in 2100.	Robert A. Heinlein
The Revolt of the Triffids.	John Wyndham (John Beynon Harris)
Revolt on Alpha C.	Robert Silverberg
The Revolving Boy.	Gertrude Friedberg
The Richest Corpse in Show Business.	Dan Morgan
Riders to the Stars.	Curt Siodmak
The Rim of Space.	A. Bertram Chandler
The Rim-World Legacy.	F. A. Javor
The Ring.	Piers Anthony & Robert E. Margroff
Ring Around the Sun.	Clifford D. Simak
The Ring of Ritornel.	Charles L. Harness
Ring of Violence.	Douglas R. Mason
Rite of Passage.	Alexei Panshin
The Rites of Ohe.	John Brunner
The Rithian Terror.	Damon Knight
The Rival Rigelians.	Mack Reynolds
River of Time.	Wallace West
The Road to the Rim.	A. Bertram Chandler
A Robert Heinlein Omnibus.	Robert A. Heinlein
The Robot Rulers.	George E. Shirley
Robots and Changelings.	Lester del Rey
Robots Have No Tails.	Lewis Padgett (C. L. Moore & Henry Kuttner)
Rocannon's World.	Ursula K. Le Guin
The Rock of Three Planets.	A. M. Lightner
Rocket from Infinity.	Lester del Rey
Rocket Jockey.	Philip St. John (Lester del Rey)
Rocket Pilot.	Philip St. John (Lester del Rey)
Rocket Ship Galileo.	Robert A. Heinlein
Rocket to Limbo.	Alan E. Nourse
Rockets to Nowhere.	Philip St. John (Lester del Rey)
Rodent Mutation.	Bron Fane
Rogue Dragon.	Avram Davidson
Rogue in Space.	Fredric Brown
Rogue Moon.	Algis Budrys
Rogue Queen.	L. Sprague de Camp
Rogue Ship.	A. E. van Vogt
The Rolling Stones.	Robert A. Heinlein
Rork!	Avram Davidson
The Rose.	Charles L. Harness
The Rule of the Door.	Lloyd Biggle, Jr.
Rule of the Pagbeasts.	J. T. McIntosh
Rulers of Men.	Hans Stefan Santesson
The Runaway Robot.	Lester del Rey (Paul W. Fairman)
The Runaway World.	Stanton A. Coblentz

The Running Man.	J. Hunter Holly
Russian Science Fiction.	Robert Magidoff
Russian Science Fiction, Series II.	Robert Magidoff
SF: Authors' Choice.	Harry Harrison
SF: '57.	Judith Merril
SF: '58.	Judith Merril
SF: '59.	Judith Merril
SF: The Best of the Best.	Judith Merril
S-F: The Year's Greatest Science-Fiction and Fantasy.	Judith Merril
S-F: The Year's Greatest Science-Fiction and Fantasy Second Annual Volume.	Judith Merril
S-F: The Year's Greatest Science-Fiction and Fantasy Third Annual Volume.	Judith Merril
SF12.	Judith Merril
S Is for Space.	Ray Bradbury
S.O.S. from Three Worlds.	Murray Leinster (Will F. Jenkins)
Saga of Lost Earths.	Emil Petaja
The Saliva Tree.	Brian W. Aldiss
Sanctuary in the Sky.	John Brunner
Sands of Mars.	Arthur C. Clarke
Sands of Time.	Peter Dagmar
The Santaroga Barrier.	Frank Herbert
Sargasso of Space.	Andrew North (Andre Norton)
Satellite.	R. Lionel Fanthorpe
Saturn Patrol.	King Lang (E. C. Tubb)
Sax Rohmer: A Bibliography.	Bradford M. Day
Scavengers in Space.	Alan E. Nourse
The Scheme of Things.	Lester del Rey
Science Fiction.	Samuel Holroyd Burton
Science Fiction by Gaslight.	Sam Moskowitz
Science Fiction Carnival.	Fredric Brown & Mack Reynolds
Science Fiction for People Who Hate Science Fiction.	Terry Carr
Science Fiction Handbook.	L. Sprague de Camp
Science Fiction Horizons No. 1.	Tom Boardman, Jr.
Science Fiction Inventions.	Damon Knight
Science Fiction Omnibus.	T. E. Dikty & Everett F. Bleiler
Science Fiction Stories.	Frederik Pohl
The Science Fiction Subtreasury.	Wilson Tucker
Science Fiction Through the Ages, Volume 1.	I. O. Evans
Science Fiction Through the Ages, Volume 2.	I. O. Evans
The Scorpions.	Robert Kelly
A Scourge of Screamers.	Daniel F. Galouye
Scourge of the Blood Cult.	George H. Smith
The Screaming Face.	John Lymington
The Sea People.	Adam Lukens (Diane Detzer)
Sea Siege.	Andre Norton
The Sea Witch.	Robert Bloch

The Search for Zei.	L. Sprague de Camp
Search the Dark Stars.	John E. Muller
Search the Sky.	Frederik Pohl & C. M. Kornbluth
Season of the Witch.	Hank Stine
A Second Arthur C. Clarke Omnibus.	Arthur C. Clarke
The Second Astounding Science Fiction Anthology.	John W. Campbell
The Second Atlantis.	Robert Moore Williams
Second Ending.	James White
Second Foundation.	Isaac Asimov
Second Foundation: Galactic Empire.	Isaac Asimov
The Second Galaxy Reader of Science Fiction.	H. L. Gold
The Second If Reader of Science Fiction.	Frederik Pohl
Second Orbit.	Geoffrey Doherty
Secret Agent of Terra.	John Brunner
The Secret Martians.	Jack Sharkey
The Secret of Saturn's Rings.	Donald A. Wollheim
The Secret of Sinharat.	Leigh Brackett
Secret of the Black Planet.	Milton Lesser
Secret of the Lost Race.	Andre Norton
The Secret of the Marauder Satellite.	Ted White
The Secret of the Martian Moons.	Donald A. Wollheim
The Secret of the Ninth Planet.	Donald A. Wollheim
The Secret of ZI.	Kenneth Bulmer
The Secret People.	John Beynon Harris
The Secret People.	Raymond F. Jones
The Secret Songs.	Fritz Leiber
Secret Under Antarctica.	Gordon R. Dickson
Secret Under the Carribbean.	Gordon R. Dickson
Secret Under the Sea.	Gordon R. Dickson
The Secret Visitors.	James White
The Seed.	Dan Thomas
The Seed of Earth.	Robert Silverberg
Seed of Light.	Edmund Cooper
The Seedling Stars.	James Blish
The Seeds of Time.	John Wyndham (John Beynon Harris)
The Seedy.	Robert Ray
Seeker from the Stars.	James Nelson Coleman
Seekers of Tomorrow.	Sam Moskowitz
Seetee Ship.	Will Stewart (Jack Williamson)
Seetee Shock.	Will Stewart (Jack Williamson)
Sense of Obligation.	Harry Harrison
A Sense of Wonder.	Sam Moskowitz
The Sensitives.	Louis Charbonneau
Sentinels from Space.	Eric Frank Russell
Sentinels of Space.	Eric Frank Russell
The Serpent.	Jane Gaskell
Seven from the Stars.	Marion Zimmer Bradley
The Seven Sexes.	William Tenn
7th Annual Edition the Year's Best S-F.	Judith Merril

The Sex Machine.	Richard E. Geis
Shadow of Tomorrow.	Frederik Pohl
Shadow on the Hearth.	Judith Merril
Shadow Over Mars.	Leigh Brackett
Shadows in the Sun.	Chad Oliver
Shadows with Eyes.	Fritz Leiber
Shambleau and Others.	C. L. Moore
The Shape of Things.	Damon Knight
Shards of Space.	Robert Sheckley
Shellbreak.	J. W. Groves
Shield.	Poul Anderson
The Ship from Atlantis.	H. Marner Munn
The Ship from Outside.	A. Bertram Chandler
The Ship That Sailed the Time Stream.	G. C. Edmondson
Ships to the Stars.	Fritz Leiber
Shock.	Richard Matheson
Shock III.	Richard Matheson
Shock II.	Richard Matheson
Shock Wave.	Leigh & Walt Richmond
Shoot at the Moon.	William F. Temple
The Shores of Space.	Richard Matheson
Shot in the Dark.	Judith Merril
The Shrinking Man.	Richard Matheson
Shrouded Planet.	Robert Randall (Randall Garrett & Robert Silverberg)
Sideslip.	Dave Van Arnam & Ted White
Sidewise in Time.	Murray Leinster (Will F. Jenkins)
Siege of the Unseen.	A. E. van Vogt
Siege Perilous.	Lester del Rey (Paul W. Fairman)
Sign of the Labrys.	Margaret St. Clair
The Silent Invaders.	Robert Silverberg
The Silent Multitude.	D. G. Compton
The Silver Eggheads.	Fritz Leiber
The Silver Locusts.	Ray Bradbury
The Silver Trumpet.	Owen Barfield
Simulacron-3.	Daniel F. Galouye
The Simulcra.	Philip K. Dick
Sin in Space.	Cyril Judd (Judith Merril & Cyril M. Kornbluth)
The Singing Stones.	Juanita Coulson
Sinister Barrier.	Eric Frank Russell
The Sioux Spaceman.	Andre Norton
The Sirens of Titan.	Kurt Vonnegut, Jr.
6 and the Silent Scream.	Ivan Howard
Six from Worlds Beyond.	T. E. Dikty
Six Gates from Limbo.	J. T. McIntosh
6 x H.	Robert A. Heinlein
Six Worlds Yonder.	Eric Frank Russell
6th Annual Edition the Year's Best S-F.	Judith Merril
Sixth Column.	Robert A. Heinlein
The Skull of Kanaima.	Victor Norwood
The Skull of the Marquis de Sade.	Robert Bloch
The Sky Is Falling and Badge of Infamy.	Lester del Rey

The Skynappers.	John Brunner
Skyport.	Curt Siodmak
Skyways for Doorian.	Zaara Van Tuyl
Slan.	A. E. van Vogt
Slave Planet.	Laurence M. Janifer
Slave Ship.	Frederik Pohl
Slavers of Space.	John Brunner
Slaves of the Klau.	Jack Vance
Slaves of the Spectrum.	Philip Kent (H. K. Bulmer)
The Sleep Eaters.	John Lymington
Sleeping Planet.	William R. Burnett, Jr.
A Small Armageddon.	Mordecai Roshwald
The Small Assassin.	Ray Bradbury
The Small Back Room.	Nigel Balchin
Snow White and the Giants.	J. T. McIntosh
The Snows of Ganymede.	Poul Anderson
So Bright the Vision.	Clifford D. Simak
So Close to Home.	James Blish
So Dark a Heritage.	Frank Belknap Long
The Soft Machine.	William Burroughs
Softly by Moonlight.	Bron Fane
Sojarr of Titan.	Manly Wade Wellman
The Solar Invation.	Manly Wade Wellman
Solar Lottery.	Philip K. Dick
The Solarians.	Norman Spinrad
Soldier, Ask Not.	Gordon R. Dickson
Solomon's Stone.	L. Sprague de Camp
Some of Your Blood.	Theodore Sturgeon
Some Will Not Die.	Algis Budrys
Something Wicked This Way Comes.	Ray Bradbury
Somewhere a Voice.	Eric Frank Russell
Somewhere Out There.	Bron Fane
Son of the Stars.	Raymond F. Jones
Son of the Tree.	Jack Vance
Sons of the Wolf.	Adam Lukens (Diane Detzer)
Sorcerer's Amulet.	Michael Moorcock
Sorcerers of Set.	Martin Thomas
The Sorceress of Qar.	Ted White
Sorceress of the Witch World.	Andre Norton
Sos the Rope.	Piers Anthony
Soul Mates.	Arthur S. Mattes
The Space Ark.	A. M. Lightner
The Space Barbarians.	Tom Godwin
Space Born.	Lan Wright
The Space-Born.	E. C. Tubb
Space-Borne.	R. Lionel Fanthorpe
Space by the Tale.	Jerome Bixby
Space Cadet.	Robert A. Heinlein
Space Captain.	Murray Leinster (Will F. Jenkins)
Space Chantey.	R. A. Lafferty
The Space Egg.	Russ Winterbotham
Space Fury.	R. Lionel Fanthorpe
Space Gypsies.	Murray Leinster (Will F. Jenkins)
Space Hostages.	Nicholas Fisk

Space Hunger.	Charles Grey (E. C. Tubb)
Space Mercenaries.	A. Bertram Chandler
The Space Merchants.	Frederik Pohl & C. M. Kornbluth
Space No Barrier.	Pel Torro
The Space Olympics.	A. M. Lightner
Space on My Hands.	Fredric Brown
Space Opera.	Jack Vance
Space Pioneer.	Mack Reynolds
Space Pioneers.	Andre Norton
The Space Pirate.	Jack Vance
The Space Plague.	A. M. Lightner
Space Platform.	Murray Leinster (Will F. Jenkins)
Space Police.	Andre Norton
Space Prison.	Tom Godwin
Space Puppet.	John Rackham
Space Salvage.	H. K. Bulmer
Space Service.	Andre Norton
Space Station #1.	Frank Belknap Long
The Space Swimmers.	Gordon R. Dickson
Space, Time and Crime.	Miriam Allen deFord
Space, Time and Nathaniel.	Brian W. Aldiss
The Space-Time Juggler.	John Brunner
Space Trap.	Thornton Bell
Space Treason.	H. K. Bulmer & A. V. Clarke
Space Tug.	Murray Leinster (Will F. Jenkins)
Space Void.	Marston Johns (John E. Muller)
Space War.	Neil R. Jones
The Space Willies.	Eric Frank Russell
Space Winners.	Gordon R. Dickson
Spacehive.	Jeff Sutton
Spacemaster I.	John Ball
Spacemen, Go Home.	Milton Lesser
Spaceship to Saturn.	Hugh Walters
Spaceways.	Charles Eric Maine
Spacial Delivery.	Gordon R. Dickson
The Spawn of the Death Machine.	Ted White
Special Delivery.	Kris Neville
Special Mission.	John E. Muller
The Specials.	Louis Charbonneau
Spectre of Darkness.	John E. Muller
Spectrum.	Kingsley Amis & Robert Conquest
Spectrum 2.	Kingsley Amis & Robert Conquest
Spectrum 3.	Kingsley Amis & Robert Conquest
Spectrum 4.	Kingsley Amis & Robert Conquest
Spectrum 5.	Kingsley Amis & Robert Conquest
The Spell of Seven.	L. Sprague de Camp
The Splintered Sunglasses Affair.	Peter Leslie
Split.	Graeme de Timms
Sprague de Camp's New Anthology of Science Fiction.	L. Sprague de Camp
Spykos 4.	Peter Dagmar
The Square Root of Man.	William Tenn

The Squares of the City.	John Brunner
Stadium Beyond the Stars.	Milton Lesser
The Stainless Steel Rat.	Harry Harrison
Stand on Zanzibar.	John Brunner
The Star Beast.	Robert A. Heinlein
Star Born.	Andre Norton
Star Bridge.	James E. Gunn & Jack Williamson
The Star Conquerors.	Ben Bova
The Star Dwellers.	James Blish
Star Fourteen.	Frederik Pohl
The Star Fox.	Poul Anderson
Star Gate.	Andre Norton
Star Gladiator.	Dave Van Arnam
Star Guard.	Andre Norton
Star Hunter.	Andre Norton
Star Hunter and Voodoo Planet.	Andre Norton
The Star King.	Jack Vance
The Star Kings.	Edmond Hamilton
The Star Magicians.	Lin Carter
Star Man's Son.	Andre Norton
The Star Mill.	Emil Petaja
Star of Danger.	Marion Zimmer Bradley
The Star of Life.	Edmond Hamilton
Star of Stars.	Frederik Pohl
Star Quest.	Dean R. Koontz
Star Rangers.	Andre Norton
Star Science Fiction Stories.	Frederik Pohl
Star Science Fiction Stories #2.	Frederik Pohl
Star Science Fiction Stories #3.	Frederik Pohl
Star Science Fiction Stories #4.	Frederik Pohl
Star Science Fiction Stories $5.	Frederik Pohl
Star Science Fiction Stories #6.	Frederik Pohl
The Star Seekers.	Milton Lesser
The Star Seekers.	F. G. Rayer
Star Shine.	Fredric Brown
Star Short Novels.	Frederik Pohl
Star Surgeon.	Alan E. Nourse
Star Surgeon.	James White
Star Trek.	James Blish
Star Trek 2.	James Blish
Star Trek: Mission to Horatius.	Mack Reynolds
The Star Wasps.	Robert Moore Williams
Star Watchman.	Ben Bova
Star Ways.	Poul Anderson
Star Well.	Alexei Panshin
The Star Witches.	John Lymington
Starburst.	Alfred Bester
Starchild.	Frederik Pohl & Jack Williamson
Starhaven.	Ivar Jorgenson (Robert Silverberg)
The Starlight Corridor.	Roger Mansfield
Starman Jones.	Robert A. Heinlein
Starman's Quest.	Robert Silverberg
The Starmen.	Leigh Brackett

The Stars and Under.	Edmund Crispin
The Stars Are Ours.	H. K. Bulmer
The Stars Are Ours!	Andre Norton
The Stars Came Down.	Richard Saxon
The Stars, Like Dust.	Isaac Asimov
The Stars My Destination.	Alfred Bester
The Stars Will Wait.	Henry L. Hasse
Starshine.	Theodore Sturgeon
Starship.	Brian W. Aldiss
Starship Troopers.	Robert A. Heinlein
Starswarm.	Brian W. Aldiss
Station in Space.	James E. Gunn
The Status Civilization.	Robert Sheckley
The Stealer of Souls.	Michael Moorcock
Steel Magic.	Andre Norton
The Stellar Legion.	E. C. Tubb
Step to the Stars.	Lester del Rey
Stepsons of Terra.	Robert Silverberg
The Still, Small Voice of Trumpets.	Lloyd Biggle, Jr.
A Stir of Echoes.	Richard Matheson
The Stolen Sun.	Emil Petaja
Store of Infinity.	Robert Sheckley
Stories from Science Fiction.	Geoffrey Doherty
Storm Over Warlock.	Andre Norton
Stormbringer.	Michael Moorcock
Stowaway to Mars.	John Beynon (Harris)
Strange Evil.	Jane Gaskell
The Strange Flight of Frank Shapar.	Alfred L. Milligan
The Strange Ones.	Pel Torro
Strange Relations.	Philip Jose Farmer
Strange Signposts.	Roger Elwood & Sam Moskowitz
The Strange World of Planet X.	Robert Ray
Stranger in a Strange Land.	Robert A. Heinlein
Stranger Than You Think.	G. C. Edmondson
Strangers from Earth.	Poul Anderson
Strangers in the Universe.	Clifford D. Simak
Sturgeon in Orbit.	Theodore Sturgeon
Subterfuge.	Charles Eric Maine
Such Men Are Dangerous.	Martin Thomas
Summoned from the Tomb.	Peter Haining
The Sun Saboteurs.	Damon Knight
The Sun Smasher.	Edmond Hamilton
Sunburst.	Phyllis Gotlieb
The Sundered Worlds.	Michael Moorcock
Sundog.	B. N. Ball
The Sunken World.	Stanton A. Coblentz
The Sunless World.	Neil R. Jones
The Super Barbarians.	John Brunner
Supermind.	Mark Phillips (Randall Garrett & Laurence M. Janifer)
The Supplemental Checklist of Fantastic Literature.	Bradford M. Day
Survival Margin.	Charles Eric Maine
Survival Project.	John E. Muller
The Survivors.	Tom Godwin
The Survivors.	Paul Tabori

Suspension.	Bron Fane
Sweeney's Island.	John Christopher
Switch on the Night.	Ray Bradbury
A Sword Above the Night.	John Lymington
The Sword of Aldones.	Marion Zimmer Bradley
The Sword of Lankor.	Howard L. Cory (Julie Ann Jardine & Larry Maddock)
The Sword of Rhiannon.	Leigh Brackett
Sword of the Dawn.	Michael Moorcock
The Sword Swallower.	Ron Goulart
Swords Against Wizardry.	Fritz Leiber
Swords and Sorcery.	L. Sprague de Camp
Swords in the Mist.	Fritz Leiber
The Swords of Lankhmar.	Fritz Leiber
Swordsmen in the Sky.	Donald A. Wollheim
The Symmetrians.	Kenneth Harker
Synthajoy.	D. G. Compton
The Synthetic Man.	Theodore Sturgeon
The Synthetic Ones.	Lionel Roberts
The Talbot Agreement.	Edmond G. Addeo & Richard M. Garvin
Talbot Mundy Biblio.	Bradford M. Day
The Tale of the Future: A Checklist.	I. F. Clarke
A Tale of Two Clocks.	James H. Schmitz
Talents, Inc.	Murray Leinster (Will F. Jenkins)
Tales from Gavagan's Bar.	L. Sprague de Camp & Fletcher Pratt
Tales from the White Hart.	Arthur C. Clarke
Tales in a Jugular Vein.	Robert Bloch
Tales of Conan.	L. Sprague de Camp & Robert E. Howard
Tales of Gooseflesh and Laughter.	John Wyndham (John Beynon Harris)
Tales of Outer Space.	Donald A. Wollheim
Tales of Science Fiction.	B. N. Ball
Tales of Ten Worlds.	Arthur C. Clarke
The Tandar Saga.	W. C. Hanna
Target: Terra.	Laurence M. Janifer & S. J. Treibich
Tarnsman of Gor.	John Norman
Tarzan and the Abominable Snowman.	Barton Werper
Tarzan and the Cave City.	Barton Werper
Tarzan and the Silver Globe.	Barton Werper
Tarzan and the Snake People.	Barton Werper
Tarzan and the Valley of Gold.	Fritz Leiber
Tarzan and the Winged Invaders.	Barton Werper
The Technicolor ® Time Machine.	Harry Harrison
Telepathist.	John Brunner
Telepower.	Lee Hoffman
The Temple of the Dead.	Victor Norwood
Ten from Infinity.	Ivar Jorgensen (Paul W. Fairman)
Ten from Tomorrow.	E. C. Tubb
Ten Million Years to Friday.	John Lymington

Title	Author
Ten Years to Doomsday.	Chester Anderson & Michael Kurland
10th Annual Edition the Year's Best S-F.	Judith Merril
The Tenth Galaxy Reader.	Frederik Pohl
The 10th Victim.	Robert Sheckley
Terminal Beach.	J. G. Ballard
Terror.	Robert Bloch
Terror!	Larry T. Shaw
Terror by Satellite.	Hugh Walters
Terror in the Modern Vein.	Donald A. Wollheim
Tessie, the Hound of Channel 1.	Shepherd Mead
Tharkol, Lord of the Unknown.	Edmond Hamilton
These Savage Futurians.	Philip E. High
They.	Marya Mannes
They Came, They Saw.	James R. Hallums
They Never Come Back.	Leo Brett
They Shall Have Stars.	James Blish
They Walked Like Men.	Clifford D. Simak
Thief of Baghdad.	Richard Wormser
Thief of Llarn.	Gardner F. Fox
The Thief of Thoth.	Lin Carter
The Thing and Other Stories.	John W. Campbell
Things.	Ivan Howard
The Third Eye.	Theodore R. Cogswell
Third from the Sun.	Richard Matheson
The Third Galaxy Reader.	H. L. Gold
The Third Level.	Jack Finney
The Thirst Quenchers.	Rick Raphael
13 French Science-Fiction Stories.	Damon Knight
The 13th Immortal.	Robert Silverberg
30-Day Wonder.	Richard Wilson
This Business of Bomfog.	Madelaine Duke
This Ever Diverse Pair.	G. A. L. Burgeon (Owen Barfield)
This Fortress World.	James E. Gunn
This Immortal.	Roger Zelazny
This Island Earth.	Raymond F. Jones
This Strange Tomorrow.	Frank Belknap Long
This World is Taboo.	Murray Leinster (Will F. Jenkins)
Thongor Against the Gods.	Lin Carter
Thongor at the End of Time.	Lin Carter
Thongor in the City of Magicians.	Lin Carter
Thongor of Lemuria.	Lin Carter
Thorns.	Robert Silverberg
Those Idiots from Earth.	Richard Wilson
Those Who Watch.	Robert Silverberg
A Thousand Ages.	D. E. Ellis
The 1000 Year Plan.	Isaac Asimov
A 1000 Years On.	John E. Muller
Three Against the Witch World.	Andre Norton
Three by Heinlein.	Robert A. Heinlein
Three from Out There.	Leo Margulies
Three Hearts and Three Lions.	Poul Anderson
Three in One.	Leo Margulies

Three Novels.	Damon Knight
Three Quarters.	Graeme de Timms
Three Steps Spaceward.	Frank Belknap Long
The Three Stigmata of Palmer Eldritch.	Philip K. Dick
The Three Suns of Amara.	William F. Temple
Three Times Infinity.	Leo Margulies
Three to Conquer.	Eric Frank Russell
Three to the Highest Power.	William F. Nolan
Three Worlds of Futurity.	Margaret St. Clair
Three Worlds to Conquer.	Poul Anderson
Threshold of Eternity.	John Brunner
Through a Glass Clearly.	Isaac Asimov
Through the Barrier.	Pel Torro
Through Time and Space with Ferdinand Feghoot.	Grendel Briarton (R. Bretnor)
The Throwbacks.	Roger Sarac
The Thunder and Lightning Man.	Colin Cooper
Thunder and Roses.	Theodore Sturgeon
Thunder of Stars.	John Kippax & Dan Morgan
The Thurb Revolution.	Alexei Panshin
The Ticket That Exploded.	William Burroughs
The Tide Went Out.	Charles Eric Maine
Tiger by the Tail.	Alan E. Nourse
Tiger Girl.	Edmond Hamilton
Tiger! Tiger!	Alfred Bester
Time and Again.	Clifford D. Simak
Time and Stars.	Poul Anderson
The Time Axis.	C. L. Moore & Henry Kuttner
The Time Before This.	Nicholas Monsarrat
The Time Bender.	Keith Laumer
Time Bomb.	Wilson Tucker
The Time Chariot.	T. Earl Hickey
The Time Curve.	Roger Elwood & Sam Moskowitz
The Time Dissolver.	Jerry Sohl
Time Echo.	Lionel Roberts
The Time Factor.	Rex Gordon
Time for a Change.	J. T. McIntosh
Time for the Stars.	Robert A. Heinlein
Time Gladiator.	Mack Reynolds
The Time Hoppers.	Robert Silverberg
Time in Advance.	William Tenn
Time Injection.	Eric C. Williams
Time Is the Simplest Thing.	Clifford D. Simak
Time Knot.	Douglas R. Mason
The Time-Lockers.	Wallace West
The Time Masters.	Wilson Tucker
The Time Mercenaries.	Philip E. High
Time of the Great Freeze.	Robert Silverberg
Time of the Hedrons.	Jack Dennis Eckstrom
Time Out for Tomorrow.	Richard Wilson
Time Out of Joint.	Philip K. Dick
Time Probe.	Arthur C. Clarke
Time to Live.	John Rackham

Title	Author
Time to Teleport.	Gordon R. Dickson
The Time Traders.	Andre Norton
Time Tunnel.	Murray Leinster (Will F. Jenkins)
The Time Tunnel.	Murray Leinster (Will F. Jenkins)
The Time Twister.	Emil Petaja
The Time Twisters.	J. Hunter Holly
Time Waits for Winthrop.	Frederik Pohl
Time: X.	Wilson Tucker
The Timeless Ones.	Pel Torro
Timeless Stories for Today and Tomorrow.	Ray Bradbury
Timeliner.	Charles Eric Maine
Timepiece.	B. N. Ball
Times Without Number.	John Brunner
Timeslip!	Murray Leinster (Will F. Jenkins)
Titan's Daughter.	James Blish
To Conquer Chaos.	John Brunner
To Live Forever.	Jack Vance
To Open the Sky.	Robert Silverberg
To Outrun Doomsday.	Kenneth Bulmer
To the End of Time.	Robert Moore Williams
To the Tombaugh Station.	Wilson Tucker
To Worlds Beyond.	Robert Silverberg
Tolkien and the Critics.	Neil D. Isaacs & Rose A. Zimbardo
The Tolkien Relation.	William Ready
Tomorrow and Tomorrow.	Lewis Padgett (C. L. Moore & Henry Kuttner)
Tomorrow and Tomorrow and The Fairy Chessmen.	Lewis Padgett (C. L. Moore & Henry Kuttner)
Tomorrow Came.	Edmund Cooper
The Tomorrow People.	Judith Merril
Tomorrow Plus X.	Wilson Tucker
Tomorrow Sometimes Comes.	F. G. Rayer
Tomorrow, the Stars.	Robert A. Heinlein
Tomorrow x 4.	Damon Knight
Tomorrow Times Seven.	Frederik Pohl
Tomorrow's Children.	Isaac Asimov
Tomorrow's Gift.	Edmund Cooper
Tomorrow's Harvest.	Albert Root
Tongues of the Moon.	Philip Jose Farmer
Too Many Magicians.	Randall Garrett
Tormented City.	Charles Grey (E. C. Tubb)
A Torrent of Faces.	James Blish & Norman L. Knight
Torture Garden.	Robert Bloch
The Touch.	Daniel Keyes
The Touch of Evil.	John Rackham
A Touch of Infinity.	Harlan Ellison
A Touch of Strange.	Theodore Sturgeon
Toward Infinity.	Damon Knight
Tower at the End of Time.	Lin Carter
The Tower of Rizwan.	Douglas R. Mason
The Tower of Zanid.	L. Sprague de Camp

The Towers of Toron.	Samuel R. Delany
The Toymaker.	Raymond F. Jones
A Trace of Memory.	Keith Laumer
Trader to the Stars.	Poul Anderson
Tramontane.	Emil Petaja
The Transcendent Man.	Jerry Sohl
Transfinite Man.	Colin Kapp
Transit.	Edmund Cooper
Trapped in Space.	Jack Williamson
The Traps of Time.	Michael Moorcock
Treasure of the Black Falcon.	John Coleman Burroughs
The Tree Lord of Imeten.	Tom Purdom
The Trial of Terra.	Jack Williamson
Triangle.	Isaac Asimov
The Triple Man.	R. Lionel Fanthorpe
The Tritonian Ring.	L. Sprague de Camp
The Triumph of Time.	James Blish
Trivana 1.	R. Cox Abel & Charles Barren
Trouble on Titan.	Alan E. Nourse
The Trouble Twisters.	Poul Anderson
Trouble with Lichen.	John Wyndham (John Beynon Harris)
The Trouble with Tycho.	Clifford D. Simak
Troyana.	S. P. Meek
Tunnel in the Sky.	Robert A. Heinlein
Tunnel Through Time.	Lester del Rey (Paul W. Fairman)
Turn Left at Thursday.	Frederik Pohl
Turning On.	Damon Knight
12 to the Moon.	Robert A. Wise
21st Century Sub.	Frank Herbert
The Twenty-Second Century.	John Christopher
Twice in Time.	Manly Wade Wellman
Twice Upon a Time.	Charles L. Fontenay
Twilight Journey.	L. P. Davies
The Twilight Man.	Michael Moorcock
Twilight World.	Poul Anderson
Twin Planets.	Philip E. High
Twin Worlds.	Neil R. Jones
Twinkle, Twinkle Little Star.	Ben Barzman
The Twisted Men.	A. E. van Vogt
The Twisters.	Vern Hansen
Twists in Time.	Murray Leinster (Will F. Jenkins)
Two Hundred Million A.D.	A. E. van Vogt
200 Years to Christmas.	J. T. McIntosh
Two Sought Adventure.	Fritz Leiber
Two Tales and Eight Tomorrows.	Harry Harrison
2001: A Space Odyssey.	Arthur C. Clarke
The Two-Timers.	Bob Shaw
U.F.O. 517.	Bron Fane
U.N. Confidential--A.D. 2000.	Thomas Blake
The Ultimate Analysis.	Phil Harbottle
The Ultimate Invader.	Donald A. Wollheim
The Ultimate Man.	John E. Muller

The Ultimate Weapon.	John W. Campbell
Ultimatum in 2050 A.D.	Jack Sharkey
Unancestral Voices.	Owen Barfield
The Uncertain Midnight.	Edmund Cooper
The Uncharted Planet.	Luan Ranzetta
The Unconfined.	R. Lionel Fanthorpe
Under Compulsion.	Thomas M. Disch
Under the Triple Suns.	Stanton A. Coblentz
Undersea City.	Frederik Pohl & Jack Williamson
Undersea Fleet.	Frederik Pohl & Jack Williamson
Undersea Quest.	Frederik Pohl & Jack Williamson
The Undesired Princess.	L. Sprague de Camp
The Unearth People.	Kris Neville
Unearthly Neighbors.	Chad Oliver
The Unending Night.	George H. Smith
The Unexpected.	Leo Margulies
The Unexpected Dimension.	Algis Budrys
The Unfair Fare Affair.	Peter Leslie
The Unfriendly Future.	Tom Boardman, Jr.
The Unholy City.	Charles G. Finney
The Uninhibited.	Dan Morgan
The Uninvited.	John E. Muller
The United Planets.	Victor Wadey
Universe.	Robert A. Heinlein
The Universe Against Her.	James H. Schmitz
The Universe Between.	Alan E. Nourse
Universe Maker.	A. E. van Vogt
The Universes of E. E. Smith.	William H. Evans & Ron Ellik
The Unknown.	Donald R. Bensen
Unknown Destiny.	Bron Fane
The Unknown Five.	Donald R. Bensen
Un-Man and Other Novellas.	Poul Anderson
The Unpleasant Profession of Jonathan Hoag.	Robert A. Heinlein
The Unpossessed.	John E. Muller
The Unseen.	Erle Barton
The Unsleep.	Diana Gillon & Meir Gillon
The Untamed.	Victor Norwood
The Unteleported Man.	Philip K. Dick
Untouched by Human Hands.	Robert Sheckley
Untravelled Worlds.	Alan Frank Barter & Raymond Wilson
Unwise Child.	Randall Garrett
The Uranium Seekers.	Karl Zeigfreid
Uranium 235.	John E. Muller
The Utopia Affair.	David McDaniel
Utopia 14.	Kurt Vonnegut, Jr.
Utopia Minus X.	Rex Gordon
Utopia 239.	Rex Gordon
The Valley of Creation.	Edmond Hamilton
Valley of the Flame.	C. L. Moore & Henry Kuttner
The Vampire Affair.	David McDaniel

Vandals of the Void.	Jack Vance
Vanguard from Alpha.	Brian W. Aldiss
The Vanished Jet.	James Blish
The Variable Man and Other Stories.	Philip K. Dick
Vassals of Venus.	Philip Kent (H. K. Bulmer)
Vault of the Ages.	Poul Anderson
The Vengeance of Siva.	John E. Muller
Venus Plus X.	Theodore Sturgeon
The Venus Venture.	Marston Johns (John E. Muller)
Venusian Adventure.	E. C. Tubb
A Very Private Life.	Michael Frayn
The Victor.	Guido Nizzi
Victory on Janus.	Andre Norton
The View from the Stars.	Walter M. Miller, Jr.
Vigilante--21st Century.	Robert Moore Williams
The Village of the Damned.	John Wyndham (John Beynon Harris)
The Vintage Anthology of Science Fantasy.	Christopher Cerf
The Vintage Bradbury.	Ray Bradbury
Virgin Planet.	Poul Anderson
Visitor from Planet Phlox.	Zeno Koomoter
The Voice from Baru.	Tom Wade
The Voice of the Dolphins.	Leo Szilard
Voices in the Dark.	Edmund Cooper
The Voices of Time.	J. G. Ballard
Voices Prophesying War, 1763-1984.	I. F. Clarke
The Void Beyond and Other Stories.	Robert Moore Williams
Voodoo Planet.	Andrew North (Andre Norton)
VOR.	James Blish
The Vortex Blasters.	Sam Moskowitz
The Voyage of the Space Beagle.	A. E. van Vogt
Voyage to the Bottom of the Sea.	Raymond F. Jones
Voyage to the Bottom of the Sea.	Theodore Sturgeon
Voyagers in Time.	Robert Silverberg
Vulcan's Hammer.	Philip K. Dick
The Wailing Asteroid.	Murray Leinster (Will F. Jenkins)
The Waiting World.	R. Lionel Fanthorpe
Waldo and Magic, Inc.	Robert A. Heinlein
Waldo: Genius in Orbit.	Robert A. Heinlein
Walk Through Tomorrow.	Karl Zeigfreid
Walk Up the Sky.	Robert Moore Williams
The Wall.	Charles Grey (E. C. Tubb)
The Wall Around the World.	Theodore R. Cogswell
Wall of Serpents.	L. Sprague de Camp & Fletcher Pratt
The Wanderer.	Fritz Leiber
The Wandering Tellurian.	Alan Schwartz
The Wanting Seed.	Anthony Burgess
The War Against the Rull.	A. E. van Vogt
War of the Wing-Men.	Poul Anderson
War of Two Worlds.	Poul Anderson

War with the Gizmos.	Murray Leinster (Will F. Jenkins)
War with the Robots.	Harry Harrison
Warlock of the Witch World.	Andre Norton
Warlord of Kor.	Terry Carr
Warrior of Llarn.	Gardner F. Fox
The Warriors of Day.	James Blish
Warriors of Mars.	Edward P. Bradbury (Michael Moorcock)
Wasp.	Eric Frank Russell
The Watch Below.	James White
Watch on Peter.	John Rackham
Watchers of the Dark.	Lloyd Biggle, Jr.
The Watching World.	R. Lionel Fanthorpe
The Water of Thought.	Fred Saberhagen
Waters of Death.	Irving A. Greenfield
A Way Home.	Theodore Sturgeon
Way of the Werewolf.	Douglas A. Hill
Way Out.	Ivan Howard
Way Station.	Clifford D. Simak
We Claim These Stars!	Poul Anderson
We, the Venusians.	John Rackham
The Weapon from Beyond.	Edmond Hamilton
The Weapon Makers.	A. E. van Vogt
The Weapon Shops of Isher.	A. E. van Vogt
The Weathermakers.	Ben Bova
Web of the Witch World.	Andre Norton
Weird Shadows from Beyond.	John Carnell
Weird Tales.	Leo Margulies
The Weirdstone of Brisingamen.	Alan Garner
The Weirwoods.	Thomas Burnett Swann
The Well of the Worlds.	C. L. Moore & Henry Kuttner
The Werewolf of Ponkert.	H. Warner Munn
The Werewolf Principle.	Clifford D. Simak
West of the Moon.	Howard Simpson
West of the Sun.	Edgar Pangborn
What Mad Universe.	Fredric Brown
What Strange Stars and Skies.	Avram Davidson
What We Did to Father.	Roy Lewis
The Wheel in the Sky.	Rafe Bernard
The Wheels of If.	L. Sprague de Camp
When the Birds Fly South.	Stanton A. Coblentz
When the Gods Came.	John Adams
When the Moon Ran Wild.	Ray Ainsbury
When the Red King Awoke.	Joseph E. Kelleam
When the Star Kings Die.	John Jakes
When the Sun Went Out.	Leslie F. Stone
When the Whites Went.	Robert Bateman
When Time Stood Still.	Ben Orkow
Where Nightmares Are.	Peter Haining
The Whisper of Death.	Vern Hansen
The White Mountains.	John Christopher
Who?	Algis Budrys
Who Can Replace a Man?	Brian W. Aldiss
Who Fears the Devil?	Manly Wade Wellman
Who Goes There?	John W. Campbell

Who He?	Alfred Bester
Who Speaks of Conquest?	Lan Wright
The Whole Man.	John Brunner
Whom the Gods Would Slay.	Ivar Jorgensen (Paul W. Fairman)
Why Call Them Back from Heaven?	Clifford D. Simak
Wild and Outside.	Allen Kim Lang
Wild Talent.	Wilson Tucker
Will It End This Way?	Vance A. Geigley
The Wind from Nowhere.	J. G. Ballard
The Wind of Liberty.	Kenneth Bulmer
Window on the Future.	Douglas A. Hill
The Winds of Gath.	E. C. Tubb
The Winds of Time.	Chad Oliver
The Winged Man.	E. Mayne Hull & A. E. van Vogt
Witch World.	Andre Norton
The Witches of Karres.	James H. Schmitz
With a Strange Device.	Eric Frank Russell
Without Sorcery.	Theodore Sturgeon
A Wizard of Earthsea.	Ursula K. Le Guin
The Wizard of Lemuria.	Lin Carter
The Wizard of Linn.	A. E. van Vogt
The Wizard of Starship Poseidon.	Kenneth Bulmer
Wolfbane.	Frederik Pohl & C. M. Kornbluth
A Woman a Day.	Philip Jose Farmer
Woman from Another Planet.	Frank Belknap Long
The Wonder Effect.	Frederik Pohl & C. M. Kornbluth
The Wonder War.	Laurence M. Janifer
The Wooden Star.	William Tenn
The Woodrow Wilson Dime.	Jack Finney
World Aflame.	H. K. Bulmer
World at Bay.	E. C. Tubb
The World Between.	Jack Vance
A World Beyond.	George E. Shirley
The World Grabbers.	Paul W. Fairman
The World in Peril.	Charles Chilton
The World in Reverse.	Luan Ranzetta
The World in Winter.	John Christopher
A World Intervenes.	Otto Viking
The World Jones Made.	Philip K. Dick
The World of Chance.	Philip K. Dick
A World of Difference.	Robert Conquest
The World of Eclos.	Rex Gordon
The World of Null-A.	A. E. van Vogt
World of Ptavvs.	Larry Niven
The World of Theda.	Tom Wade
World of the Future.	Karl Zeigfreid
World of the Gods.	Pel Torro
World of the Masterminds.	Robert Moore Williams
World of the Sleeper.	Tony Russell Wayman
World of the Starwolves.	Edmond Hamilton
World of Tomorrow.	Karl Zeigfreid
World Out of Mind.	J. T. McIntosh
The World Swappers.	John Brunner

The World That Couldn't Be.	H. L. Gold
The World That Never Was.	Karl Zeigfreid
A World Their Own.	George E. Shirley
The World Within.	Adam Lukens (Diane Detzer)
World Without Men.	Charles Eric Maine
World Without Stars.	Poul Anderson
World Without Women.	Day Keene & Leonard Pruyn
Worlds Apart.	Owen Barfield
Worlds Apart.	J. T. McIntosh
Worlds Apart.	Mably Owen & Amabel Williams-Ellis
Worlds at War.	F. G. Rayer
World's Best Science Fiction: 1965.	Terry Carr & Donald A. Wollheim
World's Best Science Fiction: 1966.	Terry Carr & Donald A. Wollheim
World's Best Science Fiction: 1967.	Terry Carr & Donald A. Wollheim
World's Best Science Fiction: 1968.	Terry Carr & Donald A. Wollheim
Worlds for the Taking.	Kenneth Bulmer
The World's Largest Cheese.	Christopher Cerf
The Worlds of Clifford Simak.	Clifford D. Simak
The Worlds of Robert A. Heinlein.	Robert A. Heinlein
The Worlds of Robert F. Young.	Robert F. Young
The Worlds of Science Fiction.	Robert P. Mills
Worlds of the Imperium.	Keith Laumer
Worlds of Weird.	Leo Margulies
Worlds to Come.	Damon Knight
Worlds Without End.	Clifford D. Simak
The Wrecks of Time.	Michael Moorcock
A Wrinkle in the Skin.	John Christopher
X.	Eunice Sudak
The X Factor.	Andre Norton
The X Machine.	John E. Muller
The Year of the Angry Rabbit.	Russell Braddon
The Year of the Comet.	John Christopher
Year of the Unicorn.	Andre Norton
Year 2018.	James Blish
The Year When Stardust Fell.	Raymond F. Jones
The Year's Best Science-Fiction and Fantasy Fourth Annual Volume.	Judith Merril
Year's Best Science Fiction No. 1.	Brian W. Aldiss & Harry Harrison
Year's Best Science Fiction Novels 1952.	T. E. Dikty & Everett F. Bleiler
Year's Best Science Fiction Novels 1953.	T. E. Dikty & Everett F. Bleiler
Year's Best Science Fiction Novels 1954.	T. E. Dikty & Everett F. Bleiler
The Yellow Inferno.	Luan Ranzetta

Yet More Penguin Science Fiction.	Brian W. Aldiss
You Sane Men.	Laurence M. Janifer
Yours Truly, Jack the Ripper.	Robert Bloch
Youth Madness.	Stanton A. Coblentz
The Youth Monopoly.	Ellen Wobig
Zanthar at Moon's Madness.	Robert Moore Williams
Zanthar at the Edge of Never.	Robert Moore Williams
Zanthar of the Many Worlds.	Robert Moore Williams
The Zap Gun.	Philip K. Dick
Zero Minus X.	Karl Zeigfreid
The Zero Stone.	Andre Norton
Zhorani.	Karl Maras (H. K. Bulmer)

LIST OF PSEUDONYMS

Anthony, Piers (Piers Anthony Dillingham Jacob)
Anvil, Christopher (Harry C. Crosby)
Arch, E. L. (Rachel Ruth Cosgrove Payes)
Archer, Ron (Ted White)
Atheling, William Jr. (James Blish)
Beynon, John (John Beynon Harris)
Binder, Eando (Otto O. Binder & sometimes Earl A. Binder)
Boyd, John (Boyd Bradfield Upchurch)
Bradbury, Edward P. (Michael Moorcock)
Briarton, Grendel (Reginald Bretnor)
Budrys, Algis (Algirdas Jonas Budrys)
Burgeon, G. A. L. (Owen Barfield)
Burgess, Anthony (John Anthony Burgess Wilson)
Cameron, Ian (Donald Gordon Payne)
Christopher, John (Christopher Samuel Youd)
Clement, Hal (Harry Clement Stubbs)
Colvin, James (Michael Moorcock)
Cory, Howard L. [Larry Maddock (Jack Owen Jardine) & Julie Jardine]
Cowper, Richard (John Middleton Murry)
Crispin, Edmund (Robert Bruce Montgomery)
Cunningham, E. V. (Howard Fast)
Deer, M. J. (M. Jane Deer & George H. Smith)
DeGraeff, Allen (Albert Paul Blaustein)
del Rey, Lester (Ramon del Rey y de los Uerdes)
Demijohn, Thom (Thomas M. Disch & John T. Sladek)
de Reyna, Jorge (Diane Detzer)
Edgar, Peter (Peter King-Scott)
Edwards, Norman (Terry Carr & Ted White)
English, Charles (Charles Nuetzel)
Finney, Jack (Walter Braden Finney)
French, Paul (Isaac Asimov)
Gaskell, Jane (Jane Lynch)
Gilman, Robert Cham (Alfred Coppel)
Gordon, Rex (Stanley Bennett Hough)
Grey, Charles (E. C. Tubb)
Gridban, Volsted (E. C. Tubb)
Grinnell, David (Donald A. Wollheim)
Harris, Johnson (John Beynon Harris)
Hatch, Gerald (Dave Foley)
Holly, J. Hunter (Joan Carol Holly)
Hunt, Gill (E. C. Tubb)
Janifer, Laurence M. (Larry Mark Harris)
Jason, Jerry (George H. Smith)
Jorgensen, Ivar (Paul W. Fairman)
Jorgenson, Ivar (Robert Silverberg)
Judd, Cyril (Cyril M. Kornbluth & Judith Merril)
Kennaway, James (James Ewing Peebles)
Kent, Philip (H. K. Bulmer)

Keyes, Noel (David Noel Keightley)
Kippax, John (John Hynam)
Knox, Calvin M. (Robert Silverberg)
Koomoter, Zeno (Joseph Marnell)
Lang, King (E. C. Tubb)
Langart, Darrel T. (Randall Garrett)
LeBaron, Anthony (Keith Laumer)
Leinster, Murray (Will F. Jenkins)
Lionel, Robert (Lionel Roberts)
Lukens, Adam (Diane Detzer)
MacApp, C. C. (Carroll M. Capps)
Macnee, Patrick (Peter Leslie)
Maddock, Larry (Jack Owen Jardine)
Maddox, Carl (E. C. Tubb)
Maine, Charles Eric (David McIlwain)
Majors, Simon (Gardner F. Fox)
Maras, Karl (H. K. Bulmer)
McArthur, John (Arthur Wise)
McCann, Edson (Lester del Rey & Frederik Pohl)
McIntosh, J. T. (James Murdoch Macgregor)
Muller, John E. (Marston Johns, Mel Jay)
Nelson, Ray (Radell Faraday Nelson)
Norman, John (John Frederick Lange, Jr.)
North, Andrew (Andre Norton)
Norton, Andre (Alice Mary Norton)
Osborne, David (Robert Silverberg)
Owen, Dean (Dudley Dean McGaughy)
Padgett, Lewis (Henry Kuttner & C. L. Moore)
Parkes, Lucas (John Beynon Harris)
Phillips, Mark (Laurence M. Janifer & Randall Garrett)
Rackham, John (John Thomas Phillifent)
Randall, Robert (Randall Garrett & Robert Silverberg)
Rankine, John (Douglas R. Mason)
Reynolds, Mack (Dallas McCord Reynolds)
Richards, Henry (Richard Saxon)
Ross, Joseph (Joseph Wrzos)
St. John, Philip (Lester del Rey)
Sarac, Roger (Roger Andrew Caras)
Saxon, Peter (Martin Thomas)
Shaw, Brian (E. C. Tubb)
Sheldon, Lee (Wayne C. Lee)
Sheldon, Roy (E. C. Tubb)
Somers, Bart (Gardner F. Fox)
Sterling, Brett (Edmond Hamilton)
Stone, Leslie F. (Mrs. William Silberberg)
Tenn, William (Philip Klass)
Thomas, Dan (Leonard M. Sanders, Jr.)
Thomas, Martin (Thomas Hector Martin)
Tyler, Theodore (Edward William Ziegler)
Van Lhin, Erik (Lester del Rey [Ramon del Rey y de los Uerdes])
Van Tuyl, Zaara (Rosealthea Van Tuyl)
Wallace, Ian (REAL NAME UNKNOWN)
Walters, Hugh (Walter Llewellyn Hughes)
Werper, Barton (Peter T. Scott)
White, Jay C. (REAL NAME UNKNOWN)
Woodcott, Keith (John Brunner)
Wright, Lan (Lionel Percy Wright)
Wyndham, John (John Beynon Harris)

AFTERWORD

This was my first book, and it reflects a certain measure of youthful exuberance, inexperience, and ignorance. The worst mistakes have been corrected in this reprint edition, and remain invisible to the user, but other, more minor, errors in design have been left as they originally appeared, both because they were too expensive to correct (I would have had to redo the entire book), and because they may serve a more useful purpose in showing the reader how not to compile a bibliography.

The key to any bibliographical work, and the primary spot at which the amateur goes wrong, is design. A bibliography should possess a simple format which provides easy access to the material it attempts to cover. The most ignorant of users should be able to flip to any page of the book and be able to understand immediately what he is looking at, and how the material is presented. Abbreviations, esoteric symbols, and exotic formats are all signs of the amateur at work. The professional will find great beauty in simplicity.

Another hallmark of the nonprofessional is lack of standards. It is essential to decide what one intends to do before starting a book, and to engrave those parameters in silver letters to the front of one's typewriter. If, for example, a prospective bibliographer intends to put together the ultimate listing on "bugs", he must first decide what he means by "bug", and whether he will only include materials on six-legged insects, or will also list arachnids, certain land crustaceans, mites and ticks, centipedes, etc. While this seems like an obvious point to make, lack of consistency in applying definitions has been the downfall of many reference books.

Bibliography is a solitary business; it requires an excellent memory, enormous patience, tenacity, a large amount of motivation, and a small amount of insanity. The professional generally works alone, verifying all of his material personally, and trusting as few other sources, and especially as few other individuals, as possible. The rewards of good work tend more towards self-satisfaction than fame or money, because there is little of either at the end of the road. In fact, the only reason I can think of that anyone would ever want to compile a bibliography is that it's a hell of a lot of fun.

R. Reginald,
28 July 1974

SCIENCE FICTION

An Arno Press Collection

FICTION

About, Edmond. **The Man with the Broken Ear.** 1872
Allen, Grant. **The British Barbarians:** A Hill-Top Novel. 1895
Arnold, Edwin L. **Lieut. Gullivar Jones:** His Vacation. 1905
Ash, Fenton. **A Trip to Mars.** 1909
Aubrey, Frank. **A Queen of Atlantis.** 1899
Bargone, Charles (Claude Farrere, pseud.). **Useless Hands.** [1926]
Beale, Charles Willing. **The Secret of the Earth.** 1899
Bell, Eric Temple (John Taine, pseud.). **Before the Dawn.** 1934
Benson, Robert Hugh. **Lord of the World.** 1908
Beresford, J. D. **The Hampdenshire Wonder.** 1911
Bradshaw, William R. **The Goddess of Atvatabar.** 1892
Capek, Karel. **Krakatit.** 1925
Chambers, Robert W. **The Gay Rebellion.** 1913
Colomb, P. et al. **The Great War of 189—.** 1893
Cook, William Wallace. **Adrift in the Unknown.** n.d.
Cummings, Ray. **The Man Who Mastered Time.** 1929
[DeMille, James]. **A Strange Manuscript Found in a Copper Cylinder.** 1888
Dixon, Thomas. **The Fall of a Nation:** A Sequel to the Birth of a Nation. 1916
England, George Allan. **The Golden Blight.** 1916
Fawcett, E. Douglas. **Hartmann the Anarchist.** 1893
Flammarion, Camille. **Omega:** The Last Days of the World. 1894
Grant, Robert et al. **The King's Men:** A Tale of To-Morrow. 1884
Grautoff, Ferdinand Heinrich (Parabellum, pseud.). **Banzai!** 1909
Graves, C. L. and E. V. Lucas. **The War of the Wenuses.** 1898
Greer, Tom. **A Modern Daedalus.** [1887]

Griffith, George. **A Honeymoon in Space.** 1901

Grousset, Paschal (A. Laurie, pseud.). **The Conquest of the Moon.** 1894

Haggard, H. Rider. **When the World Shook.** 1919

Hernaman-Johnson, F. **The Polyphemes.** 1906

Hyne, C. J. Cutcliffe. **Empire of the World.** [1910]

In The Future. [1875]

Jane, Fred T. **The Violet Flame.** 1899

Jefferies, Richard. **After London; Or, Wild England.** 1885

Le Queux, William. **The Great White Queen.** [1896]

London, Jack. **The Scarlet Plague.** 1915

Mitchell, John Ames. **Drowsy.** 1917

Morris, Ralph. **The Life and Astonishing Adventures of John Daniel.** 1751

Newcomb, Simon. **His Wisdom The Defender:** A Story. 1900

Paine, Albert Bigelow. **The Great White Way.** 1901

Pendray, Edward (Gawain Edwards, pseud.). **The Earth-Tube.** 1929

Reginald, R. and Douglas Menville. **Ancestral Voices:** An Anthology of Early Science Fiction. 1974

Russell, W. Clark. **The Frozen Pirate.** 2 vols. in 1. 1887

Shiel, M. P. **The Lord of the Sea.** 1901

Symmes, John Cleaves (Captain Adam Seaborn, pseud.). **Symzonia.** 1820

Train, Arthur and Robert W. Wood. **The Man Who Rocked the Earth.** 1915

Waterloo, Stanley. **The Story of Ab:** A Tale of the Time of the Cave Man. 1903

White, Stewart E. and Samuel H. Adams. **The Mystery.** 1907

Wicks, Mark. **To Mars Via the Moon.** 1911

Wright, Sydney Fowler. **Deluge: A Romance** and **Dawn.** 2 vols. in 1. 1928/1929

SCIENCE FICTION

NON-FICTION:
Including Bibliographies, Checklists and Literary Criticism

Aldiss, Brian and Harry Harrison. **SF Horizons.** 2 vols. in 1. 1964/1965

Amis, Kingsley. **New Maps of Hell.** 1960

Barnes, Myra. **Linguistics and Languages in Science Fiction-Fantasy.** 1974

Cockcroft, T. G. L. **Index to the Weird Fiction Magazines.** 2 vols. in 1 1962/1964

Cole, W. R. **A Checklist of Science-Fiction Anthologies.** 1964

Crawford, Joseph H. et al. **"333": A Bibliography of the Science-Fantasy Novel.** 1953

Day, Bradford M. **The Checklist of Fantastic Literature in Paperbound Books.** 1965

Day, Bradford M. **The Supplemental Checklist of Fantastic Literature.** 1963

Gove, Philip Babcock. **The Imaginary Voyage in Prose Fiction.** 1941

Green, Roger Lancelyn. **Into Other Worlds:** Space-Flight in Fiction, From Lucian to Lewis. 1958

Menville, Douglas. **A Historical and Critical Survey of the Science Fiction Film.** 1974

Reginald, R. **Contemporary Science Fiction Authors,** First Edition. 1970

Samuelson, David. **Visions of Tomorow:** Six Journeys from Outer to Inner Space. 1974